Foundation

BOOKKEEPING WITH SAGE AND SPREADSHEETS WITH EXCEL

For assessments in December 2004 and June 2005

Workbook (with Sage and Excel data files on CD)

In this April 2004 edition

- For assessments under the new standards

- Layout designed to be easier on the eye – and easy to use

- Clear language and presentation

- Practical exercises - with data supplied on CD-ROM for use with Sage Line 50 or Sage Instant (you must have access to Sage software to use this data)

- Exercises using Microsoft Excel and Microsoft Word

BPP
PROFESSIONAL EDUCATION

First edition May 2003

Second edition April 2004

ISBN 0 7517 1615 4 (previous edition 0 7517 1420 8)

British Library Cataloguing-in-Publication Data
A catalogue record for this book
is available from the British Library

Published by

BPP Professional Education
Aldine House, Aldine Place
London W12 8AW

www.bpp.com

Printed in Great Britain by WM Print
Frederick Street
Walsall
West Midlands
WS2 9NE

We are grateful to the Lead Body for Accounting for
permission to reproduce extracts from the Standards
of Competence for Accounting, and to the AAT for
permission to reproduce extracts from the mapping
and Guidance Notes.

Contents

Introduction

How to use this Workbook and CD-ROM – Foundation qualification structure –
Information Technology and the Foundation AAT Standards of competence –
Assessment – Building your portfolio

		Page	Answers to activities

PART A Spreadsheets

1	Using spreadsheets	3	169

PART B Using accounting software

2	Introducing the case study	41	171
3	Supplier invoices and credit notes	61	172
4	Customer invoices and credit notes	81	173
5	Payments to suppliers	105	176
6	Receipts from customers	123	177
7	Other cash transactions	139	178
8	Other credit transactions	151	179

		Page	Answers to assignments

PART C Assignments

1	Supplier invoices and credit notes	183	219
2	Customer invoices and credit notes	187	223
3	Payments to suppliers	195	231
4	Receipts from customers	199	237
5	Other cash transactions	205	243
6	Other credit transactions	213	249

PART **D**   Appendices

1   The Blitz nominal ledger account codes 257
2   Shortcut keys 261

Index 265

Order form

Review form & free prize draw

Introduction

How to use this Workbook and CD-ROM

Aims of this Workbook and CD-ROM

To provide knowledge that will assist students display competency in information technology skills as required at AAT Foundation Level.

To pass the assessment successfully you need a thorough understanding in all areas covered by the standards of competence.

To tie in with the other components of the BPP Effective Study Package to ensure you have the best possible chance of success.

This Workbook

Foundation Level papers require you to provide evidence of your practical computing skills. This Workbook and the accompanying CD contains practical exercises using Sage accounting software, Microsoft Excel and Microsoft Word.

Interactive Texts and Practice and Revision Kits

Computer skills and computerised systems are relevant in Foundation Units 1-4 and Unit 21. To ensure you have the knowledge you need for Foundation Level assessments ensure you study the relevant BPP Interactive Texts and Revision Kits for these units. This Workbook and CD-ROM provides additional, practical knowledge and examples.

Passcards

These short memorable notes are focused on key topics for the Foundation Units, designed to remind you of what the Interactive Text has taught you.

The Case Study in this Workbook

The case study is about a newly-established company of contract cleaners, Blitz Limited. The company has been operating for just over one month when the assignments in the book begin. The case starts in August 2000.

The data for each assignment is held in a separate Sage back-up file on the CD-ROM that accompanies this book. The files allow you to attempt 'later' assignments (eg Assignment 4) without having to do earlier assignments (eg Assignments 1, 2 and 3) first.

The book and CD contain six assignments covering credit and cash transactions and a variety of simple word processing and spreadsheet exercises. Guidance is given on how to carry out the tasks in each assignment using Sage or Microsoft Word or Microsoft Excel.

How much prior knowledge is needed?

Some basic knowledge of accounting is presumed. You should have an understanding of the logic behind the processing of accounting transactions. This book does not explain ledgers, accounts, invoices, credit notes and so on. These are explained in other AAT Units.

Explanations are given for each assignment about how the computerised accounting system is being used, and why. It is important to understand what the computerised processing being performed means in accounting terms.

Using the Sage data with your Sage software

Sage software is produced by the Sage Group plc, the leading producer of accounting software in the UK. The CD packaged with this book contains data only. To make use of this data **you need to have access to Sage software**.

The CD contains data compatible with:

- Sage Line 50 (Financial Controller) versions 6, 7, 8, 9 and 10
- Sage Instant Accounts versions 6, 8 or 10

See the section 'Loading the Sage data' in Chapter 2 for detailed instructions regarding how to use the Sage data held on the CD.

Foundation qualification structure

The competence-based Education and Training Scheme of the Association of Accounting Technicians is based on an analysis of the work of accounting staff in a wide range of industries and types of organisation. The Standards of Competence for Accounting which students are expected to meet are based on this analysis.

The AAT Standards identify the key purpose of the accounting occupation, which is to operate, maintain and improve systems to record, plan, monitor and report on the financial activities of an organisation, and a number of key roles of the occupation. Each key role is subdivided into units of competence, which are further divided into elements of competences.

By successfully completing assessments in specified units of competence, students can gain qualifications at NVQ/SVQ levels 2, 3 and 4, which correspond to the AAT Foundation, Intermediate and Technician stages of competence respectively.

Whether you are competent in a Unit is demonstrated by means of:

- *Either* an Exam Based Assessment (set and marked by AAT assessors)

- *Or* a Skills Based Assessment (where competence is judged by an Approved Assessment Centre to whom responsibility for this is devolved)

- Or *both* Exam *and* Skills Based Assessment

Below we set out the overall structure of the Foundation (NVQ/SVQ Level 2) stage, indicating how competence in each Unit is assessed. In the next section there is more detail about the computerised aspect of the Foundation Units.

All units are assessed by Skills Based Assessment, and Unit 3 is also assessed by Exam Based Assessment.

NVQ/SVQ Level 2 – Foundation

| Unit 1 Recording Income and Receipts | Element 1.1 | Process documents relating to goods and services supplied |
| | Element 1.2 | Process receipts |

| Unit 2 Making and Recording Payments | Element 2.1 | Process documents relating to goods and services received |
| | Element 2.2 | Process payments |

Unit 3 Preparing Ledger Balances and an Initial Trial Balance	Element 3.1	Balance bank transactions
	Element 3.2	Prepare ledger balances and control accounts
	Element 3.3	Draft an initial trial balance

| Unit 4 Supplying Information for Management Control | Element 4.1 | Code and extract information |
| | Element 4.2 | Provide comparisons on costs and income |

| *Unit 21 Working with Computers | Element 21.1 | Use computer systems and software |
| | Element 21.2 | Maintain the security of data |

| *Unit 22 Contribute to the Maintenance of a Healthy, Safe and Productive Working Environment | Element 22.1 | Contribute to the maintenance of a healthy, safe and productive working environment |
| | Element 22.2 | Monitor and maintain an effective and efficient working environment |

Unit 23 Achieving Personal Effectiveness	Element 23.1	Plan and organise your own work
	Element 23.2	Maintain good working relationships
	Element 23.3	Improve your own performance

* Students that have direct entry to subsequent Levels must demonstrate competence in Units 21 and 22 at those Levels.

Information Technology and the Foundation Standards of Competence

The 2002 Standards of Competence have clarified the amount of evidence the candidate is required to produce to prove competence in the Information Technology (IT) aspects at Foundation level.

In the past, Units 1, 2 and 3 always required candidates to have a knowledge and understanding of computerised accounting. Now, the revised standards clarify the evidence required through the range statements.

Unit 4, Supplying Information for Management Control, has changed little, but now requires candidates to produce a word processed report and a spreadsheet.

Unit 21, Working with Computers, requires candidates to prove competence in the generic tasks of using a computer and maintaining the security of data. Many of the competencies in this unit can be evidenced through observation whilst the candidate is producing evidence for units 1-4.

Evidence requirements

The Knowledge and Understanding for each of **Units 1-3** require candidates to understand:

- The operation of computerised accounting systems, including output

The extent of this knowledge is determined by the evidence requirements stipulated in the range statements. Therefore, candidates should be able to produce the following computerised evidence. (Different accounting packages use different terminology for the following evidence, but the essence of the requirements should not be affected.)

For Unit 1:

- Sales day book
- Sales returns day book
- Subsidiary sales ledger
- Main ledger
- Cash book
- Statements of account

For Unit 2:

- Purchases day book
- Purchases returns day book
- Subsidiary purchases ledger
- Main ledger
- Cash book
- Petty cash book

For Unit 3:

- Cash book
- Main ledger
- Subsidiary ledgers
- Bank reconciliation statement
- Journal
- Control accounts: sales ledger; purchases ledger; non-trade debtors and petty cash
- Trial balance

The Knowledge and Understanding for **Unit 4** requires the candidate to know and understand:

- Methods of analysing information in spreadsheets (Element 4.2)
- Methods of presenting information, including word-processed documents (Element 4.2)
- House style for different types of documents, including word-processed documents (Element 4.2)

The extent of this knowledge is determined by the evidence requirements stipulated in the range statements. The range statement for element 4.2 also specifies word processed documents. Therefore, candidates should be able to produce the following evidence:

- The performance criteria 'Provide comparisons to the appropriate person in the required format' includes the format of a word-processed report

- The Knowledge and Understanding regarding spreadsheets requires candidates to analyse information in a spreadsheet, in the contexts of providing comparisons on costs and income

The depth of knowledge required for **word-processed reports** is, in the context of providing comparisons, to be able to produce a short informal report using:

- Different font sizes
- Embolden
- Italicise
- Table

The depth of knowledge required for **spreadsheets**, in the context of analysing information in respect of costs and income, is to be able to produce a spreadsheet which has the following features:

- Title
- Labels and figures
- Simple formulae

Assessment

The computerised aspect of units 1, 2, 3 and 4 should be assessed through skills testing. However, as Unit 3 is also examined, candidates should also be prepared for a question on computerised accounting in the Initial Trial Balance exam.

Details of possible assessment methods can be found in the guidance notes for units 1–4 and 21 (these are reproduced in the front pages of the relevant BPP Interactive Texts). However, the opportunity exists for many of the competencies of Unit 21 to be evidenced whilst computerised evidence is being produced for Units 1–4.

Where the Approved Assessment Centre is a **college or training organisation**, skills testing will involve a combination of the following.

(a) Documentary evidence of activities carried out at the workplace, collected by you in an **accounting portfolio**

(b) Realistic **simulations** of workplace activities; these simulations may take the form of case studies and in-tray exercises and involve the use of primary documents and reference sources

(c) **Projects and assignments** designed to assess the Standards of Competence

If you are unable to provide workplace evidence, you will be able to complete the assessment requirements by the alternative methods listed above.

Students and Assessment Centres should be aware of the opportunity that exists for many of the competences of Unit 21 to be evidenced whilst computerised evidence is being produced for units 1–4 (and 7). The most powerful evidence will come from observation, but witness testimony from the workplace, personal report/checklists will also be valuable pieces of evidence. This coupled with the output produced and evidence of questioning should enable centres to ensure all performance criteria, range and knowledge and understanding are evidenced in a variety of ways.

Computer related evidence in the portfolio may be distributed through the various units or may be filed in the Unit 21 section. Either way, the use of cross-referencing in the portfolio will be of paramount importance.

Building your portfolio

What is a portfolio?

A portfolio is a collection of work that demonstrates what the owner can do. In AAT language the portfolio demonstrates **competence**.

A painter will have a collection of his paintings to exhibit in a gallery, an advertising executive will have a range of advertisements and ideas that she has produced to show to a prospective client. Both the collection of paintings and the advertisements form the portfolio of that artist or advertising executive.

Your portfolio will be unique to you just as the portfolio of the artist will be unique because no one will paint the same range of pictures in the same way. It is a very personal collection of your work and should be treated as a **confidential** record.

What evidence should a portfolio include?

No two portfolios will be the same but by following some simple guidelines you can decide which of the following suggestions will be appropriate in your case.

(a) **Your current CV**

This should be at the front. It will give your personal details as well as brief descriptions of posts you have held with the most recent one shown first.

(b) **References and testimonials**

References from previous employers may be included especially those of which you are particularly proud.

(c) **Your current job description**

You should emphasise financial **responsibilities and duties**.

(d) **Your student record sheets**

These should be supplied by AAT when you begin your studies, and your training provider should also have some if necessary.

(e) **Evidence from your current workplace**

This could take many forms including **letters, memos, reports** you have written, **copies of accounts** or **reconciliations** you have prepared, **discrepancies** you have investigated etc. Remember to obtain permission to include the evidence from your line manager because some records may be sensitive. Discuss the performance criteria that are listed in your Student Record Sheets with your training provider and employer, and think of other evidence that could be appropriate to you.

(f) **Evidence from your social activities**

For example you may be the treasurer of a club in which case examples of your cash and banking records could be appropriate.

(g) **Evidence from your studies**

Few students are able to satisfy all the requirements of competence by workplace evidence alone. They therefore rely on simulations to provide the remaining evidence to complete a unit. If you are not working or not working in a relevant post, then you may need to rely more heavily on simulations as a source of evidence.

(h) **Additional work**

Your training provider may give you work that specifically targets one or a group of performance criteria in order to complete a unit. It could take the form of questions, presentations or demonstrations. Each training provider will approach this in a different way.

(i) **Evidence from a previous workplace**

This evidence may be difficult to obtain and should be used with caution because it must satisfy the 'rules' of evidence, that is, it must be current. Only rely on this as evidence if you have changed jobs recently.

(j) **Prior achievements**

For example you may have already completed the health and safety unit during a previous course of study, and therefore there is no need to repeat this work. Advise your training provider who will check to ensure that it is the same unit and record it as complete if appropriate.

How should it be presented?

As you assemble the evidence remember to **make a note** of it on your Student Record Sheet in the space provided and **cross reference** it. In this way it is easy to check to see if your evidence is **appropriate**. Remember one piece of evidence may satisfy a number of performance criteria so remember to check this thoroughly and discuss it with your training provider if in doubt. Keep all your evidence together in a ring binder or lever arch file for safe storage.

When should evidence be assembled?

You should begin to assemble evidence **as soon as you have registered as a student**. **Don't leave it all** until the last few weeks of your studies, because you may miss vital deadlines and your resulting certificate sent by the AAT may not include all the units you have completed. Give yourself and your training provider time to examine your portfolio and report your results to AAT at regular intervals. In this way the task of assembling the portfolio will be spread out over a longer period of time and will be presented in a more professional manner.

What are the key criteria that the portfolio must fulfil?

As you assemble your evidence bear in mind that it must be:

- **Valid**. It must relate to the Standards.
- **Authentic**. It must be your own work.
- **Current**. It must refer to your current or most recent job.
- **Sufficient**. It must meet all the performance criteria by the time you have completed your portfolio.

Finally

Remember that the portfolio is **your property** and **your responsibility**. Not only could it be presented to the external verifier before your award can be confirmed; it could be used when you are seeking **promotion** or applying for a more senior and better paid post elsewhere. How your portfolio is presented can say as much about you as the evidence inside.

> For further information about portfolios, BPP have produced a book *Building Your Portfolio*.
> It can be ordered using the order form at the back of this book or at *www.bpp.com/aat.*

P A R T   A

Spreadsheets

chapter 1

Using Spreadsheets

Contents

1 Introduction
2 What is a spreadsheet?
3 Examples of spreadsheet formulae
4 Basic skills
5 Spreadsheet construction
6 Formulae with conditions
7 Charts and graphs
8 Spreadsheet format and appearance
9 Other issues: printing; controls; spreadsheets and word processing software
10 Three dimensional (multi-sheet) spreadsheets

Knowledge and understanding

Methods of analysing information in spreadsheets

1 Introduction

The vast majority of people who work in an accounting environment are required to use spreadsheets to perform their duties. This fact is reflected in the AAT Standards, which require candidates to be able to produce clear, well-presented spreadsheets, that utilise basic spreadsheet functions such as simple formulae.

2 What is a spreadsheet?

A spreadsheet is essentially an electronic piece of paper divided into **rows** (horizontal) and **columns** (vertical). The rows are numbered 1, 2, 3 . . . etc and the columns lettered A, B C . . . etc. Each individual area representing the intersection of a row and a column is called a '**cell**'. A cell address consists of its row and column reference. For example, in the spreadsheet below the word '*Jan*' is in cell B2. The cell that the cursor is currently in or over is known as the 'active cell'.

The main examples of spreadsheet packages are Lotus 1 2 3 and Microsoft Excel. We will be referring to **Microsoft Excel**, as this is the most widely-used spreadsheet. A simple Microsoft Excel spreadsheet, containing budgeted sales figures for three geographical areas for the first quarter of the year, is shown below.

	A	B	C	D	E	F
1	BUDGETED SALES FIGURES					
2		Jan	Feb	Mar	Total	
3		£'000	£'000	£'000	£'000	
4	North	2,431	3,001	2,189	7,621	
5	South	6,532	5,826	6,124	18,482	
6	West	895	432	596	1,923	
7	Total	9,858	9,259	8,909	28,026	
8						

2.1 Why use spreadsheets?

Spreadsheets provide a tool for calculating, analysing and manipulating numerical data. Spreadsheets make the calculation and manipulation of data easier and quicker. For example, the spreadsheet above has been set up to calculate the totals **automatically.** If you changed your estimate of sales in February for the North region to £3,296, when you input this figure in cell C4 the totals (in E4 and C7) would change accordingly.

2.1.1 Uses of spreadsheets

Spreadsheets can be used for a wide range of tasks. Some common applications of spreadsheets are:

- Management accounts
- Cash flow analysis and forecasting
- Reconciliations
- Revenue analysis and comparison
- Cost analysis and comparison
- Budgets and forecasts

2.1.2 Cell contents

The contents of any cell can be one of the following.

(a) **Text**. A text cell usually contains **words**. Numbers that do not represent numeric values for calculation purposes (eg a Part Number) may be entered in a way that tells Excel to treat the cell contents as text. To do this, enter an apostrophe before the number eg '451.

(b) **Values**. A value is a **number** that can be used in a calculation.

(c) **Formulae**. A formula **refers to other cells** in the spreadsheet, and performs some sort of computation with them. For example, if cell C1 contains the formula =A1-B1, cell C1 will display the result of the calculation subtracting the contents of cell B1 from the contents of cell A1. In Excel, a formula always begins with an equals sign: = . There are a wide range of formulae and functions available.

2.1.3 Formula bar

The following illustration shows the formula bar. (If the formula bar is not visible, choose **View**, **Formula bar** from Excel's main menu.)

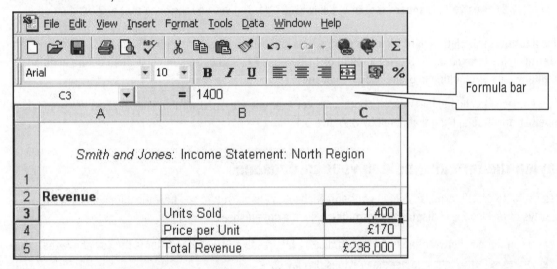

The formula bar allows you to see and edit the contents of the active cell. The bar also shows the cell address of the active cell (C3 in the example above).

3 Examples of spreadsheet formulae

Formulas in Microsoft Excel follow a specific syntax. All Excel formulae start with the equals sign =, followed by the elements to be calculated (the operands) and the calculation operators. Each operand can be a value that does not change (a constant value), a cell or range reference, a label, a name, or a worksheet function.

Formulae can be used to perform a variety of calculations. Here are some examples.

(a)   =C4*5. This formula **multiplies** the value in C4 by 5. The result will appear in the cell holding the formula.

(b)   =C4*B10. This **multiplies** the value in C4 by the value in B10.

(c)   =C4/E5. This **divides** the value in C4 by the value in E5. (* means multiply and / means divide by.)

(d)   =C4*B10-D1. This **multiplies** the value in C4 by that in B10 and then subtracts the value in D1 from the result. Note that generally Excel will perform multiplication and division before addition or subtraction. If in any doubt, use brackets (parentheses): =(C4*B10)–D1.

(e)   =C4*117.5%. This **adds** 17.5% to the value in C4. It could be used to calculate a price including 17.5% VAT.

(f)   =(C4+C5+C6)/3. Note that the **brackets** mean Excel would perform the addition first. Without the brackets, Excel would first divide the value in C6 by 3 and then add the result to the total of the values in C4 and C5.

(g)   = 2^2 gives you 2 **to the power** of 2, in other words 2^2. Likewise = 2^3 gives you 2 cubed and so on.

(h)   = 4^ (1/2) gives you the **square root** of 4. Likewise 27^(1/3) gives you the cube root of 27 and so on.

Excel calculates a formula from left to right. You can control how calculation is performed by changing the syntax of the formula. For example, the formula =5+2*3 gives a result of 11 because Excel calculates multiplication before addition. Excel would multiply 2 by 3 (resulting in 6) and would then add 5.

You may use parentheses to change the order of operations. For example =(5+2)*3 would result in Excel firstly adding the 5 and 2 together, then multiplying that result by 3 to give 21.

3.1 Displaying the formulae held in your spreadsheet

It is sometimes useful to see all formulae held in your spreadsheet to enable you to see how the spreadsheet works. There are two ways of making Excel **display the formulae** held in a spreadsheet.

(a)   You can 'toggle' between the two types of display by pressing **Ctrl** + ` (the latter is the key above the Tab key). Press Ctrl + ` again to get the previous display back.

(b)   You can also click on Tools, then on Options, then on View and tick the box next to 'Formulas'.

In the following paragraphs we provide examples of how spreadsheets and formulae may be used in an accounting context.

Example: formulae

	A	B	C	D	E	F
1	BUDGETED SALES FIGURES					
2		Jan	Feb	Mar	Total	
3		£'000	£'000	£'000	£'000	
4	North	2,431	3,001	2,189	7,621	
5	South	6,532	5,826	6,124	18,482	
6	West	895	432	596	1,923	
7	Total	9,858	9,259	8,909	28,026	
8						

(a) In the spreadsheet shown above, which of the cells have had a number typed in, and which cells display the result of calculations (ie which cells contain a formula)?

(b) What formula would you put in each of the following cells?

    (i)   Cell B7.
    (ii)   Cell E6.
    (iii) Cell E7.

(c) If the February sales figure for the South changed from £5,826 to £5,731, what other figures would change as a result? Give cell references.

Solution

(a) Cells into which you would need to enter a value are: B4, B5, B6, C4, C5, C6, D4, D5 and D6. Cells which would perform calculations are B7, C7, D7, E4, E5, E6 and E7.

(b) (i) =B4+B5+B6 *or better* =SUM(B4:B6)

    (ii) =B6+C6+D6 *or better* =SUM(B6:D6)

    (iii) =E4+E5+E6 *or better* =SUM(E4:E6) Alternatively, the three monthly totals could be added across the spreadsheet: = SUM (B7: D7)

(c) The figures which would change, besides the amount in cell C5, would be those in cells C7, E5 and E7. (The contents of E7 would change if any of the sales figures changed.)

Activity 1.1

The following spreadsheet shows sales of two products, the Ego and the Id, for the period July to September.

	A	B	C	D	E	F	G
1	**Sigmund Ltd**						
2	*Sales analysis - Q3 X7*						
3		M7	M8	M9	Total		
4		£	£	£	£		
5	Ego	3000	4000	2000	9000		
6	Id	2000	1500	4000	7500		
7	Total	5000	5500	6000	16500		
8							
9							
10							

Devise a suitable formula for each of the following cells.

(a) Cell B7.

(b) Cell E6.

(c) Cell E7.

Note: In this Workbook, Answers to Activities follow Chapter 8.

Activity 1.2

The following spreadsheet shows sales, exclusive of VAT, in row 6.

	A	B	C	D	E	F	G	H
1	**Taxable Supplies plc**							
2	*Sales analysis - Branch C*							
3	*Six months ended 30 June XX*							
4		Jan	Feb	Mar	Apr	May	Jun	Total
5		£	£	£	£	£	£	£
6	Net sales	2,491.54	5,876.75	3,485.01	5,927.70	6,744.52	3,021.28	27,546.80
7	VAT							
8	Total							
9								
10								
11								

Your manager has asked you to insert formulae to calculate VAT at 17½% in row 7 and also to produce totals.

(a) Devise a suitable formula for cell B7 and cell E8.

(b) How could the spreadsheet be better designed?

Activity 1.3

The following balances have been taken from the books of Ed Sheet, a sole trader, at 31 December 200X.

	Dr £	Cr £
Plant and machinery (NBV)	20,000	
Motor vehicles (NBV)	10,000	
Stock	2,000	
Debtors	1,000	
Cash	1,500	
Creditors		2,500
Overdraft		1,500
Drawings	1,000	
Capital (1 Jan 20XX)		28,000
Profit for year	3,500	

Your manager has started to prepare a balance sheet using Microsoft Excel. The basic structure of the spreadsheet has been set up, and the required numbers have been input. You have been asked to insert the formulae required in the cells highlighted with a border.

	A	B	C	D	E	F
1	Ed Sheet					
2	Balance sheet as at 31 Dec 200X					
3		£	£			
4	Fixed assets					
5	Plant	20000				
6	Vehicles	10000				
7						
8	Current assets					
9	Stock	2000				
10	Debtors	1000				
11	Cash	1500				
12						
13	Current liabilities					
14	Creditors	2500				
15	Overdraft	1500				
16						
17	Net current assets					
18	Net assets					
19						
20	Represented by:					
21	Opening capital		28000			
22	Profit for year		3500			
23	Drawings		1000			
24	Closing capital					
25						
26						

Devise the formulae required to go in the cells C7, B12, B16, C17, C18 and C24.

4 Basic skills

In this section we explain some **basic spreadsheeting skills**. We give instructions for Microsoft Excel, the most widely used package. Our examples should be valid with all versions of Excel released since 1997.

You should read this section while sitting at a computer and trying out the skills we describe **'hands-on'**.

4.1 Examples of useful spreadsheet skills

Start Microsoft Excel by double-clicking on the Excel **icon** or button (it will look like an X), or by choosing Excel from the **Start** menu (maybe from within the **Microsoft Office** option**)**.

4.1.1 Moving about

The F5 key is useful for moving around within large spreadsheets. If you press the function key **F5,** a **Go To** dialogue box will allow you to specify the cell address you would like to move to. Try this out.

Also experiment by holding down Ctrl and pressing each of the direction arrow keys in turn to see where you end up. Try using the **Page Up** and **Page Down** keys and also try **Home** and **End** and Ctrl + these keys. Try **Tab** and **Shift + Tab**, too. These are all useful shortcuts for moving quickly from one place to another in a large spreadsheet.

4.1.2 Editing cell contents

Suppose cell A2 currently contains the value 456. If you wish to **change the entry** in cell A2 from 456 to 123456 there are four options – as shown below.

(a) Activate cell A2, **type** 123456 and press **Enter**.

    To undo this and try the next option press **Ctrl + Z**: this will always undo what you have just done.

(b) **Double-click** in cell A2. The cell will keep its thick outline but you will now be able to see a vertical line flashing in the cell. You can move this line by using the direction arrow keys or the Home and the End keys. Move it to before the 4 and type 123. Then press Enter.

    When you have tried this press Ctrl + Z to undo it.

(c) **Click once** before the number 456 in the formula bar. Again you will get the vertical line and you can type in 123 before the 4. Then press Enter. Undo this before moving onto (d).

(d) Press the **function key F2**. The vertical line cursor will be flashing in cell A2 at the *end* of the figures entered there (after the 6). Press Home to get to a position before the 4 and then type in 123 and press Enter, as before.

4.1.3 Deleting cell contents

You may delete the contents of a cell simply by making the cell the active cell and then pressing **Delete**. The contents of the cell will disappear. You may also highlight a range of cells to delete and then delete the contents of all cells within the range.

For example, enter any value in cell A1 and any value in cell A2. Move the cursor to cell A2. Now hold down the **Shift** key (the one above the Ctrl key) and keeping it held down press the ↑ arrow. Cell A2 will stay white but cell A1 will go black.

What you have done here is **selected** the range A1 and A2. Now press the Delete key. The contents of cells A1 and A2 will be deleted.

4.1.4 Filling a range of cells

Start with a blank spreadsheet. Type the number 1 in cell A1 and the number 2 in cell A2. Now select cells A1: A2, this time by positioning the mouse pointer over cell A1, holding down the left mouse button and moving the pointer down to cell A2. When cell A2 is highlighted release the mouse button.

Now position the mouse pointer at the **bottom right hand corner** of cell A2. When you have the mouse pointer in the right place it will turn into a **black cross**.

Then, hold down the left mouse button again and move the pointer down to cell A10. You will see an outline surrounding the cells you are trying to 'fill'.

Release the mouse button when you have the pointer over cell A10. You will find that the software **automatically** fills in the numbers 3 to 10 below 1 and 2.

Try the following variations of this technique.

(a) Delete what you have just done and type in **Jan** in cell A1. See what happens if you select cell A1 and fill down to cell A12: you get the months **Feb, Mar, Apr** and so on.

(b) Type the number 2 in cell A1. Select A1 and fill down to cell A10. What happens? The cells should fill up with 2's.

(c) Type the number 2 in cell A1 and 4 in cell A2. Then select A1: A2 and fill down to cell A10. What happens? You should get 2, 4, 6, 8, and so on.

(d) Try **filling across** as well as down.

(e) If you click on the bottom right hand corner of the cell using the **right mouse button**, drag down to a lower cell and then release the button you should see a menu providing a variety of options for filling the cells.

4.1.5 The Sum button Σ

We will explain how to use the SUM button by way of a simple example. Start with a blank spreadsheet, then enter the following figures in cells A1:B5.

	A	B
1	400	582
2	250	478
3	359	264
4	476	16
5	97	125

Make cell B6 the active cell and click once on the **sum button** (the button with a Σ symbol on the Excel toolbar - the Σ symbol is the mathematical sign for 'the sum of'). A formula will appear in the cell saying =SUM(B1:B5). Above cell B6 you will see a flashing dotted line encircling cells B1:B5. Accept the suggested formula by hitting the Enter key.

The formula =SUM(B1:B5) will be entered, and the number 1465 will be appear in cell B6.

Next, make cell A6 the active cell and **double-click** on the sum button. The number 1582 should appear in cell A6.

4.1.6 Multiplication

Continuing on with our example, next select cell C1. Type in an = sign then click on cell A1. Now type in an **asterisk *** (which serves as a **multiplication sign**) and click on cell B1. Watch how the formula in cell C1 changes as you do this. (Alternatively you can enter the cell references by moving the direction arrow keys.) Finally press Enter. Cell C1 will show the result (232,800) of multiplying the figure in Cell A1 by the one in cell B1.

Your next task is to select cell C1 and **fill in** cells C2 to C5 automatically using the **dragging technique** described above. If you then click on each cell in column C and look above at the line showing what the cell contains you will find that the software has automatically filled in the correct cell references for you: A2*B2 in cell C2, A3*B3 in cell C3 and so on.

(**Note**: The forward slash **/** is used to represent division in spreadsheet formulae).

4.1.7 Inserting columns and rows

Suppose we also want to add each row, for example cells A1 and B1. The logical place to do this would be cell C1, but column C already contains data. We have three options that would enable us to place this total in column C.

(a)   Highlight cells C1 to C5 and position the mouse pointer on one of the **edges**. (It will change to an arrow shape.) Hold down the **left** mouse button and drag cells C1 to C5 into column D. There is now space in column C for our next set of sums. Any **formulae** that need to be changed as a result of moving cells using this method should be changed **automatically** – but always check them.

(b)   The second option is to highlight cells C1 to C5 as before, position the mouse pointer anywhere **within** column C and click on the **right** mouse button. A menu will appear offering you an option **Insert…** . If you click on this you will be asked where you want to shift the cells that are being moved. In this case you want to move them to the right so choose this option and click on OK.

(c)   The third option is to **insert a whole new column**. You do this by clicking on the letter at the top of the column (here C) to highlight the whole of it then proceeding as in (b). The new column will always be inserted to the left of the one you highlight.

You can now display the sum of each of the rows in column C.

You can also insert a new row in a similar way (or stretch rows).

(a)   To **insert** one row, perhaps for headings, click on the row number to highlight it, click with the right mouse button and choose insert. One row will be inserted **above** the one you highlighted. Try putting some headings above the figures in columns A to C.

(b)   To insert **several** rows click on the row number immediately **below** the point where you want the new rows to appear and, holding down the left mouse button highlight the number of rows you wish to insert. Click on the highlighted area with the right mouse button and choose Insert (or if you prefer, choose **Insert**, **Rows** from the main menu).

4.1.8 Changing column width

You may occasionally find that a cell is not wide enough to display its contents. When this occurs, the cell displays a series of hashes ######. There are two options available to solve this problem.

(a)   One is to **decide for yourself** how wide you want the columns to be. Position the mouse pointer at the head of column A directly over the little line dividing the letter A from the letter B. The mouse **pointer** will change to a sort of **cross**. Hold down the left mouse button and, by moving your mouse, stretch Column A to the right, to about the middle of column D, until the words you typed fit. You can do the same for column B. Then make your columns too narrow again so you can try option (b).

(b)   Often it is easier to **let the software decide for you**. Position the mouse pointer over the little dividing line as before and get the cross symbol. Then double-click with the left mouse button. The column automatically adjusts to an appropriate width to fit the widest cell in that column.

You can either adjust the width of each column individually or you can do them all in one go. To do the latter click on the button in the top left hand corner to **select the whole sheet** and then **double-click** on just one of the dividing lines: all the columns will adjust to the **'best fit'** width.

4.1.9 Keyboard shortcuts and toolbar buttons

Here are a few tips to improve the **appearance** of your spreadsheets and speed up your work. To do any of the following to a cell or range of cells, first **select** the cell or cells and then:

(a)   Press Ctrl + B to make the cell contents **bold.**

(b)   Press Ctrl + I to make the cell contents *italic*.

(c)   Press **Ctrl + C** to **copy** the contents of the cells.

(d)   Move the cursor and press **Ctrl + V** to **paste** the cell you just copied into the new active cell or cells.

There are also **buttons** in the Excel toolbar (shown below) that may be used to carry out these and other functions. The best way to learn about these features is to use them - enter some numbers and text into a spreadsheet and experiment with keyboard shortcuts and toolbar buttons.

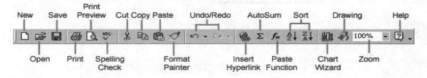

5 Spreadsheet construction

Spreadsheet models that will be used mainly as a calculation tool for various scenarios should ideally be constructed in **three sections**, as follows.

1. An inputs section containing the variables (eg the amount of a loan and the interest rate).

2. A calculations section containing formulae (eg the loan term and interest rate).

3. The results section, showing the outcome the calculations.

Here is an example arranged in this way.

	A	B	C	D	E	F	G
1	*Results*						
2		£					
3	Interest due:	200.00					
4							
5							
6							
7	*Variables*						
8	Loan	£ 2,000.00					
9	Interest rate	10%					
10							
11							
12							
13	*Calculations*						
14	Interest	200.00					
15							
16							
17							
18							
19							
20							

Cell B3 contains the formula **=B14**

The variables are typed in as numbers (just as they are shown here)

Cell B14 contains the formula **=B8*B9**

In practice, in many situations it is often **more convenient** to combine the results and calculations areas as follows.

	A	B	C	D	E	F	G
1	*Results*						
2		£					
3	Interest due:	200.00					
4							
5							
6							
7	*Variables*						
8	Loan	£ 2,000.00					
9	Interest rate	10.00%					
10							
11							
12							
13							
14							
15							

Cell B3 contains the formula **=B8*B9**

The variables are typed in as numbers (just as they are shown here)

If we took out another loan of £4,789 at an interest rate of 7.25% we would simply need to **overwrite the figures in the variable section** of the spreadsheet with the new figures to calculate the interest.

After the activity below, we look at a more complicated example. Work through this example at a PC with Excel loaded.

Activity 1.4

Answer questions (a) and (b) below, which relate to the following spreadsheet.

	A	B	C	D	E
1	**Boilermakers Ltd**				
2	*Department B*				
3					
4	*Production data*	Machine A	Machine B	Machine C	
5	Shift 1	245.84	237.49	231.79	
6	Shift 2	241.14	237.62	261.31	
7	Shift 3	244.77	201.64	242.71	
8	Shift 4	240.96	238.18	234.50	
9					
10					
11	*Usage data*	Machine A	Machine B	Machine C	
12	Maintenance	35	71	6	
13	Operational	8.47	7.98	9.31	
14	Idle	1.42	2.4	0.87	
15	Recovery	0	15	4	
16					
17					
18					
19					
20					

(a) Cell B9 needs to contain an average of all the preceding numbers in column B. Suggest a formula which would achieve this.

(b) Cell C16 contains the formula

=C12+C13/C14-C15

What would the result be, displayed in cell C16?

5.1 Example: Constructing a cash flow projection

Suppose you wanted to set up a simple six-month cash flow projection, in such a way that you could use it to estimate how the **projected cash balance** figures will **change** in total when any **individual item** in the projection is **altered**. You have the following information.

(a) Sales were £45,000 per month in 20X5, falling to £42,000 in January 20X6. Thereafter they are expected to increase by 3% per month (ie February will be 3% higher than January, and so on).

(b) Debts are collected as follows.

(i) 60% in month following sale.
(ii) 30% in second month after sale.

(iii)   7% in third month after sale.

(iv)   3% remains uncollected.

(c)   Purchases are equal to cost of sales, set at 65% of sales.

(d)   Overheads were £6,000 per month in 20X5, rising by 5% in 20X6.

(e)   Opening cash is an overdraft of £7,500.

(f)   Dividends: £10,000 final dividend on 20X5 profits payable in May.

(g)   Capital purchases: plant costing £18,000 will be ordered in January. 20% is payable with order, 70% on delivery in February and the final 10% in May.

5.1.1 Headings and layout

The first step is to put in the various **headings** required for the cash flow projection. At this stage, your spreadsheet might look as follows.

	A	B	C	D	E	F	G
1	EXCELLENT PLC						
2	*Cash flow projection - six months ending 30 June X6*						
3		*Jan*	*Feb*	*Mar*	*Apr*	*May*	*Jun*
4		£	£	£	£	£	£
5	Sales						
6	*Cash receipts*						
7	1 month in arrears						
8	2 months in arrears						
9	3 months in arrears						
10	Total operating receipts						
11							
12	Cash payments						
13	Purchases						
14	Overheads						
15	Total operating payments						
16							
17	Dividends						
18	Capital purchases						
19	Total other payments						
20							
21	Net cash flow						
22	Cash balance b/f						
23	Cash balance c/f						
24							

Note the following points.

(a)   We have **increased the width** of column A to allow longer pieces of text to be inserted. Had we not done so, only the first part of each caption would have been displayed (and printed). If you skipped Section 2 of this chapter but you don't know how to widen a column, you had better go back and read it now.

(b)   We have developed a **simple style for headings**. Headings are essential, so that users can identify what a spreadsheet does. We have **emboldened** the company name and *italicised* other headings.

(c)   When **text** is entered into a cell it is usually **left-aligned** (as for example in column A). We have **centred** the headings above each column by highlighting the cells and using the relevant buttons at the top of the screen.

(d)   **Numbers** should be **right-aligned** in cells.

(e)   We have left **spaces** in certain rows (after blocks of related items) to make the spreadsheet **easier to use and read**.

5.1.2 Inserting formulae

The next step is to enter the **formulae** required. For example, in cell B10 you want total operating receipts, =SUM(B7:B9).

Look for a moment at cell C7. We are told that sales in January were £42,000 and that 60% of customers settle their accounts one month in arrears. We could insert the formula =B5*0.6 in the cell and fill in the other cells along the row so that it is replicated in each month. However, consider the effect of a change in payment patterns to a situation where, say, 55% of customer debts are settled after one month. This would necessitate a **change to each and every cell** in which the 0.6 ratio appears.

An alternative approach, which makes **future changes much simpler** to execute, is to put the relevant ratio (here, 60% or 0.6) in a cell **outside** the main table and cross-refer each cell in the main table to that cell. This means that, if the percentage changes, the change need only be reflected in **one cell**, following which all cells which are dependent on that cell will **automatically use the new percentage**. We will therefore input such values in separate parts of the spreadsheet, as follows. Look at the other assumptions which we have inserted into this part of the spreadsheet.

	A	B	C	D	E	F	G
24							
25							
26	*This table contains the key variables for the*		*X6 cash flow projections*				
27							
28	Sales growth factor per month		1.03				
29	Purchases as % of sales		-0.65				
30							
31	Debts paid within 1 month		0.6				
32	Debts paid within 2 months		0.3				
33	Debts paid within 3 months		0.07				
34	Bad debts		0.03				
35							
36	Increase in overheads		1.05				
37							
38	Dividends (May)		-10000				
39							
40	Capital purchases		-18000				
41	January		0.2				
42	February		0.7				
43	May		0.1				
44							
45							
46	*This table contains relevant opening balance data as at Jan*		*X6*				
47							
48	Monthly sales X5		45000				
49	January X6 sales		42000				
50	Monthly overheads X5		-6000				
51	Opening cash		-7500				
52							

Now we can go back to cell C7 and input =B5*C31 and then fill this in across the '1 month in arrears' row. (Note that, as we have no December sales figure, we will have to deal with cell B7 separately.) If we assume for the moment that we are copying to cells D7 through to G7 and follow this procedure, the contents of cell D7 would be shown as =C5*D31, and so on, as shown below.

	A	B	C	D	E	F	G
3		*Jan*	*Feb*	*Mar*	*Apr*	*May*	*Jun*
4		£	£	£	£	£	£
5	Sales						
6	*Cash receipts*						
7	1 month in arrears		=B5*C31	=C5*D31	=D5*E31	=E5*F31	=F5*G31
8	2 months in arrears						
9	3 months in arrears						
10	Total operating receipts						

You may have noticed a problem. While the formula in cell C7 is fine - it multiplies January sales by 0.6 (the 1 month ratio stored in cell C31) - the remaining formulae are useless, as they **refer to empty cells** in row 31. This is what the spreadsheet would look like (assuming, for now, constant sales of £42,000 per month).

	A	B	C	D	E	F	G
3		*Jan*	*Feb*	*Mar*	*Apr*	*May*	*Jun*
4		£	£	£	£	£	£
5	Sales	42000	42000	42000	42000	42000	42000
6	*Cash receipts*						
7	1 month in arrears		25200	0	0	0	0
8	2 months in arrears						
9	3 months in arrears						
10	Total operating receipts						

This problem highlights the important distinction between **relative** cell references and **absolute** cell references. Usually, cell references are **relative**. A formula of =SUM(B7:B9) in cell B10 is relative. It does not really mean 'add up the numbers in cells B7 to B9'; it actually means '**add up the numbers in the three cells above this one**'. If this formula was copied to cell C10 (as we will do later), it would become =SUM(C7:C9).

This is what is causing the problem encountered above. The spreadsheet thinks we are asking it to 'multiply the number two up and one to the left by the number twenty-four cells down', and that is indeed the effect of the instruction we have given. But we are actually intending to ask it to 'multiply the number two up and one to the left by the number in cell C31'. This means that we need to create an **absolute** (unchanging) **reference** to cell C31.

Absolute cell references use **dollar signs** ($). A dollar sign before the column letter makes the column reference absolute, and one before the row number makes the row number absolute. You do not need to type the dollar signs - add them as follows.

(a)   Make cell C7 the active cell and press F2 to edit it.

(b)   Note where the cursor is flashing: it should be after the 1. If it is not move it with the direction arrow keys so that it is positioned somewhere next to or within the cell reference C31.

(c)   Press F4.

The **function key F4** adds dollar signs to the cell reference: it becomes $C$31. Press F4 again: the reference becomes C$31. Press it again: the reference becomes $C31. Press it once more, and the simple relative reference is restored: C31.

(a) A dollar sign **before a letter** means that the **column** reference stays the same when you copy the formula to another cell.

(b) A dollar sign **before a number** means that the **row** reference stays the same when you copy the formula to another cell.

In our example we have now altered the reference in cell C7 and filled in across to cell G7, overwriting what was there previously. This is the result.

(a) Formulae

	A	B	C	D	E	F	G
3		*Jan*	*Feb*	*Mar*	*Apr*	*May*	*Jun*
4		£	£	£	£	£	£
5	Sales	42000	42000	42000	42000	42000	42000
6	*Cash receipts*						
7	1 month in arrears		=B5*$C$31	=C5*$C$31	=D5*$C$31	=E5*$C$31	=F5*$C$31
8	2 months in arrears						
9	3 months in arrears						
10	Total operating receipts						

(b) Numbers

	A	B	C	D	E	F	G
3		*Jan*	*Feb*	*Mar*	*Apr*	*May*	*Jun*
4		£	£	£	£	£	£
5	Sales	42000	42000	42000	42000	42000	42000
6	*Cash receipts*						
7	1 month in arrears		25200	25200	25200	25200	25200
8	2 months in arrears						
9	3 months in arrears						
10	Total operating receipts						

Other formulae required for this projection are as follows.

(a) **Cell B5** refers directly to the information we are given - **sales of £42,000** in January. We have input this variable in cell C49. The other formulae in row 5 (sales) reflect the predicted sales growth of 3% per month, as entered in cell C28.

(b) Similar formulae to the one already described for row 7 are required in rows 8 and 9.

(c) **Row 10** (total operating receipts) will display simple **subtotals**, in the form =SUM(B7:B9).

(d) **Row 13 (purchases)** requires a formula based on the data in row 5 **(sales)** and the value in cell C29 **(purchases** as a % of sales). This model assumes no changes in stock levels from month to month, and that stocks are sufficiently high to enable this. The formula is B5 * $C$29. Note that C29 is negative.

(e) **Row 15** (total operating payments), like row 10, requires **formulae** to create **subtotals**.

(f) **Rows 17 and 18** refer to the **dividends and capital purchase data** input in cells C38 and C40 to 43.

(g) **Row 21** (net cash flow) requires a **total** in the form =B10 + B15 + B21.

(h) **Row 22** (balance b/f) requires the contents of the **previous month's closing cash** figure.

(i) **Row 23** (balance b/f) requires the **total** of the **opening cash** figure and the **net cash flow** for the month.

The following image shows the formulae that should now be present in the spreadsheet.

	A	B	C	D	E	F	G
1	EXCELLENT PLC						
2	Cash flow projection - six months						
3		Jan	Feb	Mar	Apr	May	Jun
4		£	£	£	£	£	£
5	Sales	=C49	=B5*$C$28	=C5*$C$28	=D5*$C$28	=E5*$C$28	=F5*$C$28
6	Cash receipts						
7	1 month in arrears	=$C$48*$C$31	=B5*$C$31	=C5*$C$31	=D5*$C$31	=E5*$C$31	=F5*$C$31
8	2 months in arrears	=$C$48*$C$32	=$C$48*$C$32	=B5*$C$32	=C5*$C$32	=D5*$C$32	=E5*$C$32
9	3 months in arrears	=$C$48*$C$33	=$C$48*$C$33	=$C$48*$C$33	=B5*$C$33	=C5*$C$33	=D5*$C$33
10	Total operating receipts	=SUM(B7:B9)	=SUM(C7:C9)	=SUM(D7:D9)	=SUM(E7:E9)	=SUM(F7:F9)	=SUM(G7:G9)
11							
12	Cash payments						
13	Purchases	=B5*$C$29	=C5*$C$29	=D5*$C$29	=E5*$C$29	=F5*$C$29	=G5*$C$29
14	Overheads	=$C$50*$C$36	=$C$50*$C$36	=$C$50*$C$36	=$C$50*$C$36	=$C$50*$C$36	=$C$50*$C$36
15	Total operating payments	=SUM(B13:B14)	=SUM(C13:C14)	=SUM(D13:D14)	=SUM(E13:E14)	=SUM(F13:F14)	=SUM(G13:G14)
16							
17	Dividends	0	0	0	0	=C38	0
18	Capital purchases	=C40*C41	=C40*C42	0	0	=C40*C43	0
19	Total other payments	=SUM(B17:B18)	=SUM(C17:C18)	=SUM(D17:D18)	=SUM(E17:E18)	=SUM(F17:F18)	=SUM(G17:G18)
20							
21	Net cash flow	=B10+B15+B19	=C10+C15+C19	=D10+D15+D19	=E10+E15+E19	=F10+F15+F19	=G10+G15+G19
22	Cash balance b/f	=C51	=B23	=C23	=D23	=E23	=F23
23	Cash balance c/f	=SUM(B21:B22)	=SUM(C21:C22)	=SUM(D21:D22)	=SUM(E21:E22)	=SUM(F21:F22)	=SUM(G21:G22)
24							

Be careful to ensure you use the correct sign (negative or positive) when manipulating numbers. For example, if total operating payments in row 15 are shown as **positive**, you would need to **subtract** them from total operating receipts in the formulae in row 23. However if you have chosen to make them **negative**, to represent outflows, then you will need to **add** them to total operating receipts.

Here is the spreadsheet in its normal 'numbers' form.

	A	B	C	D	E	F	G
1	EXCELLENT PLC						
2	Cash flow projection - six months ending 30 June X6						
3		Jan	Feb	Mar	Apr	May	Jun
4		£	£	£	£	£	£
5	Sales	42000	43260	44558	45895	47271	48690
6	Cash receipts						
7	1 month in arrears	27000	25200	25956	26735	27537	28363
8	2 months in arrears	13500	13500	12600	12978	13367	13768
9	3 months in arrears	3150	3150	3150	2940	3028	3119
10	Total operating receipts	43650	41850	41706	42653	43932	45250
11							
12	Cash payments						
13	Purchases	-27300	-28119	-28963	-29831	-30726	-31648
14	Overheads	-6300	-6300	-6300	-6300	-6300	-6300
15	Total operating payments	-33600	-34419	-35263	-36131	-37026	-37948
16							
17	Dividends					-10000	
18	Capital purchases	-3600	-12600			-1800	
19	Total other payments	-3600	-12600			-11800	
20							
21	Net cash flow	6450	-5169	6443	6521	-4894	7302
22	Cash balance b/f	-7500	-1050	-6219	224	6746	1852
23	Cash balance c/f	-1050	-6219	224	6746	1852	9154
24							

5.1.3 Tidy the spreadsheet up

Our spreadsheet needs a little **tidying up**. We will do the following.

(a)   Add in **commas** to denote thousands of pounds.

(b)   Put **zeros** in the cells with no entry in them.

(c)   Change **negative numbers** from being displayed with a **minus sign** to being displayed in **brackets**.

	A	B	C	D	E	F	G
1	EXCELLENT PLC						
2	Cash flow projection - six months ending 30 June X6						
3		Jan	Feb	Mar	Apr	May	Jun
4		£	£	£	£	£	£
5	Sales	42,000	43,260	44,558	45,895	47,271	48,690
6	Cash receipts						
7	1 month in arrears	27,000	25,200	25,956	26,735	27,537	28,363
8	2 months in arrears	13,500	13,500	12,600	12,978	13,367	13,768
9	3 months in arrears	3,150	3,150	3,150	2,940	3,028	3,119
10	Total operating receipts	43,650	41,850	41,706	42,653	43,932	45,250
11							
12	Cash payments						
13	Purchases	(27,300)	(28,119)	(28,963)	(29,831)	(30,726)	(31,648)
14	Overheads	(6,300)	(6,300)	(6,300)	(6,300)	(6,300)	(6,300)
15	Total operating payments	(33,600)	(34,419)	(35,263)	(36,131)	(37,026)	(37,948)
16							
17	Dividends	0	0	0	0	(10,000)	0
18	Capital purchases	(3,600)	(12,600)	0	0	(1,800)	0
19	Total other payments	(3,600)	(12,600)	0	0	(11,800)	0
20							
21	Net cash flow	6,450	(5,169)	6,443	6,521	(4,894)	7,302
22	Cash balance b/f	(7,500)	(1,050)	(6,219)	224	6,746	1,852
23	Cash balance c/f	(1,050)	(6,219)	224	6,746	1,852	9,154
24							

5.1.4 Changes in assumptions (what if? analysis)

We referred to earlier to the need to design a spreadsheet so that **changes in assumptions** do **not** require **major changes** to the spreadsheet. This is why we set up two separate areas of the spreadsheet, one for 20X6 assumptions and one for opening balances. Consider each of the following.

(a)   Negotiations with suppliers and gains in productivity have resulted in cost of sales being reduced to 62% of sales.

(b)   The effects of a recession have changed the cash collection profile so that receipts in any month are 50% of prior month sales, 35% of the previous month and 10% of the month before that, with bad debt experience rising to 5%.

(c)   An insurance claim made in 20X5 and successfully settled in December has resulted in the opening cash balance being an overdraft of £3,500.

(d)   Sales growth will only be 2% per month.

All of these changes can be made quickly and easily. The two tables are revised as follows.

	A	B	C	D	E	F	G
25							
26	*This table contains the key variables for the*		*X6 cash flow projections*				
27							
28	Sales growth factor per month		1.02				
29	Purchases as % of sales		-0.62				
30							
31	Debts paid within 1 month		0.5				
32	Debts paid within 2 months		0.35				
33	Debts paid within 3 months		0.1				
34	Bad debts		0.05				
35							
36	Increase in overheads		1.05				
37							
38	Dividends (May)		-10000				
39							
40	Capital purchases		-18000				
41	January		0.2				
42	February		0.7				
43	May		0.1				
44							
45							
46	*This table contains relevant opening balance data as at Jan*		*X6*				
47							
48	Monthly sales X5		45000				
49	January X6 sales		42000				
50	Monthly overheads X5		-6000				
51	Opening cash		-3500				
52							

The resulting (recalculated) spreadsheet would look like this.

	A	B	C	D	E	F	G
1	**EXCELLENT PLC**						
2	*Cash flow projection - six months ending 30 June X6*						
3		Jan	Feb	Mar	Apr	May	Jun
4		£	£	£	£	£	£
5	Sales	42,000	42,840	43,697	44,571	45,462	46,371
6	*Cash receipts*						
7	1 month in arrears	22,500	21,000	21,420	21,848	22,285	22,731
8	2 months in arrears	15,750	15,750	14,700	14,994	15,294	15,600
9	3 months in arrears	4,500	4,500	4,500	4,200	4,284	4,370
10	Total operating receipts	42,750	41,250	40,620	41,042	41,863	42,701
11							
12	*Cash payments*						
13	Purchases	-26,040	-26,561	-27,092	-27,634	-28,187	-28,750
14	Overheads	-6,300	-6,300	-6,300	-6,300	-6,300	-6,300
15	Total operating payments	-32,340	-32,861	-33,392	-33,934	-34,487	-35,050
16							
17	Dividends	0	0	0	0	-10,000	0
18	Capital purchases	-3,600	-12,600	0	0	-1,800	0
19	Total other payments	-3,600	-12,600	0	0	-11,800	0
20							
21	Net cash flow	6,810	-4,211	7,228	7,109	-4,423	7,650
22	Cash balance b/f	-3,500	3,310	-901	6,327	13,436	9,012
23	Cash balance c/f	3,310	-901	6,327	13,436	9,012	16,663
24							

Example: Commission calculations

The following four insurance salesmen each earn a basic salary of £14,000 pa. They also earn a commission of 2% of sales. The following spreadsheet has been created to process their commission and total earnings. Give an appropriate formula for each of the following cells.

- (a) Cell D4.
- (b) Cell E6.
- (c) Cell D9.
- (d) Cell E9.

	A	B	C	D	E
1	*Sales team salaries and commissions - 200X*				
2	Name	Sales	Salary	Commission	Total earnings
3		£	£	£	£
4	Northington	284,000	14,000	5,680	19,680
5	Souther	193,000	14,000	3,860	17,860
6	Weston	12,000	14,000	240	14,240
7	Easterman	152,000	14,000	3,040	17,040
8					
9	Total	641,000	56,000	12,820	68,820
10					
11					
12	*Variables*				
13	Basic Salary	14,000			
14	Commission rate	0.02			
15					

Solution

Possible formulae are as follows.

- (a) =B4*$B$14.
- (b) =C6+D6.
- (c) =SUM(D4:D7).
- (d) There are a number of possibilities here, depending on whether you set the cell as the total of the earnings of each salesman (cells E4 to E7) or as the total of the different elements of remuneration (cells C9 and D9). Even better, would be a formula that checked that both calculations gave the same answer. A suitable formula for this purpose would be:

  =IF(SUM(E4:E7)=SUM(C9:D9),SUM(E4:E7),"ERROR")

  We will explain this formula in more detail after the next example.

Example: actual sales compared with budget sales

A business will often need to compare its results with budgets or targets to see how far it has exceeded, or fallen short of, its expectations. It is useful to express **variations as a percentage of the original budget**, for example sales may be 10% higher than predicted.

Continuing the example of the insurance salesmen, a spreadsheet could be set up as follows showing differences between actual sales and target sales, and expressing the difference as a percentage of target sales.

	A	B	C	D	E	F
1	Sales team comparison of actual against budget sales					
2	Name	Sales (Budget)	Sales (Actual)	Difference	% of budget	
3		£	£	£	£	
4	Northington	275,000	284,000	9,000	3.27	
5	Souther	200,000	193,000	(7,000)	(3.50)	
6	Weston	10,000	12,000	2,000	20.00	
7	Easterman	153,000	152,000	(1,000)	(0.65)	
8						
9	Total	638,000	641,000	3,000	0.47	
10						

Give a suitable formula for each of the following cells.

(a)   Cell D4.

(b)   Cell E6.

(c)   Cell E9.

Try this for yourself, before looking at the solution.

Solution

(a)   =C4-B4.

(b)   =(D6/B6)*100.

(c)   =(D9/B9)*100. Note that in (c) you **cannot simply add up the individual percentage differences**, as the percentages are based on different quantities.

6 Formulae with conditions

Suppose the company employing the salesmen in the above example awards a bonus to those salesmen who exceed their target by more than £1,000. The spreadsheet could work out who is entitled to the bonus.

To do this we would enter the appropriate formula in cells F4 to F7. For salesperson Easterman, we would enter the following in cell F7:

=IF(D4>1000,"BONUS"," ")

We will now explain this formula.

IF statements follow the following structure (or syntax).

=IF(logical_test,value_if_true,value_if_false)

The logical_test is any value or expression that can be evaluated to Yes or No. For example, D4>1000 is a logical expression; if the value in cell D4 is over 1000, the expression evaluates to Yes. Otherwise, the expression evaluates to No.

Value_if_true is the value that is returned if the answer to the logical_test is Yes. For example, if the answer to D4>1000 is Yes, and the value_if_true is the text string "BONUS", then the cell containing the IF function will display the text "BONUS".

Value_if_false is the value that is returned if the answer to the logical_test is No. For example, if the value_if_false is two sets of quote marks "" this means display a blank cell if the answer to the logical test is No. So in our example, if D4 is not over 1000, then the cell containing the IF function will display a blank cell.

Note the following symbols which can be used in formulae with conditions:

<	less than (like L (for 'less') on its side)
<=	less than or equal to
=	equal to
>=	greater than or equal to
>	greater than
<>	not equal to

Care is required to ensure **brackets** and **commas** are entered in the right places. If, when you try out this kind of formula, you get an error message, it may well be a simple mistake, such as leaving a comma out.

6.1 Examples of formulae with conditions

A company offers a discount of 5% to customers who order more than £1,000 worth of goods. A spreadsheet showing what customers will pay might look like this.

	A	B	C	D	E	F
1	**Discount Traders Ltd**					
2	*Sales analysis – April 200X*					
3	Customer	Sales	5% discount	Sales (net)		
4		£	£	£		
5	Arthur	956.00	0.00	956.00		
6	Dent	1423.00	71.15	1351.85		
7	Ford	2894.00	144.70	2749.30		
8	Prefect	842.00	0.00	842.00		
9						
10						

The formula in cell C5 is: =IF(B5>1,000,(0.05*B5),0). This means, if the value in B5 is greater than £1,000 multiply it by 0.05, otherwise the discount will be zero. Cell D5 will calculate the amount net of discount, using the formula: =B5-C5. The same conditional formula with the cell references changed will be found in cells C6, C7 and C8. **Strictly**, the variables £1,000 and 5% should be entered in a **different part** of the spreadsheet.

Here is another example.   Suppose the pass mark for an examination is 50%. You have a spreadsheet containing candidate's scores in column B. If a score is held in cell B10, an appropriate formula for cell C10 would be:

=IF(B10<50,"FAILED","PASSED").

7 Charts and graphs

Using Microsoft Excel, It is possible to display data held in a range of spreadsheet cells in a variety of charts or graphs. We will use the Discount Traders Ltd spreadsheet shown below to generate a chart.

	A	B	C	D	E
1	**Discount Traders Ltd**				
2	*Sales analysis - April 200X*				
3	Customer	Sales	5% discount	Sales (net)	
4		£	£	£	
5	Arthur	956.00	0.00	956.00	
6	Dent	1423.00	71.15	1351.85	
7	Ford	2894.00	144.70	2749.30	
8	Prefect	842.00	0.00	842.00	
9					
10					

The data in the spreadsheet could be used to generate a chart, such as those shown below. We explain how later in this section.

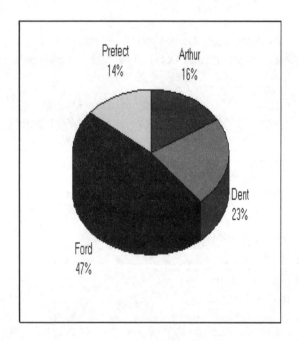

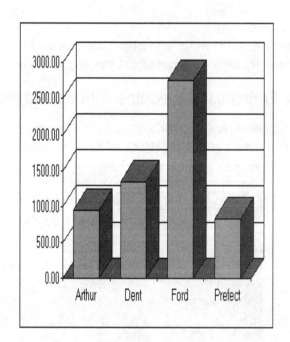

The Chart Wizard, which we explain in a moment, may also be used to generate a line graph. A line graph would normally be used to track a trend over time. For example, the chart below graphs the Total Revenue figures shown in Row 7 of the following spreadsheet.

	A	B	C	D	E	F
1			Revenue 2000-2003			
2						
3						
4	**Net revenue:**	2000	2001	2002	**2003**	
5	Products	24,001	27,552	34,823	**39,205**	
6	Services	5,306	5,720	6,104	**6,820**	
7	Total Revenue	29,307	33,272	40,927	**46,025**	
8						

Total Revenue 2000-2003

Year	£
2000	29307
2001	33272
2002	40927
2003	46025

7.1 The Chart Wizard

Charts and graphs may be generated simply by **selecting the range** of figures to be included, then using Excel's Chart Wizard. The Discount Traders spreadsheet referred to earlier is shown again below.

	A	B	C	D	E
1	Discount Traders Ltd				
2	*Sales analysis - April 200X*				
3	Customer	Sales	5% discount	Sales (net)	
4		£	£	£	
5	Arthur	956.00	0.00	956.00	
6	Dent	1423.00	71.15	1351.85	
7	Ford	2894.00	144.70	2749.30	
8	Prefect	842.00	0.00	842.00	
9					
10					

To chart the **net sales** of the different **customers**, follow the following steps.

Step 1   Highlight cells A5:A8, then move your pointer to cell D5, hold down **Ctrl** and drag to also select cells D5:D8.

Step 2   Look at the **toolbar** at the top of your spreadsheet. You should see an **icon** that looks like a small bar chart. Click on this icon to start the 'Chart Wizard'.

The following steps are taken from the Excel 2000 Chart Wizard. Other versions may differ slightly.

Step 3   Pick the type of chart you want. We will choose chart type **Column** and then select the sub-type we think will be most effective. (To produce a graph, select a type such as **Line**).

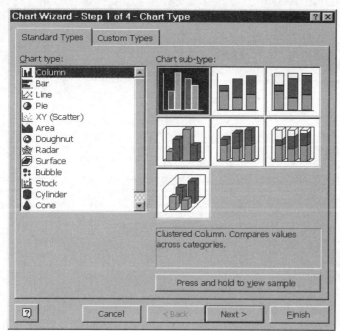

Step 4   This step gives us the opportunity to confirm that the data we selected earlier was correct and to decide whether the chart should be based on **columns** (eg Customer, Sales, Discount etc) or **rows** (Arthur, Dent etc). We can accept the default values and click Next.

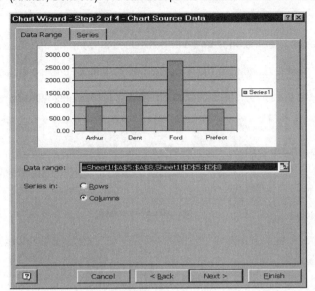

Step 5   Next, specify your chart **title** and axis **labels**. Incidentally, one way of remembering which is the **X axis** and which is the **Y axis** is to look at the letter Y: it is the only letter that has a vertical part pointing straight up, so it must be the vertical axis! Click Next to move on.

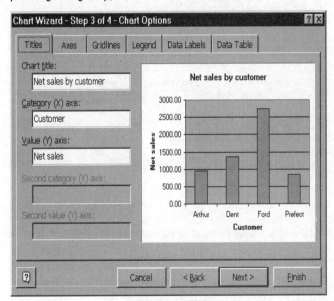

As you can see, there are other index tabs available. You can see the effect of selecting or deselecting each one in **preview** - experiment with these options as you like then click Next.

Step 6   The final step is to choose whether you want the chart to appear on the same worksheet as the data or on a separate sheet of its own. This is a matter of personal preference – for this example choose to place the chart as an object within the existing spreadsheet.

7.2 Changing existing charts

Even after your chart is 'finished' you may change it in a variety of ways.

(a) You can **resize it** simply by selecting it and dragging out its borders.

(b) You can change **each element** by **double clicking** on it then selecting from the options available.

(c) You could also select any item of **text** and alter the wording, size or font, or change the **colours** used.

(d) In the following illustration, the user has double-clicked on the Y axis to enable them to **change the scale**.

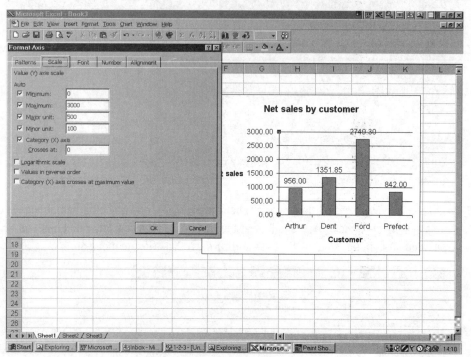

8 Spreadsheet format and appearance

Good presentation can help people understand the contents of a spreadsheet.

8.1 Titles and labels

A spreadsheet should be headed up with a title which **clearly defines its purpose**. Examples of titles are follows.

(a) Trading, profit and loss account for the year ended 30 June 200X.

(b) (i) Area A: Sales forecast for the three months to 31 March 200X.
(ii) Area B: Sales forecast for the three months to 31 March 200X.
(iii) Combined sales forecast for the three months to 31 March 200X.

(c) Salesmen: Analysis of earnings and commission for the six months ended 30 June 200X.

Row and **column** headings (or labels) should clearly identify the contents of the row/column. Any assumptions made that have influenced the spreadsheet contents should be clearly stated.

8.2 Formatting

There are a wide range of options available under the **Format** menu. Some of these functions may also be accessed through toolbar **buttons**. Formatting options include the ability to:

(a) Add **shading** or **borders** to cells.

(b) Use **different sizes of text** and different **fonts**.

(c) Choose from a range of options for presenting values, for example to present a number as a **percentage** (eg 0.05 as 5%), or with commas every third digit, or to a specified number of **decimal places** etc.

Experiment with the various formatting options yourself.

8.2.1 Formatting numbers

Most spreadsheet programs contain facilities for presenting numbers in a particular way. In Excel you simply click on **Format** and then **Cells ...**to reach these options.

(a) **Fixed format** displays the number in the cell rounded off to the number of decimal places you select.

(b) **Currency format** displays the number with a '£' in front, with commas and not more than two decimal places, eg £10,540.23.

(c) **Comma format** is the same as currency format except that the numbers are displayed without the '£'.

(d) **General format** is the format assumed unless another format is specified. In general format the number is displayed with no commas and with as many decimal places as entered or calculated that fit in the cell.

(e) **Percent format** multiplies the number in the display by 100 and follows it with a percentage sign. For example the number 0.548 in a cell would be displayed as 54.8%.

(f) **Hidden format** is a facility by which values can be entered into cells and used in calculations but are not actually displayed on the spreadsheet. The format is useful for hiding sensitive information.

8.3 Gridlines

One of the options available under the **Tools**, **Options** menu, on the **View** tab, is an option to remove the gridlines from your spreadsheet.

Compare the following two versions of the same spreadsheet. Note how the formatting applied to the second version has improved the spreadsheet presentation.

	A	B	C	D	E	F
1	Sales team salaries and commissions - 200X					
2	Name	Sales	Salary	Commi	Total earnings	
3		£	£	£	£	
4	Northingto	284000	14000	5680	19680	
5	Souther	193000	14000	3860	17860	
6	Weston	12000	14000	240	14240	
7	Eastermai	152000	14000	3040	17040	
8						
9	Total	641000	56000	12820	68820	
10						

	A	B	C	D	E
1	Sales team salaries and commissions - 200X				
2	Name	Sales	Salary	Commission	Total earnings
3		£	£	£	£
4	Northington	284,000	14,000	5,680	19,680
5	Souther	193,000	14,000	3,860	17,860
6	Weston	12,000	14,000	240	14,240
7	Easterman	152,000	14,000	3,040	17,040
8					
9	Total	641,000	56,000	12,820	68,820
10					

8.4 Rounding errors

The ability to display numbers in a variety of formats (eg to no decimal places) can result in a situation whereby totals that are correct may actually look incorrect.

Example: Rounding errors

The following example shows how apparent rounding errors can arise.

	A	B	C	D
1	*Petty cash*			
2	*Week ended 16 August 200X*			
3		£		
4	Opening balance	231		
5	Receipts	33		
6	Payments	-105		
7	Closing balance	160		
8				

	A	B	C	D
1	*Petty cash*			
2	*Week ended 16 August 200X*			
3		£		
4	Opening balance	231.34		
5	Receipts	32.99		
6	Payments	(104.67)		
7	Closing balance	159.66		
8				

Cell B7 contains the formula =SUM(B4:B6). The spreadsheet on the left shows that 231 + 33 - 105 is equal to 160, which is not true (check it). The **reason for the discrepancy** is that both spreadsheets actually contain the values shown in the spreadsheet on the right.

However, the spreadsheet on the left has been formatted to display numbers with **no decimal places**. So, individual numbers display as the nearest whole number, although the actual value held by the spreadsheet and used in calculations includes the decimals.

Solution

One solution, that will prevent the appearance of apparent errors, is to use the **ROUND function.** The ROUND function has the following structure: ROUND (value, places). 'Value' is the value to be rounded. 'Places' is the number of places to which the value is to be rounded.

The difference between using the ROUND function and formatting a value to a number of decimal places is that using the ROUND function actually **changes** the **value**, while formatting only changes the **appearance** of the value.

In the example above, the ROUND function could be used as follows. The following formulae could be inserted in cells C4 to C7.

C4 = ROUND(B4,0)   C5 = ROUND(B5,0)   C6 = ROUND(B6,0)   C7 = SUM(C4:C6)

Column B could then be hidden by highlighting the whole column (by clicking on the B at the top of the column), then selecting Format, Column, Hide from the main menu. Try this for yourself, hands-on.

Note that using the ROUND function to eliminate decimals results in slightly inaccurate calculation totals (in our example 160 is actually 'more correct' than the 159 obtained using ROUND. For this reason, some people prefer not to use the function, and to make users of the spreadsheet aware that small apparent differences are due to rounding.

9 Other issues: printing; controls; using spreadsheets with word processing software

9.1 Printing spreadsheets

The print options for your spreadsheet may be accessed by selecting **File** and then **Page Setup**. The various Tabs contain a range of options. You specify the area of the spreadsheet to be printed in the Print area box on the Sheet tab. Other options include the ability to repeat headings on all pages and the option to print gridlines if required (normally they wouldn't be!)

Experiment with these options including the options available under Header/Footer.

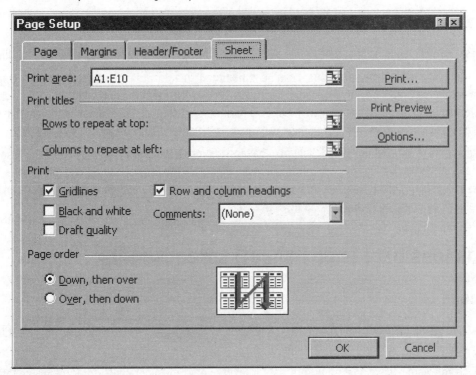

9.2 Controls

There are facilities available in spreadsheet packages which can be used as controls – to prevent unauthorised or accidental amendment or deletion of all or part of a spreadsheet.

(a)   **Saving** and **back-up**. When working on a spreadsheet, save your file regularly, as often as every ten minutes. This will prevent too much work being lost in the advent of a system crash. Spreadsheet files should be included in standard back-up procedures (back-up options and procedures are covered in detail in the BPP Interactive Text for Unit 21).

(b)   **Cell protection**. This prevents the user from inadvertently changing or erasing cells that should not be changed. Look up how to protect cells using Excel's Help facility. (Select Help from the main menu within Excel, then select Contents and Index, click on the Find tab and enter the words 'cell protection').

(c)   **Passwords.** You can set a password for any spreadsheet that you create. In Excel, simply click on **Tools,** then on **Protection,** then on **Protect Sheet** or **Protect Workbook**, as appropriate. The use of passwords with spreadsheet files is covered in detail in the BPP Interactive Text for Unit 21.

9.3 Using spreadsheets with word processing software

There may be a situation where you wish to incorporate the contents of all or part of a spreadsheet into a **word processed report**. There are a number of options available to achieve this.

(a)   The simplest, but least professional option, is to **print out** the spreadsheet and interleave the page or pages at the appropriate point in your word processed document.

(b)   A neater option if you are just including a small table is to select and **copy** the relevant cells from the spreadsheet to the computer's clipboard by selecting the cells and choosing Edit, Copy. Then switch to the word processing document, and **paste** them in at the appropriate point.

(c)   Office packages, such as Microsoft Office allow you to **link** spreadsheets and word processing files.

For example, a new, blank spreadsheet can be '**embedded**' in a document by selecting Insert, Object then, from within the Create New tab, selecting Microsoft Excel worksheet. The spreadsheet is then available to be worked upon, allowing the easy manipulation of numbers using all the facilities of the spreadsheet package. Clicking outside the spreadsheet will result in the spreadsheet being inserted in the document.

The contents of an existing spreadsheet may be inserted into a Word document by choosing Insert, Object and then activating the Create from File tab. Then click the Browse button and locate the spreadsheet file. Highlight the file, then click Insert, and then OK. You may then need to move and resize the object, by dragging its borders, to fit your document.

10 Three dimensional (multi-sheet) spreadsheets

10.1 Background

In early spreadsheet packages, a spreadsheet file consisted of a single worksheet. Excel provides the option of multi-sheet spreadsheets, consisting of a series of related sheets.

For example, suppose you were producing a profit forecast for two regions, and a combined forecast for the total of the regions. This situation would be suited to using separate worksheets for each region and another for the total. This approach is sometimes referred to as working in **three dimensions**, as you are able to flip between different sheets stacked in front or behind each other. Cells in one sheet may **refer** to cells in another sheet. So, in our example, the formulae in the cells in the total sheet would refer to the cells in the other sheets.

Excel has a series of 'tabs', one for each worksheet at the foot of the spreadsheet.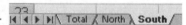

10.2 How many sheets?

Excel can be set up so that it always opens a fresh file with a certain number of worksheets ready and waiting for you. Click on **Tools ... Options** ... and then the **General** tab and set the number *Sheets in new workbook* option to the number you would like each new spreadsheet file to contain (sheets may be added or deleted later).

If you subsequently want to insert more sheets you just **right click** on the index tab after which you want the new sheet to be inserted and choose **Insert** … and then **Worksheet**. By default sheets are called **Sheet 1, Sheet 2** etc. However, these may be changed. To **rename** a sheet in **Excel, right click** on its index tab and choose the rename option.

10.3 Pasting from one sheet to another

When building a spreadsheet that will contain a number of worksheets with identical structure, users often set up one sheet, then copy that sheet and amend the sheet contents. [To copy a worksheet in Excel, from within the worksheet you wish to copy, select Edit, Move or Copy sheet, and tick the Create a copy box.] A 'Total' sheet would use the same structure, but would contain formulae totalling the individual sheets.

10.4 Linking sheets with formulae

Formulae on one sheet may refer to data held on another sheet. The links within such a formula may be established using the following steps.

Step 1	In the cell that you want to refer to a cell from another sheet, type =.
Step 2	Click on the index tab for the sheet containing the cell you want to refer to and select the cell in question.
Step 3	Press Enter or Return.

Example: Formulae linking sheets

Start with a blank spreadsheet and ensure that it contains at least two sheets.

Type the number 1,746, 243 in cell A1 of the first sheet. Then select the tab for the second sheet and select A1 in that sheet (this is step 1 from the three steps above). Type =. Follow steps 2 and 3 above. The same number will display in cell A1 of both sheets. However, what is actually contained in cell A1 of the second sheet is the formula **=Sheet1!A1**

Cell A1 in the second sheet is now linked to cell A1 in the first sheet. This method may be used regardless of the cell addresses - the two cells **do not have to be in the same place** in their respective sheets. For instance cell Z658 of one sheet could refer to cell P24 of another. If you **move cells** or insert **extra rows** or columns on the sheet with the original numbers the cell references on the other sheet will **change automatically**.

10.5 Uses for multi-sheet spreadsheets

There are a wide range of situations suited to the multi-sheet approach. A variety of possible uses follow.

(a) A model could use one sheet for variables, a second for calculations, and a third for outputs.

(b) To enable quick and easy **consolidation** of similar sets of data, for example the financial results of two subsidiaries or the budgets of two departments.

(c) To provide **different views** of the same data. For instance you could have one sheet of data sorted in product code order and another sorted in product name order.

Key learning points

☑ A **spreadsheet** is basically an electronic piece of paper divided into **rows** and **columns**. The intersection of a row and a column is known as a **cell**.

☑ Essential basic **skills** include how to **move around** within a spreadsheet, how to **enter** and **edit** data, how to **fill** cells, how to **insert** and **delete** columns and rows and how to improve the basic **layout** and **appearance** of a spreadsheet.

☑ **Relative** cell references (B3) change when you copy formulae to other locations or move data from one place to another. **Absolute** cell references ($B$3) stay the same.

☑ A wide range of **formulae** and functions are available within Excel. We looked at the use of conditional formulae that use an **IF** statement.

☑ A spreadsheet should be given a **title** which clearly defines its purpose. The contents of rows and columns should also be clearly **labelled**. **Formatting** should be used to make the data held in the spreadsheet easy to read and interpret.

☑ **Numbers** can be **formatted** in several ways, for instance with commas, as percentages, as currency or with a certain number of decimal places. **Rounding** differences may need to be dealt with.

☑ Excel includes the facility to produce a range of charts and graphs. The **Chart Wizard** provides a tool to simplify the process of chart construction.

☑ Spreadsheets can be **linked** to and exchange data with **word processing documents** - and vice versa.

☑ **Backing-up** is a key security measure. You can also use cell protection and **passwords** to prevent unauthorised access (these areas are covered in Unit 21).

☑ Spreadsheet packages permit the user to work with **multiple sheets** that refer to each other. This is sometimes referred to a three dimensional spreadsheet.

☑ Spreadsheets can be used in a variety of accounting contexts. You should practise using spreadsheets, **hands-on experience** is the key to spreadsheet proficiency.

Quick quiz

1   List three types of cell contents.

2   What do the F5 and F2 keys do in Excel?

3   What technique can you use to insert a logical series of data such as 1, 2 …. 10, or Jan, Feb, March etc?

4   How do you display formulae instead of the results of formulae in a spreadsheet?

5   List five possible changes that may improve the appearance of a spreadsheet.

6   What formula would be used in a worksheet named Calculations to refer to cell A5 in a sheet named Variables?

7   List three possible uses for a multi-sheet (3D) spreadsheet.

Answers to quick quiz

1   Text, values or formulae.

2   F5 opens a GoTo dialogue box which is useful for navigating around large spreadsheets. F2 puts the active cell into edit mode.

3   You can use the technique of 'filling' - selecting the first few items of a series and dragging the lower right corner of the selection in the appropriate direction.

4   Select Tools, Options, ensure the View tab is active then tick the Formulas box within the window options area.

5   Removing gridlines, adding shading, adding borders, using different fonts and font sizes, presenting numbers as percentages or currency or to a certain number of decimal places.

6   =Variables!A5 (you would not need to type this, you would enter = in the cell you wish the value to display, then navigate using the mouse to cell A5 in the sheet named Variables and hit Enter).

7   The construction of a spreadsheet model with separate Input, Calculation and Output sheets. They can help consolidate data from different sources. They can offer different views of the same data.

Activity checklist

This checklist shows which performance criteria, range statement or knowledge and understanding point is covered by each activity in this chapter. Tick off each activity as you complete it.

Activity

1.1   Knowledge and Understanding: Methods of analysing information in spreadsheets

1.2   Knowledge and Understanding: Methods of analysing information in spreadsheets

1.3   Knowledge and Understanding: Methods of analysing information in spreadsheets

1.4   Knowledge and Understanding: Methods of analysing information in spreadsheets

P A R T   B

Using accounting software

chapter 2

Introducing
the case study

Contents

1   Introduction
2   Using Sage
3   Loading the data for assignments
4   Account reference codes
5   The nominal ledger (or 'main ledger')
6   Using the Word and Excel files
7   Conclusion

Range statement

Relevant computerised records
Computerised records
Computerised ledgers

Knowledge and understanding

Operation of computerised accounting systems

1 Introduction

Sage is a 'user-friendly' software package and is designed to help you as much as possible. This first section describes some important features of the software.

2 Using Sage

2.1 Setting up Sage software for the first time

If Sage has not been installed on the PC you will be using, follow the instructions in the Sage manuals for installing the software. If you will be using the case study data on a network, please consult the IT department of your organisation. (the contents of the CD could be copied to a network location and accessed from there).

If you are installing Sage Line 50 or Sage Instant for the first time choose the following options:

- Create a **new** company or a new set of data files

- General Business – **Standard** chart of accounts

- The **Company Details** you enter does not matter, as when you load one of the Assignments the correct Blitz company details and chart of accounts will overwrite any existing data. But, for the record, the Blitz Company details are shown below.

    Blitz Limited
    25 Apple Road
    London
    N12 3PP

- **Financial Year** – starts in August 2000 (the case study is set in 2000 and 2001)

- All other options can be ignored (ie by clicking on **Next** or on **Finish**)

Check with your tutor or supervisor about how to gain access to the software package. The procedure is likely to be as simple as that described below for a stand-alone PC, but it may be different if your college has a larger system.

Click on the Start button and search through the menus until you find Sage. Alternatively there may be an **icon** on the 'desktop'. If so, just **double-click** on it.

The software *may* have been set up by your college so that you have to enter a password before you can get into the package. **BPP do not recommend this for the purposes of the Blitz case study**.

Activity 2.1

Make sure that you are aware of how to access the Sage software you will be using.

Once you have gained access to the package the Sage screen will look something like the illustration below. Notice the menu bar (File, Edit, View etc) and the row of icons or buttons beneath (Customers, Suppliers, Nominal, etc).

If you are using an earlier version of Sage, you may not see some of these icons, such as Period End and E-mail. The icon 'picture' may also differ depending upon the version of the software you are using – don't worry about this – the button will still do the same thing.

Later version and also show Sage Task bar. This book refers to the buttons across the top of the screen rather than using the Sage Task bar. If your version of Sage displays the Task bar, you may wish to **close this task bar** by clicking on the **X** to the right of the work Tasks.

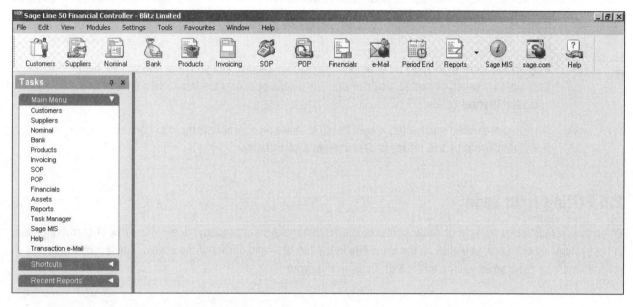

2.2 Buttons, icons and the task bar

To access the part of Sage required for a particular task you click on the appropriate 'button' or 'icon'. When you click on a button a further window will then appear, specifying more detailed areas of work within your initial selection. You click on a button within this new window to select an option. The selection process goes on until you have reached the program or 'routine' that you wish to use.

As explained above, later versions of Sage include a **Task bar** that may be displayed in the left portion of the window. This provides another way by which you may move around the software.

When you have reached the program or routine you want to use, it should be fairly clear, from instructions on the screen or from the position of the cursor, what you are expected to do next. You might, for example, enter transaction details into the computer, or give instructions for extracting information from the files.

You will be helped throughout by on-screen messages and instructions.

2.3 Keyboard or mouse?

The package can be used with a keyboard alone, but you may find it easier to use a **mixture** of keyboard and mouse.

When using the keyboard, the **Tab** key and the **Esc** (or Escape) key are particularly useful.

(a)   The **Tab** key is used to move on to the next item on screen. Using the **Shift** key and the **Tab** key together moves you back to the previous item on screen.

(b)   The Escape key (**Esc**) can be used to close the current window and move back to the previous window.

2.4 Correcting errors

If incorrect data is keyed, you may correct it in a number of ways.

(a)   If an error is spotted immediately, you will usually be able to wipe out the incorrect data using the **delete** key.

(b)   If an error occurs whilst you are entering a transaction record, and you spot the mistake before the transaction is saved or posted, you can alter the details or cancel the transaction entirely and start again, using the **Discard** option.

(c)   If errors are spotted much later, you will need to make an appropriate input to correct the error. Correcting errors by this means is described in a later chapter.

2.5 Exiting from Sage

When you have finished working on Sage, you should exit from the system properly, to avoid the risk of corrupting data in the system. To exit Sage, you click on the word **File** in the top left-hand corner of the screen. The last option on the menu that drops down when you do this is **Exit**. Click on this word.

2.5.1 Do you wish to backup your data?

A message will then appear on the screen asking you whether you wish to back up your data. In a 'live' system, you would back data up at regular intervals – probably daily. In a training system, your course supervisor might instruct you to select No. If you choose No (by clicking on the No button or pressing N) you will exit from Sage, and you will be returned to the Windows desktop screen.

When you start doing the assignments in this book you may well want to make a copy of your work on a floppy disk. Procedures for **backing up** and restoring data are described later in this chapter.

2.6 The Blitz case study

The assignments in this workbook are based on a case study of a fictional North London company, Blitz Limited. The **case study is set in late 2000 and early 2001**. Blitz Limited was established in August 2000 by two friends, Maria Green and Tim Nicholas. Each has put £20,000 into the company, and they are worker-directors.

The company provides cleaning services. Much of its business comes from office cleaning and other contract cleaning services (such as factory cleaning). However, the company also provides window cleaning services for businesses and domestic cleaning services for private individuals.

2.6.1 When does the case study begin?

The case study begins in October 2000. Blitz has had a fairly busy September, receiving 27 invoices from various suppliers and has issued 35 invoices to customers. Apart from payments of wages and salaries, there were no cash transactions in September, and all invoices are as yet unpaid.

At the beginning of October 2000, Blitz Limited has 27 supplier accounts on its purchase ledger and 35 customer accounts on its sales ledger.

3 Loading the data for assignments

In this section we explain how to use the Sage data contained on the CD that accompanies this Text. You **do not need to load the data while reading this section**. The instructions provided later in this book, at the start of each assignment, tell you when to load the data.

Blitz is the name of the fictional company on which the case study in this book is based. The CD contains data files to be used with either Sage Line 50 or Sage Instant. To use this data **you need to have access to Sage Line 50 or Sage Instant** – the **CD does not contain Sage software** (BPP is not entitled to give away Sage software!).

The data is held on the CD in standard **Line 50** and **Instant back-up files**. Each back-up file has been named to make it clear which assignment it relates to. You load the data that represents the starting point for each Assignment by starting Line 50 or Instant and then restoring the relevant back-up.

You will also be asked occasionally to **load Assignment data while working through Chapters 2-8**. This serves two purposes; it gives you practice loading Assignment data and it enables us to explain Sage functions using 'real' data.

The Assignments themselves do not start until you reach Part C of this book. When starting an Assignment you will be asked to load a fresh copy of the data so previous changes will not affect your performance in the Assignment.

3.1 Loading the Sage data

The latest version of Sage **Line 50** (at the time of publication) is version 10. As many users are still using Line 50 versions 6, 7, 8 and 9 we have also provided a set of data in these versions.

The latest version of Sage **Instant Accounts** (at the time of publication) is version 10. Previous versions were numbered 6 and 8. As many users are still using Sage Instant Accounts versions 6 and 8 we have also provided a set of data in these versions.

Sage releases Line 50 in three products – Accountant, Accountant Plus and Financial Controller. The data provided on the CD can be used with Line 50 Financial Controller.

Instant Accounts is released in two products – Instant Accounts and Instant Accounts Plus. The data provided on the CD can be used with the 'basic' Instant Accounts.

When working through the remainder of this book you will come across instructions such as 'load the data for Assignment 1'. Whenever you are instructed to load an Assignment in this book you should follow the following steps.

Step 1 Ensure the CD is in your CD-ROM drive (you will not see anything happen after inserting the CD – it is not designed to auto-run).

Step 2 Start Sage Line 50 or Sage Instant. If you do not know which version of Sage you have, start Sage then select Help, About from the Main Menu. The version number should then display – ignore any 'decimals' eg version 8.2 is version 8.

Step 3 From the Sage main menu select File, Restore. You will see a box similar to that shown below. Click on the down arrow next to the Drives box, then select the letter of your CD-ROM drive.

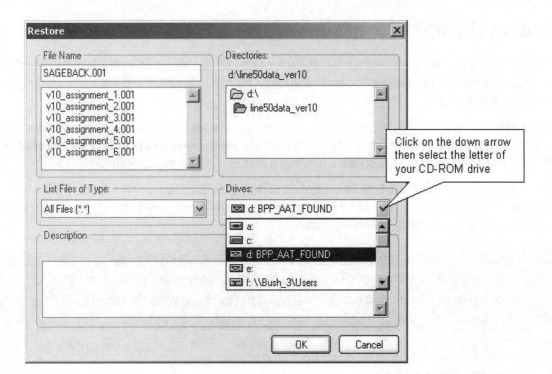

Step 4 After selecting your CD-ROM drive, you should see the contents of the CD in the 'Directories' box – as shown in the following illustration. (The CD-ROM drive shown in our illustrations is drive 'D' – your PC may use a different letter.)

Double-click the folder that relates to the Sage software you are using;

If you are using Instant version 6 double click **instantdata_ver6**

If you are using Instant version 8 double click **instantdata_ver8**

If you are using Instant version 10 double click **instantdata_ver10**

If you are using Line 50 version 6 double click **line50data_ver6**

If you are using Line 50 version 7 double click **line50data_ver7**

If you are using Line 50 version 8 double click **line50data_ver8**

If you are using Line 50 version 9 double click **line50data_ver9**

If you are using Line 50 Version 10 double click **line50data_ver10**

PROFESSIONAL EDUCATION

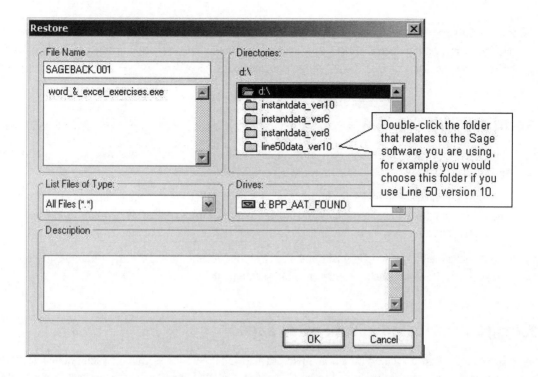

Step 5 We now need to choose the Assignment to restore. The Assignment number is the number before the dot. For example, if we are using Line 50 version 6 and we wish to load Assignment 3 we would click once on v6_assignment_3.001 to highlight it, and then click on OK.

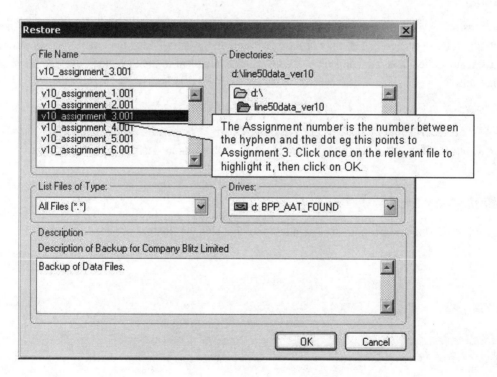

Step 6   If you are using a recent version of Sage, you will see a message warning you that the Restore will overwrite any existing data. Click Yes to proceed. You should now see a box telling you the Restore has been successful. Click on OK. The assignment is now loaded.

3.2 Overwriting Blitz data

Every time you restore an Assignment a fresh copy of the data is loaded. The program overwrites any data that was there previously, so you can, for example:

(a)   Load Assignment 1 and make any entries you like, even if they are complete nonsense, and then load Assignment 1 again to get a fresh clean version. In other words you can *experiment with the data* as much as you like.

(b)   Load Assignment 1, then load Assignment 2. Restoring Assignment 2 will overwrite the data for Assignment 1 and replace it with the data for Assignment 2.

3.3 Backing up and restoring data using Sage

As explained earlier, the data provided on the CD in effect provides a back-up of the data for each of the assignments. If you make changes to the data and wish to save theses changes, you should use Sages back-up facility to save the data to a floppy disc.

3.3.1 Backing up

The Sage package offers you the chance to back up your data onto a floppy disk or into another folder whenever you exit the program. You can also do this at other times by clicking on the word **File** at the top of the main window and choosing the **Backup** option. It is not a difficult procedure: it is very similar to the Save and Save As options in any Windows program.

If you want to keep a copy of, say, your finished versions of Assignments 1 and 2 in back up form, save the individual backup files in separate folders on your floppy disk.

A single 1.44 MB floppy disk is large enough to store backups of all six Sage assignments in this book.

3.3.2 Restoring data

You restore data by clicking on **File** in the main window and choosing the **Restore** option.

Activity 2.2

(a)   Load the data for Assignment 1. Click on Suppliers. What is the code of the first supplier listed?

(b)   Load the data for Assignment 2. Click on Suppliers. What is the code of the first supplier listed?

(c)   Click on New and use the Supplier Record Wizard to create a new supplier record with the name and *Refn* 111111. (Leave all other details blank by clicking Next each time, then Finish.) What is the code of the first account listed now?

(d)   Re-load the data for Assignment 2. Click on Suppliers. What is the code of the first supplier listed now?

3.4 Looking at the opening data

3.4.1 Suppliers ledger data

Re-load Assignment 1. Then, change the date within Sage to the timeframe when the Blitz Case study is set. To do this, from the main menu select **Settings**, **Change program date**. Enter 30/09/2000.

To view data in the suppliers ledger accounts, click on the **Suppliers** button in the main window. The following window will appear (or a similar window -depending upon the version of Sage you are using).

Still in the Suppliers window, now click on the **Aged** button. Enter 30/09/2000 in the Report date and Payments Up To boxes, and click OK. You should see the following data. Note again that the appearance of the illustrations used throughout this book may be slightly different to what you see on screen – depending upon the version of Sage you use. This does not matter – the data (account names, dates, totals etc) should be the same.

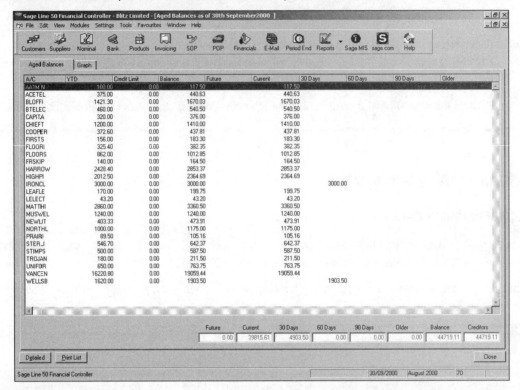

When you have had a look at this press the Esc key or click on **Close** to make this window disappear. Now click on the **Activity** button (next to the **Aged** button) and accept the defaults, except make the date range 01/09/2000 to 30/09/2000. Then click **OK**.

You may receive a warning stating 'Terms have not been agreed on this Account'. If you don't receive the warning carry on. If you do receive the warning just click OK – Blitz is a new company and has not yet finalised terms with suppliers.

The next screen you see shows you details of how the balance on an account is made up. To see details for another account click on the *button* at the right of the box labelled A/C. A list of all the supplier accounts will drop down. Just scroll around and *double-click* on any account name to see the activity for that account.

Alternatively, if you prefer not to use the mouse, press the function key F4. This will bring down the menu of accounts. You can use the up and down cursor keys to scroll from one account to another and press the **Enter** key when the account you want is highlighted.

3.4.2 Customers ledger data

Close the windows open within Sage by pressing the Escape key until you get back to the main window. When you get there, click on the **Customers** button.

From the Customers window, you should then select the **Aged** button or **Activity** button and follow the same procedures as above for the Suppliers ledger. The first customer account on the file for Assignment 1, for example, is for E T ADAMS.

Alternatively, in either the Suppliers or Customers windows you can click on the Account you wish to view, then click Activity and accept the date range.

Activity 2.3

Click on the button labelled **Customers** and then on the new button that appears labelled **Record**.

Find the cursor: it should be in a box labelled A/C. Press **Tab** several times (slowly) and watch the cursor move from one box to the next. At some times it will highlight a button such as Save instead of appearing in a box.

Now experiment with the Shift + Tab combination and watch the cursor move in reverse order.

What happens if you place your mouse pointer in a particular white space on the screen and click?

Press **Esc** when you are happy that you understand the tools you have available for moving the cursor around the screen.

Activity 2.4

Click on **Customers.** If there are any customers listed note down the A/C code (eg ADAMSE) of the first one. Now click on **Record**, and type 000000 (six noughts) in the A/C box and press **Tab**. Now click on **Discard**. What happens? Then click on Close.

4 Account reference codes

As you may already have realised, in our case study, Blitz Limited uses the first six significant letters (or numbers) in the supplier's or customer's name to create their code. For initials and surname, the first six significant letters are taken from the surname. If there are less than six characters in the name (and initials), the code is made up to 6 digits with Xs.

Examples

Name	Account reference code
Matthias Scaffolding	MATTHI
Ace Telephone Answering	ACETEL
B L Office Supplies	BLOFFI
The Tomkinson Group	TOMKIN
R C Chadwick	CHADWI
A Wyche	WYCHEA
A Rose Ltd	ROSEAL
P Wood	WOODPX
C Fry	FRYCXX

If you select Customer or Supplier, then highlight an account and click on the Activity button you can view past transactions on an account – this is useful if a customer or supplier has an account query. Try the following Activity.

Activity 2.5

Load the data for Assignment 1, then start up Sage. A customer, Mr E A Newall, has telephoned Blitz to say he has not received an invoice for some domestic cleaning work. He would like to know how much the cost will be. Can you answer his query?

5 The nominal ledger (or 'main ledger')

Load the opening data for Assignment 1 now by following the instructions given earlier in this chapter.

IMPORTANT!

To ensure Sage is operating using the timeframe the case study is set in, you must change the program date. Close all Sage windows except the main window, then select **Settings**, **Change Program Date** from the pull-down menu. Insert the date 30/09/2000 and click OK.

Blitz Limited is using the 'default' nominal ledger account codes provided in the Sage software. The sales account codes 4000, 4001, 4002 and 4100 have been renamed. A list of the codes is given in Appendix 1 to this book.

5.1 Looking at the opening data

To produce a trial balance report showing the current Nominal ledger balances, click on the **Financials** button and then on the **Trial** (Balance) button.

You will then be asked to choose the relevant Period and the output format for the report (the order in which these options are presented depends upon the version of Sage you are using. Choose the Period September 2000 and to preview the report on screen. Then click on **OK**. (Ensure you have changed the Program Date as explained above before running the report.)

The trial balance to the end of September follows (based on Assignment 1 data).

Date: 16/03/2004   **Blitz Limited**   Page: 1
Time: 11:28:47   **Period Trial Balance**

To Period: Month 2, September 2000

N/C	Name	Debit	Credit
0020	Plant and Machinery	5,734.50	
0030	Office Equipment	1,620.00	
0040	Furniture and Fixtures	1,421.30	
0050	Motor Vehicles	16,220.80	
1100	Debtors Control Account	22,620.43	
1200	Bank Current Account	33,946.07	
2100	Creditors Control Account		44,719.11
2200	Sales Tax Control Account		3,369.03
2201	Purchase Tax Control Account	6,022.38	
2210	P.A.Y.E.		1,370.00
3000	Ordinary Shares		40,000.00
4000	Sales Contract Cleaning		16,597.40
4001	Sales Window Cleaning		1,970.40
4002	Sales Domestic Services		683.60
5000	Materials Purchased	3,703.83	
6201	Advertising	2,200.00	
6203	P.R. (Literature & Brochures)	170.00	
7001	Directors Salaries	1,707.03	
7003	Staff Salaries	475.75	
7004	Wages - Regular	4,941.15	
7005	Wages - Casual	480.00	
7100	Rent	3,000.00	
7103	General Rates	1,240.00	
7200	Electricity	43.20	
7400	Travelling	100.00	
7500	Printing	500.00	
7501	Postage and Carriage	89.50	
7502	Telephone	1,155.00	
7504	Office Stationery	372.60	
7700	Equipment Hire	296.00	
8202	Clothing Costs	650.00	
	Totals:	108,709.54	108,709.54

Activity 2.6

Your supervisor has asked you for details of cash received into the bank account and paid from the bank account since the company was established. With assignment 1 loaded, can you provide this information using the Activity facility? The nominal ledger code for the bank account is 1200.

6 Using the Word and Excel files

The CD that accompanies this book includes a file called Word_&_Excel_exercises.exe. When you execute (run) this file, four Microsoft Word files and six Microsoft Excel files will be copied to your hard disk in a new folder called AATF. The files are used in exercises throughout this book.

To make use of the Word and Excel files you need:

- A CD-ROM drive
- Microsoft Windows 95/98/ME/XP or Windows NT/2000
- Microsoft Excel 97 or above – to use the six spreadsheet files
- Microsoft Word 97 or above – to use the four Word documents

The data from Word_&_Excel_exercises.exe needs to be installed on your computer's hard disk. Follow the instructions below.

6.1 Loading the Word and Excel files

To unload the files to a new folder on your hard disk (C:\AATF) follow these instructions.

6.1.1 First installation

View the CD-ROM in Windows Explorer and double-click on the Word_&_Excel_exercises.exe file. Then click on OK in the pop-up box. The files will then be extracted to your hard disk. If the screen then returns to Windows Explorer, the files have been installed on your hard disk in the folder AATF.

6.1.2 File already exists

If you see a message like the one below, the data has already been installed on your computer.

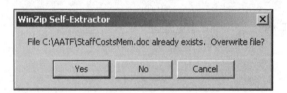

Click Yes to overwrite the file specified with a new version. Click No if you want to keep your current version of the file (for instance if you have made changes to it but saved it under its original name).

6.1.3 What next?

If you have followed the instructions above the data has been copied into a folder on your hard drive called C:\AATF. (You may need to press the F5 key to refresh your screen before you can see this folder in Windows Explorer.)

When you view the contents of the folder C:\AATF you will see the files available for use in Word (the .doc files) or Excel (the .xls files) – as shown in the following illustration. You will be told when to use each file when working through this book.

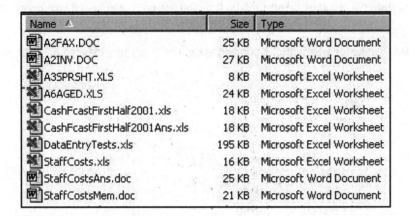

Name △	Size	Type
A2FAX.DOC	25 KB	Microsoft Word Document
A2INV.DOC	27 KB	Microsoft Word Document
A3SPRSHT.XLS	8 KB	Microsoft Excel Worksheet
A6AGED.XLS	24 KB	Microsoft Excel Worksheet
CashFcastFirstHalf2001.xls	18 KB	Microsoft Excel Worksheet
CashFcastFirstHalf2001Ans.xls	18 KB	Microsoft Excel Worksheet
DataEntryTests.xls	195 KB	Microsoft Excel Worksheet
StaffCosts.xls	16 KB	Microsoft Excel Worksheet
StaffCostsAns.doc	25 KB	Microsoft Word Document
StaffCostsMem.doc	21 KB	Microsoft Word Document

6.1.4 Using word processing software

The basics of word processing software are covered in the BPP Interactive Text for Unit 21 *Working with Computers* (Chapter 2 Section 3). Further word processing skills are covered in BPP's Interactive Text for Unit 4.

6.1.5 Using spreadsheets

The basics of spreadsheet software were covered in the previous Chapter of this book. Spreadsheets are also covered in other BPP books, for example the Unit 4 Interactive Text.

For those students who wish to develop more advanced skills, BPP has produced a Workbook, complete with Excel spreadsheet files on CD, to cover the skills required at Technician Level. Refer to the Order Form in the back of this book of you wish to purchase the *Excel exercises for Technician* Workbook with CD.

Introductory exercise: Using Excel and Word

Mr Tim Nicholas would like a memo giving details of total gross pay, total National Insurance, and total overall payroll cost for the month, and any differences from the previous months totals. A similar memo was prepared last month and saved in the file **StaffCostsMem.doc**.

On October 2 2000, Mr Nicholas handed you the following information and asked you to prepare the memo.

Month 2	Total Gross	Employers Nat. Ins.
1 T. NICHOLAS	3,000.00	300.00
2 S. LYNCH	2,125.00	212.50
3 A. PATEL	1,650.00	165.20
4 J. ESCOTT	1,500.00	150.00
5 A. CROPPER	850.00	59.64
6 A. VAUGHAN	875.00	61.32
7 K. KNIGHT	900.00	63.00
8 L. LEROY	1,083.33	108.40
9 L. BROWN	1,100.00	110.00
10 M. KORETZ	1,083.33	108.40
11 N. PARKER	1,083.33	108.40
12 G. TURNER	0.00	0.00
13 M. KOTHARI	1,067.00	106.90
14 N. FAROUK	968.00	97.00
15 L. FARROW	927.00	86.73
16 E. PARKINSON	182.00	0.00
17 N. HAZELWOOD	1,350.00	135.20
18 C. STANLEY	1069.00	107.10
19 S. BABCOCK	983.33	63.28
20 D. COOMBES	1,150.00	60.48

Unload the Word and Excel exercises the folder AATF on your hard disk if you have not already done so.

Open the file **StaffCostsMem.doc** with your word processor and **StaffCosts.xls** with your spreadsheet package. Save each file with a different name (eg Staffcosts_Sep2000....).

(a)   Using **StaffCosts.xls,** enter this month's figures and details in the appropriate columns. The totals will be calculated automatically.

(b)   Copy the spreadsheet into the memo and make any other changes that you think are appropriate.

   Hint: Highlight the relevant cells in the spreadsheet and click on **Edit**, **Copy**. Then switch to the memo in Word, place the cursor where you would like the figures to appear and click **Edit**, **Paste**.

(c)   If possible, print out a copy of the memo.

Solution to introductory exercise

A suggested solution can be found in the file **StaffCostsAns.doc**.

7 Conclusion

7.1 You should now be able to do the following

(a)   Use the BPP CD-ROM to load data for the Assignments.

(b)   Refer to individual accounts in the Suppliers ledger, Customers ledger or Nominal ledger in order to answer queries about transactions in the account.

(c)   Produce a Trial Balance.

(d)   Key in data fairly quickly and (more importantly) accurately. If you require practice using the keyboard, try the exercises contained in the Excel file **DataEntryTests.xls** – if you have installed the Word and Excel files as instructed earlier in this chapter this file will be in the AATF folder on your hard disk.

Key learning points

☑ We have looked at some important features associated with **modern accounting software** – we use Sage as an example.

☑ The assignments in this book are based on a **case study** of a fictional North London company called 'Blitz Limited'. The case study is set in late 2000 and early 2001.

☑ Every time you restore an Assignment from within Sage, using the data provided on the CD that accompanies this book, a **fresh copy of the ledger** as it exists before the Assignment begins is loaded. The program overwrites any data that was there previously.

Quick quiz

1   How do you exit from Sage?

2   What does the F4 key do within Sage?

3   What method does Blitz Limited use to devise customer and supplier account codes?

4   What range of accounts make up the Sales accounts in the Blitz nominal ledger?

5   How do you print a trial balance from Sage?

Answers to quick quiz

1   By selecting File (from in the top left-hand corner of the screen) and then selecting Exit.

2   If you are within a field that requires an entry from a list (eg an account number), the F4 key will show the list of possible entries (eg all existing account numbers).

3   Blitz Limited uses the first six significant letters (or numbers) in the supplier's or customer's name to create their code.

4   Blitz uses the nominal ledger account codes provided in the Sage software. Sales account codes start at 4000 and end at 4905 (a full list of the codes is given in Appendix 1 to this book).

5   By selecting the Financials button from the main menu, then the Trial (Balance) button. You then choose the appropriate accounting period.

Activity checklist

This checklist shows which knowledge and understanding point is covered by each activity in this chapter. Tick off each activity as you complete it.

Activity

2.1		Knowledge and Understanding: Operation of computerised accounting systems
2.2		Knowledge and Understanding: Operation of computerised accounting systems
2.3		Knowledge and Understanding: Operation of computerised accounting systems
2.5		Knowledge and Understanding: Operation of computerised accounting systems
2.5		Knowledge and Understanding: Operation of computerised accounting systems
2.6		Knowledge and Understanding: Operation of computerised accounting systems

chapter 3

Supplier invoices
and credit notes

Contents

1   Introduction
2   Suppliers
3   Supplier details
4   Entering details of invoices received
5   Entering details of credit notes received
6   Reports
7   Conclusion

Range statement

Relevant computerised records
Computerised records
Computerised ledgers

Knowledge and understanding

Operation of computerised accounting systems

1 Introduction

We will now explain some of the most important options for dealing with suppliers. The Suppliers window, which is shown below, is displayed on screen when you click on the **Suppliers** button in the main window. (In Sage, this is how you access functions associated with the **Purchase ledger**).

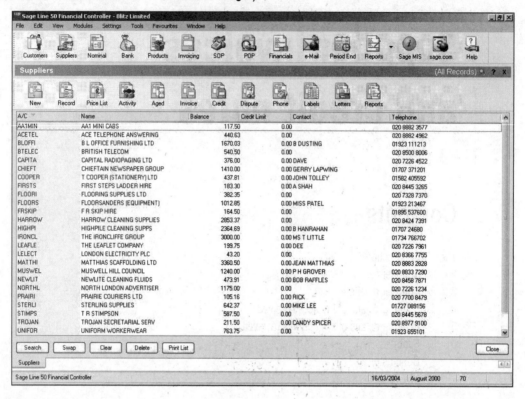

2 Suppliers

When an invoice is received from a new supplier, an account for the supplier must be set up. There are three ways of entering new supplier accounts.

    (a)   Using the Supplier **Record** button.

    (b)   Using the **Invoices** button.

    (c)   Using the **New** button from within Suppliers to access the Supplier Record Wizard.

The **Record** button method is described here. Experiment with the other two methods yourself.

3 Supplier details

To set up an account for a new supplier click on Suppliers. Then, ensure no existing supplier is highlighted (by clicking on Clear) and then click on the **Record** button. This option allows you to insert details of a new supplier (that is, create a new supplier account) or to amend details of an existing account, for example to change the supplier's address or telephone number.

Existing supplier accounts can also be deleted from the ledger in certain circumstances. When you click on the **Record** button, the following display will appear on screen. (There may be slight differences in layout depending upon the version of Sage you are using.) Note that different aspects of supplier details are depicted as index cards or tabs (Details, Defaults etc). You click on the index tab to activate the related options.

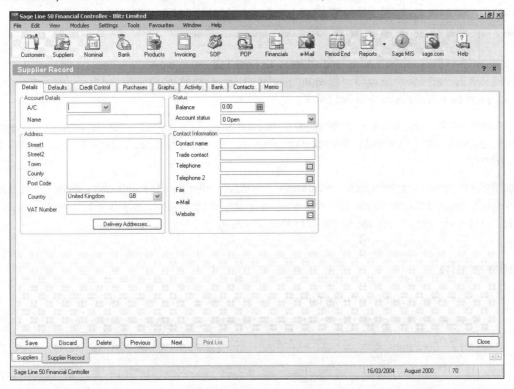

3.1 Details

The cursor starts at the **A/C box**. The supplier's reference code should be entered here. The maximum length for the code is eight digits. The coding system used by Blitz Limited uses six characters.

When you enter a code for a new supplier and press **Tab**, the words **New Account** will appear in the grey area next to the **A/C box**. The cursor will have moved down to the next line, ready for you to insert the supplier's name. Press **Tab** to move from the name line to the address section. Press the **Shift** key plus **Tab** to move *up* to the previous line. If you want to leave a line blank just press **Tab** again to move on to the next line. A typical entry is shown below.

Name	Lexington Supplies
Street 1	Billington House
Street 2	25-29 Dorchester Avenue
Town	London
County	
Postcode	W12 5TL

Activity 3.1

Load up Assignment 6 and using the A/C code LEXING enter all of the details given in the previous paragraph as a new supplier account (save the account). Between which two codes does the new account appear?

After you have entered the supplier's name and address, use the **Tab** key to move the cursor down the screen, from one item to the next. A contact name (in case of account queries), trade contact, telephone and fax numbers, e-mail and website details can be entered in the relevant fields.

In the assignments in this book you will not be required to enter any details in the box for **Vat Reg No**. However, in practice these details would be entered in the box if required. You can just press **Tab** to leave the field blank and move on to the next field.

Click on the Delivery button to enter a **Delivery Address**. You would enter here the address to which the supplier in question normally delivers the goods you buy from him – a factory in Manchester, say. Blitz Limited has all its supplies delivered to its main address, so you will not need to enter anything here.

3.2 Credit control

Now click on the third index tab labelled **Credit Control**. This gives you a new screen – shown below.

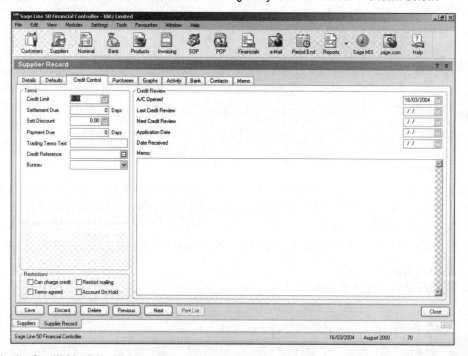

You would fill in the **Credit Limit** line if the supplier had allocated you an upper limit to the amount of credit you are allowed.

The **Sett Due Days** box refers to the terms of your account – how many days following the invoice date must payment (settlement) be made to qualify for any settlement discount. The amount of settlement discount, in percentage terms, is shown in the **Sett Discount** box. For example a supplier may offer you a 10% discount if you pay an invoice within, say, 7 days. In this case you would enter the number 7 in the **Sett Due Days** box and 10.00 in the **Sett Discount** box.

The entry in the **Pay Due Days** box is the number of *days* that you have to pay an invoice: typically a supplier might expect payment within 30 days. The **Terms** box is for a narrative description: 'Payment on delivery', or whatever is appropriate. When Terms have been agreed with a supplier the **small Terms agreed** box should be 'ticked'.

You need not be concerned with the **Credit Ref** and **Bureau** boxes. If you are interested, use the Sage on-line help facility to find out their purpose.

3.3 Defaults

The Defaults index tab allows you to specify certain details about how a transaction with the supplier will normally be posted. For example if one of your suppliers were Yorkshire Electricity you would probably be reasonably sure that all transactions on this account should be posted to the Electricity expense account in the nominal ledger.

If you make an entry in the **Def N/C** box when you first set up the Yorkshire Electricity account, then when you next have an invoice from Yorkshire Electricity the program will automatically suggest to you that it should be posted to the 'default' nominal account you specified when the account was set up. (You can, however, choose a different nominal code at the time when you are posting the transaction.)

Sage has a box for **Disc%**. This is for discounts other than settlement discounts. It is not used in the Blitz case study.

The **Def Tax Code** box will offer you a pull down list of possible VAT codes that apply to this supplier. In the assignments in the Blitz case study the default code is **T1 – 17.5%**, which is the standard rate of VAT at the time of preparation of this book.

Below the **Def Tax Code** box is a box labelled **Currency**. The default in the case study is '**1 Pound Sterling**'. If you click on this box and its downward pointing arrow you will be offered a number of other options such as French Francs or German Marks. The Blitz case study only uses UK currency, so you can just accept the default for this box.

In the assignments in this book *you will not be required* to enter any details in the boxes for **Analysis.** These are useful for management accounting purposes, but not part of the standards of competence at AAT Foundation level. In each case press **Tab** to leave the field blank and move on to the next field.

The other index tabs are not used in the assignments in this book, but you might find it interesting to have a look at them and see what happens when you click on various buttons. Don't be afraid of experimenting: you can always get a fresh copy of the data using the CD-ROM.

3.4 Checking and saving your work

When you have entered all the details that need to be entered you should *check* what you have on screen against the document you are working from (against the details given in this book in the case of the assignments).

(a) If you have made just one or two errors just press **Tab** until the entry is highlighted and type in the correct entry. If just one character is wrong it is quicker to click on the entry, and move the cursor using the cursor keys until it is in the appropriate place, delete the wrong character and insert the correct one.

(b)   If you have made a complete hash of the entries it may be better to start all over again and be more careful next time. In this case click on the button labelled **Discard.** The screen will be cleared and you can start again.

(c)   If you are happy that all your entries are correct click on **Save**. The new supplier will be added to the Suppliers ledger.

(d)   If you click on Save and only then realise you have made a mistake in posting the details you can call up the details you posted again by selecting the supplier code from the main Suppliers window, click on **Record** and edit out your mistakes. Alternatively you can call up the account and click on **Delete** to remove it entirely. However you can only delete a supplier in this way if no transactions have yet been posted to that account.

Activity 3.2

(a)   What is the post-code for account AA1MIN?

(b)   What is the contact name for account TROJAN?

(c)   What is the full account name and telephone number of the account COOPER?

Activity 3.3

Set up a supplier account for the following supplier in the same way as details have been entered for existing Blitz supplier accounts. Refer to the paragraphs above if you don't know whether you need to put an entry in a particular box or how to make the entry.

Lineker Leisurewear Limited
Bernard House
647 Spenser Street,
Birmingham, BH1 2OD
Contact: Frederic Ferinella
Phone: 0161 123 6543
Credit limit: £1,500

4 Entering details of invoices received

When invoices are received from suppliers, the details of each invoice must be entered in the Suppliers Ledger, in the appropriate supplier's account.

4.1 The Invoices option

To enter supplier invoice details, you should click on the **Invoice** button in the **Suppliers** window. The following window will be displayed. (Later versions of Sage may include additional options that are not used in our case study.)

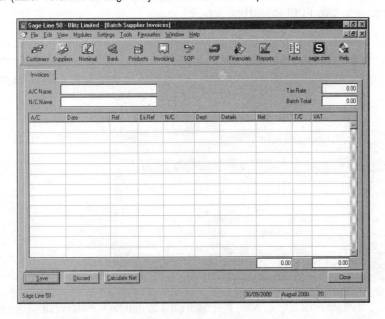

Suppose your company receives an invoice from a firm of public relations and marketing consultants as follows:

Invoice details	£	Nominal ledger item
Sales promotion expenses	2,000	Sales promotions
Advertising costs	1,500	Advertising
Public relations	600	PR
	4,100	

This invoice needs to be split into its three elements, £2,000 to charge to sales promotion expenses (nominal ledger account code 6200), £1,500 to advertising costs (N/C code 6201) and £600 to PR (N/C code 6203). You would enter three separate lines in the Supplier Invoices window.

You can enter as many lines as are necessary on each invoice. You can invoice *several different suppliers* on the same screen.

You can scroll back up and edit transactions if you realise you have made a mistake before you **Save** the invoice. If you want to delete an entire line, tab to it or click in it anywhere and then press function key F8. Other function keys are useful too. See Appendix 2 at the end of this book for a list.

Once you have finished entering the details of an invoice you click on **Save** and the screen is cleared ready for the next supplier's invoice.

4.2 A/C (account code)

Initially the cursor will be in the box labelled **A/C.** If you know the *code* for the supplier you can just type it in and press Tab. If you know some of the details for the supplier but you can't quite remember the code, Sage offers you a handy tool for finding out what you need to enter. At the right of the A/C box is a button. This is called the **Finder** button.

4.2.1 Searching for accounts: the Finder button (or F4)

When you are confronted with an empty box with the Finder button because you are required to choose one code from many possibilities. Click on the button (or press **function key F4** if you prefer to use the keyboard). Another alternative if you know, say, that the code begins with G, is to type G and then press Enter. In each case you will be presented with a selection window.

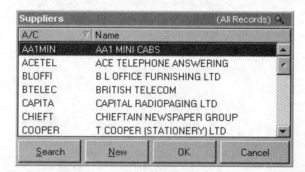

If you can see the account you want in the list immediately just click on it to highlight it and then click on OK or press Enter. If not, use the scroll bar or the cursor keys to scroll up or down until you see the name you want, then click on it and click OK.

Activity 3.4

Click the relevant buttons until you reach the Supplier Invoices window and then press F4. What appears in the A/C *Name* box at the *top* of the window when you select the account code BLOFFI and click on OK or press Enter? What if you type in the code MUSWEL?

4.2.2 Searching for accounts: the Search button

The **Search** button at the foot of the Finder window offers you a means of searching for accounts that fulfil certain conditions. Let's say, for the sake of argument, that you are in charge of the purchase ledger for accounts of suppliers who come from Watford. Click on the Search button and you will see the following screen.

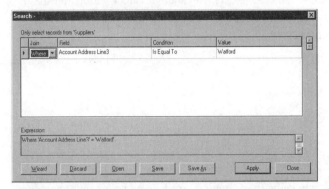

Click the down arrow to the right of the Join heading and select **Where**. Tab to the white square below the heading Field. From the drop down menu select **Account Address Line 3**. Tab through the condition field, ensuring it is set to 'Is Equal To'. In the Value field type *Watford*. Click on **Apply**, then click on **Close**. You will be returned to a window which shows only the names of those suppliers whose records indicate that they are located in Watford. If you are trying this out using Blitz data there will be now be only three account names: BLOFFI, FLOORS and UNIFOR.

You can search on more than one criteria. For example, from within the Suppliers finder window click on **Search** again, the criteria entered previously will show. Press **Tab** four times and you will be on a new line. Using the drop down menus under each heading select **And** (hit Tab), **Balance** (Tab), **Is Greater Than** (Tab), and type in 1000.00. Click **Apply** and **Close**. The suppliers in Watford with balances over £1,000.00 will be displayed.

Wherever you see the **Search** button within Sage the same principles for searching and selecting records apply.

When you close the Suppliers Record window you will notice that the 'filter' you designed still applies. Therefore, only those records that meet the criteria appear in the Suppliers window. To view all records click on the magnifying glass button. **(2 Records found)** 🔍

There are symbols that may help you with searches. For example, if you wish to find all accounts with a post code that begins with W a search on W in the postcode line would not find any records. You can, however, search using W* – the asterisk is a 'wildcard', standing for **any other character** or characters. Try it.

The magnifying glass symbol in the suppliers window has the effect of switching between all suppliers record and just those records that meet the Search Criteria. Try the button out.

Activity 3.5

Try out the techniques described in the previous paragraphs.

4.3 Date

When the right account code is entered the supplier's full name will be shown in the A/C Name box. Pressing Tab will highlight the **Date** box. The date you enter should be the date *on the supplier's invoice*.

Sage has a delightful feature for entering dates. When the cursor enters the date field another Finder button appears. If you click on this or press F4 a little calendar appears and you just have to *double-click* on the date you want. Use the arrows at the top to scroll through the months and years if necessary.

The calendar is fun, but it is probably quicker to type in the date using the numeric keypad. This is a matter of personal preference.

4.4 Ref

Press Tab again and you are taken to a box headed **Ref.** You can leave this blank but it is best to use it for the supplier's invoice number for reference purposes. There is also an extra reference box **Ex Ref** for an additional reference if required.

4.5 Entering the invoice details

Pressing Tab once more takes you to the parts of the invoicing screen that do what you would think of as the double entry in a manual system. The entries you make are as follows.

(a) The nominal ledger code (**N/C**). This is the account in the nominal ledger to which the purchase or expense relates. You can use the search facilities described above to find the nominal code you want.

A good shortcut here, if you have an approximate idea of the nominal account code, is to type in the approximate number and then press Enter, or function key F4, or click on the Finder button. This brings up the Nominal Accounts list starting from the number you typed. So, for example, if you know an invoice is an overhead and that overhead account codes are in the range 7000 to 7999 you can type in 7 and press F4.

(b) The **Dept** box can be used to analyse the information further. This is not used in the Blitz case study, so just press Tab again.

(c) In the **Details box** you type details of the goods or service supplied. Try typing a long sentence and see how the text scrolls across as you reach the end of the box.

(d)   In the **Net** box key in the amount of the invoice item *excluding value added tax* (the net amount). Just key in figures, with a decimal point between the pounds and the pence. Don't try to key in a £ sign. You don't need to key in zeros for pence at the end of a round figure amount.

- Keying 123 gives you 123.00

- Keying 123.4 gives you 123.40

- Keying 1230 gives you 1230.00

(e)   The code for the VAT rate (**T/c**) will automatically show T1, though you can alter this if necessary. The VAT codes used in the Blitz case study are:

T0   Zero-rated items (VAT = 0%)

T1   Standard-rated items (VAT currently = 17.5%)

T9   Transactions to which VAT does not apply

You will be told what code to use at AAT Foundation level.

(f)   The **Tax** is calculated automatically from the net amount of the invoice already entered and the VAT tax code.

4.5.1 The Calculate Net button

If you prefer, instead of entering the net amount of the invoice in the **Net** box, you can enter the total amount, *including VAT. Before* pressing Tab, click on the **Calculate Net** button or press function key F9. The program will now deduct VAT *at the standard rate* from the invoice amount you have keyed in, and display the VAT automatically in the **Tax** column.

When the VAT has been calculated and you have entered all the invoice details, press Tab again, and the cursor will move down to the next line of the screen. Details of another invoice item can then be entered on this line.

Note that running totals of your entries are shown at the foot of the Net column and the VAT column. You can compare the totals with the total shown on the invoice once you have posted all the items. If the totals are not the same there is a mistake somewhere. If it is your mistake you can scroll back up or tab to the error and correct it.

Remember that a whole line can be deleted by clicking on it or tabbing to it and pressing function key F8. Only use the **Discard** button if you wish to scrap *all* the details you have just entered on the screen.

Activity 3.6

With **Assignment 6** still loaded (we loaded it for Assignment 3.1), enter the following invoice details, following the instructions given earlier in this chapter. Use the features of the Sage package to calculate the correct figures for you.

A/C	Date	Refn	N/C	Details	Net	T/C	VAT
NEWLIT	01/10/2000	SW369	5000	Materials	100.00	T1	??.??
IRONCL	04/10/2000	214876	7701	Repairs	???.??	T1	??.??

The gross amount of the second invoice is £240.

Task

Find out the total amount of VAT for the two transactions, and what the N/C codes 5000 and 7701 stand for.

Save the details, once you have checked the answer.

4.6 Posting the invoice details

When you have entered details for all the items on the invoice(s) you are processing and you are satisfied that they are correct, click on the **Save** button. **Saving the transaction posts the invoice**.

When you post the details of an invoice, the **program**:

(a)   Updates the individual account of the supplier in the Suppliers Ledger;

(b)   Updates the appropriate accounts in the Nominal Ledger. The accounts that are updated are the Creditors Control Account, the VAT Control account and the various purchases, expense or fixed asset accounts to which the invoices relate (as specified in the transaction details by your choice of N/C codes). The double entry posting to the nominal ledger will be:

Debit   Nominal Ledger Account selected

Debit   Purchase Tax Control, code 2202

Credit   Creditors Control Account, code 2100

Note that in Sage there are two VAT control accounts, one for VAT on purchases (debits), the other for VAT on sales (credits).

Activity 3.7

When you have done Activity 3.6 find out the debit or credit balances on the Nominal Ledger accounts 2100, 2202, 5000 and 7701 and the Suppliers ledger accounts NEWLIT and IRONCL and make a note of them.

Now reload a fresh copy of Assignment 6. How do the balances on the accounts differ? Explain each of the differences.

5 Entering details of credit notes received

When a credit note is received from a supplier, the supplier is acknowledging that, for one reason or another, he has charged too much. Credit notes can be issued when goods are returned to the supplier as faulty or unwanted, or when there is a dispute about an invoice and the supplier agrees to reduce the bill.

Details of credit notes received from suppliers must be entered in the Suppliers Ledger, in the account of the appropriate supplier. The procedures are very similar to those for entering details of purchase invoices.

(a)   Click on the **Credit** button in the Suppliers window.

(b)   The screen will display a new window just like the Supplier Invoice window, except that the details of the credit note appear in red as you enter them.

The procedure is the same as that already described for entering details of purchase invoices. You must make sure, however, that:

(a)   The nominal ledger code you select (N/C) is the same as the code that was chosen for the original purchase invoice details.

(b)   The VAT code (T/C) is also the same as for the original purchase invoice.

Some other points should also be noted.

(a)   Enter the **Date** on the credit note, not 'today's date'.

(b)   The **Ref** item is for the credit note number, which you can copy from the credit note itself.

(c)   The **Details** item can be used for recording brief details of the reason for receiving the credit note.

After you have entered the details of your credit note(s) click on **Save** as before. When you Save a credit note, the program:

(a)   Updates the account(s) of the individual supplier(s) in the purchase ledger.

(b)   Updates the Creditors Control Account and the other relevant accounts in the nominal ledger.

Activity 3.8

With Assignment 6 data loaded (from Activity 3.7) post the invoice for £240 to supplier IRONCL again and check the balance on the IRONCL account and on the nominal ledger accounts.

Then post a credit note for the same amount to the IRONCL account and check that the balances have reverted to their previous amounts.

6 Reports

6.1 Supplier reports

When you have entered a day's batch of invoices you can print a list of the details, with totals. These listings are sometimes called 'Day Books'.

A wide range of supplier reports are available from within Sage. The procedure for printing these reports differs slightly between earlier and later versions of Sage. If you click on the Reports button from within the suppliers window in a **recent version** of Sage, you will see the screen shown below.

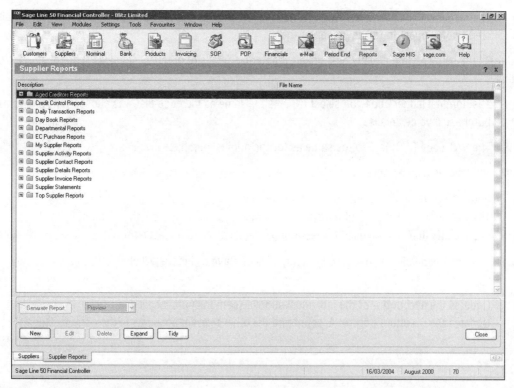

You double click on the appropriate folder, such as Day-Book Reports and then highlight the report you wish to run (for example Day Books: Supplier Invoices (detailed)).

In **older versions** of Sage you would reach this point by simply clicking on the Reports button in the Suppliers window. You will then see the following screen, from where you can choose the report you require.

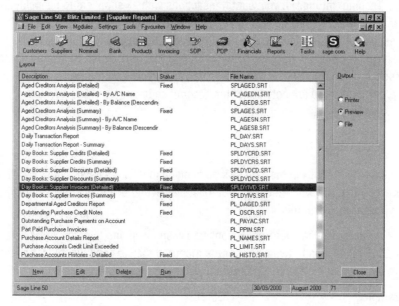

6.2 Output

In later versions, you select the type of output by using the drop down list to the right of the Generate Report button. Later versions also include the option of **e-mailing** the report (this option is not used in this book). In older versions, choose your output type by clicking in the white circle next to the appropriate label in the Output section of the screen.

(a) **Printer**. This sends your report straight to a printer to be printed out. The usual Windows Print window will appear, allowing you to choose what part of the document you want printed, what printer you want to send it to and so on. Printing things using Windows applications is explained in Chapter 2.

(b) **Preview**. This option brings up a screen display of the information that you can edit to some extent for printing purposes. For example you might want to change the font style or the width of the margins.

(c) **File**. This option allows you to save a copy of the report on disk. The usual Windows **Save As** window will appear and you will have to choose a name for report and specify the directory in which you want it to be saved. Again, see Chapter 2 if you have forgotten how to use the Save As window.

When you have selected the Report and output type you require, click on **Run** (older versions) or **Generate Report**.

6.3 Criteria

You must now choose what transactions you want to appear in your listing. There are five main criteria for doing this.

(a) By specifying a supplier range (the accounts you wish to be included).
(b) By specifying a date range (the date or dates of the transactions you wish to list).
(c) By specifying a transaction range (the range of transaction numbers for which you require a listing).
(d) By specifying a department range.
(e) By specifying a nominal account range.

6.3.1 Supplier range

Accept the defaults (by 'Tabbing' through) if you want transactions with all suppliers to be included in the report. However, you may want a report of transactions with suppliers in a certain range eg A – D. If, for example, you had a query from a specific supplier about invoices sent to you in the last month you would specify the appropriate date range, leave the transaction range as it is (ranging from the first to the most recent transaction) and then enter the supplier code in *both* boxes in the **Supplier** section. Note that you can click on the Finder button (or press F4 when the cursor is in the appropriate box) if you are not sure of the account code.

6.3.2 Specifying a date range

Press Tab if necessary until the first box in the date section is highlighted. As a default this may show the date 01/01/1980, but it is unlikely that you will want to accept this. The second box may show a date like 31/12/2019. Again it is unlikely that you will want to accept this.

Instead you should key in the earliest date for transactions you wish to list and then the latest date. Key in each date using *two digits* for the day of the month, two digits for the month of the year and two digits for the year (there is no need to type slashes or the full four digit year, the program will insert these automatically).

Examples	Enter
6th April 2000	060400
15th May 2000	150500
2nd November 2000	021100

Suppose today is 5 October and you have just entered invoices received from suppliers with various dates from 30 September to 2 October. In the first Date Range box enter 30092000 then press Tab. In the second box type 02102000. You can use the calendar button if you prefer.

You are now ready to produce your report. Just Click on **OK** and wait for the report to be output in the way you specified earlier.

6.3.3 Specifying a transaction range

Choosing the date range for a listing of purchase invoices or supplier credit notes can be a problem because the invoices or credit notes will have different dates. When an invoice has a date that is now several weeks old, it could be very difficult to be sure of including it in a report by specifying the date range, without listing other invoices you have already processed in the past.

You can specify the invoices (or credit notes) you wish to list by specifying their transaction numbers. These are unique numbers, automatically allocated to each entry into the system by the program. To specify a transaction range, you should remember to *take a note* of the first transaction number for the invoices and the credit notes when you start to process them. The second box in the Transaction section shows the total number of transactions entered so far on the system (purchase ledger, sales ledger and nominal ledger). Your next transaction will be the next number in the sequence. For example, if the box shows that 70 transactions have been processed (number of entries = 70) your next entry will be transaction 71.

You can find the last transaction number by clicking on **Financials** in the main window and jumping to the end of the list that appears.

The Transaction boxes on screen will display a transaction range from 1 to 9999999 (or to the most recent transaction number). You should alter the range, to specify the transactions you wish to list.

Don't worry about mixing purchase invoices and credit note transaction numbers. The report will contain only one type of transaction or the other (ie invoices only or credit notes only), depending on the type of report you have selected.

You are now ready to produce a report of transaction within the range specified. Just Click on **OK** and wait for the report to be output in the way you specified earlier. (Blitz does not operate with more than one Department so you can tab through this option.)

6.3.4 Nominal account range

The procedure is the same if you wanted to know about all transactions posted, say, to nominal account codes 7000 to 7999, or code 1200 to 1200 (ie account 1200 only).

Again when you have specified the range you want you are ready to produce your report as before.

Activity 3.9

Load a fresh copy of Assignment 6 data. Run the report Day Books: Supplier Invoices (Detailed). Make sure that the data range covers the period from 1 August 2000 to 30 October 2000.

What are the totals shown and what is the number of the last transaction listed.

If you use the Preview option for Output, Sage will open a Report or 'File View' window for the report. You can switch between the report and the program itself by clicking on the word **Window** at the top of the screen and then clicking on whichever window you want.

6.4 Closing a Report or File View window

Buttons at the bottom of the screen give you a variety of options for moving about in the report, viewing it in different ways, saving it, printing it, or just closing the report window.

7 Conclusion

Experiment ...

This is an important chapter because it introduces many of the widely used features of the Sage package. Spend some time going over what you have read, ideally while sitting at a computer. Try calling up windows and making entries in the way we describe. You won't break the software by experimenting with its features and you can always call up a 'clean' copy of Blitz case study data.

... and try an Assignment!

If you think you can follow the instructions in this chapter, **you should now be able to attempt Assignment 1** at the end of this Workbook. If you haven't yet attempted the **Activities** in this and the previous chapter, you should do these first.

Key learning points

☑ In Sage, you access functions associated with the **Purchase ledger** through the **Suppliers** button. Sage calls the '**Purchase ledger control account**' the '**Creditors control account**'.

☑ We have looked at some important features associated with **processing supplier invoices and credit notes**. Suppliers button in the main window.

☑ Supplier records include basic **details** such as Company Name, Address and contact details as well as **accounting data** such as payment terms and any agreed credit limit.

☑ Invoices are entered into Sage from the options accessed by selecting the **Suppliers** icon from the main menu and then clicking on the **Invoice** button.

☑ Credit Notes are entered into Sage from the options accessed by selecting the **Suppliers** icon from the main menu and then clicking on the **Credit** button.

☑ Modern accounting systems offer various **reports** and **enquiry** facilities to enable information regarding transactions to be extracted from the system easily.

Quick quiz

1   List three possible methods of setting up a new supplier account.

2   What is the purpose of the Defaults tab in the Supplier Record?

3   What is the Search button within the Finder window used for?

4   Give one reason why a credit note may be issued.

5   List three alternatives for outputting a report from Sage.

Answers to quick quiz

1   Through the options provided using the Supplier Record button; Using the Invoices button; Using the New button from within Suppliers to access the Supplier Record Wizard.

2   The Defaults index tab allows you to specify certain details about how a transaction with the supplier will normally be posted. These details are used as default values when inputting transactions – this saves time.

3   The Search button within the Finder window enables a search to be made for accounts that meet the criteria you specify.

4   Credit notes can be issued if a mistake was made in the initial invoice, or if goods are returned as faulty or unwanted, or if a dispute arises and the supplier agrees to reduce the bill.

5   The report could be output to a printer, to the screen or to a computer file. A fourth alternative is to use Sage's facility to automatically e-mail the report – but the system must be set-up to allow this.

Activity checklist

This checklist shows which knowledge and understanding point is covered by each activity in this chapter. Tick off each activity as you complete it.

Activity

3.1		Knowledge and Understanding: Operation of computerised accounting systems
3.2		Knowledge and Understanding: Operation of computerised accounting systems
3.3		Knowledge and Understanding: Operation of computerised accounting systems
3.4		Knowledge and Understanding: Operation of computerised accounting systems
3.5		Knowledge and Understanding: Operation of computerised accounting systems
3.6		Knowledge and Understanding: Operation of computerised accounting systems
3.7		Knowledge and Understanding: Operation of computerised accounting systems
3.8		Knowledge and Understanding: Operation of computerised accounting systems
3.9		Knowledge and Understanding: Operation of computerised accounting systems

chapter 4

Customer invoices and credit notes

Contents

1   Introduction
2   Customers
3   Producing invoices
4   Invoicing for services
5   Invoicing for the sale of products
6   Producing credit notes
7   Printing invoices and credit notes
8   Updating the ledgers
9   Updating the ledgers without producing invoices
10   Reports
11   Customer queries
12   Conclusion

Range statement

Relevant computerised records

Computerised records

Computerised ledgers

Knowledge and understanding

Operation of computerised accounting systems

1 Introduction

The **Customer** button in the main Sage window is used to access functions associated with the **Sales ledger**. The options available under the Customers option are shown below (earlier versions of Sage don't include some options such as the facility to build Customer price lists – these options aren't required to complete the exercises in this book). These options work in a similar way to the equivalent function relating to Suppliers, explained in the previous chapter.

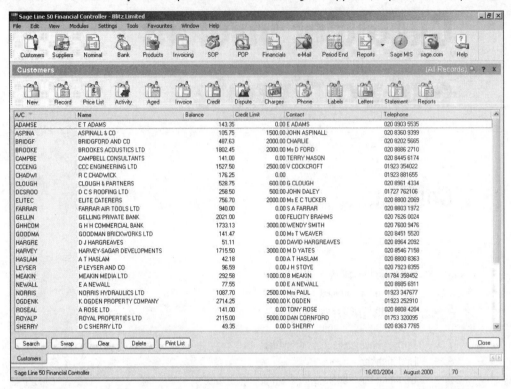

2 Customers

When an invoice has to be produced for sending to a new customer (ie a customer who has not been invoiced before by your company), an account for the customer must be set up in the customers ledger. There are four ways of entering new customer accounts in the ledger:

(a)   Using the **Record** button in the Customers window.

(b)   Using the **Invoices** button in the Customers window.

(c)   Using one of the buttons in the **Invoicing** window.

(d)   Using the **New** button from within Customers to access the Customer Record Wizard.

The **Record** button option and the Wizard option are similar to the options for entering details of new supplier accounts in the purchase ledger described in the previous chapter.

The option to set up new customer accounts from the **Invoices** button in the *Customers* window also works in a similar way to the method described in the context of the *Suppliers* window in Chapter 3.

Note that the **Invoices** option from within the Suppliers window would only be used if the actual invoices were not going to be printed from Sage. In the Blitz case study we will be producing Invoices and Credit Notes using Sage, therefore we will be using the **Invoicing** option from the **main** window.

Activity 4.1

If you have forgotten what a 'record' looks like, or what details are needed, load up any Assignment you like, click on **Customers** then on **Record** and select any account to remind yourself.

2.1 Credit limits

For the purpose of the case study and Assignment 2 you will be required to enter an amount for the maximum credit that will be allowed to the customer (ie the maximum value of goods or services that will be supplied on credit at any time). This amount should be entered as the 'Credit Limit' in the appropriate box.

How you enter new customer accounts from within the **Invoicing** window is described later in this chapter.

3 Producing invoices

If you select the **Invoicing** button from the **main** window, one of the two boxes will appear, depending on the version of Sage you are using.

3.1 Older versions of Sage

If you are using an older version of Sage you will be presented with the following window.

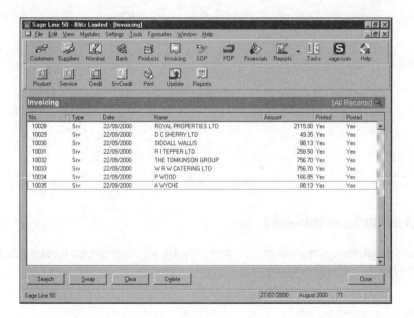

In older versions of Sage the following options are available in the Invoicing window.

Icon	Use
Product	To invoice for the sale of goods or a product
Service	To invoice for the supply of services
Credit	To produce a credit note for goods
Service Credit	To produce a credit note for services
Print	To print invoices or credit notes
Update	To post invoices and credit notes to the ledgers
Reports	To produce lists of invoices in various stages of production

As you process invoices the blank space in this window will gradually be filled up with key details of each invoice, providing a handy numerical index of all invoices in the system. The **Swap** and **Clear** buttons affect which items are selected (highlighted) in the main part of the screen. Test these functions for yourself. The **Search** button will be explained later in this chapter.

3.2 Later versions of Sage

In later versions of Sage the Invoicing window will be the same or similar to the one shown below. To produce an Invoice or a Credit Note for a product or service, you would select New/Edit. Unlike earlier versions, you specify whether you are producing an Invoice or a Credit Note, and whether this related to a product or service, later in the process.

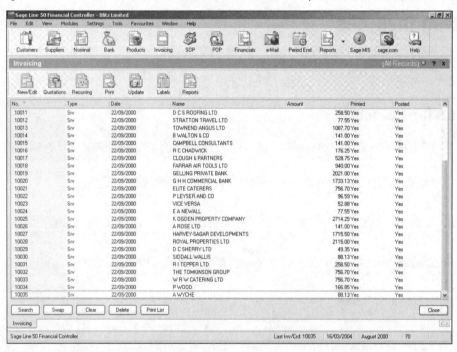

3.3 Invoice and credit note numbering

Invoices should be numbered sequentially. The program therefore allocates a number to each invoice automatically as you work, by adding 1 to the number of the previous invoice.

Activity 4.2

Familiarise yourself with the above by clicking on **Invoicing** in the main window and seeing what happens when you click on the various buttons and options available. Press **Esc** to get back to the initial Invoicing screen whenever you like.

4 Invoicing for services

In **older versions** of Sage, invoices for services can be produced using the **Service** button in the Invoicing window. In **later versions**, service invoices are produced by selecting **New/ Edit** from the **Invoicing** window. The fact that it is a Service Invoice is entered from within the 'Format' option when entering the Invoice details. The main Invoice screen from recent versions of Sage is shown below.

This window is used to enter the details for one invoice. Each invoice is for the sale of one or more services or items. There is a separate line for the details of each item, in the main (central) part of the screen.

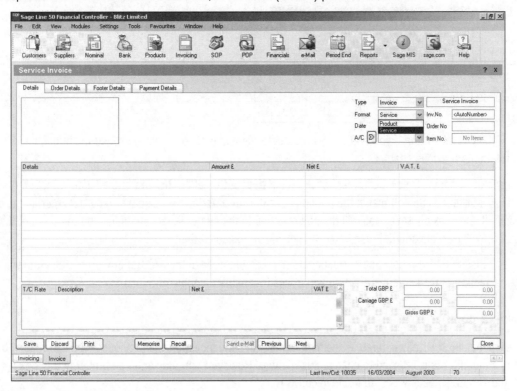

4.1 Details

Whether you are using an older version of Sage or a newer version, you will be presented with a series of options for your invoice. The Details Tab contains basic Invoice details as explained in the following paragraphs.

4.1.1 Type

Select whether you are producing an Invoice or a Credit Note. For the purposes of the case study in this book, you may ignore the other options.

4.1.2 Format

It is here, in newer versions of Sage, that you specify whether the Invoice or Credit Note refers to a Product or to a Service.

4.1.3 A/C (account)

In this box you enter the customer's account code. You can type in the code directly if you know it, or just type *part* of the code and press Tab, a list of Customer Accounts will appear with the nearest code to the one you entered highlighted. If this is correct, click on OK or press Enter to accept the code. If not you will have to scroll up or down the list in the usual way to find the customer you want. Alternately, you may bring up the list of all existing customers by clicking the 'Finder' button to the right of the A/C box.

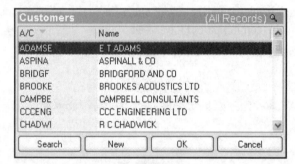

You may use the **Search** button if you don't know the Customer account code. We explained the principles of using the Search button in the previous chapter.

If the invoice is to be sent to a new customer, click on the **New** button at the bottom of the Finder window. A screen will appear that is just like the one you met in the previous chapter for entering new Supplier records. Enter all the details for the new account and click on **Save**. You will then be returned to the customer accounts list and the account that you have just set up will be highlighted. Press Enter or click on OK to accept this.

Once you are satisfied that you have the correct customer account code in the A/C Ref box press Tab. This will take you to the **Details** section of the screen, but before we proceed there are a couple of things to check.

4.1.4 Invoice number

The invoice will be automatically entered as the next number in sequence after the previous invoice produced by the system. You shouldn't (usually) need to change this number. However, you may enter a number in this box if required. (Use Shift and Tab to 'go backwards' to the Invoice No.)

4.1.5 Invoice Date

The screen will display today's date (ie the date in the computer system). To accept this date, press Tab. Another invoice date can be entered, if required. As the Assignments in this book are set back in the Year 2000, you will need to enter an appropriate date for every invoice. (Note: If you are going to enter many invoices with the same date, use the

Change Program Date function under the **Settings** menu option from the main menu before you start entering invoices.)

Activity 4.3

Load up the data for **Assignment 1** and then enter these details in a service invoice, following the instructions above.

A/C Ref:	WRWCAT
Invoice number:	20000
Date:	25 November 2000
Details:	Contract cleaning
Amount:	£100.00 plus VAT

What is the name and address details of the customer concerned?

4.1.6 The Details box

Having entered the Account, press Tab until you get to the main part of the screen. In the details box enter a description of the service that has been delivered. In the Blitz case study this will be something like 'Window Cleaning' or 'Domestic Services'.

4.1.7 Edit item line

Before tabbing on from the Details box to the Amount box you should activate the Edit Line Box to enable you to enter details such as the appropriate Nominal ledger code. To do this either:

(a)   Press function key F3, or

(b)   Click on the little button in the right corner of the Details box.

You will then be presented with the following options (the appearance of this box may alter slightly if you are using an older version of Sage).

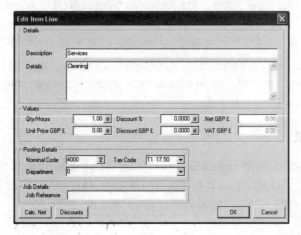

This window shows the text you entered in the details box in the main Service Invoice window. This is how the text will appear on the invoice. You can change this text if required. You may change other details such as the Tax Code if required.

You can also enter any Discount details (*not* settlement discount, which is handled elsewhere). In later versions of Sage, you may enter Discount as either a percentage or as an amount. If you click on the buttons beside these boxes (or press F4) a little drop-down calculator appears.

This can be operated by using the *numeric keypad* on the keyboard.

In fact you can bring up a calculator window at *any* time, just by pressing F2. To enter the result of a calculation into a field in a Sage screen you can press Ctrl + C, to copy the value from the calculator, then click on the field in question and press Ctrl + V.

The **Nominal code box** is where you specify the nominal code for the invoice. Each item on the invoice can have a different nominal ledger code if appropriate (in other words different items on the same invoice can be given different nominal ledger sales account codes). For each item (each line of Details you enter in the main Service invoice window) the code for the appropriate nominal ledger sales account should be entered using the Service Item Line screen.

In the Blitz Limited case study, the nominal ledger codes that are used are:

Code	Nominal ledger account
4000	Sales – Contract Cleaning
4001	Sales – Window Cleaning
4002	Sales – Domestic Services
4100	Sales – Materials

Rather than memorising these accounts, an easy approach is to key in the number 4 alone and then press Tab (or use function key F4). This brings up the list of Nominal Accounts with number 4000 highlighted. If Contract Cleaning is not the account you want then just scroll to find Window Cleaning or whatever. Once the nominal account you want is highlighted press Enter or click on OK and this account number will be entered in the right box.

There is also the option of specifying a Department for management accounting analysis purposes. This facility is not used in the Blitz case study so once you have entered the nominal code you can just press Enter or click on OK to be returned to the main Service invoice window.

4.1.8 Amount, Net and VAT

Press Tab once you have entered the details for an item and hit Tab, you will be taken to the **Amount** box. Enter the amount of the invoice *excluding VAT* and press Tab again. The Net and VAT amounts will be calculated automatically. By default VAT will be 17.5% of the Net Amount you entered. (If you need to change this you can return to the Edit Item Line window and do so.)

Later versions of Sage provide the option to use Hourly Rates within Service Invoicing. If you use this function, you would enter Details such as '2 hours heavy duty cleaning' then, within the Edit Item Line box, enter 2 in Hours and the price per hour in Unit Price. You can follow the same procedure to enter a second invoice line and a third, and so on.

Activity 4.4

Load up the data for **Assignment 6** and change the date within Sage to 25/11/2000 (use Settings, Change program data) . Prepare the following service invoices (you have to find out the Nominal code yourself). Click on **Save** when you have entered the details for each invoice.

No.	Date	A/C	Details	N/C	Price
10065	25/11/2000	ADAMSE	Window cleaning	?	£100
10066	25/11/2000	GARDEN	Contract cleaning	?	£100

When you have finished press **Esc** (or click on **Close**) to return to the initial Invoicing screen. Scroll down to the bottom and make a note of the amount of each of the invoices you entered. Explain the results.

4.2 Order details

Occasionally, you might want to include extra details about the order on the invoice, for example:

(a) To specify a delivery address when this differs from the invoice address.

(b) To specify payment terms (eg 'PAYMENT REQUIRED WITHIN 30 DAYS OF INVOICE DATE').

To add these details, you should click on the **Order Details** index tab and enter the details in this window.

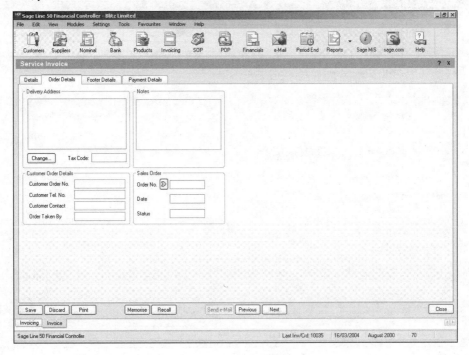

4.2.1 Customer Order No

This is where any customer reference number for this order would be entered.

4.2.2 Customer Tel. No./Contact

The customer's telephone number and contact name will be displayed automatically (from their account details).

4.2.3 Delivery Address

The delivery name and address can be entered here, when this is different from the name and address on the invoice (and in the records in the customer's account in the customers ledger).

4.2.4 Notes

Notes can be added, to appear on the invoice. These can be used, if required, to bring special information to the customer's attention; for example '5% DISCOUNT FOR SETTLEMENT WITHIN 7 DAYS OF INVOICE DATE'.

4.3 Footer Details

If you wish, you can also add details to the invoice for the following:

(a)   Charging for the delivery of goods (Carriage).
(b)   Providing details of any discounts offered to the customer for early payment (Settlement Terms).
(c)   Giving every item on the invoice the same tax code, nominal ledger code or department code (Global).

Only (a) is relevant to the Blitz case study in this book. If you click on the **Footer Details** index tab, a new window will appear, as shown below (or a similar window if you use a previous version of Sage).

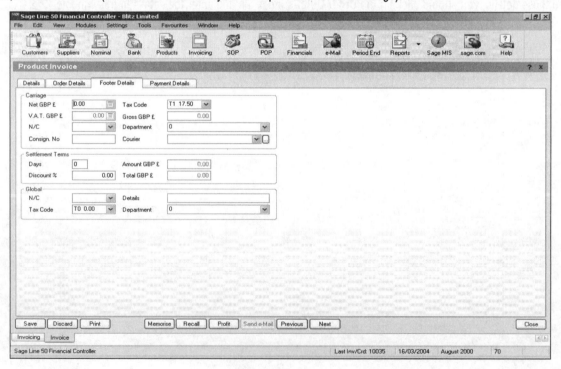

4.3.1 Carriage

The amount of charges for carriage outwards can be entered in the Net box at the top of the window. The charge for carriage, *excluding VAT*, should be keyed in.

4.3.2 Tax code (T/c)

Unless told otherwise use the same tax code for VAT as for the main invoice. It should usually be T1, meaning that VAT is chargeable at the standard rate of 17.5%.

4.3.3 Nominal code

Enter the nominal ledger code for the Carriage Outwards account in the nominal ledger. In the Blitz Limited system, this code is 4905. Otherwise you may need to click on the Finder button beside this box to find the right code.

Activity 4.5

Re-load the data for Assignment 6. Enter the following details, referring back to the previous paragraphs for instructions if necessary.

No.	Date	A/C	Details	N/C	Price
10065	31/12/2000	OWENLO	Sundry	4101	£100

Delivery address: 14 Woodgate Street, Barnet, N16 3BB
Order no.: 14879
Telephone number: 020-7734 2843
Customer contact: Jennifer
Carriage: £5
Settlement discount: 5% if settled within 30 days

What is the total amount of the invoice as shown on screen? Did any discrepancies arise as you were doing this activity, and if so what should you do about them?

4.4 Saving the invoice details

When you have entered all the details of the invoice (which might or might not include footer details) click on the **Save** button. This adds the main details of the invoice to the index shown in the main Invoicing window. The Service Invoice window will be cleared and you can start entering details for a new invoice. However:

(a)   The invoice you have saved is *not yet posted* to the customers ledger and nominal ledger.
(b)   An invoice is not printed.

This feature of the Sage package very sensibly recognises that in practice you might realise that you want to change the details to be posted and printed at a later stage.

We shall see how to print and post invoices later in this chapter.

4.5 Discard

As an alternative to Saving the details you have entered, the **Discard** button allows you to cancel all the details of the invoice you have just entered. It is sometimes easier and safer to start again than trying to edit an incorrect set of entries.

4.6 Editing saved entries

You can change any of the entries you have made so far, so long as you haven't posted them (updated the ledgers). Click on the relevant invoice (which you will now see listed in the main Invoicing window) and then click on the **Service** button again. Alternatively, just double-click the invoice you wish to edit.

Activity 4.6

Firstly, re-load the data for Assignment 6, and find out the balance on the Customer account WOODPX.

Then enter the following service invoice details (accept the invoice number offered by Sage and find out the nominal code for yourself). Then click on **Close** and respond **Yes** to the question 'do you want to save changes?'

Date	A/C	Details	Price
31/12/2000	WOODPX	Domestic services	£600

What is the balance on customer account WOODPX now?

5 Invoicing for the sale of products

5.1 Invoices in the case study

In the Blitz case study all invoices and credit notes are processed as Service Invoices or Service Credits. The reason for this is that, as a cleaning company, Blitz is essentially a service provider.

The few sales of materials Blitz does make are processed on 'Service' invoices for simplicity and consistency. For example, a customer can then be invoiced for cleaning services and purchases of cleaning materials on the same invoice.

However, it is perfectly acceptable to invoice these sales using the Product Invoice option. The important thing, from an accounting point of view, is to ensure sales of products are **posted to the correct nominal account** – in Blitz's case account 4100 – Sales Materials.

5.2 Product invoices in recent versions

In later versions of Sage, the procedure for Invoicing for the sale of products is very similar to the process of invoicing for services explained in the previous section. This involves selecting Invoicing from the main menu, then the New/ Edit option, and then choosing the product format from within the Invoice Details.

5.3 Product invoices in older versions

If you use an older version of Sage to produce an invoice for the sale of products, you use the **Product** button in the Invoicing window. When you click on this button, the screen will display windows similar to those that appear when you select the **Service** invoice option.

5.4 Product code

The main difference between a Service Invoice and a Product Invoice is the use of Product codes. On each line of the Invoice you enter the relevant Product code for items to be included in the Invoice.

If you don't know the code for the product you can use the Finder button beside the Product Code heading. A window will appear with a list of items and their codes. There is also the facility to set up a new Product if you wish. This is much like setting up a new customer or supplier account. When the item you want is highlighted, press Enter or click on the OK button and this code will be shown in the Product Code field in the main screen, together with its description.

A company might not use product codes in its Sage system, perhaps because, like Blitz Ltd in the case study, selling materials is just a sideline, or because stock is set up on a different system. There may also be times when an item sold is 'non-standard' and does not have a stock code because it is not usually carried in stock. In this case you can make one of three entries in the Product Code field.

M	This simply allows you to type a message in the Description box. You might want to type something like '*Thank you for ordering the following items*' before listing out the items ordered with their prices.
S1	This code is used for a non-stock item to which VAT applies.
S2	This code is used for a non-stock item to which VAT does not apply.

You will only use the **S1** code in the Blitz case study. Type in S1 and press Tab. A window headed Edit Item Line will appear. This is very similar to the Edit Item Line that we explained when we explained Service Invoices in the previous section.

5.5 Edit item line

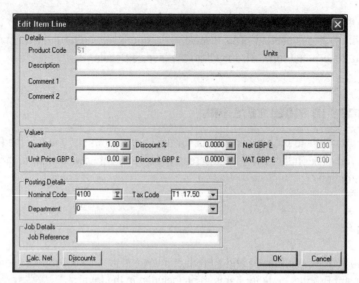

The entries to make are as follows.

(a) *Description.* One line's worth of description can be entered. You can follow this with two lines of *Comments* which might describe the item further, or make it clear that it is a non-stock item, or explain how the item is packaged ('box of 12'), or whatever else you like.

(b) Once you have entered your description and comments, Tab down to the *Quantity* box and key in the number of items you are selling. Note that if the item is sold and priced in, say, boxes of twelve you should key in the number of *boxes*, not the number of individual items.

(c) Pressing Tab takes you to the *Unit Price*. This is the price of one unit of sale (eg a box), not of an individual item.

Suppose for example an item's price is £2 per can and cans are sold in boxes of 12. If you were selling somebody 36 cans you could enter this in two ways.

Method 1		Method 2	
Quantity	36	Quantity	3
Unit Price	2	Unit Price	24

Method 2 is generally preferable. To make things crystal clear on the invoice you might include the words 'box of 12 cans' in your description or comments

(d) *Discount %.* This is zero, unless the customer is entitled to a trade discount on the net price; for example, a discount for bulk purchasing. You can simply Tab on to the next item when there is no trade discount. If you do offer a discount of, say, 2%, key in 2.

(e) *Nominal Code.* This is the nominal ledger code for the sales account to which the sales item relates. In the Blitz system, this will be the code for the Sales – Materials account, which is code 4100.

(f) *Department.* This can be used to enter a code for the department which has made the sale. In the Blitz system, department codes are *not used*, and you should leave this item blank simply by pressing Tab.

(g)   The same *Tax Codes* apply as described previously. In the Blitz system, these are as follows.

- T0 for zero-rated items

- T1 for standard-rated items (with VAT currently at 17.5%)

- T9 for items to which VAT does not apply

(h)   *Net, Discount and VAT*. The total net amount payable for the item (Quantity × Unit Price), the amount of discount and the VAT payable are displayed automatically.

Once you have completed all the details you want to enter in this window click on OK. If the Quantity, the Tax Code or the Nominal account are blank you will get a message telling you so. Click on OK in the message box or press Enter to clear the message, type in the entry required, then click on OK.

This will take you back to the main Invoice window. The details you have just specified will now be shown in the relevant boxes. The cursor will be flashing in the Description box and you add whatever details you like. Once you have done this and you are satisfied that the figures are correct (change them if not), press Tab until you reach the next line of the invoice.

The main invoice screen also gives you options for Order Details and Footer Details. These features were described in the previous section of this chapter.

When the invoice is complete and correct Save it by clicking on the **Save** button and the screen will be cleared ready for the next invoice. If you have entered details of all the invoices you have to process click on Close or press Esc to get back to the main Invoicing window.

Activity 4.7

On 21 October 2000 a customer R I Tepper Ltd purchased 4 cases of Gleamo. One case contains 12 tins and costs £10.68.

Re-load Assignment 6 and enter this transaction as a **Product** invoice number 10065, following the instructions given in the preceding paragraphs (use Product Code 51).

What is the total amount of the invoice? Which nominal code should be used?

6 Producing Credit Notes

6.1 Older versions

In older versions of Sage Credit Notes are entered using the **Credit** or **SRV Credit** button from the Invoicing window.

6.2 Later versions

In later versions Credit Notes are entered exactly the same way as invoices, that is, by using the New/Edit button from within the invoicing window. You are then able to select **Credit** in the **Type** field, and **Product** or **Service** in the **Format** field.

7 Printing invoices and credit notes

To print invoices and credit notes you have two main options.

(a)   At any time during the preparation of an invoice you can print out a hard copy,

To print out a copy of the invoice while you are preparing it click on the **Print** button at the bottom of the invoice window. Further windows will appear as explained below.

(b)   You Save each invoice or credit note before leaving the input screen. A list of invoices and credit notes will be shown in the main Invoicing window and from this you can select invoices to print.

7.1 The Print button (on the main Invoicing screen)

If you are going to use the **Print** button you must first select which invoices you want to print out. One way of doing this is simply to highlight the invoice(s) concerned in the index list in the main Invoicing window by clicking on them. This is the easiest option if you only want to print one or two invoices.

If you want to highlight *all* the invoices in an index list quickly, first use the **Clear** button at the bottom of the main invoicing window (this takes away any odd highlighting there might be) and then click on the **Swap** button (this will now highlight *all* the invoices). Every time the **Swap** button is clicked it changes highlighted invoices into unhighlighted invoices and vice versa.

7.1.1 The Search button

You may want only to print or look at some invoices and credit notes rather than all of them. To cope with this problem you can use the **Search** button at the bottom of the main invoicing screen. Click on this and the following window will appear.

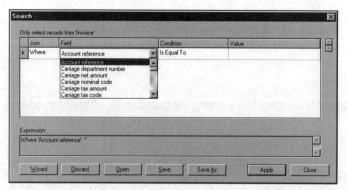

The search button appears in many places throughout Sage and always works in the same way. Re-read section 4.2.2 of Chapter 3 now, then attempt Activity 4.8.

Activity 4.8

Load **Assignment 5** and click on the Invoicing button. Use the Search button to produce the following lists in the Invoicing window.

    (a)   A list of Service invoices with an Invoice Total greater than £1,500.00, with an invoice number less than 10040.

    (b)   A list of invoices or credit notes that have not been posted.

    (c)   A list devised by you using the wildcard symbol (*).

    (d)   A full list of all invoices and credit notes on the system.

7.2 Printing

After clicking the Print button in the main Invoicing window (and answering Yes if asked if you wish to continue), another window will appear. If you are using an older version of Sage, the window will appear as shown below.

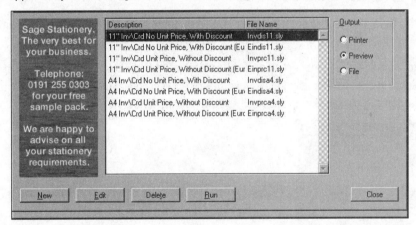

In more recent versions, you will see a similar window, but the options are laid out slightly differently and a **Generate Report** button has replaced the **Run** button.

You are given the options of sending the invoice(s) straight to the Printer, seeing a Preview on screen or creating a File copy of the invoice. (The file option has nothing to do with posting the invoice to the ledgers: it is a file copy of the invoice document.)

You get a list of possible layouts for your invoice in the Description box. We suggest you use the layout INVDIS. You have two of each of these – one set for 11" paper and one set for A4 paper. Alternatively your tutor might tell you to use a special layout designed by your college.

When you have selected your layout, click in the **Preview** circle and then click on **Run** (or in later versions ensure Preview is selected and click on **Generate Report**). A screen display of your invoice will shortly appear. Click on **Zoom** and then Page Width to get a decent view of your invoice. If you are happy with what you see click on **Print.**

7.3 Extra copies

Once you have printed an invoice or credit note a Yes will appear in the Print column in the main Invoicing window. This is a useful check if you are not sure whether or not an invoice has been printed, but *you can still print out a duplicate copy* of the invoice if you want to. An invoice might get lost in the post or damaged before it is sent, for example. To print another copy just select the invoice in the main Invoicing window, click on the **Print Invoices** button and proceed as usual.

Activity 4.9

Load Assignment 6 and print out a copy of Invoice No. 10042.

8 Updating the ledgers

When you click on the **Save** button after processing an invoice or credit note, the details are *not* posted to the customers ledger or nominal ledger.

To post the details to the ledgers, you must click on the **Update** button in the Invoicing window. Just like printing, you can post many invoices (or credit notes) all at the same time, or you can select individual ones for posting. After you have made your selection and clicked Update, you will see the following window.

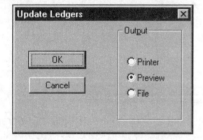

This procedure will generate a report telling you what has been posted. Decide whether you want a printed report or just a screen display or preview, or if you want a file copy of the report. Then click on OK or press Enter.

The Update Ledgers report is a list of the invoices or credit notes you have just posted to the ledger, showing details of each item posted. The listing shows:

- Invoice number or credit note number
- Invoice date
- Customer's account code
- Transaction number given to the entry by the accounts
- Product code, if any

- Nominal ledger code for each transaction
- Department code (if any) for the transaction
- Description of the goods or services sold (and quantity)
- Net amount of the invoice (or credit note)
- Tax code for the VAT
- Amount of the VAT
- Total of each invoice and a grand total for all invoices posted

Activity 4.10

Re-load up Assignment 5 and confirm the balances on the following accounts.

GOODMA	0.00
HASLAM	0.00
Sales – Window cleaning (4001)	2,634.40

Now enter the following details exactly as shown and **Save** each invoice.

Invoice.	Date	A/C	Details	Nominal code	Amount (net)
10053	25/10/2000	GOODMA	Window cleaning	4001	£100.00
10054	25/10/2000	HASLAM	Window cleaning	4001	£100.00

(a)   What is the balance on the three accounts now?

(b)   In the Invoicing window click on **Clear** at the bottom of the screen and then on the option **Update** at the top of the screen. Say **Yes** to the message that appears and choose whether you want a print-out or just a screen preview.

What is the balance on the three accounts now?

9 Updating the ledgers without producing invoices

In some companies, invoices could be produced manually or on a different system. When this situation occurs, the accounting system is used to post invoice and credit note details to the customers ledger and nominal ledger, but not to produce invoices.

To update the ledgers without producing invoices, you should click on the **Customers** button in the main Sage window and then on the **Invoices** button in the Customers window. Entering and posting invoice and credit note details can then be done in the same way as entering and posting details of invoices and credit notes from suppliers. These procedures have already been described in Chapter 3.

10 Reports

When you have entered a batch of invoices or credit notes (or several batches of invoices or credit notes) you can print a list of the details, with totals. This is often called a day book listing. In Sage these reports can be generated by clicking on the **Reports** button in the *Customers* window, then selecting the report required eg Day Books: Customer Invoices (Detailed).

You can choose between detailed and summary reports, and specify a particular Date Range, Transaction Range, Customer Account Range or Nominal Account Range. You should look through the various options available.

11 Customer queries

Customers often telephone the accounts department of a company with queries about invoices or credit notes. These queries can often be answered by looking up the invoice details on the system. Typical queries could be:

(a)   I haven't received the credit note you promised. Have you sent it yet?

(b)   I haven't had an invoice from you yet. Can you tell me how much will it be?

(c)   I haven't received your invoice yet. It might be lost in the post. Can you send me a duplicate copy?

11.1 Invoice or credit note details

You can look up the details of an invoice or credit note, to find out:

(a)   Whether it is on the system.

(b)   Whether the invoice or credit note has been printed (and presumably sent).

You can also obtain details of the invoice or credit note. To look up these details, you can use **Invoicing** button to display a complete list of all invoices then use the **Search** button to specify the customer's account code as your condition (for example you would set your criterion as, say, Where Account Reference Is Equal to ADAMSE). You can narrow the field further by specifying additional criteria, such as a date range.

11.1.1 Example

You receive a telephone enquiry from David Hargreaves, asking about an invoice that had been expected but not yet received. You might know the customer's account reference number already. In the case study of Blitz Limited, the customer's code would start with the first letters of the surname. There are two ways of finding the details you want.

(a)   Call up the Invoicing window, set your Search criteria as Account Reference Is Equal to HAR* and click on **Apply** and then on **Close**. All accounts with codes beginning with the letters HAR will be shown. Highlight the account and click on the **Service** button. You will probably get a warning telling you that the invoice has been posted and that amendments will not be saved. You only want to *look* at the details, so just click on OK and the invoice window that you used to prepare the invoice will be displayed once more.

(b)   Alternatively click on the **Customers** button in the main Sage window. This too has a **Search** button and you might find it quicker to use this than to scroll right through the list. Once you find the account code for D Hargreaves click on it to highlight it, click on **Activity** and on **OK**. You will see on screen details of the account. However this will not tell you whether the invoice has been printed yet. Take a note of the number and use the Invoicing window to find this information.

11.1.2 Duplicate invoices

We saw how to print extra copies of invoices in section 7.3 of this chapter.

12 Conclusion

If you can follow the instructions in this chapter, you should be ready to attempt **Assignment 2.**

Key learning points

☑ In Sage, you access functions associated with the **Sales ledger** through the **Customers** button. Sage calls the '**Sales ledger control account**' the '**Debtors control account**'.

☑ Customers who deal regularly with an organisation should have an account in the **customers ledger** (or sales ledger).

☑ In Sage, there are four ways of entering **new customer accounts** in the ledger:

- Using the Record button in the Customers window

- Using the Invoices button in the Customers window

- Using one of the buttons in the Invoicing window

- Using the New button from within Customers to access the Customer Record Wizard

☑ Customers who purchase products or services can be **invoiced** through the Invoicing window in Sage.

☑ **Invoices** (and **credit notes**) are built up in sections, and the appropriate details must be entered in each section.

☑ If you use Sage software, you click on the **Save** button after processing an invoice or credit note. This saves the details entered, but **does not post the transaction** to the customers' ledger or nominal ledger.

☑ To post the details to the ledgers, you must click on the **Update** button in the Invoicing window.

Quick quiz

1   List four methods for setting up a new customer account.

2   Are you able to change the default invoice number allocated by Sage if required?

3   You have just entered all the details of a new invoice to Sage, and clicked on the Save button. The new Invoice appears within the list of invoices shown in the main Invoicing window. Has details of this Invoice been posted to the customers ledger and nominal ledger?

4   If an organisation uses Sage, but elects to produce their Invoices using a different system, should invoice and credit note details be entered through the Invoicing option?

5   How would you print a Sales Ledger day book listing?

Answers to quick quiz

1   Using the Record button in the Customers window; Using the Invoices button in the Customers window; Using one of the buttons in the Invoicing window; Using the New button from within Customers to access the Customer Record Wizard.

2   Yes, the number can be altered if required simply by typing in a new number. (Use Shift and Tab to 'go backwards' to the Invoice No.).

3   No, to post the details to the ledgers, you must click on the Update button in the Invoicing window.

4   No, in this situation it would make more sense to update the ledgers without producing invoices. This can be done by selecting the Customers button in the main Sage window, and then selecting the Invoices button from within the Customers window. The processing of invoice and credit note details can be done from here.

5   These can be generated by clicking on the Reports button in the Customers window, then selecting the report required eg Day Books: Customer Invoices (Detailed).

Activity checklist

This checklist shows which knowledge and understanding point is covered by each activity in this chapter. Tick off each activity as you complete it.

Activity

4.1		Knowledge and Understanding: Operation of computerised accounting systems
4.2		Knowledge and Understanding: Operation of computerised accounting systems
4.3		Knowledge and Understanding: Operation of computerised accounting systems
4.4		Knowledge and Understanding: Operation of computerised accounting systems
4.5		Knowledge and Understanding: Operation of computerised accounting systems
4.6		Knowledge and Understanding: Operation of computerised accounting systems
4.7		Knowledge and Understanding: Operation of computerised accounting systems
4.8		Knowledge and Understanding: Operation of computerised accounting systems
4.9		Knowledge and Understanding: Operation of computerised accounting systems
4.10		Knowledge and Understanding: Operation of computerised accounting systems

chapter 5

Payments to suppliers

Contents

1   Introduction
2   Source documents
3   Identifying invoices for payment – Aged analysis
4   Posting payments
5   Discounts
6   Credit notes
7   Payments on account
8   'One-off' payments: cheque requisitions
9   Producing cheques
10   Reports
11   Queries about payments to suppliers
12   Conclusion

Range statement

Relevant computerised records

Computerised records

Computerised ledgers

Knowledge and understanding

Operation of computerised accounting systems

1 Introduction

Suppliers who have provided goods or services, and have invoiced us for these goods or services, require payment. In this chapter, we look at how payments to suppliers are processed.

2 Source documents

Cheques for payments may be produced manually or printed from within Sage. Regardless of which method is used, the payment must be correctly authorised. Therefore, those signing the cheques may need to see the source documents which may include:

(a)   The *invoice* or *invoices* for payment, and possibly a statement from the supplier listing all invoices still outstanding and unpaid;

(b)   Any *credit note* or *credit notes* from the supplier; and

(c)   Possibly *goods received note*, to confirm receipt of the goods that are being paid for.

The invoice must be signed or initialled by an *authorised* person, giving authority for the invoice to be paid. This signature could be written on the invoice itself, and dated. If any invoice has not been properly authorised, it should be referred to your supervisor.

A payment could be made for which there is an authorised *cheque requisition* form, instead of an invoice from regular supplier with an account in the Suppliers Ledger. The procedures for recording such transactions in the accounts are different, and are explained later.

3 Identifying invoices for payment – Aged analysis

If your supervisor tells you, say, to pay all invoices that have been outstanding for over one month, your first task would be to find the relevant source documents.

(a)   If your department keeps unpaid invoices in date order in a separate file, this is usually a simple manual task. You can take the invoices for payment out of the file.

(b)   Alternatively, you can identify which suppliers to pay by checking the records in the Suppliers Ledger. The most efficient way of doing this is to use an Aged Analysis.

3.1 Aged Analysis

An aged analysis is a listing of all accounts or selected accounts with the invoices analysed according to how long they have been outstanding. Start by clicking on **Suppliers** and then on **Aged.** You should see the following dialogue box.

(a)   *Aged Balances Report Date*. This will show the Program Date which will be today's date unless you have changed it (under Settings, Change Program Date).

You should enter the date you want to use to calculate the aged balances: the program will count back 30 days, 60 days, 90 days and so on from this date and analyse the balances accordingly. For example, if you enter 31/10/2000 you will get balances that were 30, 60, 90 etc days old as at 31/10/2000.

(b)   *Include Payments Up To*. You might have paid lots of invoices in early November but this might not be relevant to your report on the state of affairs at the end of October. You might only wish to include payments made up to 31/10/2000 (or another date): if so specify this here.

Click on **OK** and the following report will appear – the figures shown below were obtained using Assignment 1 data.

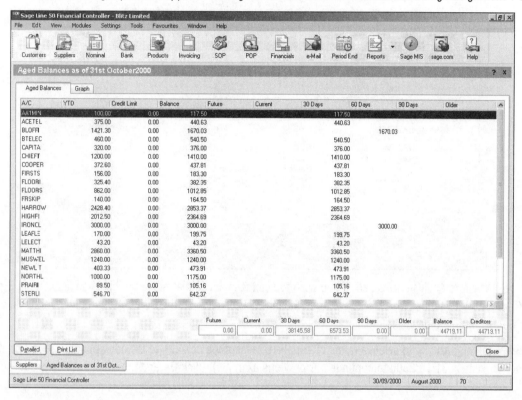

You can see at a glance how long each amount making up the current balance on each account has been outstanding.

3.1.1 Future

If you are using dates for your reports that are prior to the actual date, the report will show the value of transactions that have been posted between the report date and the actual date in the **Future** column. For example, if you received and posted £5,000 of new invoices on 1 November, but ran a report on that day for 31 October the report would show an amount of £5,000 in the Future column.

3.2 Aged analysis report

In the later version of Sage, the on-screen aged analysis can be printed using the Print List button that displays when the analysis is on-screen.

A more detailed report, that includes contact names and phone numbers may be produced. Such a report can be obtained by using the **Reports** button in the Suppliers window. Close the Aged analysis window.

You should now be back in the Suppliers window. Click on the **Report** button. In older versions of Sage the Report is selected as shown below. To see a similar screen in later versions of Sage, double click on the **Aged Creditors Reports** folder.

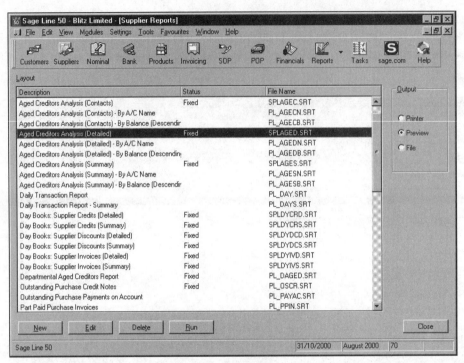

Click on Aged Creditors Analysis (Detailed) if you wish to see the invoices that make up the balance, or Aged Creditors Analysis (Summary) if you just wish to see the Aged Balances. Then click on the **Run** button in older versions, or the **Generate Report** button in new versions.

You then have the opportunity to select a range of suppliers (accept the defaults to include all) and transaction dates (ensure the 'To' date is 31/10/2000 to continue our previous example). Click **OK** and the report will be produced.

Activity 5.1

The Search button was explained in the previous chapter in relation to customers, but can also be used in the Suppliers Window. To practice using the Search button, load up the data for Assignment 2 and try getting listings of Suppliers' accounts according to a variety of criteria: all those with codes in the alphabetical range P to S, say, or all those with a balance over or under a certain amount, all those that do not have an address in London, or anything else you think of.

4 Posting payments

When payments are processed to suppliers accounts entries are made to:

- The suppliers' individual accounts in the Suppliers Ledger
- The creditors control account in the Nominal Ledger (debit)
- The bank account in the Nominal Ledger (credit)

To post a payment, you should have the following data:

(a)   The nominal ledger code for the bank account. In the Blitz case study, this is code 1200.
(b)   The supplier's account reference code.
(c)   The date of the payment.
(d)   If possible, the cheque number.
(e)   Usually, the cheque amount.

If you want to check the previous transaction details on a supplier's account before recording the payment, you can use the **Activity** button.

4.1 Allocation of payments to invoices

Normally, a payment is made to pay off one or more outstanding invoices. Instead of just recording a payment in the supplier's account, the payment should be allocated to the invoice or invoices to which it relates.

4.2 How to post payments

If you Click on the **Bank** button in the main Sage window a bank accounts window will appear with a number of buttons and a list of all the company's bank accounts. Highlight the Account the payments will be made from - in this case the Bank Current Account.

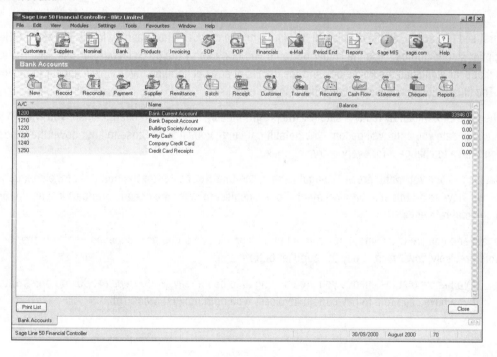

Click on the **Supplier** button and you will get a new window the top of which looks very much like a cheque book and the lower half of which tells you about outstanding invoices on a supplier's account. The following illustration assumes the data for Assignment 2 is currently loaded.

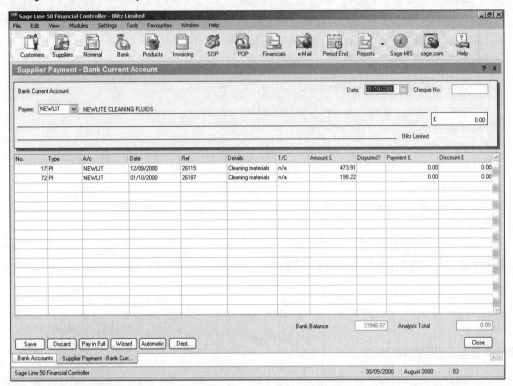

Most of the headings are self-explanatory. As you will see, the **Tp** or **Type** column in the lower half of the screen identifies the type of transaction as a purchase invoice (PI), a purchase credit note (PC), or a purchase payment on account (PA).

When you first see this screen all the details will be blank and the cursor will be flashing in the **Payee** box. Here you type the supplier's code number (use the Finder button if you don't know the precise code). Press Tab. The supplier's full name will appear alongside the Payee box and the details of any outstanding invoices will appear in the lower half of the screen. The illustration above shows you what this will look like.

By default the **Date** box will show today's date (or the program date), but you can change this if you wish. If you do change it, the new date you enter will become the default date until you click on Close to shut down the window, so you probably won't have to change it for every entry you make.

When the date is the one you want, press Tab again and in the **Chq No.** box enter the number of the cheque you are posting. You will have to do this for *every* payment. Do not neglect to enter the cheque number: it is an important control and a useful reference.

Press Tab again and you are taken into a box with a pound sign. What you do next depends upon whether or not you have been told precisely *how much* to pay the supplier beforehand.

(a) If you know that the cheque you are entering is to be for, say, £500, *type in* 500 and press Tab.

(b) If you have been told to pay certain invoices, type nothing: just press Tab.

On the previous illustration relating to Newlite Cleaning Fluids two outstanding invoices are shown, one for £473.91 and another for £198.22 - a total of £672.13. The information and instructions you might have could be as follows.

(a) A cheque for £473.91 is to be sent to Newlite Cleaning Fluids. **OR**

(b) Any invoices received from Newlite Cleaning Fluids in September 2000 should be paid. **OR**

(c) The balance on the Newlite Cleaning Fluids account should be paid in full.

4.3 Predetermined cheque amount

If you have been told the amount of the cheque, type it into the box with the pound sign. Press Tab and two things will happen.

(a) The amount that you typed in figures (eg '473.91') will appear in words ('Four hundred seventy-three Pounds and 91p'), just like on a real cheque.

(b) You will be taken to the first **Payment** box in the lower half of the screen. The amount shown (highlighted) in this box will at this point be 0.00. Look also at the Analysis Total box at the bottom of the window, which also shows 0.00 at this point.

Now click on the **Pay in Full** button at the bottom of the screen. The amount in the first Payment box (next to the invoice Amount box) will change to £473.91. The amount in the Analysis Total box will also change to £473.91. This is the total amount of the invoice you are paying.

The cursor, meanwhile will have moved down a line to the next Payment box and 0.00 will be highlighted. If you click on the Pay in Full button nothing will happen. This is because there is no difference between the amount in the £ sign box (the amount of the cheque) and the amount in the Analysis Total box match: the cheque total has already been allocated.

4.4 Posting payments

You can now click on the **Save** button. The payment is then posted and the screen is cleared for the next payment. Payments will only be posted if the amount in the analysis total box equals the amount of the cheque.

Activity 5.2

(a) Load the data for Assignment 3. Change the program date to 31/10/2000 (from the main menu choose Settings, Change program Date). What is the balance on the Supplier account NEWLIT and the Bank account (1200)?

(b) Enter the details for a cheque to NEWLIT for £473.91 dated 10 October 2000, cheque number 010203. Print out a remittance advice, then save your entry.

(c) What is the balance on the account NEWLIT and the bank account now?

4.5 Paying specific invoices

Our second scenario suggested that you had been told to pay invoices with a September 2000 date only. If you look back to the Newlite illustration you will see that the only invoice that fits into this category is the one for £473.91. You proceed as follows.

(a)   When you reach the box with the pound sign, just press Tab, leaving the box blank.

(b)   The cursor will move to the September 2000 invoice's Payment box with an amount 0.00 highlighted.

(c)   Click on the Pay in Full button. The amount in the first Payment box will change to £473.91, and so will the amount in the cheque amount box, and the amount in the Analysis Total box.

(d)   The cursor will move to the next Payment box, beside the outstanding invoice amount of £198.22.

(e)   You *do not* want to pay this second invoice because it is not a September 2000 invoice. Therefore (unless you first want to print a remittance advice note) just click on the **Save** button. The payment is posted and the screen will clear for the next entry.

Activity 5.3

Load Assignment 3 again. Change the program date to 31/10/2000. Following the above, pay any invoices received from Newlite Cleaning Supplies in September 2000. Cheque number is 010203. Also pay any received from British Telecom in September 2000. Cheque number is 010204.

4.6 Paying off the balance

The final scenario suggested that you were told to pay off the balance on the account. The procedure is exactly the same as the procedure for paying specific invoices, except that instead of Saving at step (e) you click on Pay in Full. You continue to do this for each invoice listed until all the invoice Amount boxes on screen have an equivalent amount in the Payment box. The cheque amount and the amount in the Analysis Total box will increase by the amount of each invoice that you Pay in Full. When all the invoices shown are paid, print a remittance advice if you want to and then click on the **Save** button.

To finish processing payments click on the **Close** button or press Esc.

4.7 Part payments

If you had been instructed, say, to pay Newlite Cleaning Fluids an amount of only £150 (perhaps because of a dispute), you would enter a 'part payment'. The procedure is exactly as for any other predetermined cheque amount. Enter the amount of the cheque, then press Tab until you reach the Payment box of the invoice you want to part pay. In this example you would enter £150 here. When you save the payment the outstanding amount will be reduced by £150.

If you want to pay the whole of some invoices but only part of others, use the Pay in Full button on those invoices you wish to pay all of, but enter the amount you wish to part pay when in the Payment box of an invoice you are part paying.

Activity 5.4

Load Assignment 3 again. Change the program date to 31/10/2000.

Pay off the balance on the Newlite Cleaning Fluids account. Cheque number is 914785.

Pay Prairie Couriers Ltd £50.

What is the balance on these two accounts, now?

4.8 Remittance advices

A remittance advice can be sent with a payment to a supplier, indicating the invoices that are being paid, together with discounts taken and credit notes being used. It is, quite simply, a statement to show what the payment is for.

To produce and print a remittance advice, once you have entered the details of a payment click on the **Remittance** button. In later versions of Sage you will be presented with a list of payments available for Remittance Advice printing. Clicking on the Print button will bring up the following window.

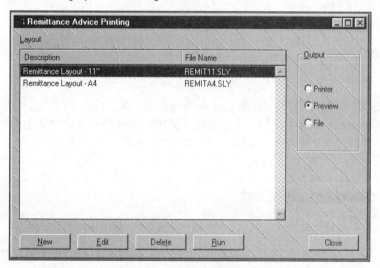

Pick one of the default layouts, REMIT11 or REMITA4, depending on your printer's paper size. Choose what sort of Output you want – printed, preview or file – and then click on Run.

Activity 5.5

Load Assignment 3. Change the program date to 31/10/2000.

Pay Newlite Cleaning Fluids £198.22. Cheque number is 246264.

Print a remittance advice.

5 Discounts

5.1 Settlement discount

As mentioned in Chapter 3, some suppliers offer a discount for early payment of an invoice. For example, payment terms of '30 days net, 3% discount 7 days' means that the invoice should be paid in full within 30 days, but a discount of 3% is available if payment is made within 7 days of the invoice date.

When such a discount (a 'settlement discount') is taken, you will need to calculate the amount of the discount. VAT rules stipulate that VAT should be charged on the discounted *net* amount (whether or not the discount is taken). Check that you can do the calculation accurately. For example, suppose that a supplier offers a 3% settlement discount for the following invoice.

	Taking the discount	*Not taking the discount*
	£	£
Net amount	1,600.00	1,600.00
Discount (3%)	(48.00)	
VAT-able amount	1,552.00	
VAT at 17.5%	271.60	271.60
Total payable	1,823.60	1,871.60

In other words, if you pay up within 7 days you can save your company £48. The VAT authorities are also happy, because your supplier's accounts show a VAT *output* (sales) tax amount of £271.60 and yours show a VAT *input* (purchases) tax amount of £271.60, whether you take the discount or not.

5.2 Recording settlement discount

To record a payment when a settlement discount is being taken the procedure is as follows.

(a) As before, click on **Bank** in the main window and then **Supplier** in the Bank Accounts window. Enter the supplier code, date and cheque number.

(b) When you get to the box with the pound sign in it leave it blank by pressing Tab to take you on the Payment box. Make no entry here.

(c) Press Tab again to take you to the Discount box. Type in the amount of the discount in pounds (for example type in 48.00). You may have to calculate this yourself, or it might be shown on the invoice already.

(d) Press Tab. The amount in the Payment box will automatically be calculated as the amount of the invoice minus the discount. The cursor will move to the next payment line.

(e) **Save** the payment as usual.

Activity 5.6

Load Assignment 3. Change the program date to 31/10/2000.

Pay off the full balance on the account SAMURA, taking a discount of 5% on the total amount owing. The cheque number is 222354

How much do you actually pay? What is the VAT element?

6 Credit notes

6.1 Offsetting credit notes

When a credit note has been posted to a supplier's account, this can be offset against an invoice that is being paid. For example, if a supplier has submitted an invoice for £100 and there is a credit note for £25, only £75 has to be paid to settle the account. Credit notes that have been posted to suppliers' accounts will appear with invoices in the list on the cheque screen.

To use a credit note, enter the details on the cheque in the usual way, leaving the cheque amount box with the pound sign blank by Tabbing through it. Press tab until you reach the *credit note's* Payment box. Click on the **Pay in Full** button. You will see the amount in the Payment box change to the amount of the credit note – in the example given it would be £25.

Now Tab up or down to the Payment box of the invoice you want to pay. Click on **Pay in Full**. The amount in the invoice's Payment box will now be equal to the amount of the invoice (£100, say), but the Analysis Total box and the cheque amount box will show the amount of the invoice less the amount of the credit note: £75 in our example.

If the amount of the credit note is greater than the amount of any outstanding invoice, proceed as follows. Without entering a cheque amount, Tab down to the Payment boxes of the invoices in question and click on Pay in Full. Then Tab to the Payment box of the credit note and *type in* the amount shown in the Analysis Total box. Press Tab.

The cheque amount will then be nil – in other words no cheque needs to be sent. This will be relatively rare, but if it happens Tab back up to the cheque number box and clear any number you typed there by pressing Delete. When you click on **Save** this has the effect of clearing off the invoices that have been offset against the credit note, and reducing the amount of the credit note outstanding.

Activity 5.7

Load up Assignment 3. Change the program date to 31/10/2000.

Pay Trojan Secretarial Services £141. Cheque number is 147853.

7 Payments on account

7.1 What is a payment on account?

Occasionally, a payment might be made to a supplier 'on account', before an invoice is received. When this happens, the amount shown in the cheque amount box will still be greater than the amount shown in the Analysis Total box, even after you have paid any invoices you want to pay in full.

7.2 Making a payment on account

To make a payment on account, enter the supplier, date and cheque number details and then *type into* the pound sign box the total amount you want to pay.

When the total cheque amount is entered Tab down to the Payment box and click on **Pay in Full** for each invoice in the normal way. When you have finished, assuming that you do not want to generate a remittance advice (see below), click on **Save**. A message like the one shown below will appear. Click on Yes (or key in Y or press Enter) to accept this.

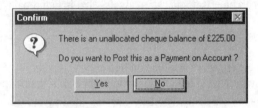

If you do want to send a remittance advice you must do this *before* you click on Save. Use the **Remittance** button in the way already described.

7.3 Offsetting payments on account against invoices

Later, when invoices have been received, the payment on account should be offset against them. This is done in the same way as using a credit note. Without entering a cheque amount, Tab down to the Payment boxes of the invoices in question and click on Pay in Full. Then Tab to the payment on account item, and *type in* the *smaller* of:

- The total of the payment on account.
- The amount now shown in the Analysis Total box.

If the payment on account is not large enough to cover the newly-received invoices there will now be an amount shown on the cheque to make up the difference.

If the amount of the payment on account still exceeds the amount of any invoices received the cheque amount will be nil – in other words no cheque will be sent. Again, this will be relatively rare, but if it happens Tab back up to the cheque number box and clear it by pressing Delete. If you click on **Save** this has the effect of clearing off the invoices that have been offset against the payment on account, and reducing the amount of the outstanding payment on account.

Activity 5.8

Load up Assignment 6. Change the program date to 31/10/2000.

Pay the Leaflet Company £500 (cheque number 278400), part of which is a payment on account. Note down how much.

Post an invoice for leaflets dated 5 November 2000 (number WE4582) received from The Leaflet Company for £700 (gross). The Nominal account is the Printing account.

Change the program date to 15/11/2000 and clear the balance on this supplier's account (cheque number 278487).

Tasks

(a)   How much was the payment on account?

(b)   What is the amount of the cheque needed to clear the balance?

8 'One-off' payments: cheque requisitions

Payments are sometimes made against a cheque requisition.

(a)   If an invoice from a supplier will be received in due course, the payment can be entered as a payment on account, as described above.

(b)   If the supplier does not have or need an account, there won't be an entry for the transaction in the suppliers ledger.

A cheque payment for a bank transaction that will not be processed through the suppliers ledger should be recorded directly to the nominal ledger accounts. The payment should be processed as follows.

(a)   Click on the **Bank** button in the main window.

(b)   If different bank accounts are used for nominal ledger payments and Supplier payments, make sure the correct one is highlighted. (Only one account is used in the Blitz case study.)

(c)   Click on the **Payment** button in the Bank Accounts window.

The following box, or a similar box if using a later version, will appear.

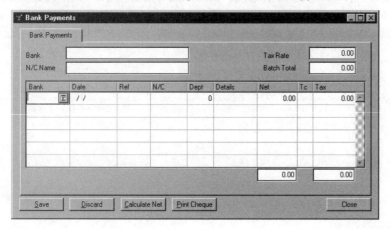

The cursor begins in the Bank column with the usual finder button. This is because many businesses make non-suppliers ledger payments from a separate bank account to the main one for purchases, although this does not apply in the case of Blitz, where you would simply choose A/C 1200 as usual.

Enter the **Date** in the usual way. The **Ref** should be the cheque number.

Press Tab again to take you to the **N/C** box. Here you enter the nominal ledger account code for the account to which the payment refers. For example, a cheque payment for the hire of a motor car should be given the nominal account code 7401 in the Sage system. This is the account code for Car Hire expenses. As usual, a list of codes can be displayed on screen by clicking on the Finder button or pressing the F4 function key.

In the Blitz case study you can Tab straight through the **Dept** box, then type in an appropriate brief description of what the payment is for in **Details**.

In the **Net** box you have two options.

(a)   Enter the *net amount of the payment (excluding VAT)* and press Tab. The cursor will move to the **T/c** (Tax code) box. The default code T1 for standard rate VAT will already be shown and the **Tax** box will already show VAT calculated at this rate. You can, however alter the tax code (usually to T0 for zero rated items). If you do this and press Tab the VAT will automatically be recalculated at the appropriate rate.

(b)   Alternatively you can enter the *total payment inclusive of VAT* in the **Net** box. Before pressing Tab click on the **Calc Net** button at the foot of the window. This will automatically calculate VAT at the standard rate and divide the total amount that you entered into net and VAT amounts. The tax code T1 will be shown in the **T/c** box. You can change this to another rate (in which case the figures will be recalculated) if necessary.

When you click on **Save** the transactions will be automatically posted to the appropriate nominal ledger accounts:

Credit: Bank Account (probably code 1200)

Debit: Nominal ledger account specified in the N/C field for the transaction.

Activity 5.9

Your supervisor has asked you, on 5 October 2000, to record a cheque payment to Goodtime Ltd for £1,410.00 (£1,200.00 net plus £210.00 for VAT at the standard rate.) The cheque is for UK Entertainment (nominal ledger code 7403). There is no invoice, and the request for payment has been submitted on a cheque requisition form. The cheque number is 345432.

Record this transaction. (It does not matter which Assignment you have loaded.)

9 Producing cheques

To print cheques using Sage follow the following instructions.

Step 1   The date of your printed cheques are retrieved from the computer system date. To create post-dated cheques, change your computer's system date.

Step 2   From the main Sage toolbar, choose the Bank option.

Step 3   From the Bank Accounts window, select the account that you want to make the payments from - **1200**.

Step 4   Click on the Cheques button. The Print Cheques window appears listing all remittances for all purchase invoices), purchase credit notes and purchase payments on account that have not been printed before and have blank references. Remittances for bank payments that selected to print the cheque during processing are also shown.

Step 5   To restrict the transactions that appear to a certain date range, select the Date Range checkbox and enter the range you require.

Step 6   If you want to include cheques that have already been printed, select the Show Printed Items checkbox. If you have already printed a cheque it appears in a different colour in the Print Cheques window and a 'Y' appears in the Prn or Printed column.

Step 7   The starting cheque number is automatically entered for you. You can change this number if required.

Step 8   Select the transactions you want to print cheques for.

Step 9   Print the cheques you have selected by clicking on the Print cheques button. If you have not selected any transactions cheques will be printed for all listed transactions.

Step 10   Select the layout you require and click Run. The cheques are printed and you are asked to confirm that they have all printed correctly. If your cheques have printed correctly, each cheque is given a reference number.

10 Reports

To see on screen a list of all the *transactions* on the bank account, click on **Nominal,** highlight account number 1200 and click on **Activity,** and then on OK.

To get an equivalent print-out, click on **Nominal** as before, click on **Reports,** and choose Nominal Activity from the options you are offered. You will need to specify the relevant date range and account range (1200 to 1200).

To get reports on *payments* click on **Bank** in the main window, ensure the account you want is highlighted (A/c 1200 in the Blitz case study), and then click on **Reports**. The options you are then presented with depends upon the version of Sage you are using. Experiment with the reports available on-screen.

11 Queries about payments to suppliers

You might be asked to deal with a query from a supplier who wants to know when you are going to pay an outstanding invoice.

Simply highlight the account in the main supplier window and click on Activity. To see all transactions relating to that supplier accept the defaults by clicking **OK**.

12 Conclusion

If you were able to follow the instructions in this chapter, you should now be ready to attempt Assignment 3.

Key learning points

☑ **Cheques** for payments may be produced manually or printed from within an accounting software package such as Sage. Regardless of which method is used, payments must be correctly **authorised**.

☑ An **aged analysis** is a listing of all accounts or selected accounts with the invoices analysed according to how long they have been outstanding.

☑ Payments can be posted in Sage from the **Bank** button in the main Sage window. The user selects the bank account the payments will be made from (usually the Bank Current Account) and then clicks on the **Supplier** button.

☑ Details of the payment are **entered on-screen** into a form that looks very much like a cheque.

☑ Modern accounting software packages also include the option of printing **Remittance Advices** to be sent with cheques detailing the invoices paid.

☑ Sage and other similar packages can also handle '**payments on account**' and automate **discount** calculations.

Quick quiz

1   List three possible source documents that may be required to be viewed before payment is made to a supplier.

2   What is an Aged Analysis report?

3   To post a payment to Sage, you will need certain information. List three pieces of information you will need.

4   What is a remittance advice?

5   What is a 'payment on account'?

Answers to quick quiz

1   Source documents may include: The invoice or invoices for payment; Possibly a statement from the supplier listing all invoices still outstanding and unpaid; Any credit notes offset from the invoice totals; and possibly a goods received note.

2   An aged analysis report is a listing of all accounts or selected accounts with the invoices analysed according to how long they have been outstanding.

3   Any three of the following: The nominal ledger code for the bank account; the supplier's name or account code, the date of the payment; possibly the cheque number, the cheque amount or invoices to be paid.

4   A remittance advice is a document showing the invoices that are being paid by a cheque, together with discounts taken and credit notes being used. It's purpose is to show exactly what the payment is for.

5   A 'payment on account is a payment made to a supplier 'on account', before an invoice has been received.

Activity checklist

This checklist shows which knowledge and understanding point is covered by each activity in this chapter. Tick off each activity as you complete it.

Activity

5.1		Knowledge and Understanding: Operation of computerised accounting systems
5.2		Knowledge and Understanding: Operation of computerised accounting systems
5.3		Knowledge and Understanding: Operation of computerised accounting systems
5.4		Knowledge and Understanding: Operation of computerised accounting systems
5.5		Knowledge and Understanding: Operation of computerised accounting systems
5.6		Knowledge and Understanding: Operation of computerised accounting systems
5.7		Knowledge and Understanding: Operation of computerised accounting systems
5.8		Knowledge and Understanding: Operation of computerised accounting systems
5.9		Knowledge and Understanding: Operation of computerised accounting systems

chapter 6

Receipts from customers

Contents

1   Introduction
2   Receipts
3   Credit notes and customer receipts
4   Discounts
5   Returned cheques
6   Refunding paid invoices
7   Writing off small amounts
8   Account balances
9   Payments with order (bank receipts)
10 Reports
11 Conclusion

Range statement

Relevant computerised records

Computerised records

Computerised ledgers

Knowledge and understanding

Operation of computerised accounting systems

1 Introduction

In this chapter we explain the process of recording payments sent to us from customers.

2 Receipts

2.1 Recording customer receipts

The information required to process the payment to the customer's Sales ledger account includes:

(a)   The nominal ledger code of the bank account (1200 in the Blitz case study).

(b)   The name of the customer and the customer's account reference code.

(c)   The date of the receipt.

(d)   The customer's cheque number (although this is not essential).

(e)   The cheque amount.

(f)   The amount of early settlement discount taken, if any.

You should also receive information showing which invoice (or invoices) the customer is paying, such as a remittance advice. This should also identify any credit notes that are being used.

Click on the **Bank** button in the main Sage window. As you learned in the previous chapter this gives a list of all the company's bank accounts. If there is more than one, highlight the one to which customer receipts are posted (probably account 1200, as in the Blitz case study) and then click on the **Customer** button. The following window, or a similar one depending upon the version of Sage you are using, will appear.

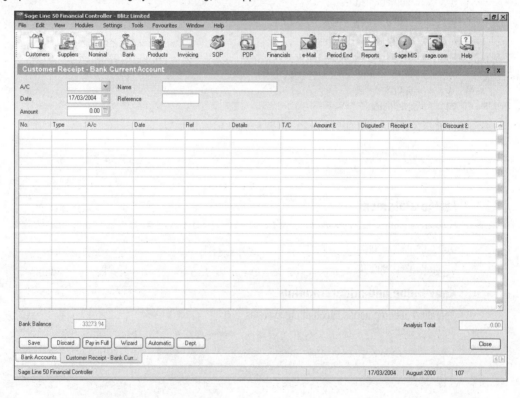

The cursor will be positioned the A/C box. Here you enter the customer account code. You can use the Finder button on the right of the A/C box to find the code. When you enter a code and press Tab the full name of the customer appears in the Name box and details of any outstanding transactions on the account appear in the lower half of the screen.

The Tp (or Type) column shows the type of transaction on each line:

(a)   SI means sales invoice.

(b)   SC means sales credit note.

(c)   SA means sales payment on account.

Enter the Date of payment. By default this field will show today's date, as recorded in the computer system, but you can alter this. If you do so the new date will appear each time you start a fresh receipt until you close the window, so there is no need to change it every time.

Pressing Tab takes you to the Ref box. Here you can enter something like the customer's cheque number or the number of the customer's remittance advice or the number of the invoice being paid, or some other identifying reference. *Do not* leave this field blank: enter a unique reference of some kind.

2.2 Allocating receipts

When you reach the Amount box you have two options.

(a)   If you can see at a glance that the amount of the cheque that you have received is the same as the amount of the outstanding invoice(s) shown in the lower half of the screen, leave the Amount box empty: just press Tab.

(b)   If you are not sure what invoices are being paid it is safer to key in the amount of the cheque in the Amount box and press Tab. (A £ sign is not required.)

You must now allocate the receipt of the customer's payment to the outstanding invoice or invoices in the account, to indicate which invoice or invoices have been paid. The procedure is just like the procedure for allocating payments, as described in the previous chapter.

When you press Tab you will be taken to the **Receipt** box and an amount of 0.00 will be highlighted. If you click on the **Pay in Full** button this will change to the full amount of the invoice.

(a)   If you left the Amount box blank this will also change to the amount of the invoice, as will the amount in the Analysis Total box. Press Tab again to move to the next line and repeat the procedure until the amount in the Amount box and the Analysis Total box equal the amount of your receipt. Click on **Save** and the screen will clear.

(b)   If you did key in the amount of the receipt in the Amount box there are three possibilities.

(i)   If the amount you entered was *less than* the amount of any invoice, it is a part payment by the customer. When you click on the **Pay in Full** button the amount you keyed in will appear in the Receipt box and in the Analysis Total box. There is no more money to allocate so you can just click on **Save**.

(ii)   If the amount you keyed in was exactly the *same as* the amount of an invoice (or the same as the total of several invoices), then clicking on the **Pay in Full** button for the invoice or invoices will make an amount equal to the amount of the invoice(s) appear in the Receipt box and the Analysis Total box. Click on **Save** when there is no more money to allocate.

(iii)   If the amount you keyed in was *greater than* the total of all the outstanding invoices you have received a payment on account. Click on the **Pay in Full** button each time you Tab to the next Receipt box until any outstanding invoices are paid. The total will accumulate in the Analysis Total box, but when you have finished the Amount box will still show a greater total than the Analysis Total box. Click on **Save** and you will get a message telling you that there is an unallocated cheque balance of £X, and asking if you want to post it as a payment on account. Assuming that this is what you want, click on Yes.

This might sound complicated, but it is not really when you start using the system. The following table summarises what we have said so far.

Amount received	Amount(s) outstanding	Action
£254.31	£254.31	Leave the Amount box blank and Tab to the Receipt box beside the invoice amount £254.31. Click on Pay in Full then Save.
£500	£200 £300	You can see at a glance that what you have received is the same as the amount outstanding. Proceed as in the previous example for the two invoice amounts.
£193.46	£247.82 £193.46	The customer is clearly paying the second of the two invoices. Leave the Amount box blank and Tab to the Receipt box beside the amount £193.46. Click on Pay in Full and then Save.
£752.57	£466.18 £286.39	Key in the amount £752.57 in the Amount box and press Tab. Click on Pay in Full for each of the two invoices. The total in the Analysis Box will show £466.18 the first time you do this and increase to £752.57 the second time. The two invoices have been paid in full. Click on Save.
£200 (Part payment)	£350	Key in the amount £200 in the Amount box and press Tab. Click on Pay in Full. The amount in the Receipt box will show £200, as will the total in the Analysis Box. Click on Save. When you next call up the account it will show that £150 is still outstanding.
£500 (Payment on account)	£350	Key in the amount £500 in the Amount box and press Tab. Click on Pay in Full. The amount in the Receipt box will show £350, as will the total in the Analysis Box. However the Amount box will still show £500. Click on Save and respond Yes when you get a message asking if you want to post a payment on account of £150.

Activity 6.1

Load Assignment 6 and find out the balances on the bank account and the debtors ledger control account.

Post the following receipts from customers, all dated 15/11/2000, following the procedures described above. Use the number of the first invoice that is being paid as your reference number.

ASPINA £211.50

BRADLE £500.00

DCSROO£200.00

ELITEC £941.11

ROSEAL £146.00

What are the balances on the bank account and the debtors ledger control account now?

Print out a report of the activity on the ELITEC account.

3 Credit notes and customer receipts

Customers will generally pay the balance due – which is the total of Invoices due less the total of any Credit Notes relating to those invoices.

The best way of recording a receipt in the customer's account where a credit note is being used is to include the credit note in the allocations as follows.

(a)   Enter the *actual cheque amount* in the Amount box.

(b)   Tab down to the Receipt box of the credit note transaction and click on **Pay in Full**.

(c)   Tab to the Receipt box of the other outstanding invoice or invoices being paid and click on **Pay in Full** until the total amount of the cheque is used up.

Activity 6.2

Load up Assignment 3.

You have received a cheque for £1,762.50 from Royal Properties Ltd. Post this receipt as you think appropriate.

4 Discounts

A customer might take advantage of an early settlement discount, when this is offered. When a customer takes a discount, you will need to be informed of the amount of discount that has been taken. (You might also be asked to check that the customer has calculated the discount correctly. You can do this with the calculator buttons if you like.)

Recording a receipt net of discount is similar to recording a payment to a supplier net of discount.

(a)   In the Discount box type in the amount of the discount in pounds. Press Tab.

(b)   The Receipt box will automatically show the reduced balanced due.

Activity 6.3

Load up Assignment 3.

You have decided to offer Harvey-Sagar Developments a settlement discount of 2% on all future invoices.

(a)   Amend the record of this customer accordingly.

(b)   Post an invoice to Harvey-Sagar Developments dated 15 November 2000 for £850 (net) for Office Cleaning. (Accept the default invoice number offered by Sage.)

(c)   Post a receipt dated 20 November 2000 from Harvey-Sagar Developments for £2,694.28, following the instructions above.

5 Returned cheques

Occasionally, a cheque received from a customer might be 'bounced' and returned by the bank marked 'Refer to Drawer'. The customer's bank is refusing to pay the cheque possibly because there are insufficient funds in the customer's bank account.

When a cheque bounces, the receipt will already have been recorded in the customer's account. This must now be corrected. The following instructions apply to Sage Line 50 and Sage Instant Accounts Plus only. Sage Instant Accounts users should read through these sections, but will not be able to perform the operations on-screen.

Click on **Tools** at the top of the main window and choose the option **Write Off, Refund, Return** from the menu that drops down, as shown in the following illustration.

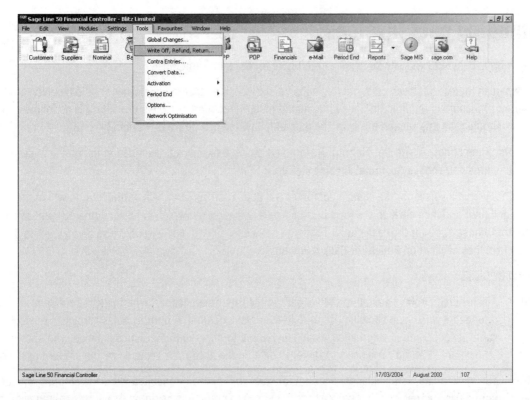

You are then asked to choose whether amendments will be made to the Sales ledger or the Purchase ledger. Choose the Sales Ledger option and click on **Next**.

You will see a list. This includes the item Customer Cheque Returns. Highlight this and click on the **Next** button at the foot of the window. A list of customer accounts will appear. Highlight the one you require and click on Next.

Next, select the cheque that has 'bounced', then click on Next. Enter the date of the transaction, which would usually be the date the cheque was dishonoured, and click Next. You will see a summary of what you are asking to be done. If you are happy with this, click on **Finish** to post the transaction. If not there is a **Back** option, allowing you to go back through these steps and change your decisions as necessary.

Activity 6.4

Load Assignment 6.

It is 31 October 2000. A cheque from A Wyche for £88.13 has bounced.

(a)   What is the initial balance on A Wyche's account and on the bank account?

(b)   Record the bounced cheque, following the instructions given above.

(c)   What is the balance on the two accounts now?

(d)   How is the transaction shown in A Wyche's customer's ledger account?

6 Refunding paid invoices

To cancel an *unpaid* invoice, you should issue a credit note for the same amount.

However, when an invoice has been paid, but it is subsequently decided that the customer should be given a refund in full, a different procedure is required. In Sage Line 50 and Instant Accounts Plus this procedure is as follows. (Sage Instant users should read this section but won't be able to follow the procedure on-screen.)

Click on **Tools.** Then choose **Write Off, Refund, Return** and proceed exactly as described in the previous section, except that this time you choose **Customer Invoice Refunds**.

Details of all *fully-paid* invoices for the chosen customer will appear on screen. Click on the item to which the refund applies to highlight it and then click on the **Next** button. You are then asked which bank account you want to post the adjustment to. Choose 1200 for the case study. Then you get a summary of what you have said you want to do and are asked to confirm it by clicking on **Finish** (or Back if you are not happy).

The effect of this is as follows.

(a) A sales credit note is posted to the account in the Customers ledger, with the same reference as the refunded invoice, and showing 'Refund' in the details column. A dummy sales invoice is posted to the same account, and is automatically allocated in full to the credit note. The details column shows 'Allocation – Refund'. The sales turnover to date on the account is reduced by the amount of the refund.

(b) The appropriate Nominal ledger account for sales is reduced by (debited with) the amount refunded. The nominal ledger bank control account, out of which the refund is being paid, will be credited with the amount refunded (in other words the bank balance will be reduced).

Activity 6.5

Load Assignment 6.

What is the balance on the accounts for Bridgford and Co and Sales – Contract cleaning?

On 31 October 2000 it has been decided that Bridgford and Co should be given a refund for invoice number 10003.

Post this transaction. What is the new balance on Bridgford and Co's account and on the Sales – Contract cleaning account?

How does this transaction appear in Bridgford and Co's account?

7 Writing off small amounts

It is quite common in practice for customers to mistakenly pay a few pence less than they owe. For example, a customer might remit a cheque for £76.00 to pay an invoice for £76.38.

When a company receives payments that are less than the invoiced amount, but only by a small amount, a decision might be taken to write-off the unpaid amount, because it is too small to worry about. It would cost too much (time-wise) to chase the customer for payment and the effort wouldn't be worthwhile.

Sage Line 50 includes a facility that automates the process of writing off small amounts on customer accounts. (This facility is not available in Sage Instant). Users of Line 50 and Instant Accounts Plus can write off small amounts by following the following steps. Choose the **Tools** menu and then **Write Off, Refund, Return.** Pick the option *Write off Customer Transactions below a value* in the **Sales ledger** list.

A screen prompt asks you to 'Enter the value below which a transaction will be written off', and you must key in the amount below which the balance on any customer account will be written off as uncollectable. The value can be as little as 0.02 (ie. £0.02).

When you have keyed in this write-off and clicked on **Next**, the screen will automatically display every customer account and transaction for which the unpaid balance is currently less than the value you have entered.

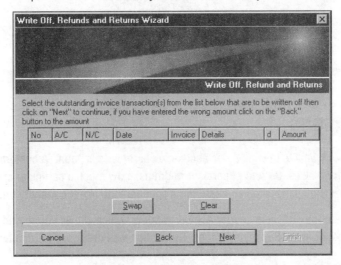

To write off the unpaid balance on an account firstly highlight the account by clicking on it. You will then see a list of transactions displayed in a box like that shown above. To highlight all transactions shown, click on the **Swap** button at the foot of the window.

When you have made your selection or selections, click on **Next.** A further screen will ask the date of the write off. Enter this, click **Next** and then **Finish**.

(a) The account(s) in the Customers ledger will be credited with the amount written off, with 'Bad Debt Write Off' shown as the details.

(b) In the Nominal ledger, the debtors control account (code 1100) will be credited with the amount written off, and the bad debt write off account (code 8100) is debited.

Activity 6.6

If you use Line 50, load up Assignment 5. (Users of Sage Instant should skip this activity.)

It is 31/10/2000 (for the purpose of these exercises, whenever you are told 'it is .....' change the program date within Sage to that date) .

Post the following receipts from customers.

ASPINA £105.00

CHADWI £176.00

NORRIS £1,087.27

Now, following the instructions above, write off any balances below £1.00.

What is the total amount written off?

Which nominal ledger accounts are affected?

8 Account balances

You might be asked to find out what is the unpaid balance on a customer's account. A customer might telephone, for example, and ask how much he owes. Or your supervisor might ask how much a particular customer still owes. The simplest way of finding the unpaid balance on an customer's account is to use the **Activity** button.

This gives a window similar to the Suppliers Ledger Activity window, which allows you to find the current unpaid balance on any supplier account in the Suppliers Ledger. This option was described in Chapter 5.

9 Payments with order (bank receipts)

9.1 Receipts from 'Cash Sale' customers

Customers might pay by cheque or credit card for goods or services when they make their order. The customer is not asking for credit; any may not want or need an account in the Customers Ledger. The transaction should be recorded as a sale and a bank receipt.

To record a cheque or credit card receipt for items that will not be processed through the Customers ledger, click on the **Bank** button in the main Sage window, and then (after selecting the appropriate bank account if there is more than one) on the **Receipt** button.

To enter the details of the receipt, you will need the following information:

 (a) The bank account to which the transaction will be posted (1200 in the Blitz case study).

 (b) The transaction date.

 (c) The reference number your company uses for cash sales transactions.

(d) The nominal account code to which the credit will be posted (ie the sales account or other income account in the nominal ledger).

(e) The department code, if any.

(f) A description of the item for which the payment has been received (also optional).

(g) The net value of the item (excluding VAT).

(h) The VAT code for the item.

9.2 Entering bank receipt details

When you click on the **Receipt** button, the following window will appear (or a similar window if you are using an earlier version of Sage).

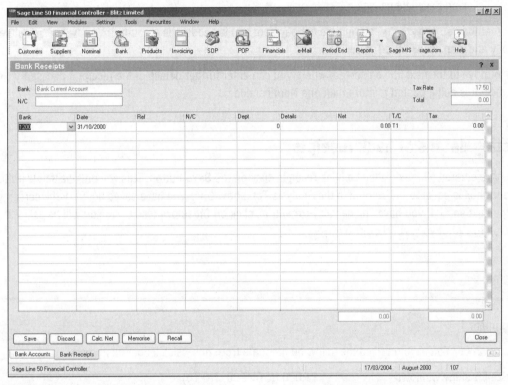

Enter the bank account code (1200 in Blitz) and the date as usual. For the **Ref** you can enter a reference for the transaction such as the customer's cheque number or your own paying-in slip number. Press Tab again.

Key in the code of the nominal ledger account (for sales or income) to which the receipt refers, then press Tab (the N/C name will then appear in the N/C Name box at the top of the window). In the Blitz case study, the code will be one of the following:

4000	Sales – contract cleaning
4001	Sales – window cleaning
4002	Sales – domestic services
4100	Sales – materials

In the **Dept** and **Details** boxes you can enter the code of the Department concerned if any and a description of the purpose of the payment from the customer.

You can enter either the net amount of the receipt (excluding VAT) or the gross amount (including VAT).

(a)   If you enter the net amount, press Tab and the cursor will move to the T/c column. This may show a default code such as T1, but you can alter it if you wish. In the Blitz case study, the codes are:

T0 For zero-rated items

T1 For standard-rate items (currently taxed at the rate of 17.5%)

(b)   If you key in the gross receipt in the Net column and click on **Calculate Net** (or press F9) this automatically deducts VAT at the standard rate (assuming tax code T1 applies). If you than press Tab you can change the tax code if you like and the amounts will be recalculated as appropriate. (If the code has to be altered from, say T0 to T1, you may need to Tab back to the Net box, re-enter the gross amount and click on Calculate net again.

Whichever method you choose for entering the net payment and tax code, the amount of VAT will be calculated automatically and displayed in the Tax column.

Press Tab to move to the next line on screen, where you can enter further details of the receipt if necessary (for example if a single receipt is being posted to more than one Nominal code).

9.3 Posting details of bank receipts

When you have entered all the details of a bank receipts click on the **Save** button. This will only be active if the amount in the Amount box is equal to the amount in the Analysis Total box. Once you have saved an entry the screen will clear, ready for the next entry. If you have finished all your entries click on **Close** or press Esc. (You will be asked if you are sure you wish to Exit. If you are, click on Yes.)

Activity 6.7

Load Assignment 1.

It is 8 October 2000. You have received the following amounts from non-sales ledger customers.

Gleamo Prize for shiny windows: £1,000 (N/C 4900; T/C T0)

D. Spenser, one-off payment for domestic services: £100 (gross)

Post these transactions using the paying-in slip reference 123478.

What is the balance on the bank account after you have done this?

10 Reports

A wide variety of reports are available to display and analyse receipts from customers. Again, the process for producing reports differs slightly depending upon the version of Sage you are using.

Explore the options available under the **Reports** button in the **Bank** window. Ensure you are able to print the Day Books: Bank Receipts (Detailed) Report.

11 Conclusion

When you feel you have a reasonable understanding of this chapter, you should be ready to attempt **Assignment 4**.

Key learning points

☑   When customers make payments for invoices, the **receipt** should be recorded in the **Customers ledger**, sometimes known as the Sales ledger.

☑   Receipts can be posted in Sage from the **Bank** button in the main Sage window. The user selects the bank account the payments will be made from (usually the Bank Current Account) and then clicks on the **Customer** button.

☑   Details of the receipt are **entered on-screen**, and there is the opportunity to **allocate** the receipt to outstanding transactions.

☑   Customer receipts will usually comprise the value of outstanding **invoices**, less any **credit notes** issued and **discount** agreed.

☑   Occasionally, a cheque issued by a customer may not be paid after they have been submitted for banking. Such cheques are often said to have '**bounced**'. Modern accounting packages such as Sage include facilities for processing bounced cheques.

☑   Accounting packages such as Sage also **simplify** the **accounting procedures** for issuing refunds for previously paid invoices, writing off very small balances and accounting for sales paid for immediately.

☑   A range of **reports** are available from within Sage that allow you to analyse receipts from customers.

Quick quiz

1 List the information required to post a receipt to the Customers ledger.

2 What is 'settlement discount'?

3 What is the most common reason for a cheque to 'bounce'?

4 In Sage, how would you record a transaction involving a new customer who pays with cash and does not want or need an account in the Customers Ledger.

5 How would you print a listing of bank receipts from Sage?

Answers to quick quiz

1 The information required is: The nominal ledger code (or at least the nominal ledger account name) of the bank account into which the receipt will be banked; The name of the customer or the customer's account reference code; The date of the receipt; The customer's cheque number (not essential); The cheque amount; The amount of early settlement discount taken, if any.

2 'Settlement discount' is the amount that can be deducted from the total owed if payment is received before a specified date. For example, a customer may purchase an item for £100, but the supplier states that if they make payment within 7 days (example only), £95 will be accepted as full payment. In this case, £5 settlement discount must be accounted for.

3 The most common reason a customer's bank refuses to pay a cheque is because there are insufficient funds in the customer's bank account. Other reasons could include an unauthorised signature on the cheque or only one signature when two are required.

4 The transaction should be recorded as a sale and a bank receipt. To do this in Sage, you would click on the Bank button from the main Sage window, and then (after selecting the appropriate bank account if there is more than one) on the Receipt button. You are required to enter a range of details, including the code of the nominal ledger account (for sales or income) to which the receipt should be posted.

5 To get a report on receipts, you would click on Bank from the Sage main window, ensure that the account you want is highlighted, and then click on Reports. You would select the Day Books: Bank Receipts (Detailed) report, and specify the criteria for your report.

Activity checklist

This checklist shows which knowledge and understanding point is covered by each activity in this chapter. Tick off each activity as you complete it.

Activity

6.1   Knowledge and Understanding: Operation of computerised accounting systems

6.2   Knowledge and Understanding: Operation of computerised accounting systems

6.3   Knowledge and Understanding: Operation of computerised accounting systems

6.4   Knowledge and Understanding: Operation of computerised accounting systems

6.5   Knowledge and Understanding: Operation of computerised accounting systems

6.6   Knowledge and Understanding: Operation of computerised accounting systems

6.7   Knowledge and Understanding: Operation of computerised accounting systems

chapter 7

Other cash transactions

Contents

1 Introduction
2 Petty cash transactions
3 Nominal ledger journal entries and bank-cash transactions
4 Bank transactions not involving sales or purchases
5 Bank reconciliations
6 Conclusion

Range statement

Relevant computerised records
Computerised records
Computerised ledgers

Knowledge and understanding

Operation of computerised accounting systems

1 Introduction

In this chapter we explain the procedures for processing a range of cash transactions not related to receipts from customers.

2 Petty cash transactions

2.1 Petty cash account

A petty cash account is a record of relatively small cash payments and cash receipts. The balance on the petty cash account at any time should be the amount of cash (notes and coins) held within the business. Petty cash is commonly kept in a locked metal box, in a safe or locked drawer. The box will contain notes and coins, vouchers recording amounts of cash withdrawn (and the reasons for using the cash) and vouchers for petty cash receipts.

The accounting records for petty cash are often maintained in a book, or a spreadsheet. Transactions are recorded from the petty cash vouchers into the petty cash book.

A petty cash account must also be maintained in the nominal ledger. The person responsible for petty cash needs to ensure entries from the petty cash book are entered into the into 'main' accounting system. Requests for petty cash **must be authorised** in line with stated policy.

For payments of cash out of petty cash, details must be entered of

    (a)   The amount withdrawn.

    (b)   The purpose. This will be used to allocate the nominal ledger account to which the item of expense relates.

Similarly, for receipts of cash into petty cash, details must be entered of

    (a)   The amount received.

    (b)   The reason for the receipt – used to allocated the nominal ledger account.

2.2 Recording petty cash transactions

The information you need to record a cash payment or cash receipt is as follows.

    (a)   The code of the nominal ledger account to which the payment will be debited or the receipt credited.

    (b)   The transaction date.

    (c)   If appropriate, a reference number such as the petty cash voucher number.

    (d)   A description of the reason for the payment or receipt unless the nominal account code used means this is obvious.

    (e)   Either the net value of the item (excluding VAT), or the gross amount of the item (including VAT).

    (f)   The appropriate VAT code.

The petty cash account is included in the list in the Bank window. Just select the Petty Cash account (code 1230) instead of the main bank account (code 1230).

Transactions are posted **exactly as for Bank receipts and payments**. Try the following Activity.

Activity 7.1

Load up Assignment 3.

Post the following transactions to the petty cash account. Transactions are numbered consecutively, beginning at PC013. VAT receipts have not been obtained, so no VAT applies.

25 Oct   Stationery: £5.26.

28 Oct   Refreshments: £4.45

24 Oct   Present for new baby: £27.99 (N/C 6202)

25 Oct   Loan (Joan Davies): £50 (N/C 9998)

31 Oct   Received from Joan Davies: £50.

What is the balance on the petty cash account and on account 7504 now?

3 Nominal ledger journal entries and bank-cash transactions

3.1 Nominal ledger journal entries

A nominal ledger journal entry is used to record transactions and accounting entries that will not be recorded in any other book of prime entry.

Although a journal can be thought of as a 'book' for recording transactions to be posted to the nominal ledger, it is common for journal transactions to be recorded on sheets of paper, known as journal vouchers.

Entries in the journal must subsequently be posted to the appropriate accounts in the nominal ledger. For every journal transaction, there will have to be:

(a)   A debit entry in one nominal ledger account.
(b)   A corresponding credit entry in another nominal ledger account.

In other words, there are two sides to every transaction, the debit entry and the credit entry.

A transaction recorded in the journal, for example, could relate to a transfer between accounts in the nominal ledger. In the Sage system, a journal entry is used, for example, to record transfers of petty cash from the bank account to the cash account.

Movements of money between the bank account and petty cash are known as bank-cash transactions.

3.2 Recording bank-cash transactions

To record a movement of money from the bank account to cash (that is, a cash withdrawal) or to record the payment of cash (notes and coin) into the bank, click on the **Nominal** button in the main Sage window and then on the **Journals** button in the Nominal Ledger window. The window shown below will be displayed (or a similar window depending upon the version of Sage you use).

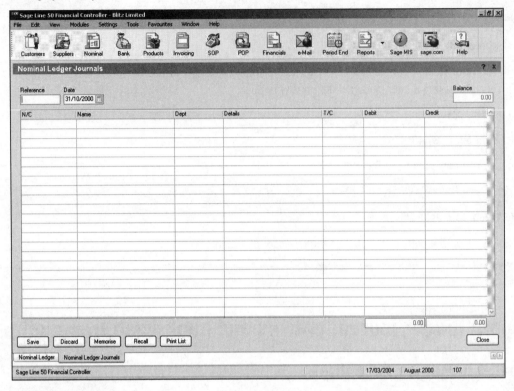

3.2.1 Ref or Reference

This is an optional item, which can be used to identify the transaction. The journal voucher number could be inserted here (up to a maximum of six characters).

3.2.2 Date

If necessary, enter the transaction date, as an eight-digit code in the format DDMMYYYY or use the calendar button. The cursor will then move past the box labelled Balance, down to the main part of the screen. Here, you enter the details of the debit item and the credit item, one per line, for the transaction.

For a bank-cash transaction, the debit and credit entries are as follows.

(a) When *cash is withdrawn* from the bank.

		Nominal ledger code
DEBIT	Petty cash	1230
CREDIT	Bank current account	1200

(b)   When *cash is paid into* the bank from petty cash.

		Nominal ledger code
DEBIT	Bank current account	1200
CREDIT	Petty cash	1230

3.2.3 N/C and Name

Enter the nominal ledger code of the bank account (1200) or the petty cash account (1230). It does not matter which code you enter on the first line. You will need to enter both, one per line, to complete the input details. When you enter the code, the account name will appear in the Name box automatically. (To find other codes you can use the Finder button in the normal way: click on it or press function key F4 when the cursor is in this box.)

For our purposes we can ignore the Dept box and Tab through to Details.

3.2.4 Details

You can enter brief details of the transaction. For example:

N/C	Name	Description	T/c	Debit	Credit
1230	PETTY CASH	Received from bank a/c	T9	100.00	
1200	BANK CURRENT A/C	To petty cash float	T9		100.00

The description for one side of the entry should always indicate the other nominal ledger account to which the transaction relates. In the example above, the details for the withdrawal of £100 from the bank (the credit of 100.00 for N/C 1200) refer to petty cash which is the recipient of the money.

3.2.5 T/c (Tax Code)

A bank-cash transaction does not involve VAT. Enter tax code T9.

3.2.6 Debit/Credit

Enter the amount of the transaction, in the debit or the credit column, according to whether the nominal ledger account should be debited or credited.

Remember that there must be two entries for a bank-cash transaction, one a debit and one a matching credit, to complete a journal entry. In fact the system will not allow you to post your journal until Debits equal Credits and the amount shown in the Balance box is nil.

When you have completed the entry, Click on **Save** as usual and the nominal ledger accounts will be updated with the transaction details.

Activity 7.2

Load Assignment 6.

A payment of £1200 has been incorrectly analysed as Legal Fees. In fact £500 of this related to consultancy fees and £300 was advertising. All figures are stated net.

Post a journal to correct this (reference J23) dated 6 November 2000. What is the balance on the advertising account now?

4 Bank transactions not involving sales or purchases

A business will occasionally receive or make payments by cheque (that is, through its bank account, not in cash) that do not involve sales or purchases, receipts from customers or payments to suppliers. These cash payments or receipts should be recorded using the **Payment** and **Receipt** buttons in the **Bank** window. These options were described in Chapter 5 (payments) and Chapter 6 (receipts).

Examples of transactions you could be expected to record are suggested below.

    (a)   Payment of PAYE income tax to the Inland Revenue authorities.

    (b)   Payment of a court fine (eg a parking ticket fine).

    (c)   Payment for a road vehicle licence (car tax).

    (d)   The receipt of a loan.

5 Bank reconciliations

5.1 The Sage bank reconciliation

Sage includes a facility for making a bank reconciliation – ie checking the bank account records in the nominal ledger against a bank statement sent by the bank.

If a transaction is the same in both the bank statement and the nominal ledger account it is said to be 'reconciled'. The reconciliation process therefore involves checking every item on the bank statement against the transactions listed in the nominal ledger bank account and matching the transactions. Any differences should then be identified, to complete the reconciliation.

Note that you always work *from* the bank statement *to* the nominal ledger account. *Unreconciled* items are those that have *not yet appeared in the bank statement*, even though they have been recorded in the nominal ledger account.

5.2 Documents for checking

You will obviously need a bank statement from the bank to carry out a reconciliation. Paying in slips will also probably be needed, as we shall see. You will also need a list of transactions in the nominal ledger bank account.

To produce a print-out of the bank transactions, you can click on the **Bank Statement** button (the simpler option), or else (in all versions) click on the **Nominal** button in the main Sage window and select the bank account (account 1200) by scrolling down to it and clicking on it to highlight it. Then click on the **Report** button in the Nominal Ledger window. The reason why you need this report is explained in a moment.

Four standard reports are listed – Day Books: Nominal Ledger, Nominal Activity, Nominal Balances and Nominal List. You want the one called *Nominal Activity*, so click on this to highlight it. If possible the Output option to choose is Printer, but if you do not have access to a printer, choose Preview. Then click on Run. Specify account code 1200 in the Report Criteria or Additional Report Filter window. You don't actually need to do this if you highlighted account 1200 before clicking on **Reports,** but it is good practice to do so.

If you are printing the report a series of windows will give you printing options and instructions.

5.3 Performing the bank reconciliation

Click on the **Bank** button in the main Sage window, Select the account you want to reconcile then click on the **Reconcile** button. The program will display the window shown below, or a similar window if you use an earlier version.

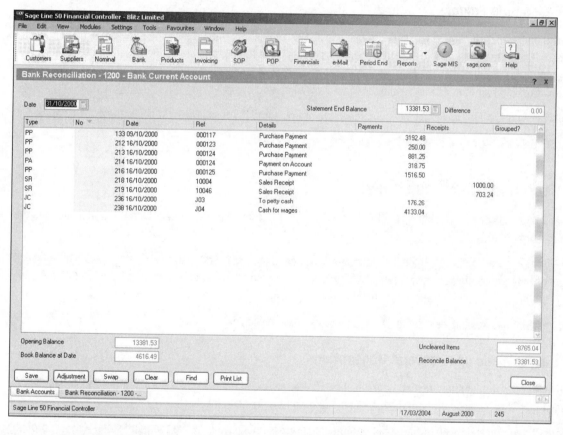

Key in the date of the *bank statement* and the closing balance shown at the end of the bank statement. You can use the scroll bar or the cursor direction keys ↓ and ↑ to look through the list, and the Page Up, Page Down, Home and End keys to speed up the process. We will now explain the four main boxes on the screen.

5.3.1 Opening Balance

This is the bank Reconcile Balance brought forward from the last time a bank reconciliation was done using the Sage software. It should reflect the opening balance on the bank statement. If there has not been a previous bank statement, or if the procedure has never been carried out before, the balance brought forward will be 0.00.

5.3.2 Uncleared items

This is the net total (debits plus credits) of all items or receipts that are left unreconciled on the screen. Each time you reconcile an item listed in the bank statement with an item on the screen, you will find that the balance in this box changes.

5.3.3 Book Balance (at Date)

This is the current account balance for the bank account in the nominal ledger. The main reason why this balance is different to the bank Reconcile Balance is because, unlike the bank statement, it takes into account any receipts or payments that were in the process of clearing through the banking system when the bank statement was produced.

5.3.4 Reconcile Balance

When the bank reconciliation is finished, the balance shown in this box must match the ending balance on the bank statement. Each time an item is identified as being reconciled, the total in this box is increased (if it is a receipt) or decreased (if it is a payment). The first time you ever do a bank reconciliation the box will show 0.00; subsequently it will show the same amount as the Opening Balance box when you begin.

You will find that the Reconcile Balance plus the value of uncleared items is always equal to the book balance.

Reconcile Balance + Uncleared Items = Book Balance

5.4 Reconciliation procedures

In a bank reconciliation, you must match the transactions listed in the bank statement with the transactions in the nominal ledger bank account.

When you find a transaction on the bank statement is matched by a transaction in the nominal bank account click on it to highlight the transaction on the screen. The figures in the Reconcile Balance box and the Uncleared Items box will change by the amount of the transaction that you just highlighted.

If you make a mistake, and want to de-select a transaction, just click on it again.

5.4.1 Items made up of several transactions

You may have a problem in matching items because there may be some that are the total of several smaller transactions. This happens on both the bank statement and on the screen listing.

(a) If several receipts were paid into the bank on a single paying-in slip the bank statement will probably only show the total. You need to consult the paying-in slips to see how these items are made up, and match individual receipts.

(b)   The reconciliation screen will lump together any transactions of the same type (eg five customer receipts) that were posted one after the other and had the same date, unless they were given a unique *reference* number when they were posted. A single total will then be shown for all of these individual transactions, making matching far more difficult. The details will just say 'Customer Deposit'.

You may remember that we emphasised the importance of giving receipts a unique reference number when we were describing how they should be posted. This is the reason why.

(A possible solution, that would make a *virtue* of these 'problems', would be to post receipts from paying-in slips, giving each batch of receipts the same reference as the paying-in slip number. In fact this would make it *easier* to match items on the bank statement and the reconciliation screen.)

5.4.2 Items in the bank statement but not in the ledger account

There could be some items in the bank statement that have not been entered in the nominal ledger bank account. For example, there could be some bank charges that have not yet been recorded in the account.

You can make an adjustment, and post the receipt or payment to the bank account in the nominal ledger. To do this click on the **Adjustment** button at the foot of the window. A new window will appear, as shown below.

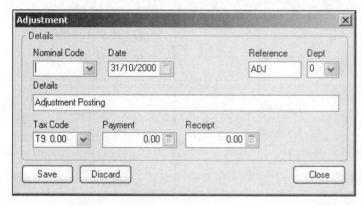

The entries to make are as follows.

(a)   *N/C (Nominal Code).* Enter the nominal ledger code for the account to which the item of income or expense relates. In the Blitz case study, for example, a deduction of bank interest would be coded 7900 and a deduction of bank charges would be coded 7901.

(b)   *Date.* Enter the date of the receipt or payment.

(c)   *Details.* By default this says 'Adjustment Posting but it is better to enter your own brief narrative details of the item.

(d)   *Tax Code.* The VAT code would be T9 for bank charges, but for other items (for example, some direct debits) it would be T1. Check with your supervisor if you are not sure.

(e)   *Payment / Receipt.* Enter the gross value of the receipt or payment, in the appropriate box. (The other box is left as 0.00.)

Click on **Save** when you are satisfied that your adjustment details are correct. The transaction will be posted in the appropriate nominal ledger accounts.

5.5 Completing the reconciliation

When you have checked the items in the bank statement against the nominal bank account, the value in the Reconcile Balance box should equal the balance on the bank statement itself.

If it does reconcile, click on the **Save** button. This will clear the reconciled transactions (ie the transactions that you have matched and highlighted in the nominal bank account and the bank statement). The unreconciled items will be displayed on screen the next time you do a bank reconciliation. The reconciled transactions will not be listed next time, provided you have cleared them.

To get a list of unreconciled payments and receipts use the Bank Reports option and find these reports in the list that appears.

Activity 7.3

Load Assignment 6. On 20 October you receive the following bank statement.

Date	Details	Withdrawals	Deposits	Balance
10-Oct-2000	Balance from sheet 5			13,381.53
11-Oct-2000	000117	3,192.48		10,189.05
14-Oct-2000	BGC		1,000.00	11,189.05
18-Oct-2000	000124	1,200.00		
18-Oct-2000	000125	1,516.50		8,472.55
20-Oct-2000	BACS	4,133.04		4,339.51
20-Oct-2000	Bank interest	74.50		4265.01

Perform a bank reconciliation as at 20 October 2000, following the procedures explained in the preceding section. What are the outstanding items, if any?

6 Conclusion

You may want more practice with a bank reconciliation. This is included in **Assignment 5**, which you can now attempt.

Key learning points

☑ Organisations often keep a relatively small amount of cash in a locked metal box, in a safe or locked drawer. This is known as '**petty cash**' and is used for small cash purchases and receipts.

☑ A **petty cash account** must be maintained in the nominal ledger. Records of individual petty cash transactions are recorded using **petty cash vouchers**, which may be entered into a **book** or a spreadsheet – from which the **nominal ledger journal** is prepared.

☑ In Sage, the petty cash account is included in the list in the Bank Accounts window. After selecting the petty cash account (rather than the main bank account), transactions are posted exactly as for Bank **receipts** and **payments**.

☑ Transactions and accounting entries that are not recorded in any other book of prime entry are entered using **nominal ledger journal entries**. Each journal entry comprises two sides – a debit entry and a credit entry.

☑ Sage includes a facility for automating the process of conducting a **bank reconciliation**.

Quick quiz

1   How are the notes and coins that make up the petty cash usually stored?

2   No record of petty cash is required to be kept in the nominal ledger. TRUE or FALSE?

3   As petty cash amounts are small, there is no need to know the purpose of the funds. TRUE or FALSE?

4   What are journal entries used for?

5   How do you access the bank reconciliation function in Sage?

Answers to quick quiz

1   Petty cash is commonly kept in a locked metal box, in a safe or locked drawer.

2   FALSE. A petty cash account must be maintained in the nominal ledger.

3   FALSE. The purpose of the funds is required so the transaction can be posted to the correct nominal ledger account – and to prevent fraud.

4   Nominal ledger journal entries are used to enter transactions and accounting entries that are not recorded in any other book of prime entry.

5   You click on the Bank button in the main Sage window, select the account you want to reconcile, then click on the Reconcile button.

Activity checklist

This checklist shows which knowledge and understanding point is covered by each activity in this chapter. Tick off each activity as you complete it.

Activity

7.1 ☐ Knowledge and Understanding: Operation of computerised accounting systems

7.2 ☐ Knowledge and Understanding: Operation of computerised accounting systems

7.3 ☐ Knowledge and Understanding: Operation of computerised accounting systems

chapter 8

Other credit transactions

Contents

1   Introduction
2   Contra entries
3   Credit limits
4   Writing off bad debts
5   Chasing overdue customer payments
6   Correcting errors
7   Conclusion

Range statement

Relevant computerised records

Computerised records

Computerised ledgers

Knowledge and understanding

Operation of computerised accounting systems

1 Introduction

This chapter explains the procedures for processing a range of other transactions that may occur on customer and supplier accounts.

2 Contra entries

2.1 What is a contra entry?

Contra is an accounting term that means against, or on the opposite side. A contra entry is made in the accounts of a business when a debit entry can be matched with a credit entry so that one cancels out the other. A common type of contra entry occurs when a supplier is also a customer. The amount owed as a supplier and the amount owing as a customer can be offset, to leave just a net amount owed or owing.

For example, suppose that ABC Limited is both a customer of your business, currently owing £1,000, and a supplier to your business who is currently owed £700. ABC Ltd pays £300 to settle the debt. The £700 owed has been offset against the £1,000 owing, and ABC Limited has simply paid the net debt of £300. This would be recorded in the accounts as a

(a)   A cash receipt of £300; and

(b)   A contra entry for £700, to cancel the debt to ABC as a supplier and the remaining £700 owed by ABC as a customer.

The accounting entries done for contra transactions are as follows.

(a)   In the sales ledger, the customer's account is credited with the amount of the contra entry. This reduces the customer's outstanding debt.

(b)   In the purchase ledger, the supplier's account is debited with the same amount.

(c)   In the nominal ledger, the double entry transactions are:

CREDIT	Debtors Control Account (code 1100)
DEBIT	Bank Current Account (code 1200)
	(or any other specified bank account)
DEBIT	Creditors Control Account (code 2100)
CREDIT	Bank Current Account (code 1200)
	(or any other specified bank account)

Sage Line 50 includes a facility that automates contra entries (Sage Instant does not include this function).

2.2 Posting a contra entry

2.2.1 Post the payment or receipt first

Before you post a contra entry, you should record the actual cash payment (or receipt) in the purchase ledger (or sales ledger). For example, suppose that your company owes ABC Ltd £700, ABC Ltd owes your company £1,000 and ABC Ltd sends you a cheque for £300 to settle the difference. Your first step should be to record the £300 received as a part payment of an invoice in the account for ABC Ltd in the sales ledger. This will make the outstanding balance on the customer account (£700) equal to the outstanding balance on the supplier account (£700).

You can find out the balances on the two accounts by looking at them in the windows that appear when you click on the **Customers** button and the **Suppliers** button. Subtract one from the other to find out the amount due.

In Line 50 it is *not* essential that there are equal amounts owed and owing before you post a contra entry, but it is good accounting practice, so always post the payment (and/or) receipt that brings this about *first*.

2.2.2 Making the contra

Users of Line 50 can post a contra entry as follows (Sage Instant does not include this facility). Click on the word **Tools** at the top of the screen. A menu will appear from which you should select **Contra Entries.** A window will display, as shown below. Check the correct Bank account is displayed (eg Current Account), then Tab into the Sales Ledger A/C Ref box.

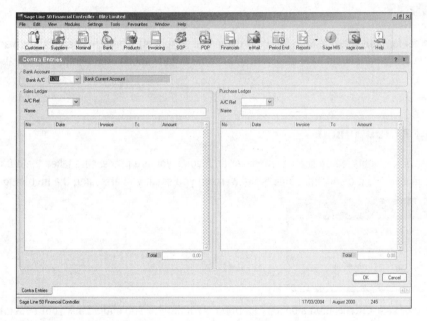

2.2.3 Sales Ledger A/C (Customer Account)

Enter the customer's account reference code if you know it (or use the Finder button or press function key F4 if not). When you press Tab the customer's name will be displayed automatically, and a list of outstanding invoices on that customer's account will appear in the left-hand box below. (Credit notes and payments on account are not listed.)

2.2.4 Purchase Ledger A/C (Supplier Account)

Enter the supplier's account reference code. This would normally be the same as the customer's code, but not necessarily so – for instance, a customer might trade under a different name when making supplies. When the code is entered, pressing Tab brings up the supplier's name and a list of outstanding invoices appears in the right hand box below it.

Now that the two accounts are shown side-by-side, you should be able to identify the matching transactions for which you want to make the contra entry.

To make the contra entry, select the appropriate transaction (sales invoice) in the customer account, by clicking on it. The amount in the Total box for sales invoices at the bottom of the screen is increased by the value of the transaction. (Note: you can de-select an invoice by clicking on it again.)

When you have selected the appropriate sales invoice find the appropriate purchase invoice in the other box, and select it by clicking. The amount in the Total box for purchase invoices at the bottom of the screen is increased by the value of the transaction you have selected.

So long as you first posted any payment that was due or receipt that had been received the two totals will now be equal.

Click on OK to save the transaction, which will be posted to the appropriate accounts in the sales, purchase and nominal ledgers.

3 Credit limits

Credit limits can be set for individual customers (or by individual suppliers). These fix the maximum amount of credit (unpaid invoices) the customer should have at any time. In some organisations credit limits are not always strictly observed.

3.1 Exceeding a credit limit

A warning message will be displayed on screen whenever an invoice you are processing takes the outstanding balance on the account above its current credit limit. This is the warning you see if you are using the **Invoicing** option.

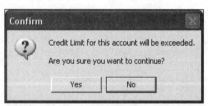

You should be aware of your organisation's policy regarding credit limits. You should ask your supervisor what to do whenever you are not sure.

If you know that you should proceed, perhaps on instructions from your supervisor, you can select the **Yes** option. The program will then allow you to continue with the entry, despite the warning.

If your supervisor instructs you to increase the customer's credit limit, click on **No** and then (without closing the current **Invoice** window) click on the **Customers** button, select the Customer's account from the list and then click on **Record.**

Activate the Credit Control Tab and click into the Credit Limit box, key in the new limit and then click on **Save.** Then press Esc twice to get back to the invoice window. The invoice will now be accepted without the warning.

A customer who is over their credit limit is listed *in red* in the main Customers window.

Activity 8.1

Load Assignment 3.

Post an invoice for £400 (net) to School of Dance. The invoice is for Window cleaning, is numbered 21785, and is dated 14 November 2000.

By how much is School of Dance over its credit limit and what is the new balance on the Sales – Window Cleaning account?

4 Writing off bad debts

4.1 Bad debts

Occasionally, a customer who has been invoiced will fail to pay, and the debt must eventually be 'written off' as uncollectable. There are various reasons why a debt could become a 'bad debt'. Three common reasons are:

    (a)   The customer proves unreliable and is unlikely to pay.

    (b)   The customer goes out of business.

    (c)   There is a dispute with the customer relating to items billed on a particular invoice.

In each of these situations, it may eventually be decided to write off the money owed as a bad debt.

When a debt is written off as uncollectable, one of two possible situations could apply.

    (a)   The customer will not be granted credit ever again. The customer's entire debt is written off, and the customer's account will eventually be deleted from the sales ledger.

    (b)   An individual transaction is written off, but the company will continue to sell on credit to the customer. A dispute about one transaction is not allowed to affect the long-term relationship with the customer.

Sage Line 50 automates the process of writing off bad debts (Sage Instant does not include this feature).

4.2 Writing off an account

To write off all the outstanding debts in a customer's account users of Line 50 start by clicking on the word **Tools** at the top of the screen and then on **Write Off, Refund, Return**.

To write off a customers account you would then select the **Sales ledger** option, and click next. You will then see the following box.

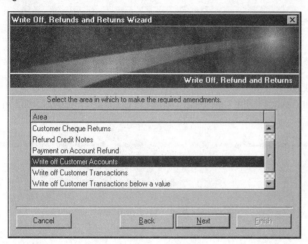

This gives you a number of options (a similar list appears if you select the Purchase ledger). The one we want on this occasion is **Write Off Customer Accounts**. Select this and then click on **Next**. Select the account you want and then click on **Next**.

As this option writes off Customer Accounts rather than individual transactions, clicking on **Next** will write off *all* the transactions listed.

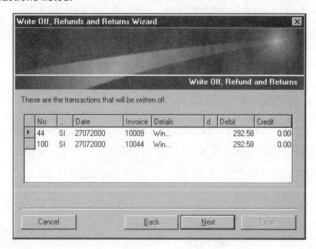

You will be asked to select a date for the write off. Enter the appropriate **date**, then click Next again, and you will see the following.

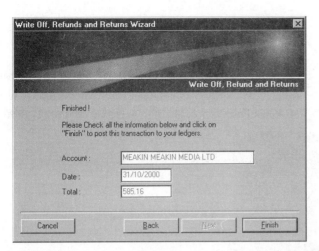

Click on **Finish** and you are returned to the main screen. The effect of all this is as follows.

(a)   The customer's account in the Customers ledger will be updated automatically when you select the Yes option to write off the outstanding debts on the account. The account will remain, however, in the sales ledger and will not be deleted.

(b)   The appropriate accounts in the nominal ledger will also be updated automatically:

CREDIT   Debtors control account (N/C code 1100)

DEBIT   Bad debt write off account (N/C code 8100)

If you check the Customers account and Nominal accounts Activity records you will see the entry that has been made.

You could be forgiven for thinking that, having chosen the option **Write off Account,** the account will no longer appear in the ledger. However, the customer account will not be completely removed. This is because it is needed to provide a complete record of transactions, and for auditing purposes. The customer record therefore remains on the system.

Activity 8.2

Load up Assignment 2.

It is 15 November 2000. Write off the account of the customer named Vice Versa.

What entries are shown in the customer's Activity record once you have done this?

What accounts are affected in the nominal ledger?

4.3 Writing off a transaction

To write off a single outstanding invoice users of Line 50 start by clicking on the word **Tools** at the top of the screen, then on **Write Off, Refund, Return** and selecting the Sales ledger option. The amendment you want this time is **Write Off Customer Transactions.** Select this, click on Next, then select the account. Clicking on Next brings you to this box.

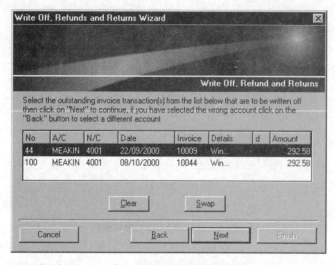

In the example above, to write off Invoice 10009, click on this to select it, then enter the **date** for the write off, click Next again then click on Finish.

Activity 8.3

Users of Line 50 should now load Assignment 5 and follow the instructions below. (Users of Sage Instant should skip this activity.)

It is 20 November 2000. Write off invoice number 10025, following the instructions above as appropriate.

What is the amount of the write off and the new balance on the Debtors Control account?

5 Chasing overdue customer payments

It is an unfortunate fact of business life that many customers delay payment of invoices. They will pay eventually, and there will not be a bad debt. However, unless a determined effort is made to collect the unpaid invoice or invoices, the customer might continue to delay payment for as long as possible. In most businesses, there are procedures for:

(a)   Producing a regular list of unpaid invoices, analysing the length of time for which each invoice has been outstanding (an 'aged debtors list').

(b)   Producing statements of unpaid invoices for individual customers, for sending out to the customer as a reminder.

(c)   Producing and sending reminder letters to customers whose invoices are overdue for payment.

5.1 Aged debtors list

To produce a list of unpaid debts, analysed by age, print out an Aged debtors analysis (Detailed) using the **Reports** option in the Customers window. The procedures for producing an aged debtors were described in Chapter 6.

5.2 Statements

A printed statement of account shows the transactions and balance outstanding on an account at the date the statement was issued. Statements are sent to customers to assist with debt collection.

For the case study in this book, a standard layout provided by Sage (Statement With Tear Off Remit Advice) is used. This shows the following details.

(a)   Customer name, address and account code.
(b)   The statement date.
(c)   Brought forward figures at the beginning of the period covered by the statement.
(d)   Details of transactions in the period (date, invoice number, description, amount).
(e)   An analysis of outstanding amounts by age.
(f)   A total of the amounts outstanding.

To produce statements, use the **Statement** button in the **Customers** window. The following window will appear (a slightly different window appears if you are using an earlier version of Sage).

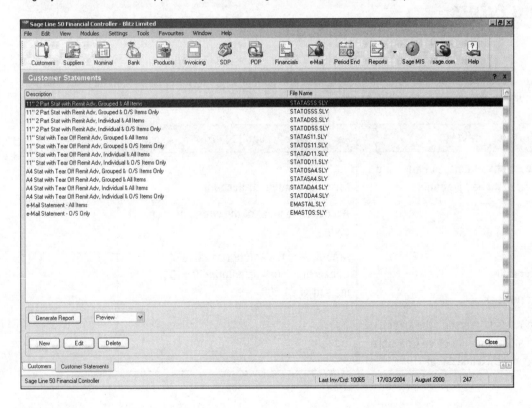

Clicking on **Generate Report**, or **Run**, in earlier versions, will bring up the **Criteria** window which requires you to specify an Account Range and a Date Range. The dates you enter affect how the information is shown. All transactions dated before the first date in your range will be lumped together in a single brought forward figure. After entering the dates, clicking **OK** will produce the statements.

5.3 Reminder letters

Reminder letters can be sent to customers to urge them to settle invoices that are overdue for payment. The Sage package includes standard letters and also allows users to create their own.

The Letters function is accessed through the **Letters** button in the Customers window. We will not be explaining this feature further as it is not included in the AAT Foundation Standards. However, you may wish to experiment with the function yourself.

Activity 8.4

Load Assignment 3. It is 31 December 2000 (change the Program Date to 31/12/2000).

Print out a statement and as stern a reminder letter as you can for Townend Angus Ltd.

How many days overdue is payment of the invoice?

6 Correcting errors

6.1 Errors

Sometimes, errors are noticed after transactions have been input and posted to the system. Errors can be grouped into two types; **Non-accounting errors** and **Accounting errors**.

Non-accounting errors	Accounting errors
Errors in descriptive items, not affecting account code or money amounts	**Errors in amount or account**
Date	Account – ie input of the wrong account code
Reference items	Amount – ie the amount or value of a transaction, such as entering £1,100 instead of £1,000
Transaction details	
Department number	
Tax code (provided correcting the error does not affect the amount of VAT payable, eg. using tax code T0 instead of T2)	

If you notice an error, you should note down the details, including the transaction number. This may involve you looking through a list of sales invoices (call up the **Activity** of the Debtors Ledger Control Account or the Creditors Ledger Control Account), or looking through a particular customer or supplier account (again using the **Activity** option).

Locate the transaction in the appropriate ledger and, if possible, select the relevant account and print out an Activity report for that account. If you cannot get a print-out, note down:

- Transaction number
- Date
- Account codes concerned (customer/supplier and nominal accounts)
- Invoice number or other reference number
- Details
- Amount (net and VAT)

6.2 Correcting non-accounting errors

We will now explain the feature available within Sage to edit existing transactions Many organisations may prefer not to use such a feature – preferring to use traditional journal entries or new transactions to correct errors. If you use Sage at work, do not use this function without the approval of your manager.

To use the corrections facility provided within Sage, first close any windows that are currently open until you have only the main Sage window in front of you.

At the top of the screen you will see the word **File.** Click on this and a menu appears. The item you want is **Maintenance**. If you click on this window the same as, or similar to, the following appears.

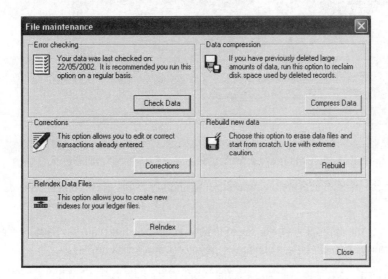

6.3 Posting error corrections

To correct errors you use the **Corrections** button. If you click on this the following screen will appear. This lists all the transactions currently on the system, in transaction number order.

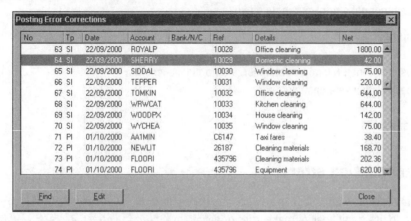

Your first job is to locate the transaction. If you noted down the transaction number this should be easy enough. Highlight the transaction and click on the **Edit** button. A new window will appear, the same as or similar to the following.

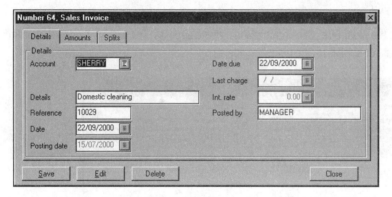

The **Details** section of the transaction will now be on screen and are available for editing.

To change the Amount you need to activate the **Amounts** Tab and to change the nominal code you should activate the **Splits** Tab.

To correct an error, Tab to the appropriate field, key in the correct details then click on **Save**. A message will appear asking you if you 'Do you wish to post these changes?'. If you are sure, click on Yes.

In the **Amounts** Tab you may correct the Net and Tax fields only if the Paid in Full flag box does is not ticked.

6.4 Correcting errors in account code or amount

You may only correct an *accounting* error using the **Maintenance** option if the transaction has not already been settled: in other words if a receipt or payment relating to the invoice has not yet been recorded on the system.

Journal entries will be required to correct errors in transactions that have been recorded as being paid. Two entries would be required, a reversing entry to cancel out the existing entry and another to input the transaction correctly.

Activity 8.5

Load the data for Assignment 3.

The details for a purchase invoice from the Ironcliffe Group posted on 26 August 2000 should have read 'Rent to 31 October 2000'.

Correct the details, as described above.

Activity 8.6

Still with Assignment 3 loaded, find the balance on each of the sales accounts. Then alter the amount of invoice number 10018 to £1000 plus VAT, and alter the details and nominal code to that for Window Cleaning.

What appears in the Activity record of the relevant customer's account after you have done this?

How have the balances on the sales accounts changed?

7 Conclusion

You should now be ready to attempt **Assignment 6**.

Key learning points

☑ A **contra entry** is made in the accounts of a business when a debit entry can be matched with a credit entry. A common type of contra entry occurs when a supplier is also a customer – the amount owed as a supplier and the amount owing as a customer can be offset.

☑ Modern accounting software packages such as Sage allow **credit limits** to be set for customers. Credit limits show the maximum amount of credit (outstanding balance) the customer is allowed.

☑ A **warning message** will be displayed on screen whenever an invoice you are processing takes the outstanding balance on the account above its current credit limit.

☑ Occasionally, a customer who has been invoiced will fail to pay, and the debt must eventually be 'written off' as a **bad debt**.

☑ A range of reports are available from within Sage to help establish the effectiveness of credit control activities, for example an **Aged debtors analysis**.

☑ A **statement** of account shows the transactions and balance outstanding on a customer's account at the date the statement was issued.

☑ **Errors** can be corrected through reversing the transaction, for example posting a correcting **journal** or issuing a Credit Note to cancel an invoice. Sage allows some errors to be corrected by **editing existing transactions** through the File, Maintenance, Corrections option.

Quick quiz

1   What is a contra entry?

2   How do you access the contra entries facility for offsetting Customer and Supplier accounts in Sage Line 50 (the automated contra feature is not included in Instant Accounts)?

3   How would you increase a customer's credit limit?

4   List three reasons why a customer may not pay an invoice.

5   Give two examples of accounting errors.

Answers to quick quiz

1   A contra entry is an accounting entry that is offset by an opposite entry. A common type of contra entry occurs when a supplier is also a customer – the amount owed as a supplier and the amount owing as a customer can be offset.

2   From the main Sage Line 50 menu, you select Tools from the top of the screen and then select Contra Entries. You can then choose the relevant accounts and transactions.

3   You would click on the Customers button, select the Customer's account from the list and then click on Record. Activate the Credit Control Tab and click into the Credit Limit box, key in the new limit and then click on Save.

4   Three common reasons are: The customer proves unreliable and simply refuses to pay; The customer goes out of business; There is a dispute with the customer relating to the goods or services supplied and billed on a particular invoice.

5   Two examples are mistakes relating to the account number such as input of the wrong account code, and entering the wrong amount or value of a transaction.

Activity checklist

This checklist shows which knowledge and understanding point is covered by each activity in this chapter. Tick off each activity as you complete it.

Activity

Activity		Knowledge and Understanding
8.1		Knowledge and Understanding: Operation of computerised accounting systems
8.2		Knowledge and Understanding: Operation of computerised accounting systems
8.3		Knowledge and Understanding: Operation of computerised accounting systems
8.4		Knowledge and Understanding: Operation of computerised accounting systems
8.5		Knowledge and Understanding: Operation of computerised accounting systems
8.6		Knowledge and Understanding: Operation of computerised accounting systems

Answers to Activities

Answers to activities

Chapter 1

Answer 1.1

(a) =SUM(B5:B6)

(b) =SUM(B6:D6)

(c) =SUM (E5:E6) *or* =SUM(B7:D7)

> *or* (best of all) =IF(SUM(E5:E6) =SUM(B7:D7),SUM(B7:D7),"ERROR") Don't worry if you don't understand this formula when first attempting this Activity - we cover IF statements later in this Chapter.

Answer 1.2

(a) For cell B7   =B6*0.175   For cell E8   =SUM(E6:E7)

(b) By using a separate 'variables' holding the VAT rate and possibly the Sales figures. The formulae could then refer to these cells as shown below.

	A	B	C	D	E	F	G	H
1	**Taxable Supplies plc**							
2	*Sales analysis - Branch C*							
3	*Six months ended 30 June 200X*							
4		Jan	Feb	Mar	Apr	May	Jun	Total
5		£	£	£	£	£	£	£
6	Net sales	=B12	=C12	=D12	=E12	=F12	=G12	=SUM(B6:G6)
7	VAT	=B6*$B$13	=C6*$B$13	=D6*$B$13	=E6*$B$13	=F6*$B$13	=G6*$B$13	=SUM(B7:G7)
8	Total	=SUM(B6:B7)	=SUM(C6:C7)	=SUM(D6:D7)	=SUM(E6:E7)	=SUM(F6:F7)	=SUM(G6:G7)	=SUM(H6:H7)
9								
10								
11	*Variables*							
12	Sales	2491.54	5876.75	3485.01	5927.7	6744.52	3021.28	
13	VAT rate	0.175						
14								

Answer 1.3

(a)   *Cell*   *Formulae*

       C7   =SUM(B5:B6)
       B12   =SUM(B9:B11)
       B16   =SUM(B14:B15)
       C17   =B12-B16
       C18   =SUM (C4:C17)
       C24   =C21+C22–C23

(b)   The finished spreadsheet follows. Further improvements could be made eg formatting numbers, clearer layout.

	A	B	C	D	E	F
1	**Ed Sheet**					
2	*Balance sheet as at 31 Dec 200X*					
3		£	£			
4	*Fixed assets*					
5	Plant	20000				
6	Vehicles	10000				
7			30000			
8	*Current assets*					
9	Stock	2000				
10	Debtors	1000				
11	Cash	1500				
12		4500				
13	*Current liabilities*					
14	Creditors	2500				
15	Overdraft	1500				
16		4000				
17	Net current assets		500			
18	Net assets		30500			
19						
20	*Represented by*					
21	Opening capital		28000			
22	Profit for year		3500			
23	Drawings		1000			
24	Closing capital		30500			
25						

Answer 1.4

Tutorial note. This activity tests whether you can evaluate formulae in the correct order. In part (a) you must remember to put brackets around the numbers required to be added, otherwise the formula will automatically divide cell B8 by 4 first and add the result to the other numbers. Similarly, in part (b), the formula performs the multiplication before the addition and subtraction.

Solution

(a)   =SUM(B5:B8)/4   An alternative is = AVERAGE(B5:B8).

(b)   59.325

Chapter 2

Answer 2.2

(a)   AA1MIN

(b)   3DTECH

(c)   111111

(d)   3DTECH. You have a fresh copy of the assignment 2 data, free of any entries you made yourself.

This Activity is to encourage you to experiment with any entries you like, safe in the knowledge that you cannot damage the Blitz data.

Answer 2.4

The 000000 should disappear.

Answer 2.5

The query is from a credit customer, so you begin by clicking on the Customers button. To find Mr Newall's account use the down arrow in the scroll bar to the right of the list of accounts. When you see NEWALL, click on that name to highlight it, then click on the Activity button. Accept the Defaults suggested by clicking on OK. The next screen will show you the current balance on Mr Newall's account.

The display on screen should show you that there is only one invoice outstanding, an amount for domestic cleaning invoiced on 22/09/2000 for £77.55.

Answer 2.6

The supervisor has requested the Transactions on the Bank Current account. Select the Nominal button, scroll down to account 1200, highlight it, click on the Activity button and accept the Defaults. You should see the following.

1200 Bank Current Account

No.	Tp	Date	Ref	Details	Amount	Debit	Credit
1	BR	19/08/2000		M Green – shares	20000.00	20000.00	
2	BR	19/08/2000		T Nicholas – shares	20000.00	20000.00	
8	JC	16/09/2000		Wages and salaries	6053.93		6053.93
						40000.00	6053.93
						33946.07	

The Tp (Type) column shows the type of transaction. BR is a bank receipt. JC is a journal entry (credit entry). The three figures at the foot of the display show total debits and credits and the balance.

Chapter 3

Answer 3.1

It should appear between LERWIC and MATTHI.

Answer 3.2

(a)   N14 6TS
(b)   Candy Spicer
(c)   T Cooper (Stationery) Ltd, 01582 405592

Answer 3.3

Check the details you have entered on screen very carefully to make sure that all the spelling and numbers are exactly as you see them here. Have you got the right combination of letters and numbers in the post-code, for instance?

Answer 3.4

You should get BL OFFICE FURNISHING LTD and MUSWELL HILL COUNCIL.

Answer 3.5

(a)   This is a hands on activity.

(b)   FLOORI, HARDIN and LERWIC. This will only work if you follow the instructions given above and avoid the pitfalls.

Answer 3.6

You should get the answers £53.24, Materials Purchases and Office Machine Maintenance.

(Incidentally, unless we tell you otherwise, it does not normally matter whether you save information entered for activities or close without saving.)

Answer 3.7

These are the results you should get.

Account	With new transactions Dr	With new transactions Cr	Fresh Assignment 6 data Dr	Fresh Assignment 6 data Cr	Difference Dr	Difference Cr
2100		8034.78		7677.28		357.50
2202	7030.74		6977.50		53.24	
5000	6336.89		6236.89		100.00	
7701	204.26				204.26	
IRONCL		240.00		0.00		240.00
NEWLIT		789.63		672.13		117.50

The differences are entirely due to the transactions you posted in the Activity. You should trace through each figure until you are happy about this, using your knowledge of double entry from Units 1 and 2. Ideally, write out all the T-accounts.

This Activity is to reassure you that Sage follows the same principles of double entry as a manual system and to highlight how much easier it is to use a computerised package.

Answer 3.9

The last transaction listed should be number 194. You should get the following totals.

Net	Tax	Gross
54,742.89	8,119.29	62,862.18

Chapter 4

Answer 4.3

The screen should show the full details in the white box at the top left.
W R W CATERING LTD
11 STATION PARADE
BARNET
HERTS

BT5 2KC

Answer 4.4

You should have got an amount of £117.50 for ADAMSE (N/C 4001) and of £116.63 for GARDEN (N/C 4000). Although the net amount of both invoices is £100, GARDEN's record is set up to receive settlement discount of 5%, so the Sage package automatically charges VAT on the discounted amount (£100 − 5% = £95). £95 × 17.5% = £16.63

You can check the records of ADAMSE and GARDEN to confirm that one is set up to receive settlement discount and the other is not.

Answer 4.5

You should have got the amount £122.51. First, set up the customer's record to receive 5% settlement discount. Delivery address, order number, telephone number and contact name should be entered on the Order Details tab, but not before you have checked why the phone number shown above is different to the one contained in the customer record (020 7734 2043). The number may have changed, or it may have been entered into the system incorrectly, or it may be an additional number. Likewise you should check whether the customer's record should be amended to show the contact name Jennifer. Other details are entered on the Footer tab.

Answer 4.6

The initial balance should be £0.00. The balance should still be £0.00 at the end of the activity, because you have not posted the invoice.

Answer 4.7

You should get the answer £50.20. The nominal code is 4100.

Answer 4.8

(a)   Only eight invoices should appear.

(b)   No invoices should appear.

(c)   Did you get the result you expected and wanted?

(d)   Credit notes 1 to 4 and invoices 10001 to 10052 should all appear.

Answer 4.9

The invoice is shown on the following page.

Answer 4.10

(a)   It is the same as when you started because you have not posted anything yet.

(b)   GOODMA now has a balance of £117.50. HASLAM has a balance of £117.50. The Sales – Window Cleaning account has increased by £200 to £2,834.40.

Invoice	Page 1

BLITZ LTD

25 APPLE ROAD
LONDON
N12 3PP

D J HARGREAVES		Invoice No.	10042
6 COLLEGE PARK		Invoice/Tax Date	08/10/2000
LONDON		Cust. Order No.	
NW10 5CD		**Account No.**	HARGRE

Quantity Details	Disc%	Disc Amount	Net Amount	VAT Amount
Domestic services	0.00	0.00	43.50	7.61

Total Net Amount	43.50
Total VAT Amount	7.61
Carriage	0.00
Invoice Total	51.11

Chapter 5

Answer 5.2

(a)   The initial balances should be:

NEWLIT: £672.13
Bank   £33,946.07

(b)   You cannot print out a remittance advice after you have saved a bank transaction.

(c)   The balances should now be:

NEWLIT: £198.22
Bank   £33,472.16

Answer 5.4

The balances should be nil and £55.16.

Answer 5.5

View the Remittance advice on-screen if you don't have access to a printer.

Answer 5.6

The cheque is for £3,044.75. The discount has to be allocated between three separate items: £82.50 + £56.25 + £21.50 = £160.25. You should have used the (F4) calculator button.

There is no VAT on insurance. You could check this by finding the transaction numbers (Suppliers ... Activity), which are numbers 76, 77 and 78 and then looking up these numbers by clicking on Financials.

Well done if you got this activity right.

Answer 5.7

You should take advantage of the credit note.

Answer 5.8

(a)   £300.25
(b)   £399.75

Answer 5.9

Ensure you process the cheque through the **Bank**, **Payment** option.

Chapter 6

Answer 6.1

The opening balance on the bank account is £4,616.49 and the closing balance is £6,615.10. the opening balance on the Debtors ledger control account is £25,486.83 and the closing balance is £23,488.22.

The receipt from ELITEC is likely to have been the most difficult to deal with: it does match up precisely to existing invoice amounts, however. Note that ROSEAL has underpaid by a small amount. You should be left with a balance of £0.88 on this account.

Here are the sort of details that your report on ELITEC should have contained. (This is an extract from a Customer Activity (Detailed) report.)

No	Tp	Date	Refn	N/C	Details	T/C	Value	O/S	Debit	Credit
56	SI	22/09/2000	10021	4000	Kitchen cleaning	T1	756.70 p	556.70	756.70	
96	SI	08/10/2000	10043	4000	KITCHEN CLEANING	T1	756.70		756.70	
97	SI	08/10/2000	10043	4100	OVEN CLEANER	T1	71.68		71.68	
98	SI	08/10/2000	10043	4100	FLAME DETERGENT	T1	84.60		84.60	
99	SI	08/10/2000	10043	4100	BRUSHES	T1	28.13		28.13	
161	SR	10/10/2000	10021	1200	Sales Receipt	T9	200.00			200.00
196	SI	16/10/2000	10054	4000	Kitchen cleaning	T1	223.25 *	223.25	223.25	
246	SR	15/11/2000	10043	1200	Sales Receipt	T9	941.11			941.11
							779.95	779.95	1,921.06	1,141. 11

Answer 6.2

Follow the instructions in section 3 of Chapter 6.

Answer 6.3

The customer should end up with £17 discount and a balance of £0.00 if you do all of this correctly.

Answer 6.4

(a)   £0.00 and £4,616.49.

(b)   Follow the instructions in section 5 of Chapter 6.

(c)   £88.13 and £4,528.36.

(d)   As follows. The cheque receipt on 10 October is now shown as a cancelled cheque and the invoice from 22 September is reinstated.

No	Tp	Date	Refn	Details	Amount	O/S	Debit	Credit
70	SI	22/09/2000	10035	Window cleaning	88.13		88.13	
150	SR	10/10/2000	CANCEL	Cancelled cheque	88.13			88.13
246	SI	31/10/2000	CANCEL	Cancelled cheque	88.13	88.13	88.13	

Answer 6.5

The initial balances are £0.00 and £27,167.80. The new balances are £0.00 and £26,752.80.

Here is the activity as recorded in Bridgford's account (shown on the following page).

No	Tp	Date	Refn	Details	Amount	O/S	Debit	Credit
38	SI	22/09/2000	10003	Office cleaning	487.63		487.63	
94	SI	08/10/2000	10041	Office cleaning at inv	493.50		493.50	
145	SR	10/10/2000	10003	Sales Receipt	981.13			981.13
246	SC	31/10/2000	REFUND	Refund – 10003	487.63			487.63
247	SI	31/10/2000	REFUND	Allocation – 10003	487.63		487.63	

Answer 6.6

The three amounts written off are £0.75, £0.43, and £0.25, a total of £1.43. This is debited to the Bad Debt Write Off account (8100) and credited to the Debtors Ledger Control account (1100). Check the activity on these accounts to see the transactions for yourself.

Answer 6.7

It should be £35,046.07 (debit).

Chapter 7

Answer 7.1

You should get £262.30 (Dr) for petty cash and £415.10 (Dr) for account 7504.

Answer 7.2

The balance on the advertising account should be £3050.00

(Cr Legal Fees (7600) £800; Dr Consultancy (7602) £500, Dr Advertising (6201) £300.)

Answer 7.3

If you have ever performed a manual bank reconciliation you should find the computerised method much easier. The outstanding items are as follows.

Cheque 000123	250.00
Cheque 000126	176.26
Receipt	(703.24)
Total	(276.98)

Chapter 8

Answer 8.1

School of Dance is £163.75 over the limit. The new balance on the Sales – Window Cleaning account is £2,920.40.

Activity 8.2

Here is what you should see in Vice Versa's account.

No	Tp	Date	Refn	Details	Amount	O/S	Debit	Credit
58	SI	22/09/2000	10035	Window cleaning	52.88		52.88	
84	SC	15/11/2000	BADDBT	Bad Debt Write Off	52.88			52.88

The write off affects the Debtors control account (1100) and the Bad Debt Write Off account (8100).

Activity 8.3

The write off is for £2,714.25. The new balance on the Debtors Control account is £17,235.19.

Activity 8.4

More than 90 days.

Answer 8.5

You should see the following activity.

No	Tp	Date	Refn	Details	Amount	O/S	Debit	Credit
53	SI	22/09/2000	10018	Window cleaning	1175.00	1175.00	1175.00	
107	SI	22/09/2000	10018	Deleted – see tran 53	940.00			

Answer 8.6

The balances change as follows.

Account	Before £	After £	Change £
4000	20,807.80	20,007.80	800.00
4001	2,520.40	3,520.40	1,000.00
4002	853.10	853.10	None
4100	980.14	980.14	None

PART C

Assignments

		Assignment	Answer to assignment	Done
1	Supplier invoices and credit notes	183	219	
2	Customer invoices and credit notes	187	223	
3	Payments to suppliers	195	231	
4	Receipts from customers	199	237	
5	Other cash transactions	205	243	
6	Other credit transactions	213	249	

Assignment 1:
Supplier invoices and credit notes

Loading and carrying out the assignment

Load assignment 1 into Sage now!

For instructions on how to load the data for assignments refer to Section 3 of Chapter 2. Check with your tutor in case special instructions apply to your college's system.

If you need to break off from this assignment part-way through, back-up your work to a floppy disk, following the instructions given on screen when you quit the Sage program. You can restore your entries when you wish to re-start working on this assignment.

If you want to keep a permanent copy of your finished work, back it up and save the back-up file with a suitable name.

Purpose

Assignment 1 tests your ability to set up accounts for new suppliers in the purchase ledger, to process invoices and credit notes from suppliers, to post the entries to the appropriate accounts in the suppliers and nominal ledgers, to produce reports and to check the current balance on the creditors control account.

The **Tasks** for this assignment follow the **Information.** Read the information and all the tasks *before* commencing work.

Information

Your supervisor asks you to process eight invoices and two credit notes received from suppliers. Today's date is 2 October 2000. Details are as follows.

Invoices from existing suppliers

Invoice No	Supplier	A/C Ref	Details	Nominal ledger account	Net amount (excluding VAT) £	£
C6147	AA1 Mini Cabs	AA1MIN	Taxi fares	Travelling		38.40
26187	Newlite Cleaning Fluids	NEWLIT	Cleaning materials	Materials purchases		168.70
435796	Flooring Supplies Ltd	FLOORI	Cleaning materials	Materials purchases	202.36	
			Equipment	Plant and machinery	620.00	
						822.36
4821	First Steps Ladder Hire	FIRSTS	Ladder hire	Equipment hire		126.75

All these invoices are subject to VAT at the standard rate of 17.5%. All invoices are dated 1 October 2000.

Invoices from new suppliers

(a) Samurai Insurance Brokers
     15 Osnabruck Street
     London EC3 5JG
     Tel: 020-7488 1066

A/C ref	Inv no	Inv date	Nominal ledger account	Net amount	VAT
SAMURA	02381	1 Oct 2000	Premises insurance	1,650.00	
			Vehicle insurance	1,125.00	
			Miscellaneous insurance	430.00	
				3,205.00	

This invoice has a Post-It note attached by your supervisor saying 'Insurance is exempt from VAT - code T2.'

(b) 3D Technical Bookshops
     116 Albert Road
     Wood Green
     London N22 7RB
     Tel: 020-8889 3539
     Contact: Adrian

A/C ref	Inv no	Inv date	Nominal ledger account	Net amount	VAT
3DTECH	001462	30 Sep 2000	Books	179.95	0%

(c)   Thames Water
        Umbrella House
        Weather Street
        London WC1 9JK
        Tel: 020-7837 4411

A/C ref	Inv no	Inv date	Nominal ledger account	Net amount	VAT
THAMES	132157	1 Oct 2000	Water rates	420.00	0%

(d)   ANS Newspaper Group
        19 Cecil Road
        London NW10 4PP
        Tel: 020-8453 2926
        Contact: Mandy Walker

A/C ref	Inv no	Inv date	Nominal ledger account	Net amount	VAT
ANSNEW	621014	29 Sep 2000	Advertising	750.00	17.5%

For all invoices, you have been given details of the item purchased, and you have been instructed to allocate each item to an appropriate nominal ledger account. Refer to the nominal ledger codes in Appendix 1 of this book if necessary.

Credit Notes from Suppliers

Credit note no	Supplier	A/C ref	Net amount	VAT
K0320	B L Office Furnishing	BLOFFI	150.00	17.5%
C0259	Trojan Secretarial Service	TROJAN	60.00	17.5%

Both credit notes are dated 1 October 2000.

The credit note from B L Office Furnishing is for the return of office furniture supplied in damaged condition. The credit note from the Trojan Secretarial Service is for overcharging; a temporary secretary had been employed for two days, but Trojan, the agency supplying the secretary, had charged for three days.

Your supervisor has asked you to identify the nominal ledger accounts for the credit note transactions, but has told you that the credit note for B L Office Furnishing relates to fixed assets (furniture and fixtures) and the credit note for Trojan Secretarial Service relates to casual wages.

Tasks

(a) Enter these transactions in the Suppliers Ledger and post the details. Use the tax code T0 for items with 0% VAT.

(b) Print a detailed suppliers invoices day book listing and suppliers credits day books listing covering *only* the transactions you have posted. If you do not have access to a printer, you should display these listings (one at a time) on your screen. Check that the number of entries in the system so far is 83. What is the total amount of transactions in each day book listing?

(c) Obtain the balance on the Creditors Control Account, after all the entries have been posted. (This is the total amount currently owed to suppliers for goods or services obtained on credit.) The nominal ledger code for this account is 2100. You can obtain the balance on the account either by looking at an appropriate screen display or by printing a copy of the Activity for the account.

Assignment 2:
Customer invoices and credit notes

Loading and carrying out the assignment

Load assignment 2 into Sage now!

For instructions on how to load the data for assignments refer to Section 3 of Chapter 2. Check with your tutor in case special instructions apply to your college's system.

If you need to break off from this assignment part-way through, back-up your work to a floppy disk, following the instructions given on screen when you quit the Sage program. You can restore your entries when you wish to re-start working on this assignment.

If you want to keep a permanent copy of your finished work, back it up and save the back-up file with a suitable name.

Purpose

Assignment 2 tests your ability to set up accounts for new customers in the customers ledger, to process invoices and credit notes to customers, to post the entries to the appropriate accounts in the customers and nominal ledgers, to produce listings and to answer queries from customers by searching the ledger files. If you have access to a printer, the assignment also tests your ability to produce invoices and credit notes.

The **Tasks** for this assignment follow the **Information.** Read the information and all the tasks *before* commencing work.

Information

It is now 8 October 2000. You have been asked to process a batch of invoices and credit notes, using the Sage Invoicing option from the main menu.

Invoices

The invoice details for processing are as follows. All invoices are subject to VAT at the standard rate (17.5%): code T1.

(1)	*Customer Name*	R P Marwood
	New Customer?	Yes
	Address	17 Eton Villas
		Harrow Road
		London NW3 0JS
	Telephone	020-7722 4488
	Contact	Mr Marwood
	Credit Limit?	No

Details	*Net Amount*
Domestic services	£66.00

(2)	*Customer Name*	School of Dance
	New Customer?	Yes
	Address	10 Underwood Street
		London N1 6SD
	Telephone	020-7490 2449
	Contact	Bernice
	Credit Limit?	Yes, £600

Details	*Net Amount*
Cleaning school property	£250.00

(3)	*Customer Name*	B & T Fashions Ltd
	New Customer?	Yes
	Address	8 Green Lanes
		London N16 4LM
	Telephone	020-7226 2703
	Contact	Peter Bruce
	Credit Limit?	No

Details	*Net Amount*
Window cleaning	£144.00

(4)
Customer Name	The Keith Group
New Customer?	Yes
Address	3 Sheringham Avenue
	London N14 2TT
Telephone	020-8360 7723
Contact	Pat Walker
Credit Limit?	Yes, £2,500

Details	*Net Amount*
Office cleaning at Grants Parade	£1,420.00
London N14 and Spur House, Watford	

(5)
Customer Name	Rapid Pizzas
New Customer?	Yes
Address	90 Upper Street
	London N10 4ZX
Telephone	020-8444 4136
Contact	Luciano Palmarozza
Credit Limit?	No
Settlement discount	5%

Details
5 cases of Flame detergent at £12 per case
3 boxes of Bream cleaner at £30.40 per box
50 pairs of cleaning gloves at £0.84 per pair

(6)
Customer Name	Bridgford & Co
New Customer?	No

Details	*Net Amount*
Office cleaning at invoice	£420.00
address	

(7)
Customer Name	D J Hargreaves
New Customer?	No

Details	*Net Amount*
Domestic services	£43.50

(8)   *Customer Name*   Elite Caterers
       New Customer?   No

       Details   *Net Amount*
       Kitchen cleaning   £644.00
       In addition, supply of materials
       10 boxes of oven cleaner at £6.10 per box
       6 cases of Flame detergent at £12 per case
       7 brushes at £3.42 each

(9)   *Customer Name*   Meakin Media Services Ltd
       New Customer?   No

       Details   *Net Amount*
       Window cleaning   £249.00

(10)   *Customer Name*   A Rose Ltd
       New Customer?   Not sure
       Address   8 Mill Mead Road
                               London N17 7HP
       Telephone   020-8808 4204
       Credit Limit?   No

       Details   *Net Amount*
       Window cleaning   £125.00

(11)   *Customer Name*   Gardeners Delight
       New Customer?   Not sure
       Invoice Address   212 Spa Road
                               London NW3 3DQ
       Delivery Address   Gardeners Delight Centre
                               Buckmans Road
                               London NW3
       Telephone   020-8368 2115
       Contact   Joe Grundy
       Credit Limit?   No
       Settlement discount   5%

       Details
       30 cases of window cleaning fluid at £21.00 per case

(12) *Customer Name*   Payne Properties Ltd
      New Customer?   Yes
      Address   18 Caledonian Road
                             London N1 9PN
      Telephone   020-7837 3442
      Contact   Carl Megson
      Credit Limit?   Yes, £2,500
      Settlement discount 5%

      Details   *Net Amount*
      Office cleaning at invoice address and 8 Richardson Street   £1,210.00

(13) *Customer Name*   T P Paul
      New Customer?   Yes
      Address   1 Arcola Street
                             London N8 1QB
      Telephone   020-8348 5453
      Contact   Mrs Paul
      Credit Limit?   No

      Details   *Net Amount*
      Domestic services   £60.00

(14) *Customer Name*   Siddall Wallis
      New Customer?   No

      Details   *Net Amount*
      Window cleaning   £182.00

(15) *Customer Name*   Norris Hydraulics Ltd
      New Customer?   No

      Details   *Net Amount*
      Factory and office cleaning   £816.40

Credit Notes

The following service credit notes are to be produced. Make sure these are numbered 1, 2 and 3, and all dated 8 October 2000.

(1)   *Customer*   Gelling Private Bank
        Details   Credit note for £250 (plus VAT), following a customer complaint about the poor quality of
                        cleaning at one of the office premises.

(2)   *Customer*   Royal Properties Ltd
        Details   Credit note for £300 (plus VAT), following an agreement with the customer that the scale
                        of the office cleaning service provided was less than originally anticipated.

(3)   *Customer*   DCS Roofing
        Details   Credit note for £150.00 (plus VAT), after customer complaint about a window broken by a
                        Blitz window cleaner.

Tasks

(a)   Enter the service invoice and credit note details into Sage. Make sure that the first invoice in the series is
        numbered 10036. Where appropriate, establish new customer accounts.

        Check the nominal ledger accounts used by Blitz Limited to account for sales. These are included in the list in
        Appendix 1.

(b)   Print (or Preview) the invoices and credit notes. If you can, back-up your work *before* posting the invoices, so
        that you can correct any errors discovered later without re-entering all the data.

(c)   Post the invoice and credit note details to the appropriate accounts in the customers ledger and nominal ledger.

(d)   Produce day book listings of customer invoices and customer credits for these transactions. Print the listings if
        you have access to a printer. Otherwise, display each listing on screen.

(e)   Your supervisor wants to know the current balance on the Debtors Control Account in the nominal ledger. Find
        out what this is. If you have access to a printer, print out the details of this account.

(f)   Your supervisor also wants to know the current debit, credit and net total balances on each of the four sales
        accounts (codes 4000, 4001, 4002 and 4100 in the nominal ledger). After you have entered the invoice and
        credit note details, find out what these balances are.

(g)   *This task can only be carried out if you have access to a printer.*

        The invoice you have produced for the School of Dance has been damaged accidentally. Coffee has been spilled
        over it. Produce another invoice for sending to the customer.

(h)   You receive a telephone call from your contact at CCC Engineering Limited. They have not yet received an invoice
        for factory cleaning services, but need to know what the cost will be, for a management meeting that afternoon.
        Find out the amount of the invoice.

(i)   *Word-processing exercise*

Unload the Word and Excel exercises from the CD-ROM onto your hard disk (see Chapter 2 for detailed instructions).

Without closing Sage switch to your word processing application such as Microsoft Word. Open the document A2FAX which will now be in the folder C:\AATF on your hard drive and *save* it with another appropriate name.

Prepare a fax to send to CCC Engineering in time for their management meeting this afternoon. The fax number is 01923 354071. Other details can be found from CCC Engineering's customer record or from an audit trail report. Copy from Sage and Paste into your word processing document if you wish to, and can work out how.

Note. To switch between applications use Alt + Tab.

(j)   *Word-processing exercise*

For the purpose of this exercise we will assume that the missing invoice was one of an early batch that was prepared manually, not using the Sage system.

Open the document A2INV and prepare a duplicate invoice for CCC Engineering. The details are those you found for the previous task.

Mention the duplicate invoice in your fax produced for the previous task. (Alter it if you have saved and closed it already.)

If you have access to a printer, print out the fax and the duplicate invoice.

Assignment 3:
Payments to suppliers

Loading and carrying out the assignment

Load assignment 3 into Sage now!

For instructions on how to load the data for assignments refer to Section 3 of Chapter 2. Check with your tutor in case special instructions apply to your college's system.

If you need to break off from this assignment part-way through, back-up your work to a floppy disk, following the instructions given on screen when you quit the Sage program. You can restore your entries when you wish to re-start working on this assignment.

If you want to keep a permanent copy of your finished work, back it up and save the back-up file with a suitable name.

Purpose

Assignment 3 tests your ability to process payments to suppliers, to post the transactions to the appropriate accounts in the purchase ledger and nominal ledger, to deal with part payments, credit notes, settlement discounts and payments in advance, to deal with payments for cheque requisitions, to produce reports for payments, and to check the current balance on the bank account and creditors control account in the nominal ledger. If you have access to a printer, the Assignment also tests your ability to produce remittance advices.

The **Tasks** for this assignment will be found following the **Information.** Read the information and all the tasks *before* commencing work.

Information

(Read this information now, but don't post any transactions until attempting the tasks on the following page.)

It is now 9 October 2000. You have been asked to process a batch of payments.

(1)   Your supervisor has provided you with a list of payment transactions (don't post these yet).

Supplier	Code	Amount	Cheque no
AA1 Mini Cabs	AA1MIN	£117.50	000100
British Telecom plc	BTELEC	£540.50	000101
Capital Radiopaging	CAPITA	£376.00	000102
B L Office Furnishing	BLOFFI	£1,493.78	000103
First Steps Ladder Hire	FIRSTS	£332.23	000104
Samurai Insurance Brokers	SAMURA	£3,205.00	000105
3D Technical Bookshops	3DTECH	£179.95	000106
The Ironcliffe Group	IRONCL	£3,000.00	000107
Trojan Secretarial Services	TROJAN	£141.00	000108
Muswell Hill Council	MUSWEL	£1,240.00	000109
North London Advertiser	NORTHL	£1,175.00	000110
Sterling Supplies	STERLI	£642.37	000111
Uniform Workerwear	UNIFOR	£763.75	000112
Van Centre	VANCEN	£19,059.44	000113

The payments to B L Office Furnishing and Trojan Secretarial Services are net of credit notes outstanding on these accounts.

(2)   You have also been asked to process a newly-received credit note of £235 (£200 plus VAT of £35) from the Chieftain Newspaper Group (because of an error in an advertisement printed in a newspaper), and a cheque (number 000114) to this supplier for the balance outstanding on the account of £1,175. The credit note number is SC0108. The nominal account code is 6201.

(3)   You have been given the following note by your supervisor.

> We have received full credit notes and revised invoices from three suppliers because they offered us early settlement discounts over the phone but did not reflect this on their original invoices, which have already been posted. The suppliers and the relevant Nominal Codes are:
>
> Floorsanders (Equipment) (FLOORS)   0020
> Harrow Cleaning Supplies (HARROW)   5000
> Matthias Scaffolding (MATTHI)   0020
>
> Please proceed as follows.
>
> (a)   Post the credit notes, which are each for the full amount currently shown as outstanding on these accounts. Use the reference 'Disc'.
>
> (b)   Post the revised invoices shown below. Use code T3 and post VAT manually.
>
> (c)   Pay the invoices taking advantage of the discounts.
>
> (d)   We are still negotiating long-term terms, so hold off making any changes to the suppliers record settlement discount % until terms are finalised.

The revised invoice details are as follows.

Supplier	Invoice no	Gross	VAT	Net
FLOORS	34005	1,005.31	143.31	862.00
HARROW	HC1213	2,840.62	412.22	2,428.40
MATTHI	63041	3,335.48	475.48	2,860.00

(4)   Blitz Limited will be purchasing more equipment from Highpile Cleaning Supplies (code HIGHPI). It has been agreed with the supplier that Blitz should make a payment of £3,500, to settle its outstanding debt and as a payment in advance for future purchases. You have been asked to record the payment. The cheque number is 000118.

(5)   You have also been asked to prepare cheques and record the payments for the following cheque requisitions. The supplier names will be filled in manually.

Cheque no	Amount	Purpose	Nominal code
000119	£258.50 (inc VAT at 17.5%)	Training course	8203
000120	£105.50 (no VAT)	Train ticket	7400
000121	£98.70 (inc VAT at 17.5%)	Refreshments	8205

Tasks

(a)   Print a remittance advice for Samurai Insurance Brokers and B L Office Furnishing. Do this *before* you post the payment transactions listed at the start of this assignment.

(b)   Post the transactions listed at the start of this assignment to the appropriate ledger accounts.

(c)   Print a report for the payments to suppliers and the bank transaction payments. If you do not have access to a printer, produce a screen display for the report. What is the total amount of payments?

(d)   Print a copy of the bank account transactions (nominal ledger code 1200) to date (9 October 2000), and establish how much money, according to the records, is remaining in this account. If you do not have access to a printer, obtain a screen display of the account to establish the remaining cash balance.

(e)   Establish the current balance on the creditors control account (nominal ledger account code 2100).

(f)   *Spreadsheet exercise*

To do this exercise you require access to Microsoft Excel.

If you have not already done so, unload the Word and Excel exercises into the folder c:\AATF as explained in Chapter 2. Then open the spreadsheet file named A3SPRSHT and save it with a new name.

Your supervisor has manually keyed some information from Sage into a spreadsheet.

(i)   Explain the meaning of the numbers in the columns headed No. and Ref.

(ii)   Your supervisor cannot understand why the totals do not match those shown in your payments report. Can you work out why? Alter the spreadsheet so that it produces the correct totals. The *totals* are calculated automatically, but you can alter the other amounts.

(iii)   Use the skills you have acquired in working with word processors to improve the appearance of this document. (If you are using both Word and Excel you will see strong similarities in the features available.)

(iv)   If you have access to a printer, print out your revised version of the spreadsheet.

Assignment 4:
Receipts from customers

Loading and carrying out the assignment

Load assignment 4 into Sage now!

For instructions on how to load the data for assignments, refer to Section 3 of Chapter 2. Check with your tutor in case special instructions apply to your college's system.

If you need to break off from this assignment part-way through, back-up your work to a floppy disk, following the instructions given on screen when you quit the Sage program. You can restore your entries when you wish to re-start working on this assignment.

If you want to keep a permanent copy of your finished work, back it up and save the back-up file with a suitable name.

Purpose

The purpose of this assignment is to test your ability to enter details of payments received from customers and to post these details to the appropriate ledgers. The transactions include payments in full and part payments, receipts with a deduction for a credit note, receipts with a deduction for an early settlement discount, payments on account, payments with order, writing off small unpaid balances on a customer account and a customer refund. The completeness and accuracy of your input will be checked by a further test of your ability to produce reports and listings, and to find the current balance on the bank current account and the debtors control account.

The **Tasks** for this assignment will be found following the **Information.** Read the information and all the tasks *before* commencing work.

Information

You are asked by your supervisor to process the following transactions. The transactions are for processing on 12 October 2000, unless otherwise indicated.

(1)   You have been given the following two customer invoices to process. You have been asked to enter and post the invoice details. If you have access to a printer, you should also produce invoices for these customers, as well as posting the invoice details to the ledgers.

Customer name	Bradley Fashions Ltd
A/C Reference Code	BRADLE
New Customer?	Yes
Address	18 Hospital Bridge Road
	St Albans, Herts
	SA5 9QT
Telephone	01727 532678
Credit Limit?	Yes, £2,500
Contact	Lee
Details	For contract cleaning services, £820 plus VAT at the standard rate

Customer name	A Rathod
A/C Reference Code	RATHOD
New Customer?	Yes
Address	200 West Road
	London N17 4GN
Telephone	020-8808 7814
Credit Limit?	No
Details	For domestic services, £75 plus VAT at the standard rate

(2)   The following payments have been received from existing customers. You have been asked to post the details to the ledgers. Your supervisor instructs you that you must use the relevant invoice number as the reference (or the first invoice number if several are being paid).

Customer	Code	Amount
E T Adams	ADAMSE	143.35
Farrar Air Tools Ltd	FARRAR	940.00
000D J Hargreaves	HARGRE	51.11
A Rose Ltd	ROSEAL	141.00
CCC Engineering	CCCENG	1527.50
Bridgford and Co	BRIDGF	981.13
Goodman Brickworks Ltd	GOODMA	141.47
Townend Angus Ltd	TOWNEN	1087.70
P Wood	WOODPX	166.85
P Leyser & Co	LEYSER	96.59
A Wyche	WYCHEA	88.13
D C Sherry	SHERRY	49.35

(3)   You have been asked to cancel an invoice of £70.50 for T P Paul. This was an invoice for domestic cleaning services, nominal account code 4002.

(4)   You have also been asked to post details of the following payments from customers, for which each customer has taken advantage of an early settlement discount of 5%.

Customer	A/C ref code	Cheque amount	Discount taken
Payne Properties	PAYNEP	1350.66	60.50
Rapid Pizzas	RAPIDP	215.66	9.66

(5)   The following payments have been received, where the customer has reduced the payment to allow for a credit note.

Customer	A/C ref code	Cheque amount
Gelling Private Bank	GELLIN	1727.25
DCS Roofing	DCSROO	82.25

Note. It may be advisable to take a back-up at this point, if you are happy with all the entries you have made, in case you make an error in posting the remaining transactions.

(6)   The following part-payments have been received:

Customer	A/C ref code	Cheque amount
Elite Caterers	ELITEC	200.00
Campbell Consultants	CAMPBE	70.00

(7)   You have been asked to enter and post details of a payment of £828.75 by Clough and Partners. This payment is partly to settle an outstanding invoice and partly a payment in advance for services not yet provided by Blitz Limited.

(8)   A payment on account has been received from the following new customer.

Customer name	M Zakis Ltd
A/C Reference Code	MZAKIS
Address	43 Ballards Lane
	London N12 0DG
Telephone	020-8445 2993
Credit Limit?	No
Amount of	
payment on account.	£500

(9)   The following payments have been received:

Customer	A/C ref code	Cheque amount
A T Haslam	HASLAM	42.00
R P Marwood	MARWOO	77.50

In each case, the customer has not paid the full invoice amount, but it has been decided to write off the small unpaid amount in each case. Post the details of the amounts to be written off. (Hint. Take a note of the unpaid amount in each case. If you forget to do this, can you think of a way of searching for this information in the Customers ledger?)

(10)   Immediate payments have been received (by cheque) for the following items, without a requirement to supply an invoice or give credit to the customer. Payments *include* VAT at the standard rate of 17.5% in each case.

Item	Amount received	Paying-in slip number
Window cleaning	47.00	500000
Domestic services	101.05	500001
Domestic services	61.10	500002
Materials sales	117.50	500003
Window cleaning	86.95	500004

These receipts must be entered and posted to the appropriate accounts.

Tasks

(a) Enter and post the transactions as described in information items (1) to (10) above. Make all the necessary entries, including the set up of new customer accounts where appropriate.

(b) Produce a report for:

(i) Amounts received from credit customers on 12 October 2000.

(ii) Bank receipts (ie amounts received from sources other than credit customers) on 12 October 2000.

Print the report if you have access to a printer; otherwise produce a screen display. What is the total amount received?

(c) After you have printed these reports, you are asked to process a refund of £96.59 to P Leyser for a payment already received. The refund has been agreed by the chief accountant with the customer.

(d) As at the end of processing, establish the total debits, credits and overall balances on the following accounts in the nominal ledger

	Account Code
Bank current account	1200
Debtors control account	1100

(e) Your supervisor wants to know how much is still owed by the customer Elite Caterers. What is the outstanding balance on this account?

Assignment 5:
Other cash transactions

Loading and carrying out the assignment

Load assignment 5 into Sage now!

For instructions on how to load the data for assignments, refer to Section 3 of Chapter 2. Check with your tutor in case special instructions apply to your college's system.

If you need to break off from this assignment part-way through, back-up your work to a floppy disk, following the instructions given on screen when you quit the Sage program. You can restore your entries when you wish to re-start working on this assignment.

If you want to keep a permanent copy of your finished work, back it up and save the back-up file with a suitable name.

Purpose

The purpose of Assignment 5 is to test your ability to post entries for petty cash in the nominal ledger and to make a small number of journal entries, and to carry out a bank reconciliation. In addition, the assignment includes a further test of your ability to post transactions for customer and supplier invoices, and customer and supplier payments.

The **Tasks** for this assignment will be found following the **Information**. Read the information and all the tasks *before* commencing work.

Information

(1)   On 13 October 2000, Blitz Limited's directors decided to set up a petty cash system with a float of £300. A cheque (number 000122) for £300 in cash was drawn on the company's bank account that day.

(2)   The following invoices have been received from suppliers.

Supplier	New supplier	Invoice number	Date	Details	Net amount £	VAT £
Hardin & Nobbs Chapel Place White Hart Lane London N17 4HA 020-8801 1907 A/C Ref HARDIN	Yes	2641	12 Oct 2000	Legal fees (N/C 7600)	1200.00	210.00
Flooring Supplies Ltd	No	435850	8 Oct 2000	Cleaning materials (N/C 5000)	762.00	133.35
Trojan Secretarial Services	No	03012	12 Oct 2000	Casual labour (N/C 7005)	210.00	36.75
AA1 Mini Cabs	No	C6281	15 Oct 2000	Taxis (N/C 7401)	134.70	23.57
Great North Hotel 75 Park Road Ealing London W5 6RU 020-8997 6005 A/C Ref GREATN	Yes	6601	7 Oct 2000	Hotel room (N/C 7402)	110.00	19.25
				Hotel meal (N/C 7406)	26.00	4.55
				Hotel telephone (N/C 7502)	3.40	0.60
				Total	139.40	24.40
Lerwick Cleaning Co Ryelands Road Norwich, NH7 4DB 01603 590624	Yes	S4031	14 Oct 2000	Cleaning materials (N/C 5000)	1400.00	245.00
				Carriage (N/C 5100)	20.00	3.50
A/C Ref LERWIC				Total	1420.00	248.50

Continued on the following page

Supplier	New supplier	Invoice number	Date	Details	Net amount £	VAT £
First Steps Ladder Hire	No	5024	8 Oct 2000	Ladder hire (N/C 7700)	81.00	14.18
Prairie Couriers Ltd	No	T34228	14 Oct 2000	Couriers (N/C 7501)	92.50	16.19
Amin Launderers 16 Southey Road London N15 3AK 020-8802 2541 A/C Ref AMINLA	Yes	0877	8 Oct 2000	Laundry (N/C 7802)	145.00	25.38

(3) The following invoices are to be sent out to customers, all dated 16 October 2000, with VAT charged at the standard rate.

Customer	New customer?	Invoice number	Details	Net amount £
Aspinall & Co	No	10053	Window cleaning	90.00
Elite Caterers	No	10054	Kitchen cleaning	190.00
S T Chana 78 Katherine Road London N9 8UL 020-8803 0147 No credit limit A/C Ref CHANAS	Yes	10055	Domestic services	135.00
L Haynes & Co 14 Millmead Road London N17 2XD 020-8885 3731 No credit limit A/C Ref HAYNES	Yes	10056	Window cleaning Materials sales Total	82.00 45.20 127.20
Brookes Acoustics Ltd	No	10057	Warehouse cleaning	670.00
CCC Engineering	No	10058	Factory cleaning	850.00
Tek Systems 115 Cricklewood Broadway London NW2 5ES 020-8452 9442 Credit limit £2,000 A/C Ref TEKSYS	Yes	10059	Contract cleaning Materials sales Total	450.00 63.00 513.00

Continued on the following page

Customer	New customer?	Invoice number	Details	Net amount £
Telefilm Latinamerica 100 Tower Bridge Road London SE1 6FJ 020-7403 2144 Credit limit £2,500 A/C Ref TELEFI	Yes	10060	Contract cleaning	830.00
GHH Commercial Bank	No	10061	Contract cleaning	950.00
The Keith Group	No	10062	Office cleaning	850.00
Owen of London 19 Piccadilly London W1 9CD 020-7734 2043 Credit limit £3,000 A/C Ref OWENLO	Yes	10063	Contract cleaning Window cleaning Materials sales Total	750.00 130.00 55.40 935.40
Biophysica Orbit Court 33 Fairfax Road London NW6 4LL 020-7624 2002 No credit limit A/C Ref BIOPHY	Yes	10064	Window cleaning Domestic services Total	63.00 45.00 108.00

(4)   The following payments to suppliers were made on 16 October 2000.

Date	Supplier	Cheque number	Amount £	Details
16 Oct 2000	Ace Telephone Answering	000123	250.00	Part payment of invoice
16 Oct 2000	ANS Newspaper Group	000124	1200.00	Payment of invoice plus payment on account
16 Oct 2000	Wells Business Systems	000125	1516.50	Payment of invoice, net of credit note CN4245 for £387 (gross) dated 14/10/2000. Nominal code 0030.

(5)   The following payments have been received from customers.

Date	Supplier	Amount £	Details
14 Oct 2000	Campbell Consultants	70.00	Part payment of invoice
15 Oct 2000	Brookes Acoustics Ltd	1000.00	Part payment of invoice
16 Oct 2000	Gardeners Delight	703.24	Payment of invoice, discount of £31.50 taken

(6) The company has received a cheque from Mr V J Richardson, a relative of one of the directors, for £10,000. The money was banked on 12 October 2000. It represents a loan from Mr Richardson to the company. A journal voucher has been prepared as follows:

JOURNAL VOUCHER			J02
	N/C	Debit £	Credit £
Cash	1200	10,000	
Loan account	2300		10,000
Loan from Mr V J Richardson			

(7) In the period to 16 October 2000, petty cash vouchers for expenditure items were as follows. (VAT is only shown where the company has obtained a valid VAT invoice.)

Ref	Date	Item	N/C code	Net amount £	VAT £	Gross amount £
PC001	13/10/2000	Postage stamps	7501	24.00	0	24.00
PC002	13/10/2000	Biscuits, coffee	8205	32.49	0	32.49
PC003	13/10/2000	Milk	8205	15.20	0	15.20
PC004	13/10/2000	Taxis	7400	25.00	0	25.00
PC005	14/10/2000	Train fares	7400	9.20	0	9.20
PC006	14/10/2000	Washing up liquid	8205	1.75	0	1.75
PC007	14/10/2000	Photocopying	7500	24.00	4.20	28.20
PC008	15/10/2000	Stationery	7504	37.24	6.52	43.76
PC009	15/10/2000	Taxis	7400	15.00	0	15.00
PC010	16/10/2000	Sandwiches, cakes	8205	38.26	0	38.26
PC011	16/10/2000	Parking	7304	7.00	0	7.00
PC012	16/10/2000	Train fares	7400	8.40	0	8.40

Notes and coin totalling £72.00 were paid into petty cash on 16 October. This was money received for various small window cleaning jobs, for which VAT should be recorded at the standard rate.

(8) Blitz Limited has not yet set up a computerised payroll system. Wages were paid by bank transfer on 16 October 2000, and the following transactions need to be accounted for.

	Code	Debit £	Credit £
Bank account	1200		4133.04
PAYE	2210		2217.96
National Insurance	2211		975.20
Directors salaries	7001	1350.80	
Staff salaries	7003	475.75	
Wages – regular	6000	4859.65	
Employers NI	7006	640.00	
		7326.20	7326.20

(9) On 19 October 2000, the following bank statement was received from Blitz's bank.

Account 11765444

BLITZ LIMITED
25 APPLE ROAD
LONDON N12 3PP

Centre Bank
Apple Road Branch
38 Apple Road
London N22

Particulars	Date	Withdrawn £	Paid in £	Balance £
BGC	21 AUG		20000.00	
BGC	21 AUG		20000.00	40000.00
BAC	16 SEP	6053.93		
				33946.07
000100	12 OCT	117.50		
000103	12 OCT	1493.78		
000104	12 OCT	332.23		
000105	12 OCT	3205.00		
000107	12 OCT	3000.00		
000111	12 OCT	642.37		
000113	12 OCT	19059.44		
000114	12 OCT	1175.00		4920.75
000101	13 OCT	540.50		
000102	13 OCT	376.00		
000106	13 OCT	179.95		
000108	13 OCT	141.00		
000109	13 OCT	1240.00		
000112	13 OCT	763.75		
000116	13 OCT	2767.77		1088.22DR
BGC	13 OCT		143.35	
BGC	13 OCT		51.11	
BGC	13 OCT		1527.50	
BGC	13 OCT		981.13	
BGC	13 OCT		940.00	

Particulars	Date	Withdrawn £	Paid in £	Balance £
BGC	13 OCT		1087.70	
BGC	13 OCT		88.13	
BGC	13 OCT		141.00	
BGC	13 OCT		141.47	
BGC	13 OCT		166.85	
BGC	13 OCT		49.35	
BGC	13 OCT		96.59	
BGC	13 OCT		1350.66	
BGC	13 OCT		215.66	
BGC	13 OCT		1727.25	
BGC	13 OCT		200.00	
BGC	13 OCT		70.00	
BGC	13 OCT		828.75	
BGC	13 OCT		82.25	
BGC	13 OCT		101.05	
BGC	13 OCT		42.00	
BGC	13 OCT		500.00	
BGC	13 OCT		47.00	
BGC	13 OCT		77.50	
BGC	13 OCT		86.95	
BGC	13 OCT		61.10	
BGC	13 OCT		117.50	9833.63
000110	13 OCT	1175.00		
000115	13 OCT	962.21		
000118	13 OCT	3500.00		
000119	13 OCT	258.50		
000120	13 OCT	105.50		
000121	13 OCT	98.70		
CASH WITHDRAWAL	16 OCT	300.00		
TRANSFER-LEYSER	16 OCT	96.59		3337.13
BGC	16 OCT		70.00	
BGC	16 OCT		10000.00	13407.13
BANK CHARGES	16 OCT	25.60		13381.53

Tasks

(a)   Post the transaction for withdrawing cash from the company's bank account to set up a petty cash system. Use the cheque number as a reference for the transaction (information item [1]).

(b)   Post the transactions for invoices received from suppliers (information item [2]).

(c)   Post the transactions for invoices sent out to customers (information item [3]).

(d)   Post the payments to suppliers (information item [4]).

(e)   Post the receipts from customers (information item [5]).

(f)   Post the receipt of the money as a loan from Mr V J Richardson, using the journal voucher as your source document. The transaction reference should be the journal voucher number. The tax reference code should be T9.

(g)   Post the petty cash transactions to the nominal ledger, for both expenditure and income items. Enter the income items as a single transaction, with reference PCR001. Produce a listing for the petty cash payments. Print the listing if you have access to a printer.

(h)   The company uses an imprest system for petty cash. On 16 October 2000, the money in petty cash should be topped up to £300. A cheque (number 000126) is to be drawn on the bank account to withdraw cash.

       (i)   What should be the cheque amount?

       (ii)   Assume that a cheque for this amount is drawn, and petty cash is restored to £300. Post this cash withdrawal transaction. Give it a reference code 000126 and a tax code T9.

(i)   Post the wages and salaries transactions, shown in information item (8), to the appropriate nominal ledger accounts. Post the transactions by means of a journal entry. Give the transaction a reference of J04. Use tax code T9.

(j)   Your supervisor wishes to know the balances on the following nominal ledger accounts after you have dealt with tasks (a) to (i).

	Nominal ledger account code
Debtors control account	1100
Bank - current account	1200
Creditors control account	2100
Staff salaries	7003
Travelling	7400
Equipment hire	7700
Sales – contract cleaning	4000
Sales – window cleaning	4001
Sales – domestic services	4002
Sales – materials	4100
Petty cash	1230
Discounts allowed	4009

Report the balances on these accounts.

(k)   Carry out a bank reconciliation on 19 October 2000, after you have completed tasks (a) to (j). How many unreconciled transactions are there and what are the amounts for:
      (i)   Statement balance.
      (ii)   Uncleared items.
      (iii) Trial balance.

A word of advice - your supervisor has advised that an error was made when posting cheque 000118. The cheque was for £3,500.00, but was mistakenly entered into Line 50 as £2,364.69. A correcting entry has been made for £1,135.31. You should match these two entries from your nominal account listing of account 1200 against the £3,500.00 that will show on the bank statement for cheque 000118.

Assignment 6:
Other credit transactions

Loading and carrying out the assignment

Load assignment 6 into Sage now!

For instructions on how to load the data for assignments, refer to Section 3 of Chapter 2. Check with your tutor in case special instructions apply to your college's system.

If you need to break off from this assignment part-way through, back-up your work to a floppy disk, following the instructions given on screen when you quit the Sage program. You can restore your entries when you wish to re-start working on this assignment.

If you want to keep a permanent copy of your finished work, back it up and save the back-up file with a suitable name.

Purpose

This assignment tests your ability to post contra entries and write-offs for bad debts and to correct errors. It also tests your ability to deal with a variety of customer problems: customers who exceed their credit limit and late payers, and chasing customers for payment by producing an aged debtors list, statements and reminder letters.

The **Tasks** for this assignment will be found following the **Information.** Read the information and all the tasks *before* commencing work.

Information

Tim Nicholas and Maria Green, the directors of Blitz Limited, are quite pleased with the first few months of trading by the company. They are very aware, however, that the company must continue to win more sales if it is to be successful. This could mean having to take the risk of selling services to customers who might not be creditworthy. In addition, cash flow could be a problem. The company has already borrowed £10,000 from Mr V Richardson, and has used a bank overdraft facility. The directors have therefore recognised a need to collect money from debtors efficiently, to make sure that cash keeps coming into the business.

(1)   Credit limits have been set for some of Blitz Limited's customers. If a customer exceeds his credit limit, however, the company's policy from now onwards will be to supply the goods or services and increase the customer's credit limit by £1,000. However, the directors wish to be informed of any such change.

(2)   On 21 October 2000, you have been asked to process the following transactions. All sales are subject to VAT at the standard rate.

Credit Sales

Customer	New customer?	Invoice number	Details	Net amount
ANS Newspaper Group 19 Cecil Road London NW10 5CD 020-8453 2926 No credit limit A/C code ANSNEW	Yes	10065	Window cleaning	150.00
Brookes Acoustics Ltd	No	10066	Window cleaning	120.00
CCC Engineering Ltd	No	10067	Contract cleaning	630.00
R C Chadwick	No	10068	Domestic services	50.00
South Sea Airtours Girton House 62 Appendale Road London N17 1RA 020-8885 5553 Credit limit £2,500 A/C code SOUTHS	Yes	10069	Contract cleaning Materials sales Total	480.00 75.00 555.00
Clough & Partners	No	10070	Window cleaning	70.00
GHH Commercial Bank	No	10071	Contract cleaning	500.00
The Keith Group	No	10072	Contract cleaning Window cleaning Total	350.00 140.00 490.00
D J Hargreaves	No	10073	Domestic services	60.00
Meakin Media	No	10074	Window cleaning	100.00
Norris Hydraulics Ltd	No	10075	Contract cleaning	620.00
K Ogden Property Co	No	10076	Contract cleaning	480.00
Owen of London	No	10077	Window cleaning	150.00
School of Dance	No	10078	Contract cleaning	320.00
R I Tepper	No	10079	Contract cleaning	250.00
B Walton & Co	No	10080	Window cleaning	150.00

Continued on the following page

Customer	New customer?	Invoice number	Details	Net amount
WRW Catering	No	10081	Contract cleaning	370.00
The Lapsley Agency	Yes	10082	Window cleaning	144.00
105 Thetford Road			Domestic services	105.00
London N9 0PB			Total	249.00
020-8803 0147				
No credit limit				
A/C code LAPSLE				

Cash sales

The following amounts were received from cash sales to customers.

Date	Details	Gross amount (including VAT)	Method of payment	Paying in slip
21 October 2000	Domestic services	51.70	Cheque	500005
21 October 2000	Domestic services	44.00	Cheque	500006
21 October 2000	Materials sales	37.60	Cheque	500007
22 October 2000	Materials sales	25.38	Notes and coin	
23 October 2000	Domestic services	35.25	Notes and coin	
23 October 2000	Materials sales	52.88	Cheque	500008

The cheque payments were banked on 23 October 2000. The two receipts in notes and coin were put into petty cash (with reference codes PCR002 and PCR003 respectively).

Invoices from suppliers

The following invoices were received from suppliers. All three suppliers are credit customers.

Supplier	New supplier?	Invoice number	Date	Details	Net amount £	VAT £
ANS Newspaper Group	No	621347	20 Oct 2000	Advertising (N/C 6201)	471.28	82.47
Elite Caterers 85B Crowland Road London N15 9KW 020-8800 2069 A/C ref ELITEC	Yes	2046	20 Oct 2000	Catering (N/C 7403)	250.00	43.75
Meakin Media Ltd 4 Nursery Road Ashford Middlesex, AF8 5TS 01784 358452 A/C ref MEAKIN	Yes	10035	20 Oct 2000	Advertising (N/C 6201)	200.00	35.00

Receipts from customers

The following receipts from customers were obtained on 22 October 2000.

Customer	A/C ref	Amount £	Details
A Rathod	RATHOD	88.13	
A Rose Ltd	ROSEAL	146.88	
S T Chanas	CHANAS	158.00	
Biophysica	BIOPHY	52.88	To settle a part of an invoice relating to domestic services
Aspinall & Co	ASPINA	105.75	
Elite Caterers	ELITEC	1427.31	
Meakin Media Ltd	MEAKIN	350.16	

Tasks

(a)   Post the credit sales transactions using the Service invoice option from the Invoicing menu.

    (i)   Prepare a list of customers who have exceeded their current credit limit.

    (ii)   Increase the credit limit for each of these customers by £1,000 each.

(b)   Post the cash sales transactions (both the bank transactions and the petty cash transactions).

(c)   Post the three invoices received from suppliers.

(d)   Post the receipts from customers. The accounts of Elite Caterers and Meakin Media should be settled by means of *contra entries*.

(e)   A cheque is being prepared to settle the account with ANS Newspaper group (cheque number 000127, dated 22 October 2000). The amount owed by ANS Newspaper Group should be offset against amounts owed to ANS, and the amount of the cheque should be for the difference.

    (i)   What is the amount of the cheque?

    (ii)   Post this cheque, and settle the accounts in the Suppliers and Customers ledgers by means of a contra entry (Sage Line 50 only).

(f)   On 23 October 2000, you are instructed to write off small unpaid balances in any customer's account. Unpaid balances of £1 or less should be written off.

    (i)   Write off these small unpaid balances.

    (ii)   What is the total amount of bad debts written off in this exercise?

(g)   Information has been received that the following customers have gone out of business.

Name	*A/C ref*
E T Adams	ADAMSE
L Haynes & Co	HAYNES

You are instructed that if there are any unpaid debts outstanding on the account of E T Adams or L Haynes & Co, the debts should be written off.

(h)   A credit note (reference 004) was issued to Owen of London on 22 October 2000 for £150 (plus VAT). Post this transaction, giving it a N/C code of 4000. (You are not required to produce the credit note itself.) Preview on screen a statement showing all transactions to date for GHH Commercial Bank.

(i)   An invoice from AA1 Mini Cabs for £158.27 in October was entered in the accounts with a nominal ledger account code of 7401. Your supervisor tells you that the code should have been 7400. You are required to alter the code.

(j)   A badly printed invoice from Newlite Cleaning Fluids dated 12 September was entered in the accounts incorrectly as £473.91 including VAT. The net amount, which is all that can be seen on the invoice, was actually £403. You are required to correct the error. What is the corrected figure?

(k)   What are the current balances on the following nominal ledger accounts?

	Code
Bank current account	1200
Debtors control account	1100
Creditors control account	2100
Bad debt write off account	8100
Advertising account	6201
Sales – contract cleaning	4000
Sales – window cleaning	4001
Sales – domestic services	4002
Sales – materials	4100

(l)   *Spreadsheet exercise: Aged Debtors Analysis*

Suppose that no more payments are received from customers before 5 November 2000. On 5 November, it is decided to review the current state of debtors, and take action to chase late payers.

However, due to a small fire which affected some of Blitz's computer hardware, it proves impossible to use the Sage system on 5 November.

Fortunately, the data from an aged debtors analysis dated 4 November is available in a spreadsheet file called A6AGED.xls.

(i)   Open A6AGED.xls and save it with a new name. (The file A6AGED.xls will be in the folder C:\AATF if you have unloaded the Word and Excel files from the CD. Refer to Chapter 2.)

(ii)   Check that the total value of debtors outstanding agrees with the value on your Sage system now that you have posted all the transactions for this assignment.

(iii)   Sort the data in order of value of overall balance: largest first. Which five customers owe the largest amounts? (See the note below if you don't know how to sort the data.)

(iv)   Sort the data in order of largest balance outstanding for over 30 days. Make a list of customers with a balance of over £1,000 that has been outstanding for more than 30 days.

(v)   Resort the data into customer account code order.

(*Hint.* In Microsoft Excel you can sort data by clicking on the word **Data** at the top of the screen and then on **Sort** in the menu that drops down.)

(m)   *Spreadsheet exercise: Cash flow forecast*

Blitz has been asked to submit a brief cash flow forecast to the bank for the first six months of next year (which is 2001 as the case is set in the year 2000).

A colleague has started to prepare the forecast, but is not sure how to continue.

(i) Open the file CashFcastFirstHalf2001.xls from the folder C:\AATF.

(ii) The relevant figures are:

Cash Balance Jan 1 2001	5,500
Cash Receipts Jan – June	4,500
Collections from Credit Sales Jan - June	130,000
Payments (materials)	25,000
Wages and salaries	52,000
Rent	8,000
Other payments	22,000

Enter this data into the spreadsheet, and enter formula to correctly calculate the required subtotals and totals.

Save the file with a different name.

Answer to Assignment 1
Supplier invoices and credit notes

You can enter the new supplier accounts in the Suppliers Ledger using either the Invoices button or the Record button.

If you use the Record button, as suggested in Chapter 4, you should set up accounts for the four new suppliers before entering any invoice details. Having set up the new accounts, you can switch to the Invoices window to process the 8 invoices.

Having processed and posted the invoice details, you should then close the Invoices window and open the Credits window to process and post the details of the 2 credit notes.

Points to check

You should check the following points.

Date

For each invoice (or credit note) you should enter the actual date of the invoice (or credit note), rather than simply using today's date.

Nominal ledger codes

Carefully check transaction details shown below in the two listings. These list the entry details for the transactions. Make sure that you have specified the correct nominal ledger code for each transaction. To find the correct N/C codes for the credit notes, you should have looked for the account codes for Furniture and Fixtures (0040) and Wages - Casual (7005).

When an invoice is for purchases or items of expense for more than one nominal ledger account, you should enter each part of the invoice separately. This means that you should have entered:

(a)   2 lines of details for the invoice from Flooring Supplies Ltd, one for the purchase of cleaning materials (code 5000) and one for the purchase of plant and machinery (code 0020); and

(b)   3 lines of details for the invoice from Samurai Insurance Brokers, one for the premises insurance (code 7104), one for the vehicle insurance (code 7303) and one for miscellaneous items of insurance (code 8204).

Listings

When you have entered and posted the details of the invoices and credit notes, you can print the 'day book' listings.

Use the Reports button in the *Suppliers ledger* window and select Day Books: Supplier Invoices (detailed) and then Day Books: Supplier Credits (detailed).

You should specify the date ranges 29/09/2000 to 02/10/2000 for supplier invoices and 01/10/2000 to 01/10/2000 for credit notes.

The printouts should appear as follows, with 11 entries in the purchases day book and 2 entries in the purchases returns day book. (However, the sequence of transactions and the transaction numbers can vary, according to the order in which you entered them in the system.) The gross value of transactions is shown at the bottom of each listing.

Blitz Limited

Day Books : Supplier Invoices (Detailed)

Date from: 29/09/2000
Date to: 02/10/2000

Supplier From:
Supplier To: ZZZZZZZZ

Trans From: 1
Trans To: 83

N/C From:
N/C To: 99999999

Dept From: 0
Dept To: 999

No	Tp	A/c	N/C	Date	Ref.	Details	Net	T/C	VAT	Total
71	PI	AA1MIN	7400	01102000	C6147	Taxi fares	38.40	T1	6.72	45.12
72	PI	NEWLIT	5000	01102000	26187	Cleaning materials	168.70	T1	29.52	198.22
73	PI	FLOORI	5000	01102000	435796	Cleaning materials	202.36	T1	35.41	237.77
74	PI	FLOORI	0020	01102000	435796	Equipment	620.00	T1	108.50	728.50
75	PI	FIRSTS	7700	01102000	4821	Ladder hire	126.75	T1	22.18	148.93
76	PI	SAMURA	7104	01102000	02381	Premises insurance	1650.00	T2	0.00	1650.00
77	PI	SAMURA	7303	01102000	02381	Vehicle insurance	1125.00	T2	0.00	1125.00
78	PI	SAMURA	8204	01102000	02381	Misc insurance	430.00	T2	0.00	430.00
79	PI	3DTECH	7505	30092000	001462	Books	179.95	T0	0.00	179.95
80	PI	THAMES	7102	01102000	132157	Water rates	420.00	T0	0.00	420.00
81	PI	ANSNEW	6201	29092000	621014	Advertising	750.00	T1	131.25	881.25
						Totals	5711.16		333.58	6044.74

PROFESSIONAL EDUCATION

Blitz Limited

Day Books : Supplier Credits (Detailed)

Date from: 01/10/2000
Date to: 01/10/2000

Supplier From:
Supplier To: ZZZZZZZZ

Trans From: 1
Trans To: 83

N/C From:
N/C To: 99999999

Dept From: 0
Dept To: 999

No	Tp	A/c	N/C	Date	Ref.	Details				
82	PC	BLOFFI	0040	01102000	K0320	Damaged furniture	150.00	T1	26.25	176.25
83	PC	TROJAN	7005	01102000	C0259	Temp overcharge	60.00	T1	10.50	70.50
						Totals :	210.00		36.75	246.75

Creditors control account

The balance on the creditors control account is £50,517.10.

	£
Total credits (invoices)	50,763.85
Total debits (credit notes)	246.75
Balance	50,517.10

This can be obtained by Escaping from the Suppliers Ledger to the main screen, and clicking on the Nominal Ledger button. In the Nominal Ledger window, click on Clear to ensure that no accounts are selected, then scroll down to account 2100 and select it by clicking on it. Then click on the Activity button and accept the defaults you are offered. At the bottom of the screen you will find the total balances.

Answer to Assignment 2
Customer invoices and credit notes

Invoices

When using the Invoicing window options, you should *save* each transaction when you have input the details, print the invoices in batches, and then update the ledgers.

Make sure you specify the nominal account code correctly for each item in each invoice.

Code	Account
4000	Sales - contract cleaning
4001	Sales - window cleaning
4002	Sales - domestic services
4100	Sales - materials

Where appropriate, enter new customer details, following the screen prompts. The default tax code is T1 if you choose to set this (we recommend you do). The suggested reference codes to use are as follows:

Customer	Ref code
R P Marwood	MARWOO
School of Dance	SCHOOL
B & T Fashions Ltd	BTFASH
The Keith Group	KEITHG
Rapid Pizzas	RAPIDP
Gardeners Delight	GARDEN
Payne Properties	PAYNEP
T P Paul	PAULTP

You must decide whether invoices (or credit notes) should be entered using the Product button or the Service button. You may prefer to use the Service option for materials sales this is ok as long as you ensure the invoice is posted to the correct nominal ledger sales account. (A business that sold mainly products rather than services would obviously use the Product Invoice.)

Order details

You should insert order details into an invoice where appropriate. Clicking on the Order Details index tab will give you a pop-up window for adding information about the delivery address. In this assignment, you need to add order details for the invoice to Gardeners Delight - ie you need to add details of the delivery address, which is different from the invoice address.

Details

You should add details for the invoice, based on the information given in the assignment. If you prepared a Service invoice that includes materials (the Elite Caterers invoice), you should have calculated yourself the amount payable (net of VAT) for materials, and entered this amount in the invoice.

Use tax code T1 for every invoice. The VAT and total amount payable are calculated automatically.

Footer

There is no requirement on any invoice for footer details, and you will not need to use the Footer index tab (or button).

Printing

To print the invoices, you must first select the invoices and then click on the Print Invoices button in the Invoicing window. Ensure you select the correct layout and paper-size for your printer.

Posting

When you use the Invoicing window options, you must post the transactions to the ledgers using the Update Ledgers button. Select all of the items listed in the Invoicing window: you can do this by clicking on Clear and then on Swap. Decide whether you want a print-out when the Update Ledgers window appears, and then simply click on OK. Follow the screen prompt for printing. A part of a printed listing of the invoices that might be produced is shown below. The invoice numbers may not be the same as yours, depending on the order in which you entered the data. Columns for Stock Code and Quantity have been omitted for lack of space.

Blitz Limited

Update Ledgers Report

Inv/Crd	Audit	Date	A/C	N/C	Details	Net	VAT	Total
2	85	08102000	ROYALP	4000	Revised scale of cleaning	−300.00	−52.50	−352.50
					Invoice Totals:	−300.00	−52.50	−352.50
10041	94	08102000	BRIDGF	4000	Office cleaning	420.00	73.50	493.50
					Invoice Totals:	420.00	73.50	493.50
10042	95	08102000	HARGRE	4002	Domestic services	43.50	7.61	51.11
					Invoice Totals:	43.50	7.61	51.11
10043	96	08102000	ELITEC	4000	KITCHEN CLEANING	644.00	112.70	756.70
	97			4100	10 BOXES OF OVEN CLEANER	61.00	10.68	71.68
	98			4100	6 CASES OF FLAME DETERGENT	72.00	12.60	84.60
	99			4100	7 BRUSHES	23.94	4.19	28.13
					Invoice Totals:	800.94	140.17	941.11
10044	100	08102000	MEAKIN	4001	Window cleaning	249.00	43.58	292.58
					Invoice Totals:	249.00	43.58	292.58

Credit notes

In older versions use the SrvCredit option, in newer versions specify Service and Credit Note during processing.

Listings

Click on the reports button in the *Customers* window.

(a)   Use the Day Books: Customer Invoices (Detailed) option to preview or print the sales day book listing for invoices.

(b)   Use the Day Books: Customer Credits (Detailed) option to preview or print the sales day book listing for credit notes.

In selecting the items for listing, you can specify the date range from 08/10/2000 to 08/10/2000.

Extracts from the listings are shown below. (The Dept column is omitted.) Check the totals shown. You should have obtained these same *totals* yourself (invoice numbers for particular customers may be different: it depends on the order in which you post the details.)

Blitz Limited

Day Books : Customer Invoices (Detailed)

Date from: 08/10/2000
Date to: 08/10/2000

Supplier From:
Supplier To: ZZZZZZZZ

Trans From: 1
Trans To: 106

N/C From:
N/C To: 99999999

Dept From: 0
Dept To: 999

No.	Tp	A/c	N/C	Date	Refn.	Details	Net	VAT	T/c	Total
87	SI	MARWOO	4002	08102000	10036	Domestic services	66.00	11.55	T1	77.55
88	SI	SCHOOL	4000	08102000	10037	Cleaning school	250.00	43.75	T1	293.75
89	SI	BTFASH	4001	08102000	10038	Window cleaning	144.00	25.20	T1	169.20
90	SI	KEITHG	4000	08102000	10039	Office cleaning	1420.00	248.50	T1	1668.50
91	SI	RAPIDP	4100	08102000	10040	FLAME DETERGENT	60.00	9.98	T1	69.98
92	SI	RAPIDP	4100	08102000	10040	BREAM CLEANER	91.20	15.16	T1	106.36
93	SI	RAPIDP	4100	08102000	10040	CLEANING GLOVES	42.00	6.98	T1	48.98
94	SI	BRIDGF	4000	08102000	10041	Office cleaning	420.00	73.50	T1	493.50
95	SI	HARGRE	4002	08102000	10042	Domestic services	43.50	7.61	T1	51.11
96	SI	ELITEC	4000	08102000	10043	KITCHEN CLEANING	644.00	112.70	T1	756.70
97	SI	ELITEC	4100	08102000	10043	OVEN CLEANER	61.00	10.68	T1	71.68
98	SI	ELITEC	4100	08102000	10043	FLAME DETERGENT	72.00	12.60	T1	84.60
99	SI	ELITEC	4100	08102000	10043	BRUSHES	23.94	4.19	T1	28.13
100	SI	MEAKIN	4001	08102000	10044	Window cleaning	249.00	43.58	T1	292.58
101	SI	ROSEAL	4001	08102000	10045	Window cleaning	125.00	21.88	T1	146.88
102	SI	GARDEN	4100	08102000	10046	WIND. CLEAN FLUID	630.00	104.74	T1	734.74
103	SI	PAYNEP	4000	08102000	10047	Office cleaning	1210.00	201.16	T1	1411.16
104	SI	PAULTP	4002	08102000	10050	Domestic services	60.00	10.50	T1	70.50
105	SI	SIDDAL	4001	08102000	10048	Window cleaning	182.00	31.85	T1	213.85
106	SI	NORRIS	4000	08102000	10049	Factory and office	816.40	142.87	T1	959.27
:						Totals	6610.04	1138.98		7749.02

Blitz Limited

Day Books : Customer Credits (Detailed)

Date from: 08/10/2000
Date to: 08/10/2000

Supplier From:
Supplier To: ZZZZZZZZ

Trans From: 1
Trans To: 106

N/C From:
N/C To: 99999999

Dept From: 0
Dept To: 999

No.	Tp	A/c	N/C	Date	Refn.	Details	Net	VAT	T/c	Total
84	SC	GELLIN	4000	08102000	1	Poor quality cleaning	250.00	43.75	T1	293.75
85	SC	ROYALP	4000	08102000	2	Revised scale of cleaning	300.00	52.50	T1	352.50
86	SC	DCSROO	4001	08102000	3	Broken window	150.00	26.25	T1	176.25
		:				Totals	700.00	122.50		822.50

Balance on the debtors control account

Escape to the main window, and click on the Nominal Ledger button. Then select the Debtors Control Account (code 1100) and click on Activity. Accept the default transaction range you are offered. If you check the totals at the foot of the account, you should find that they are as follows.

	Debit	Credit
Totals:	30369.45	822.50
Balance:	29546.95	

Sales accounts

You can find the balances for each sales account using the Nominal Ledger Activity window. Click on the Nominal Ledger button, scroll down to the accounts concerned and highlight them, then click on Activity. Accept the defaults you are offered. Use the < and > buttons at the bottom of the screen to move from one account to the next.

The current balances shown in the box at the foot of each account's Activity window should be as follows:

Account		Debit £	Credit £	Balance £
4000	Sales - contract cleaning	550.00	21,357.80	20,807.80
4001	Sales - window cleaning	150.00	2,670.40	2,520.40
4002	Sales - domestic services	0.00	853.10	853.10
4100	Sales – materials	0.00	980.14	980.14

227

School of Dance

(a) One method is to use the Search button in the Invoicing window where the Account Reference field Is Equal to SCHOOL. If you click on Apply and Close this will give you a window that includes only the relevant invoice.

(b) Select this invoice and click on the Print button in the Invoicing window.

CCC Engineering

Click on Customers and select the CCCENG account. Then click on the Activity button. You can find the amount currently owed by the customer, but not whether an invoice has been printed. The invoice amount is £1,527.50.

Word processing exercises

The next two pages show suggested solutions to the two Word exercises in this assignment.

For your duplicate invoice you will need to know the original invoice details including the VAT. An audit trail report for transaction number 40 is the best source. Use the Reports button in the main window and specify a transaction range 40 to 40 (and a date range ending on or after 8/10/2000). Alternatively you can look at CCC Engineering's transaction history and calculate the VAT manually.

To copy from one application to the other, select (highlight) the item press Ctrl + C to copy, switch to the other application and position your cursor, then press Ctrl + V.

Blitz Limited

25 Apple Road
London N12 3PP

Fax Cover Sheet

DATE:	October 8, 2000	**TIME:**	11:15
TO:	V Cockcroft CCC Engineering Ltd	**PHONE:** **FAX:**	01923 354022 01923 354071
FROM:	Your name Blitz Limited	**PHONE:** **FAX:**	020 8912 2013 020 8912 6387
RE:	Invoice number 10005		

Number of pages including cover sheet: Two

Message

This is in response to your telephone call earlier this morning.

The amount due is £1,527.50 (including VAT of £227.50). For your reference a copy of the invoice accompanies this cover note. Payment is due within 30 days of the date of the invoice.

Blitz Limited

25 Apple Road
London
N12 3PP
Tel: 020 8912 2013
Fax: 020 8912 6387

INVOICE

INVOICE NO: 10005
DATE: 22 September, 2000

To:

CCC Engineering Limited
28 Gardener Road
Watford
WF3 7GH

Deliver To:
Invoice address

QUANTITY	DESCRIPTION	UNIT PRICE	AMOUNT
	Factory cleaning	N/A	1300.00
		SUBTOTAL	1300.00
		VAT	227.50
		SHIPPING & HANDLING	-
		TOTAL DUE	**1527.50**

Make all cheques payable to: Blitz Limited
If you have any questions concerning this invoice, call: Your name, 020 8912 2013

THANK YOU FOR YOUR BUSINESS!

BPP
PROFESSIONAL EDUCATION

Answer to Assignment 3
Payments to suppliers

Remittance advice notes

If you intend to print the remittance advice notes (Task (b) of the assignment), you should produce the remittance advice notes before you save the payments in question.

Payments to suppliers

You should now process the payment transactions for the 14 payments shown in paragraph (1) in Assignment 3. Click on Bank in the main Sage window and then on the Supplier button. Follow the procedures described in Chapter 5.

It is simpler to use the Pay in Full button for these payments, rather than typing in the amount of the cheque (though it is worth trying both methods to see the difference). In the former case, press Tab when you reach the £ sign box. Click on Pay in Full when the cursor is in the Payment boxes until the £ sign box shows the correct amount.

Save each transaction after you have printed a remittance advice if required.

Chieftain Newspaper Group

To process the payment to the Chieftain Newspaper group, you must first post the credit note transaction to the relevant account in the Suppliers Ledger. There is no need to close down the Bank option and return to the main Sage window if you do not want to. Just click on Suppliers and then Credit to input the credit note details – as explained in Chapter 3.

When you have entered and posted the credit note transaction, press Esc to return to the Supplier payments window (or open it up again if you closed it). You can then process the payment to the supplier.

Credit notes and early settlement discounts

You will first need to find out the amount of the credit notes by looking at the Activity for each of the accounts mentioned. The amounts you should have posted are as follows.

Account	Gross	VAT	Net
FLOORS	1,012.85	150.85	862.00
HARROW	2,853.37	424.97	2,428.40
MATTHI	3,360.50	500.50	2,860.00

Post the new invoices as you have done in previous assignments except that instead of accepting tax code T1 and letting the program calculate VAT at 17.5% on the full amount, use code T3 and type in the amount of VAT shown on the invoice.

To pay the new invoices, you will have to calculate the discount to establish what the amount of each cheque payment should be. You should have produced the following results:

Supplier code	Gross amount £	Net amount £	Discount %	Discount £	Cheque payment (gross less discount) £
FLOORS	1,005.31	862.00	5%	43.10	962.21
HARROW	2,840.62	2,428.40	3%	72.85	2767.77
MATTHI	3,335.48	2,860.00	5%	143.00	3192.48

To enter the payment details, Tab past the £ sign box and click on Pay in Full when you reach the Payment box. Then type in the amount of the discount in the Discount box.

Highpile Cleaning Supplies

Here, you are paying an invoice and also making a payment on account for invoices not yet received. Type 3500 in the £ sign box and then when you reach the Payment box click on Pay in Full.

Now click on Save. You will be told that there is an unallocated cheque balance of £1,135.31. Click on Yes to post it as a payment on account.

Bank transaction payments

To make the payments for the cheque requisitions, from the Bank Accounts window and click on Payment. For each payment that includes VAT (cheques 000119 and 000121) you can enter the gross payment in the Net column and then click on Calc Net. The VAT will be calculated automatically, and the Net amount adjusted to exclude VAT. The tax code for the train ticket (cheque 000120) should be T0.

Listing

You have processed payments to suppliers (Suppliers Ledger) and for three bank transactions (Nominal Ledger). There are several ways of doing this in Line 50. We suggest that you click on Reports in the Bank accounts window and select:

(a)   Day Books: Bank Payments (Summary); and also

(b)   Day Books: Supplier Payments (Summary).

Enter 09/10/2000 as the date in both date boxes, when making your specifications for the listing.

The output in printed form should be as follows. (Check that your totals match the totals shown here.)

Blitz Limited
Day Books: Supplier Payments (Summary)

Date from: 09/10/2000
Date to: 09/10/2000

Bank From:
Bank To: 99999999

Transaction From: 1
Transaction To: 136

Supplier From:
Supplier To: ZZZZZZZZ :

No.	Bank	A/c	Date	Refn.	Details	Net	VAT	Total
107	1200	AA1MIN	09102000	000100	Purchase Payment	117.50	0.00	117.50
108	1200	BTELEC	09102000	000101	Purchase Payment	540.50	0.00	540.50
109	1200	CAPITA	09102000	000102	Purchase Payment	376.00	0.00	376.00
110	1200	BLOFFI	09102000	000103	Purchase Payment	1493.78	0.00	1493.78
111	1200	FIRSTS	09102000	000104	Purchase Payment	332.23	0.00	332.23
112	1200	SAMURA	09102000	000105	Purchase Payment	3205.00	0.00	3205.00
113	1200	3DTECH	09102000	000106	Purchase Payment	179.95	0.00	179.95
114	1200	IRONCL	09102000	000107	Purchase Payment	3000.00	0.00	3000.00
115	1200	TROJAN	09102000	000108	Purchase Payment	141.00	0.00	141.00
116	1200	MUSWEL	09102000	000109	Purchase Payment	1240.00	0.00	1240.00
117	1200	NORTHL	09102000	000110	Purchase Payment	1175.00	0.00	1175.00
118	1200	STERLI	09102000	000111	Purchase Payment	642.37	0.00	642.37
119	1200	UNIFOR	09102000	000112	Purchase Payment	763.75	0.00	763.75
120	1200	VANCEN	09102000	000113	Purchase Payment	19059.44	0.00	19059.44
122	1200	CHIEFT	09102000	000114	Purchase Payment	1175.00	0.00	1175.00
129	1200	FLOORS	09102000	000115	Purchase Payment	962.21	0.00	962.21
131	1200	HARROW	09102000	000116	Purchase Payment	2767.77	0.00	2767.77
133	1200	MATTHI	09102000	000117	Purchase Payment	3192.48	0.00	3192.48
135	1200	HIGHPI	09102000	000118	Purchase Payment	2364.69	0.00	2364.69
136	1200	HIGHPI	09102000	000118	Payment on Account	1135.31	0.00	1135.31

| | | | **Totals** | : | | 43,863.98 | 0.00 | 43,863.98 |

Blitz Limited
Day Books: Bank Payments (Summary)

Date from: 09/10/2000   Bank From:
Date to: 09/10/2000   Bank To: 99999999

Transaction From: 1   N/C **From**:
Transaction To: 133   N/C **To**: ZZZZZZZZ :

Dept From: 0
Dept To: 999

No	Tp	A/C	Date	Chq. No	Details	Net	VAT	T/c	
137	BP	8203	09102000	000119	Training course	220.00	38.50	T1	258.50
138	BP	7400	09102000	000120	Train ticket	105.50	0.00	T0	105.50
139	BP	8205	09102000	000121	Refreshments	84.00	14.70	T1	98.70
			Totals			409.50	53.20		462.70

Bank balance

You can print or display the Activity on the bank current account by selecting it in the Nominal Ledger (code 1200). Accept the default 'From' date and specify a 'To' date of 09/10/2000. You should get a credit balance of £10,380.61.

(Note: the Tp column indicates bank receipt [BR], purchase payment [PP], payment on account [PA], or bank payment [BP]).

Nominal Activity

Date from: 09/10/2000   N/C **1200**
Date to: 09/10/2000   N/C **To: 1200**

Transaction From: 1
Transaction To: 133

No.	Tp	Date	Refn	Details	Value	Debit	Credit
1	BR	19082000		M Green - shares	20000.00	20000.00	
2	BR	19082000		T Nicholas - shares	20000.00	20000.00	
8	JC	16092000	xxxxx	Wages and salaries	6053.93		6053.93
107	PP	09102000	100	Purchase Payment	117.50		117.50
108	PP	09102000	101	Purchase Payment	540.50		540.50
109	PP	09102000	100102	Purchase Payment	376.00		376.00
110	PP	09102000	103	Purchase Payment	1493.78		1493.78
111	PP	09102000	104	Purchase Payment	332.23		332.23
112	PP	09102000	105	Purchase Payment	3205.00		3205.00
113	PP	09102000	106	Purchase Payment	179.95		179.95
114	PP	09102000	107	Purchase Payment	3000.00		3000.00
115	PP	09102000	108	Purchase Payment	141.00		141.00
116	PP	09102000	109	Purchase Payment	1240.00		1240.00
117	PP	09102000	110	Purchase Payment	1175.00		1175.00
118	PP	09102000	111	Purchase Payment	642.37		642.37
119	PP	09102000	112	Purchase Payment	763.75		763.75
120	PP	09102000	113	Purchase Payment	19059.44		19059.44
122	PP	09102000	114	Purchase Payment	1175.00		1175.00
129	PP	09102000	115	Purchase Payment	962.21		962.21
131	PP	09102000	116	Purchase Payment	2767.77		2767.77
133	PP	09102000	117	Purchase Payment	3192.48		3192.48
135	PP	09102000	118	Purchase Payment	2364.69		2364.69
136	PA	09102000	118	Payment on Account	1135.31		1135.31
137	BP	09102000	119	Training course	258.50		258.50
138	BP	09102000	120	Train ticket	105.50		105.50
139	BP	09102000	121	Refreshments	98.70		98.70
				Totals :		40000.00	50380.61
				History Balance :			10380.61

Balance on the creditors control account

You should repeat the same exercise but this time select the creditors control account - account code 2100. The balance on the account is now £6,113.86.

Spreadsheet

If you did this exercise you should fairly easily have been able to explain that the No. column lists the number of the transaction – the number allocated by the Sage package to each consecutive transaction that you post. The Ref column shows either the cheque number or the credit note number or, in the case of discounts, the original invoice number.

The problem with the totals is that some items have been included that should not have been included and one item has been omitted. To put things right you should have deleted the amounts shown in boxes ('cells') 16, 19, 21 and 23 in columns G and I, and you should have entered the amount 1,135.31 in cell I25.

As part of your tidying up exercise you could have changed the lines in capitals to small letters, made the headings italic, given the spreadsheet a title, and so on. No 'answer' is shown because many 'answers' are acceptable, although they will be different in appearance.

Answer to Assignment 4
Receipts from customers

The assignment requires you to process a variety of transactions.

Posting new invoices

The procedures for entering details of new customer accounts and producing invoices were described in Chapter 5. You should use the Invoicing option in the main window, and:

(a)   The Service window to produce the invoice.

(b)   The Print Invoices button to print the invoices.

(c)   The Update Ledgers button to post the transactions to the ledgers.

The nominal account code should be 4000 for the invoice to Bradley Fashions (contract cleaning) and 4002 for the invoice to A Rathod (domestic services).

One of the two invoices is reproduced on the next page. If you have forgotten how to produce invoices, look again at Chapter 4.

Receipts - payment in full for invoices

Posting the 12 receipts transactions listed in item (2) in the information for the assignment should not present any difficulties. Click on the Bank button and then on the Customer button.

These are all payments in full for one or more outstanding invoices. In every case, you can use the Pay in Full button for allocating the receipt to an invoice. Make sure you include references for each receipt.

Click on Save when you have posted the details for each customer and move on to the next customer.

In the case of two customers (D J Hargreaves and A Rose Ltd) the amount received is in payment for just one invoice, when there are two outstanding invoices on the account. In cases where it is not clear what is being paid you should either allocate the payment to the earliest invoices on the account or record the payment as a payment on account - until it can be established which invoices are being paid.

Invoice   Page 1
10051
12/10/2000

BLITZ LTD

25 APPLE ROAD
LONDON
N12 3PP

BRADLEY FASHIONS LTD
18 HOSPITAL BRIDGE
ROAD
ST ALBANS
HERTS

BRADLE

Quantity Details	Disc%	Disc Amount	Net Amount	VAT Amount
Contract cleaning services	0.00	0.00	820.00	143.50

Total Net	820.00
Total VAT	143.50
Carriage	0.00
Invoice Total	963.50

T P Paul

The invoice of £70.50 for T P Paul can be cancelled by creating a credit note for £70.50. You can do this by using the SrvCredit option in the Invoicing window.

Discounts

Begin by checking that the discount has been correctly calculated. If you disagree with the customer's calculation, you would have to speak to your supervisor or (if authorised to do so) telephone the customer to query the mistake.

To check the calculation you first need to find out the transaction number(s) by looking up the customers' Activity and then the net amount due by looking at these transactions in the Financials listing.

The transactions are numbers 103 and numbers 91, 92 and 93. In the case of Rapid Pizzas, the discount of £9.66 must be divided into three chunks.

Transaction no	Net amount	Discount (5%)
103	1210.00	60.50
91	60.00	3.00
92	91.20	4.56
93	42.00	2.10
		9.66

Post this by returning to the Bank Customer receipts window and entering the relevant account code. In each case (Payne Properties and Rapid Pizzas) you should remember to follow these procedures.

(a) Make sure you enter a reference for the invoice being paid.

(b) Tab through the Amount box leaving it blank.

(c) Tab through the Receipt box leaving it blank.

(d) Enter the amount of the discount in the appropriate box and press Tab. The amount in the Receipt box will automatically be calculated.

(e) Click on Save.

Deductions for credit notes

Stay in the Bank Customer window. For each customer account, enter the invoice as the reference number. Leave the Amount box blank and Tab to the Receipt box. Click on Pay in Full in each case.

Part payments

The part payments by Elite Caterers and Campbell Consultants should be processed either:

(a)   By *keying in* the amount of the payment in the Amount box, and then Tabbing to the Receipt box of the first invoice listed and clicking on Pay in Full; *or*

(b)   By Tabbing through the Amount box and then *keying in* the amount of the payment in the first Receipt box you come to. Then you can just click on Save.

Clough and Partners

This payment of an invoice plus a payment on account must be processed by *typing* the amount received in the Amount box. When you click on Save after entering the receipt details, accept the Post as a Payment on Account message.

M Zakis Ltd

Before you process the receipt from M Zakis, you must set up an account for the (new) customer in the Customers ledger. Type in the code MZAKIS and press Tab. Click on **New** when the Customer Account window appears.

When you have set up and saved the account, return to the Bank Customer window and process the receipt.

Writing off small unpaid balances

Process the payments from A T Haslam and R P Marwood in the same way as the part payments from other customers. There will be unpaid balances of £0.18 and £0.05 respectively. (If you forgot to take a note of these amounts you can find the unpaid balance by searching the list in the Customers window.)

Click on Tools at the top of the screen, then on Write Off, Refund, Return. Choose the Sales Ledger amendments option. From the area list pick Write off Customer Transactions below a value. To be safe a good value to enter is 0.50, although you could put in a higher amount – say 1 (£1.00) – if you wish. Select both the accounts by highlighting them and click on Next. Confirm that you are writing off 23p by clicking on Finish.

Bank receipts

The five items of bank receipts from non-credit customers should be entered by using the Receipt button in the Bank Accounts window.

For each transaction, select the correct nominal ledger code (N/C). This should be 4001 for window cleaning, 4002 for domestic services and 4100 for materials sales. Enter the five transactions separately. Just key in the single number 4 and then click on the Finder button (or press F4) if you forget which nominal Sales account is which.

Reports

You should print, preview or display a *Day Books: Customer Receipts* Summary report and a *Day Books: Bank Receipts* Summary report, using the reports button in the Bank window.

The Reports window will allow you to specify the parameters for items to be listed. Specify a Date Range of 12/10/2000 to 12/10/2000.

The total amount for the report is as follows.

	Net £	Tax £	Gross £
Customer Receipts	10,508.25	0.00	10,508.25
Bank Receipts	352.00	61.60	413.60
Total	10,860.25	61.60	10,921.85

P Leyser refund

Click on Tools (at the top of the screen, then on Write Off, Refund, Return, and choose the Sales Ledger option. Choose Customer Invoice Refund from the list that appears as you click on Next. Scroll down to the LEYSER account and click on Next. The payment will appear in the window. Select it and click on Next again. You are asked which account you want to post the refund to the bank account 1200. Select this and click on Next. If the information given in the next window is correct, click on Finish.

Account balances - nominal ledger

You can establish these using the Activity button in the Nominal window. The balances should be:

Account	N/C code	Debit entries	Credit entries	Balance
Bank current account	1200	50,921.85	50,477.20	444.65
Debtors control account	1100	31,517.67	11,568.23	19,949.44

Account balances - sales ledger

Click on the Customers button and scroll down until you find the account ELITEC. You should find that the balance outstanding on this account is £1,497.81.

Answer to Assignment 5
Other cash transactions

Many of the tasks for this assignment are similar to tasks that were set in Assignments 1-4. There are invoices from new and existing suppliers, invoices to new and existing customers, and payments and receipts. In addition, however, some of the tasks relate to petty cash transactions, journal transactions and a bank reconciliation. Assignment 5 is therefore a wide-ranging test of your competence with Sage.

Setting up the petty cash system

The petty cash system is set up by withdrawing £300 in cash from the bank. This bank-cash transaction should be recorded in the nominal ledger as a journal entry. Click on the Journals button in the Nominal Ledger window. The fields should be completed as follows.

(a)   Reference. Use the cheque number as a reference for the transaction. This is 000122.

(b)   Date 13/10/2000.

(c)   The double entry is as follows. (It doesn't matter whether you do the debit or the credit entry first.)

N/C	Details	T/c	Debit £	Credit £
1200	To petty cash	T9		300.00
1230	From bank account	T9	300.00	

Save the transaction, then press Esc or click on Close.

Invoices from suppliers

The invoices from suppliers can be entered using the Invoices button in the Suppliers window. This allows you to enter new supplier details, where appropriate. The transaction date should be the invoice date, not the date on which you are processing the transactions. Some invoices relate to different items of expense, and so different nominal ledger account codes. For example, the invoice from Great North Hotel should be recorded on three lines, for nominal ledger account codes 7402, 7406 and 7502 respectively. All the purchase invoice transactions should have a tax code T1. Your accuracy in entering the transactions is tested by a later task in the assignment. If you cannot remember how to process supplier invoices, refer back to Chapter 3.

Customer invoices

You should now be familiar with the procedure for entering invoices. Ensure you assign each sales item to the appropriate nominal ledger account code - 4000 for contract cleaning, 4001 for window cleaning, 4002 for domestic services and 4100 for materials sales. All transactions should have a T1 tax code, and a date of 16/10/2000.

Payments to suppliers

To record the payments to suppliers, Click on Bank and then on the Supplier button. Look up the supplier account reference codes if you need to, using the Finder button or the F4 function key to display the supplier accounts on screen.

For the Ace Telephone Answering and ANS Newspaper Group invoices, *key in* the amount paid in the Amount box, then Tab to the Payment box and click on Pay in Full. With the ANS Newspaper Group payment, confirm that the payment on account should be posted.

Before you record the payment from Wells Business Systems you should post the credit note. Use the Calc Net option to allocate the amount correctly.

Receipts from customers

Click on the Customer button in the Bank Accounts window. The receipts from the three customers can be processed in a similar way to the payments to suppliers. Don't forget that there *must* be a reference number. Use the number of the invoice being paid.

V J Richardson cheque

This transaction can be posted as a journal entry. Click on the Journals button in the Nominal Ledger window. The entries in the main part of the screen should be:

N/C	Details	T/c	Debit £	Credit £
1200	Loan - V J Richardson	T9	10000.00	
2300	To bank account	T9		10000.00

Alternatively, you can post the transaction as a bank receipt, using the Receipt button in the Bank Accounts window. The N/C code for the receipt should be 2300, the net amount 10000 and the tax code T9.

Petty cash transactions

Click on the Bank button and then select account 1230 Petty Cash.

To post the payments out of petty cash, just click on the Payments button and a window that will be familiar by now will appear.

To post the receipt into petty cash the N/C code 4001 should be used (for window cleaning sales). Enter 72 as the Net amount, then click on the Calc Net button to calculate the VAT automatically. The final entry should be for a net cash receipt of £61.28 and VAT of £10.72.

To produce reports of Cash Payments (or Receipts), click on the Reports button in the Bank window and scroll down until you find the appropriate option. Select the date range 13/10/2000 to 16/10/2000. Print the listing if you have access to a printer. Otherwise, display the listing on screen. An extract from the listing follows.

Blitz Limited

Cash Payments (Summary)

Date from: 13/10/2000
Date to 16/10/2000

Bank From:
Bank To: 99999999

Transaction from: 1
Transaction To: 235

No.	Tp	A/C	Date	Refn	Details	Net	VAT	Total
223	CP	7501	13102000	PC001	POSTAGE STAMPS	24.00	0.00	24.00
224	CP	8205	13102000	PC002	BISCUITS, COFFEE	32.49	0.00	32.49
225	CP	8205	13102000	PC003	MILK	15.20	0.00	15.20
226	CP	7400	13102000	PC004	TAXIS	25.00	0.00	25.00
227	CP	7400	14102000	PC005	TRAIN FARES	9.20	0.00	9.20
228	CP	8205	14102000	PC006	WASHING UP LIQUID	1.75	0.00	1.75
229	CP	7500	14102000	PC007	PHOTOCOPYING	24.00	4.20	28.20
230	CP	7504	15102000	PC008	STATIONERY	37.24	6.52	43.76
231	CP	7400	15102000	PC009	TAXIS	15.00	0.00	15.00
232	CP	8205	16102000	PC010	SANDWICHES, CAKES	38.26	0.00	38.26
233	CP	7304	16102000	PC011	PARKING	7.00	0.00	7.00
234	CP	7400	16102000	PC012	TRAIN FARES	8.40	0.00	8.40
					Totals	237.54	10.72	248.26

Topping up petty cash

Check the balance on the Petty Cash account (N/C 1230) by looking at the list of accounts in and balances in the main Nominal Ledger window. This should show a balance of £123.74.

A cheque for £176.26 cash (£300 - £123.74) must be drawn to top up the petty cash balance to £300.

To post this entry, click on the Journals button in the Nominal Ledger window. The main part of the entry is as follows:

N/C	Details	T/c	Debit £	Credit £
1200	To petty cash	T9		176.26
1230	From bank account	T9	176.26	

Check that the balance on the petty cash account (N/C 1230) is now £300 (look again at the list in the Nominal Ledger window).

Wages and salaries

These transactions can be entered in the nominal ledger accounts as a single journal entry. Click on Journals in the Nominal Ledger window. Key in the date 16/10/2000 and (as instructed) reference J04. The remaining entries should be as follows:

N/C	Description	T/c	Debit £	Credit £
1200	Cash for wages	T9		4133.04
2210	PAYE, 16 Oct	T9		2217.96
2211	Nat Ins, 16 Oct	T9		975.20
7001	Directors salaries	T9	1350.80	
7003	Staff salaries	T9	475.75	
6000	Wages	T9	4859.65	
7006	Employers NI	T9	640.00	

The total debits equal the total credits, therefore you can post these transactions as a single journal entry.

BPP
PROFESSIONAL EDUCATION

Account balances

You can just scroll through the Nominal Ledger window to search for the account balances required by your supervisor. Check that you have the following balances.

N/C		Debit £	Credit £
1100	Debtors control account	25486.83	
1200	Bank – current account	4642.09	
2100	Creditors control account		7677.28
7003	Staff salaries	951.50	
7400	Travelling	301.50	
7700	Equipment hire	503.75	
4000	Sales – contract cleaning		27167.80
4001	Sales – window cleaning		3060.68
4002	Sales – domestic services		1103.90
4100	Sales – materials		1243.74
1230	Petty cash	300.00	
4009	Discounts allowed	101.66	
5009	Discounts taken		258.95

Bank reconciliation

Doing a bank reconciliation can seem a fairly complex task, and you need to be thorough. Your source document is the bank statement itself. You must match every item on the bank statement against a corresponding entry in the nominal ledger bank account.

If you have access to a printer, print out a listing of activity on the Bank Account (1200). Ensure all Sage Windows except the main menu are closed, and select **Settings**, **Change Program Date** from the menu. Key in the date of the bank statement 16/10/2000.

Now click on the Bank and Reconcile. A listing of transactions in the nominal ledger bank account will appear on screen. It is probably best to *maximise* the window for this sort of detailed screen work: click on the upward-pointing triangle in the top right hand corner of the Bank Reconciliation window. Key in the bank statement end balance in the box provided.

The matching process can now begin. When you match a transaction in the nominal ledger bank account with an item on the statement sent by the bank, you must note the match. Do this by clicking on the transaction on screen. The matched transaction will be highlighted in a different colour. Use the Page Down and Page Up keys, the ↑ and ↓ cursor keys, or the scroll bar to search through the list of transactions on screen.

You should be able to match nearly every item on the bank's statement against a transaction in the nominal ledger account. In this exercise, there is an additional item on the bank statement for bank charges. You should post this item to the nominal ledger (N/C code 7901 for bank charges) and you can do this by:

(a) Clicking on the Adjustment button.

(b) Completing the relevant fields in the window that pops up.

When you have matched *every* transaction on the bank's statement against the nominal ledger transactions on screen and you have also entered the bank charges details, you are nearing the end of the bank reconciliation exercise.

Check the balance in the Reconcile Balance field on the screen. This should equal the balance on the bank statement itself (13,381.53). If you have achieved this reconciliation, click on Save.

You can now display or print out a list of reconciled and unreconciled transactions. Click on Reports in the Bank window and obtain reports of Unreconciled Payments and Unreconciled Receipts. Extracts from these are shown below.

Blitz Limited

Unreconciled Payments

Date From: 01/01/2000
Date To: 31/12/2000

Bank From:
Bank To: 99999999

Tp	Date	Refn.	Details	Amount
PP	09102000	000117	Purchase Payment	3192.48
PP	16102000	000123	Purchase Payment	250.00
PP	16102000	000124	Purchase Payment	881.25
PA	16102000	000124	Payment on Account	318.75
PP	16102000	000125	Purchase Payment	1516.50
JC	16102000	000126	TO PETTY CASH	176.26
JC	16102000	J04	CASH FOR WAGES	4133.04
				10468.28

Unreconciled Receipts

Tp	Date	Refn.	Details	Receipts
SR	15102000	10004	Sales Receipt	1000.00
SR	16102000	10046	Sales Receipt	703.24
				1703.24

Overall the position is as follows.

	£
Statement balance	13,381.53
Unpresented payments	(10,468.28)
Unpresented receipts	1,703.24
Trial balance	4,616.49

The trial balance figure is different (by £25.60) from the account balance figure you gave your supervisor earlier. This is because you have now posted the bank charges.

If you load up Assignment 6 you will be able to view the completed reconciliation. (Ensure you change the Program Date to 16/10/2000 or later.)

Answer to Assignment 6: Other credit transactions

Posting credit sales transactions

Remember to code each item for the correct sales account in the nominal ledger, and use tax code T1 for every transaction. Whenever a customer exceeds the existing credit limit, make a note of the name, but continue to process the transaction.

The customers who have exceeded their existing credit limit are:

GHH Commercial Bank
The Keith Group
Norris Hydraulics Ltd
School of Dance
R I Tepper Ltd

Their credit limit should be increased by £1,000 in each case. To do this, after receiving the 'exceeding credit limit' warning and proceeding with the transaction, without closing the Customers Invoice window click on the Customers button, select the relevant customer account and click on Record. The customer details will then appear on screen. Move to the credit limit field (on the Credit Control tab) and key in a new credit limit (overwriting the old limit) by adding 1000 to the limit. Then click on Save and press Esc twice - you will be back in the Service Invoice Window.

Alternatively, you can post all the invoices first and then alter the credit limits of the Customers later.

Cash sales

The cheques received should be posted as Receipts in the Bank Accounts window. Enter each transaction in turn selecting the correct N/C code. The four entries should be as follows, if the tax code is entered as T1.

Deposit No.	N/C	Date	Amount	Description	Amount and tax code
500005	4002	21102000	–	Domestic services	51.7 then Calc Net button
500006	4002	21102000	–	Domestic services	44 then Calc Net
500007	4100	21102000	–	Materials sales	37.6 then Calc Net
500008	4100	23102000	–	Materials sales	52.88 then Calc Net

Save each transaction when you have entered the details. You then get a blank window for the next transaction.

The cash receipts should be posted in account 1230 as Petty Cash Receipts. The two entries should be:

Ref	Date	N/C	Details	Net and Tax
PCR002	22102000	4100	Materials sales	25.38 then Calc Net
PCR003	23102000	4002	Domestic services	35.25 then Calc Net

Invoices received from suppliers

Click on the Service button in the Invoicing window. Enter the three transactions, setting up new supplier accounts where appropriate. The tax code is T1 for all three transactions.

Receipts from customers

Click on the Customer button in the Bank Accounts window. Post the seven transactions. Check the instructions in Chapter 7 if you have forgotten how to do this.

Tab through the main Amount box if you can see at a glance which invoice(s) are being settled. Just click on Pay in Full when you get to the relevant Receipt box (Plus2: Paid box). If it is not clear how the payment should be allocated, *type in* the amount received in the main Amount box and then click on Pay in Full in each of the Receipt boxes. When there is no more money to allocate, click on Save.

You should type in the amounts for S T Chanas, Elite Caterers, and Meakin Media.

Contra entries (Sage Line 50 only)

The accounts of Elite Caterers and Meakin Media can now be settled by contra entries. Take each customer/supplier in turn.

Click on Tools, then on Contra Entries.

(a)   For Elite Caterers, enter both the Sales Ledger A/C and the Purchase Ledger A/C as ELITEC. The screen will display the unpaid invoice balances in the customer account (left-hand side) and the supplier account (right-hand side) for Elite Caterers. Click on each transaction in the sales account and then click on the supplier account transaction. The totals should be the same, and can therefore be set off in full against each other, so just click on OK to post the contra entry.

(b)   For Meakin Media, repeat the procedure. The A/C code is MEAKIN for both the Customers Ledger account and the Suppliers Ledger account. The *first* entry in the customer account and the entry in the supplier account should be selected.

ANS Newspaper Group

Click on Bank, then on Supplier. Post a payment to ANSNEW for £58.75, dated 22 October 2000, cheque number 000127.

Note: The **£58.75** is made up of:

Invoice 621347	553.75
Less Sales invoice 10065 contra	(176.25)
Less payment on account (from assignment 5)	(318.75)
Balance outstanding	**58.75**

Key the amount 58.75 into the £ sign box, then tab down to the *invoice* for advertising (amount £553.75) and click on Pay in Full. Then Save this transaction.

Return to the Contra Entries window and process a contra entry for ANS Newspaper Group, accepting the offer to process a 'part contra'.

If you look at the balance of the ANSNEW account in both the Customers and Suppliers ledgers they should both show a nil balance.

Writing off small unpaid balances

Click on Tools, then on Write Off, Refund, Return and opt for the Sales Ledger. Choose Write Off Customer transaction below a value.

Enter a value of 1.01 (£1.01). The screen will display two unpaid balances.

       CAMPBE   1.00
       CHANAS   0.63

Click on both of these and then click on Next. Use a date of 31/10/2000, click Next and confirm the write offs when asked to do so. The total amount written off is £1.63.

Writing off accounts

Look at the Customers window to find the balances on the accounts ADAMSE and HAYNES. You should do this to establish that E T Adams currently owes nothing to Blitz.

With L Haynes & Co, however, there is an unpaid balance on the account. This must be written off as a bad debt.

To write off the bad debt for L Haynes & Co, click on Tools then on Write Off, Refund, Return, and choose the Sales Ledger. This time select the Write off Customer Accounts option. Choose the account reference HAYNES. Two lines are shown, but both relate to the same invoice. Click Next, enter the date of the write-off and click next again. The amount and date of the write-off will show, if these are correct click Finish.

Credit note

The sales credit note to Owen of London should be posted using the SrvCredit button in the Invoicing window. The entry should be:

A/C	Date	Ref	N/C	Description	Amount	T/c
OWENLO	22102000	004	4000	Credit note	150.00	T1

Correcting the N/C code

A correction to an account code is an accounting error. You must first find the transaction reference number. Open the Suppliers window and select the account AA1MIN. Click on Activity. The transaction history of the account will show the October invoice for £158.27. (This includes VAT.) The transaction number is 186.

Click on File, then on Maintenance then on Corrections. In the window that appears scroll to transaction number 186, highlight it and click on Edit.

Activate the *Splits* tab, Click on Edit again and alter the N/C code. Then click on Close, then on Save and confirm that you wish to post the changes. If you scroll down to the end of the list you can see that the correction has been posted.

Newlite Cleaning Fluids

Check the Activity for NEWLIT in the Suppliers window. You should take a note of the transaction number (17) and the details of the invoice that has been posted incorrectly. Then use File … Maintenance to correct the transaction as just explained.

The details should be:

A/C	NEWLIT
Date	12092000
Inv No	26115
N/C	5000
Details	Cleaning materials
Net Amount	403.00
T/c	T1

The corrected invoice figure is £403.00 net plus VAT of £70.53 giving a total invoice amount of £473.53.

Current balances

To find the current balances on the nominal ledger accounts, simply call up the Nominal Ledger window. Scroll through each account in turn and copy down the balances shown. These should be as follows.

	Code	Balance £	
Bank current account	1200	7073.03	(debit)
Debtors control account	1100	28369.34	(debit)
Creditors control account	2100	7995.65	(credit)
Bad debt write off account	8100	151.32	(debit)
Advertising account	6201	3421.28	(debit)
Sales - contract cleaning	4000	31017.80	(credit)
Sales - window cleaning	4001	4084.68	(credit)
Sales - domestic services	4002	1430.35	(credit)
Sales – materials	4100	1417.34	(credit)

Spreadsheet exercise - Aged Debtors Analysis

The customers owing the five largest amounts are:

A/C	Balance
GHHCOM	3,436.88
OGDENK	3,278.25
KEITHG	3,243.00
NORRIS	2,775.47
ROYALP	1,762.50

You could have found this information in Sage simply by clicking on the word Balance in the main Customers window. This re-sorts the data (smallest balance first), clicking on Balance again will sort in the opposite order (largest balance first).

Customers with a balance of over £1,000 that has been outstanding for more than 30 days are as follows.

A/C	Balance	Current	30 days
OGDENK	3,278.25	564.00	2,714.25
ROYALP	1,762.50	–352.50	2,115.00
GHHCOM	3,436.88	1,703.75	1,733.13
HARVEY	1,715.50	0.00	1,715.50
NORRIS	2,775.47	1,687.77	1,087.70

Spreadsheet exercise – Cash Flow Forecast

The spreadsheet is shown below – in normal format and with formulae displayed. This file is available within the data from the Word and Excel exercises unloaded from the CD (see Chapter 2 for full instructions).

This file is called CashFcastFirstHalf2001Ans.xls.

	A	B	C	D
1	Blitz Limited cashflow forecast			
2	January 2001 - June 2001			
3				
4				£
5				
6	Forecast cash balance, January 1, 2001			5,500
7				
8	Forecast receipts			
9	Cash receipts		4,500	
10	Collections from credit sales		130,000	
11	Total receipts		134,500	
12				
13	Forecast payments			
14	Payments for materials purchased		25,000	
15	Wages and salary payments		52,000	
16	Rent payment		8,000	
17	Power, phone and other payments		22,000	
18	Total payments		107,000	
19				
20	Cash balance, June 30, 2001			33,000
21				

	A	B	C	D
1	Blitz Limited cashflow forecast			
2	January 2001 - June 2001			
3				
4				£
5				
6	Forecast cash balance, January 1, 2001			5500
7				
8	Forecast receipts			
9	Cash receipts		4500	
10	Collections from credit sales		130000	
11	Total receipts		=SUM(C9:C10)	
12				
13	Forecast payments			
14	Payments for materials purchased		25000	
15	Wages and salary payments		52000	
16	Rent payment		8000	
17	Power, phone and other payments		22000	
18	Total payments		=SUM(C14:C17)	
19				
20	Cash balance, June 30, 2001			=D6+C11-C18
21				

P A R T   D

Appendices

Appendix 1:
The Blitz Nominal Ledger –
account codes

The following is a list of the accounts in the nominal ledger of Blitz Limited.

Fixed assets

0010	FREEHOLD PROPERTY
0011	LEASEHOLD PROPERTY
0020	PLANT AND MACHINERY
0021	PLANT AND MACHINERY DEPRECIATION
0030	OFFICE EQUIPMENT
0031	OFFICE EQUIPMENT DEPRECIATION
0040	FURNITURE AND FIXTURES
0041	FURNITURE AND FIXTURES DEPRECIATION
0050	MOTOR VEHICLES
0051	MOTOR VEHICLES DEPRECIATION

Current assets

1001	STOCK
1002	WORK IN PROGRESS
1003	FINISHED GOODS
1100	DEBTORS CONTROL ACCOUNT
1101	SUNDRY DEBTORS
1102	OTHER DEBTORS
1103	PREPAYMENTS
1200	BANK CURRENT ACCOUNT
1210	BANK DEPOSIT ACCOUNT
1220	BUILDING SOCIETY ACCOUNT
1230	PETTY CASH
1240	COMPANY CREDIT CARD
1250	CREDIT CARD RECEIPTS

Current liabilities

2100	CREDITORS CONTROL ACCOUNT
2101	SUNDRY CREDITORS
2102	OTHER CREDITORS
2109	ACCRUALS
2200	SALES TAX CONTROL ACCOUNT
2201	PURCHASE TAX CONTROL LIABILITY
2210	PAYE
2211	NATIONAL INSURANCE
2230	PENSION FUND
2300	LOANS
2310	HIRE PURCHASE
2320	CORPORATION TAX
2330	MORTGAGES

Financed by

3000	ORDINARY SHARES
3001	PREFERENCE SHARES
3100	RESERVES
3101	UNDISTRIBUTED RESERVES
3200	PROFIT AND LOSS ACCOUNT

Sales

4000	SALES - CONTRACT CLEANING
4001	SALES - WINDOW CLEANING
4002	SALES - DOMESTIC SERVICES
4009	DISCOUNTS ALLOWED
4100	SALES MATERIALS
4101	SALES TYPE E
4200	SALES OF ASSETS
4400	CREDIT CHARGES (LATE PAYMENTS)
4900	MISCELLANEOUS INCOME
4901	ROYALTIES RECEIVED
4902	COMMISSIONS RECEIVED
4903	INSURANCE CLAIMS
4904	RENT INCOME
4905	DISTRIBUTION AND CARRIAGE

Purchases

5000	MATERIALS PURCHASED
5001	MATERIALS IMPORTED
5002	MISCELLANEOUS PURCHASES
5003	PACKAGING
5009	DISCOUNTS TAKEN
5100	CARRIAGE

5101	DUTY
5102	TRANSPORT INSURANCE
5200	OPENING STOCK
5201	CLOSING STOCK

Direct expenses

6000	PRODUCTIVE LABOUR
6001	COST OF SALES LABOUR
6002	SUB-CONTRACTORS
6100	SALES COMMISSIONS
6200	SALES PROMOTIONS
6201	ADVERTISING
6202	GIFTS AND SAMPLES
6203	PUBLIC RELATIONS (LIT & BROCHURES)
6900	MISCELLANEOUS EXPENSES

Overheads

7001	DIRECTORS SALARIES
7002	DIRECTORS REMUNERATION
7003	STAFF SALARIES
7004	WAGES - REGULAR
7005	WAGES - CASUAL TEMPORARY STAFF
7006	EMPLOYERS NI
7007	EMPLOYERS PENSIONS
7008	RECRUITMENT EXPENSES
7100	RENT
7102	WATER RATES
7103	GENERAL RATES
7104	PREMISES INSURANCE
7200	ELECTRICITY
7201	GAS
7202	OIL
7203	OTHER HEATING COSTS
7300	FUEL AND OIL
7301	REPAIRS AND SERVICING
7302	LICENCES
7303	VEHICLE INSURANCE
7304	MISCELLANEOUS MOTOR EXPENSES
7400	TRAVELLING
7401	CAR HIRE
7402	HOTELS
7403	UK ENTERTAINMENT
7404	OVERSEAS ENTERTAINMENT
7405	OVERSEAS TRAVELLING
7406	SUBSISTENCE
7500	PRINTING

7501	POSTAGE AND CARRIAGE
7502	TELEPHONE
7503	TELEX/TELEGRAM/FACSIMILE
7504	OFFICE STATIONERY
7505	BOOKS ETC
7600	LEGAL FEES
7601	AUDIT & ACCOUNTANCY FEES
7602	CONSULTANCY FEES
7603	PROFESSIONAL FEES
7700	EQUIPMENT HIRE
7701	OFFICE MACHINE MAINTENANCE
7800	REPAIRS AND RENEWALS
7801	CLEANING
7802	LAUNDRY
7803	PREMISES EXPENSES (MISC)
7900	BANK INTEREST PAID
7901	BANK CHARGES
7902	CURRENCY CHARGES
7903	LOAN INTEREST PAID
7904	HP INTEREST
7905	CREDIT CHARGES

Miscellaneous

8000	DEPRECIATION
8001	PLANT & MACHINERY DEPRECIATION
8002	FURNITURE/FIX/FITTINGS DEPRECIATION
8003	VEHICLE DEPRECIATION
8004	OFFICE EQUIPMENT DEPRECIATION
8100	BAD DEBT WRITE OFF
8102	BAD DEBT PROVISION
8200	DONATIONS
8201	SUBSCRIPTIONS
8202	CLOTHING COSTS
8203	TRAINING COSTS
8204	INSURANCE
8205	REFRESHMENTS
9998	SUSPENSE ACCOUNT
9999	MISPOSTINGS ACCOUNT

Appendix 2:
Shortcut keys

The table below shows the various functions assigned in Sage to the F keys along the top of the keyboard. You can view this key from within Sage by selecting **Help**, **Shortcut Keys** from the pull-down menu.

Index

Absolute cell references	18
Account balances	132
Account reference codes	51
Accounting errors	160
Active cell	4
Activity window	50
Aged debtors analysis	159
Aged debtors list	159
Allocating receipts	125
Analysis Total box	125
Assignments: loading data	45
Assumptions	30
Back ups	44
Back-up	33
Bad debt	155
Bank button	109, 124
Bank charges	147
Bank reconciliations	144
Bank statement	147
Bank transactions	144
Bank-cash transactions	141
Blitz Limited	44
Book Balance (at Date)	146
Bounced cheques	128
Buttons	43
Calculate Net button	71, 118, 134
Calculator	88
Carriage	91
Case study	44
Cash flow projection	15
Cell	4, 5
Cell protection.	33
Chart wizard	28
Charts	26
Cheque No.	110
Cheque printing	119
Collecting unpaid invoices	158
Column	4
Column width	13
Columns	12
Conditions	24
Contra entries	152
Control	33
Corrections button	162

Credit limit exceeded	154
Credit limits	83
Credit notes	95, 96, 115, 127
Credit notes received	73
Credits button	73
Criteria button	69, 96
Ctrl + Z	10
Currency	65
Currency format	31
Customer button (receipts)	124
Customer Order No.	90
Customer queries	100
Customer receipts	127
Customers: new	82
Customers window	50, 82
Date	70
Date Range	76
Day books	74
Debit and credit entries	142
Debit/Credit (journals)	143
Def N/C box	65
Def Tax Code box	65
Defaults	65
Delete	10
Delivery Address	90
Details	87
Discard option	92
Discounts	114, 128
Division	12
Duplicate copies	98
Duplicate invoices	101
Editing data	10
Errors	44, 160
Escape key	44, 50
F2 (edit)	10
F4 ('Quick Reference') function key	118
F8	71
F9	71
File output option	75
File Maintenance	161
File View windows	77
Filling	11

Financials button 52
Finder button 68
Finish 157
Fixed format 31
Footer button 90
Formatting 31
Formatting numbers 31
Formula bar 5
Formulae 5, 17, 21
Formulae with conditions 25
Function key F2 (edit) 10
Function key F4 18, 50, 68, 70
Function key F8 67, 71
Function key F9 71

General format 31
Go To (F5) 10
Graphs 26
Gridlines 31

Headings and layout 16
Hidden format 31

Icons 43
Index of invoices 84, 91
Index tabs 63
Inserting 12
Invoice 67, 85
Invoice Date 86
Invoice details 91
Invoice number 70, 86
Invoice numbers 84
Invoices: locating 106
Invoices: allocation of payments to 109
Invoices: duplicate 101
Invoices: printing 96
Invoices: refunding if already paid 130
Invoicing for the sale of goods 92
Invoicing window 83

Journal entries 141, 143
Journal vouchers 141
Journals button 142

Keyboard 44
Keyboard shortcut 13

Labels 30
Ledgers: updating 98
Letters 160
Linking worksheets 35
Loading the data for assignments 45

Maintenance 161
Microsft excel 54
Microsft word 54
Mouse 44
Multiplication 12
Multi-sheet spreadsheets 34

Net amount 71
New customers 82
Nominal accounts and codes 52
Nominal code 88, 91
Nominal ledger 52
Nominal Ledger button 52
Non-accounting errors 160
Notes 90
Number format 31

Opening Balance 146
Opening data 49
Order Details 89
Output 75
Overdue payments 158

Page Width 98
Paid in Full 111, 125, 162
Part payment 125
Part payments 112
Password 42
Passwords 34
Pay in Full button 111, 125
Paying off the balance on an account 112
Paying specific invoices 112
Payment button 117
Payment on account 126
Payments:posting 109
Payments on account 116
Payments with order (bank receipts) 132
Percent format 31
Petty cash transactions 140
Posting invoices 72

Power (^)	6
Predetermined cheque amount	111
Preview	75, 98
Price box	88
Print button	96
Printer output option	75
Printing	97
Producing cheques	119
Producing invoices	83
Product button	83, 93
Product code	93
Purchase ledger (see Suppliers)	62
Queries	100, 120
Range	11
Receipt button (bank)	132
Receipts	124, 125, 134
Reconcile Balance	146
Reconciliation procedures	146
Refunds	130
Relative cell references	18
Reminder letters	160
Reports	74, 119, 135
Reports for receipts	135
Returned cheques	128
Rounding errors	32
Rows	4, 12
SA (sales payment on account)	125
Sales ledger (see Sales ledger)	82
Sage software: quitting	44
Sales account codes	52
SC (sales credit note)	125
Service button	83
SI (sales invoice)	125
Spreadsheet calculations	23
Spreadsheet formatting	30
Spreadsheet formulae	5
Spreadsheet rounding errors	32
Spreadsheets and word processing software	34
Statement Balance	146
Statement button	159
Statements	159
Sum	5, 11
Supplier details	62

Suppliers: new	62
Suppliers button	49
Suppliers ledger data	49
Suppliers window	50
Tab key	44
Task bar	43
Tax code (VAT)	71, 91, 118
Three dimensional spreadsheets	34
Titles	30
Toolbar	13
Tp column	110, 125
Transaction numbers	76
Transaction Range	76
Trial balance	52
Uncleared items	146
Undoing actions (Ctrl + Z)	10
Unit Price	94
Unpaid invoices	158
Update Ledgers report	98
Updating the ledgers	98, 99
What if? analysis	21
Wildcard character	69
Word	54
Word processing software	55
Writing off a transaction	158
Writing off an account	156
Writing off bad debts	155
Writing off small amounts	130
Zoom	98

See overleaf for information on other
BPP products and how to order

AAT Order

To BPP Professional Education, Aldine Place, London W12 8AW

Tel: 020 8740 2211. Fax: 020 8740 1184

E-mail: Publishing@bpp.com Web:www.bpp.com

Mr/Mrs/Ms (Full name)

Daytime delivery address

Postcode

E-mail

Daytime Tel

	4/04 Texts	4/04 Kits	Special offer	8/04 Passcards	Success CDs
FOUNDATION (£14.95 except as indicated)				Foundation	
Units 1 & 2 Receipts and Payments	☐	☐	Foundation Sage Bookeeping and Excel Spreadsheets CD-ROM free if ordering all Foundation Text and Kits, including Units 21 and 22/23	£6.95 ☐	£14.95 ☐
Unit 3 Ledger Balances and Initial Trial Balance	(Combined Text & Kit) ☐				
Unit 4 Supplying Information for Mgmt Control	(Combined Text & Kit) ☐				
Unit 21 Working with Computers (£9.95)	☐				
Unit 22/23 Healthy Workplace/Personal Effectiveness (£9.95)	☐				
Sage and Excel for Foundation (Workbook with CD-ROM £9.95)	☐				
INTERMEDIATE (£9.95 except as indicated)					
Unit 5 Financial Records and Accounts	☐	☐	☐	£5.95 ☐	£14.95 ☐
Unit 6/7 Costs and Reports (Combined Text £14.95)	☐	☐		£5.95 ☐	
Unit 6 Costs and Revenues		☐			£14.95 ☐
Unit 7 Reports and Returns		☐			
TECHNICIAN (£9.95 except as indicated)					
Unit 8/9 Core Managing Performance and Controlling Resources	☐	☐		£5.95 ☐	£14.95 ☐
Spreadsheets for Technician (Workbook with CD-ROM)	☐		Spreadsheets for Technicians CD-ROM free if take Unit 8/9 Text and Kit		
Unit 10 Core Managing Systems and People (£14.95)	☐	☐	☐	£5.95 ☐	£14.95 ☐
Unit 11 Option Financial Statements (A/c Practice)	(Combined Text & Kit) ☐	☐			
Unit 12 Option Financial Statements (Central Govnmt)	☐	☐		£5.95 ☐	
Unit 15 Option Cash Management and Credit Control	☐	☐		£5.95 ☐	
Unit 17 Option Implementing Audit Procedures	☐	☐		£5.95 ☐	
Unit 18 Option Business Tax FA04 (8/04) (£14.95)	(Combined Text & Kit) ☐	☐		£5.95 ☐	
Unit 19 Option Personal Tax FA04 (8/04) (£14.95)	(Combined Text & Kit) ☐	☐		£5.95 ☐	
TECHNICIAN 2003 (£9.95)					
Unit 18 Option Business Tax FA03 (8/03 Text & Kit)	☐	☐			
Unit 19 Option Personal Tax FA03 (8/03 Text & Kit)	☐	☐			
SUBTOTAL	£	£	£	£	£

TOTAL FOR PRODUCTS £

POSTAGE & PACKING

Texts/Kits	First	Each extra
UK	£3.00	£3.00
Europe*	£6.00	£4.00
Rest of world	£20.00	£10.00 £
Passcards		
UK	£2.00	£1.00
Europe*	£3.00	£2.00
Rest of world	£8.00	£8.00 £
Success CDs		
UK	£2.00	£1.00
Europe*	£3.00	£2.00
Rest of world	£8.00	£8.00 £

TOTAL FOR POSTAGE & PACKING £

(Max £12 Texts/Kits/Passcards - deliveries in UK)

Grand Total (Cheques to *BPP Professional Education*)

I enclose a cheque for (incl. Postage) £

Or charge to Access/Visa/Switch

Card Number

CV2 No *last 3 digits on signature strip*

Expiry date

Start Date

Issue Number (Switch Only)

Signature

We aim to deliver to all UK addresses inside 5 working days; a signature will be required. Orders to all EU addresses should be delivered within 6 working days. All other orders to overseas addresses should be delivered within 8 working days. * Europe includes the Republic of Ireland and the Channel Islands.

See overleaf for information on other
BPP products and how to order

AAT Order

To BPP Professional Education, Aldine Place, London W12 8AW
Tel: 020 8740 2211. Fax: 020 8740 1184
E-mail: Publishing@bpp.com Web:www.bpp.com

Mr/Mrs/Ms (Full name) _____
Daytime delivery address _____
_____ Postcode _____
Daytime Tel _____ E-mail _____

OTHER MATERIAL FOR AAT STUDENTS	8/04 Texts	3/03 Text	3/04 Text
FOUNDATION (£5.95)			
Basic Maths and English	☐		
INTERMEDIATE (£5.95)			
Basic Bookkeeping (for students exempt from Foundation)	☐	☐	
FOR ALL STUDENTS (£5.95)			
Building Your Portfolio (old standards)	☐		
Building Your Portfolio (new standards)			
Basic Costing			☐

AAT PAYROLL

	Finance Act 2004 **8/04** December 2004 and June 2005 assessments	**Finance Act 2003** **9/03** June 2004 exams only

Special offer Take Text and Kit together £44.95 ☐ (Finance Act 2004)
Special offer Take Text and Kit together £44.95 ☐ (Finance Act 2003)

For assessments in 2005 £44.95 ☐
For assessments in 2004 £44.95 ☐

LEVEL 2 Text (£29.95)	☐
LEVEL 2 Kit (£19.95)	☐
	£ ___
LEVEL 3 Text (£29.95)	☐
LEVEL 3 Kit (£19.95)	☐
	£ ___
SUBTOTAL	£ ___

TOTAL FOR PRODUCTS £ ___

POSTAGE & PACKING

Texts/Kits	First	Each extra	
UK	£3.00	£3.00	£
Europe*	£6.00	£4.00	£
Rest of world	£20.00	£10.00	£
Passcards			
UK	£2.00	£1.00	£
Europe*	£3.00	£2.00	£
Rest of world	£8.00	£8.00	£
Tapes			
UK	£2.00	£1.00	£
Europe*	£3.00	£2.00	£
Rest of world	£8.00	£8.00	£

TOTAL FOR POSTAGE & PACKING £ ___
(Max £12 Texts/Kits/Passcards - deliveries in UK)

Grand Total (Cheques to *BPP Professional Education*) £ ___
I enclose a cheque for (incl. Postage) ☐
Or charge to Access/Visa/Switch
Card Number ☐☐☐☐ ☐☐☐☐ ☐☐☐☐ ☐☐☐☐
CV2 No ☐☐☐ last 3 digits on signature strip

Expiry date ___ / ___ Start Date ___ / ___

Issue Number (Switch Only) ___

Signature _____

We aim to deliver to all UK addresses inside 5 working days; a signature will be required. Orders to all EU addresses should be delivered within 6 working days. All other orders to overseas addresses should be delivered within 8 working days. * Europe includes the Republic of Ireland and the Channel Islands.

Review Form & Free Prize Draw – Bookkeeping with Sage and Spreadsheets with Excel (4/04)

All original review forms from the entire BPP range, completed with genuine comments, will be entered into one of two draws on 31 January 2005 and 31 July 2005. The names on the first four forms picked out on each occasion will be sent a cheque for £50.

Name: _____   Address: _____

_____

_____

How have you used this Workbook?
(Tick one box only)

☐ Home study (book only)

☐ On a course: college _____

☐ With 'correspondence' package

☐ Other _____

Why did you decide to purchase this Workbook? *(Tick one box only)*

☐ Have used BPP Texts/Kits in the past

☐ Recommendation by friend/colleague

☐ Recommendation by a lecturer at college

☐ Saw advertising

☐ Other _____

During the past six months do you recall seeing/receiving any of the following?
(Tick as many boxes as are relevant)

☐ Our advertisement in *Accounting Technician* magazine

☐ Our advertisement in *Pass*

☐ Our brochure with a letter through the post

Which (if any) aspects of our advertising do you find useful?
(Tick as many boxes as are relevant)

☐ Prices and publication dates of new editions

☐ Information on Interactive Text content

☐ Facility to order books off-the-page

☐ None of the above

Have you used other BPP Texts and Kits?   ☐ Yes   ☐ No

Your ratings, comments and suggestions would be appreciated on the following areas

	Very useful	Useful	Not useful
Files on CD	☐	☐	☐
Activities and answers	☐	☐	☐
Assignments and answers	☐	☐	☐

	Excellent	Good	Adequate	Poor
Overall opinion of this Workbook	☐	☐	☐	☐

Do you intend to continue using BPP products?   ☐ Yes   ☐ No

The BPP author of this edition can be e-mailed at: barrywalsh@bpp.com

Please return this form to Janice Ross, BPP Professional Education, FREEPOST, London W12 8BR

Please note any further comments and suggestions/errors on the reverse of this page.

Review Form & Free Prize Draw (continued)

Please note any further comments and suggestions/errors below

Free Prize Draw Rules

1 Closing date for 31 January 2005 draw is 31 December 2004. Closing date for 31 July 2005 draw is 30 June 2005.

2 Restricted to entries with UK and Eire addresses only. BPP employees, their families and business associates are excluded.

3 No purchase necessary. Entry forms are available upon request from BPP Professional Education. No more than one entry per title, per person. Draw restricted to persons aged 16 and over.

4 Winners will be notified by post and receive their cheques not later than 6 weeks after the relevant draw date.

5 The decision of the promoter in all matters is final and binding. No correspondence will be entered into.

AAT

Business Tax FA 2020

Level 4

Professional Diploma in Accounting

Course Book

For assessments from January to December 2021

Fifth edition 2020

ISBN 9781 5097 3407 8
ISBN (for internal use only) 9781 5097 3406 1

British Library Cataloguing-in-Publication Data
A catalogue record for this book is available from the British Library

Published by

BPP Learning Media Ltd
BPP House, Aldine Place
142-144 Uxbridge Road
London W12 8AA

www.bpp.com/learningmedia

Printed in the United Kingdom

Your learning materials, published by BPP Learning Media Ltd, are printed on paper obtained from traceable sustainable sources.

Contents

		Page
Introduction to the course		iv
Skills bank		vii
Chapter 1	Tax framework	1
Chapter 2	Computing trading income	15
Chapter 3	Capital allowances	37
Chapter 4	Computing corporation tax	63
Chapter 5	Taxing unincorporated businesses	79
Chapter 6	Partnerships	101
Chapter 7	National insurance	119
Chapter 8	Losses	127
Chapter 9	Self-assessment for individuals	147
Chapter 10	Self-assessment for companies	165
Chapter 11	Chargeable gains – the basics	181
Chapter 12	Further aspects of chargeable gains	201
Chapter 13	Share disposals	215
Chapter 14	Reliefs for chargeable gains	239
Activity answers		265
Test your learning: answers		311
Tax tables and reference material		349
Bibliography		377
Index		379

Introduction to the course

Syllabus overview

This unit introduces the student to UK taxation relevant to businesses. It is about the computing of business taxation, preparation of tax returns and how taxation has an impact on the running of a business for sole traders, partnerships and limited companies.

In learning how to prepare tax computations, students will gain skills in the tax treatment of capital expenditure, and the adjustment of accounting profits for tax purposes for sole traders, partnerships and limited companies. In addition, they will be able to allocate profits between partners in a partnership and be able to calculate National Insurance (NI) contributions for the self-employed.

The student will become familiar with the completion of tax returns. They will know when these returns need to be filed with the UK's Revenue and Customs authority (HMRC), and the implications of errors in tax returns, the late filing of returns and the late payment of tax. They will understand how to compute tax on the sale of capital assets and they will have an introduction to some of the tax reliefs available to businesses.

Tax advice is an important part of many accountancy roles. Students will be able to discuss the ethical issues facing business owners and managers in reporting their business tax and the responsibilities that an agent has in giving advice on tax issues to business clients.

Business Tax is an optional unit.

Test specification for this unit assessment

Assessment method	Marking type	Duration of assessment
Computer based assessment	Partially computer / partially human marked	2 hours

	Learning outcomes	Approximate weighting
1	Complete tax returns for sole traders and partnerships and prepare supporting tax computations	29%
2	Complete tax returns for limited companies and prepare supporting tax computations	19%
3	Provide advice on the UK's tax regime and its impact on sole traders, partnerships and limited companies	15%
4	Advise business clients on tax reliefs, and their responsibilities and their agents' responsibilities in reporting taxation to HMRC	19%
5	Prepare tax computations for the sale of capital assets	18%
Total		**100%**

Assessment structure

2 hours duration

Competency is 70%

Analysis of the sample paper

The **sample assessment** consisted of 11 tasks as follows:

*Note that this is only a guideline as to what might come up based on the sample paper. The format and content of each task may vary from what we have listed below.

Task	Expected content	Max marks	Chapter ref	Study complete
Task 1	**Adjustment of profits, identification of basis periods, assessable profit and overlap profits for a sole trader.**	10	2,5	
Task 2	**Split of partnership profits for continuing partners** **National insurance**	10	6,7	
Task 3	**Capital allowance computation for a sole trader**	13	3	
Task 4	**A tax return**	6	2,6	
Task 5	**Corporation tax long period of account and losses**	9	4,8	
Task 6	**Payments on account for sole trader** **Filing date for limited company**	7	9,10	
Task 7	**Penalties for sole trader and limited company**	8	1,9,10	
Task 8	**Limited company losses**	5	8	
Task 9	**Current tax issues: IR35**	14	10	
Task 10	**Chargeable gains calculations for limited company**	8	11,12	
Task 11	**Disposal of shares by a limited company**	10	13	

Skills bank

Our experience of preparing students for this type of assessment suggests that to obtain competency, you will need to develop a number of key skills.

What do I need to know to do well in the assessment?

This unit is one of the optional Level 4 units.

To be successful in the assessment you need to:

- Calculate business taxation, prepare tax returns and understand how tax has an impact on the running of a business for sole traders, partnerships and limited companies.

- Apply the tax rules to scenarios given to calculate tax due, be knowledgeable with regard to the administration of tax, the implications of errors, late payment of tax, late filing of returns and also ethical issues facing business owners.

Assumed knowledge

Business Tax is an **optional** unit which requires no assumed knowledge. The Level 4 unit, *Personal Tax*, is associated with this unit, although these units can be taken separately. Knowledge developed in either of these units will be useful in the later study of the other unit.

Assessment style

In the assessment you will complete tasks by:

1   Entering narrative by selecting from drop-down menus of narrative options known as **picklists**

2   Using **drag and drop** menus to enter narrative

3   Typing in numbers, known as **gapfill** entry

4   Entering **ticks**

5   Entering **dates** by selecting from a calendar

6   Writing written explanations in a very basic word processing environment which has limited editing and no spelling or grammar checking functionality

7   Entering detailed calculations in a very basic spreadsheet environment that has limited editing functionality and will not perform calculations for you

You must familiarise yourself with the style of the online questions and the AAT software before taking the assessment. As part of your revision, login to the **AAT website** and attempt their **online practice assessments**.

Answering written questions

In your assessment there will be a written question. The main verbs used for these type of question requirements are as follows, along with their meaning:

- Identify – analyse and select for presentation
- Explain – set out in detail the meaning of
- Discuss – by argument, discuss the pros and cons

Analysing the scenario

Before answering the question set, you need to carefully review the scenario given in order to consider what questions need to be answered, and what needs to be discussed. A simple framework that could be used to answer the question is as follows:

- Point – make the point
- Evidence – use information from the scenario as evidence
- Explain – explain why the evidence links to the point

For example if an assessment task asked us to explain which three of the fundamental ethical principles are most threatened in the following situation:

You are working on a company's corporation tax return, and notice some errors in the previous year's return which has already been filed. Your manager is concerned about the implications for their own career if the errors are disclosed, and has said that you would be considered for promotion if you agreed to keep quiet about the errors.

We could answer as follows:

1   Point – state which principles are most threatened – objectivity, integrity, professional behaviour

2   Evidence – use information from the scenario – the manager is asking me to keep quiet about an error and offered to consider me for promotion if I keep quiet

3   Explain – explain why the evidence links to the point – the manager is trying to influence my behaviour (objectivity), the manager wants me to act in a way that is not straightforward and honest (integrity), the manager wants me to behave in a way that is not legal and may discredit the profession (professional behaviour)

Introduction to the assessment

The question practice you do will prepare you for the format of tasks you will see in the *Business Tax* assessment. It is also useful to familiarise yourself with the introductory information you **may** be given at the start of the assessment.

You have **2 hours** to complete this practise assessment.

This assessment contains **11 tasks** and you should attempt to complete every task. Each task is independent. You will not need to refer to your answers in previous tasks. Read every task carefully to make sure you understand what is required.

Task 9 requires extended writing as part of your response to the questions. You should make sure you allow adequate time to complete this task.

Where the date is relevant, it is given in the task data.

You may use minus signs or brackets to indicate negative numbers **unless** task instructions say otherwise.

You must use a full stop to indicate a decimal point.

For example, write 100.57 NOT 100,57 or 100 57

You may use a comma to indicate a number in the thousands, but you don't have to.

For example, 10000 and 10,000 are both acceptable.

If rounding is required, normal mathematical rounding rules should be applied **unless** task instructions say otherwise.

---

1   As you revise, use the **BPP Passcards** to consolidate your knowledge. They are a pocket-sized revision tool, perfect for packing in that last-minute revision.

2   Attempt as many tasks as possible in the **Question Bank**. There are plenty of assessment-style tasks which are excellent preparation for the real assessment.

3   Always **check** through your own answers as you will in the real assessment, before looking at the solutions in the back of the Question Bank.

Key to icons

Key term

A key definition which is important to be aware of for the assessment

Formula to learn

A formula you will need to learn as it will not be provided in the assessment

Formula provided

A formula which is provided within the assessment and generally available as a pop-up on screen

Activity

An example which allows you to apply your knowledge to the technique covered in the Course Book. The solution is provided at the end of the chapter

Illustration

A worked example which can be used to review and see how an assessment question could be answered

Assessment focus point

A high priority point for the assessment

Open book reference

Where use of an open book will be allowed for the assessment

Real life examples

A practical real life scenario

AAT qualifications

The material in this book may support the following AAT qualifications:

AAT Professional Diploma in Accounting Level 4 and AAT Professional Diploma in Accounting at SCQF Level 8.

Supplements

From time to time we may need to publish supplementary materials to one of our titles. This can be for a variety of reasons, from a small change in the AAT unit guidance to new legislation coming into effect between editions.

You should check our supplements page regularly for anything that may affect your learning materials. All supplements are available free of charge on our supplements page on our website at:

www.bpp.com/learning-media/about/students

Improving material and removing errors

There is a constant need to update and enhance our study materials in line with both regulatory changes and new insights into the assessments.

From our team of authors BPP appoints a subject expert to update and improve these materials for each new edition.

Their updated draft is subsequently technically checked by another author and from time to time non-technically checked by a proof reader.

We are very keen to remove as many numerical errors and narrative typos as we can but given the volume of detailed information being changed in a short space of time we know that a few errors will sometimes get through our net.

We apologise in advance for any inconvenience that an error might cause. We continue to look for new ways to improve these study materials and would welcome your suggestions. If you have any comments about this book, please use the review form at the back.

These learning materials are based on the qualification specification released by the AAT in January 2020.

Tax framework

1

Learning outcomes

4.3	Discuss the responsibilities relating to tax for the business and its agents
	• The distinction between tax planning, tax avoidance and tax evasion
	• AAT's ethical standards relating to tax advice and professional conduct in relation to taxation

Assessment context

This chapter provides you with important background to your syllabus and helps you to distinguish between illegal and legal tax measures as well as ethical and unethical behaviour.

You probably will not have to calculate income tax payable in your assessment but you need to know how this works so you can understand other parts of the syllabus (eg loss relief).

Qualification context

You will not see these areas again unless you study the *Personal Tax* unit.

Business context

A tax practitioner needs to know the duties and obligations the taxpayer owes to HMRC.

A tax practitioner needs to know and understand the detailed tax rules.

A tax practitioner needs to adhere to AAT's ethical standards when giving tax advice and dealing with clients.

Chapter overview

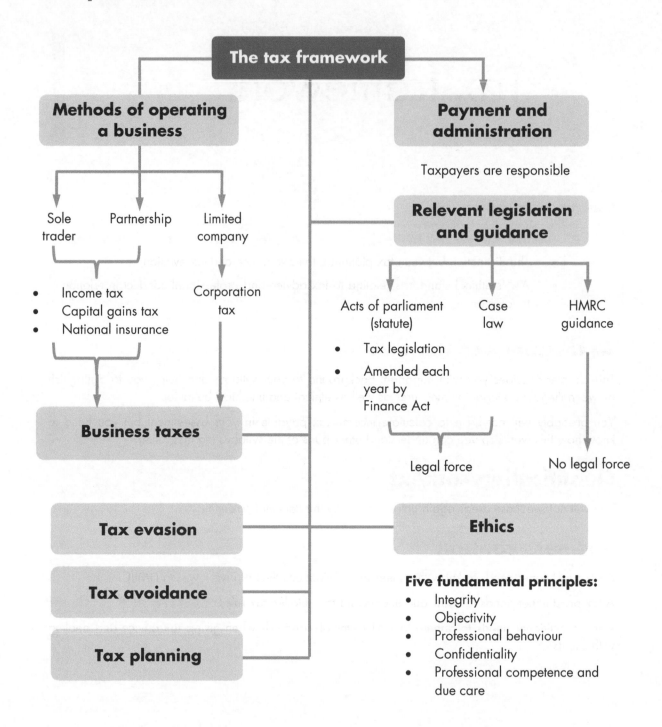

The tax framework

Methods of operating a business

Sole trader Partnership Limited company

- Income tax
- Capital gains tax
- National insurance

Corporation tax

Business taxes

Payment and administration

Taxpayers are responsible

Relevant legislation and guidance

Acts of parliament (statute)
- Tax legislation
- Amended each year by Finance Act

Case law

HMRC guidance

Legal force

No legal force

Tax evasion

Tax avoidance

Tax planning

Ethics

Five fundamental principles:
- Integrity
- Objectivity
- Professional behaviour
- Confidentiality
- Professional competence and due care

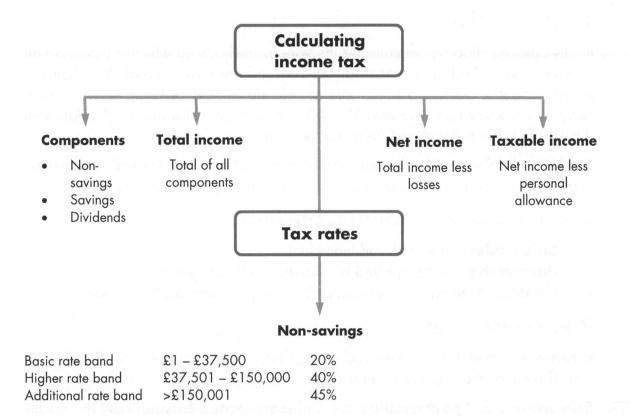

	Non-savings	
Basic rate band	£1 – £37,500	20%
Higher rate band	£37,501 – £150,000	40%
Additional rate band	>£150,001	45%

1 Introduction

In this opening chapter, we consider the various methods by which a business can operate. The method of operation affects how the business is taxed. We then see that the tax law governing businesses is included in Acts of Parliament and in a body of law known as case law. We will also look at ethics and the fundamental differences between legal and illegal tax planning.

Finally, we briefly consider the basics of how to calculate an individual's income tax liability. You may need to be aware of this when dealing with business losses.

2 Method of operating a business

- **Sole trader** – self-employed individual
- **Partnership** – self-employed individuals working together
- **Limited company** – incorporated body legally separate from owners

3 Business taxes

Income is a receipt that is expected to recur (eg trading income) while a **gain** is a one-off profit on the disposal of an asset (eg a factory).

Introduction to business tax

Sole traders and **partnerships are unincorporated businesses**. This means that there is no legal separation between the individual(s) carrying on the business and the business itself.

As a result the individual(s) concerned must pay:

- Income tax on trading income
- Class 2 and Class 4 national insurance contributions (NICs)
- Capital gains tax on disposal of assets

Companies are incorporated businesses. This means they are taxed as separate legal entities independently of their owners.

Companies must pay corporation tax on all profits, including gains on disposal of assets.

4 Payment and administration

Taxpayers who are required to perform self-assessment have a legal responsibility to pay their tax on time and submit a tax return before the deadline.

Employees have tax deducted at source by their employer so, for most people other than the self-employed, there is no need to submit a tax return.

5 Relevant legislation and guidance from HMRC

5.1 Statute law

Most of the rules governing income tax, capital gains tax and corporation tax are laid down in **statute law**, which consists of:

- **Acts of Parliament** (the tax legislation), which are created directly by the Government and amended annually by that year's Finance Act. This text includes the provisions of the **Finance Act 2020.** Assessments will test the provisions of the Finance Act 2020 until 31 December 2021.

- **Statutory Instruments**, which are detailed rules created on behalf of the Government by civil servants to amend/alter an act without parliament having to pass a new act.

5.2 HMRC guidance

To help taxpayers, **HM Revenue & Customs (HMRC)**, which administers tax in the UK, publishes a wide range of guidance material on how it interprets the various acts. Much of this information can be found on HMRC's website **www.hmrc.gov.uk.**

None of this guidance material has the force of law.

5.3 Decided tax cases

A taxpayer and HMRC may disagree over the interpretation of the legislation.

Either party may appeal to the tax tribunal. The tax tribunal is independent of the Government and will listen to both sides of the argument before making a decision.

A judge will rule in favour of one party.

Cases decided by the courts provide guidance on how legislation should be interpreted, and collectively form a second source of tax law known as **case law**.

You will not be expected to quote the names of decided cases in your assessment but you may need to know the principle decided in a case. Where relevant, this will be noted within this Course Book.

6 AAT guidelines on professional ethics

A member shall comply with the following five fundamental principles: (AAT, 2017)

Fundamental principle	What it means
Professional competence and due care	You must maintain professional knowledge and skill (in practice, legislation and techniques) to ensure that a client or employer receives competent professional service.

Fundamental principle	What it means
Integrity	You must be straightforward and honest in all professional and business relationships.
Professional behaviour	You must comply with relevant laws and regulations, and avoid any action that may bring disrepute to the profession.
Confidentiality	You must not disclose confidential professional or business information or use it to your personal advantage, unless you have explicit permission to disclose it, or a legal or professional right or duty to disclose it.
Objectivity	You must not compromise professional or business judgment because of bias, conflict of interest or the undue influence of others.

7 Tax avoidance, tax evasion and tax planning

Introduction to business tax

7.1 Tax evasion

Tax evasion is always illegal. It is when people or businesses deliberately do not declare and account for the taxes that they owe. It includes the hidden economy, where people conceal their presence or taxable sources of income.

Tax evasion can result in fines/imprisonment.

Introduction to business tax

7.2 Tax avoidance

Tax avoidance involves bending the rules of the tax system to gain a tax advantage that Parliament never intended. It often involves contrived, artificial transactions that serve little or no purpose other than to produce this advantage. It involves operating within the letter – but not the spirit – of the law. Most tax avoidance schemes simply do not work, and those who engage in it can find they pay more than the tax they attempted to save once HMRC has successfully challenged them.

7.3 Tax planning

Tax planning involves using tax reliefs for the purpose for which they were intended. For example, claiming tax relief on capital investment, or saving via ISAs or for retirement by making contributions to a pension scheme. However, tax reliefs can be used excessively or aggressively by others than those intended to benefit from them or in ways that clearly go beyond the intention of Parliament. Where this is the case, it is right to take action, because it is important that the tax system is fair and perceived to be so. (HMRC, 2018 (a))

8 Calculating an individual's income tax liability

Illustration 1: Income tax computation for fiscal year (6.4 – 5.4)

	Non-savings income £
Trading income	22,750
Less carry forward loss relief	(5,000)
Employment income	15,200
Property income	3,400
Total income	36,350
Less carry back loss relief	(2,000)
Net income	34,350
Less personal allowance	(12,500)
Taxable income	21,850

8.1 Types of income

An individual may receive different 'components' of income which are taxed at different rates dependant on whether they are non-savings income, savings income or dividend income. In the Business Tax assessment, we only consider income tax on non-savings income. Savings and dividend income are covered in the Personal Tax unit.

We prepare an income tax computation for a **tax year** (or fiscal year) which runs from 6 April to 5 April. The 2020/21 tax year is the tax year on which you will be assessed so we will consider the income an individual receives between 6 April 2020 and 5 April 2021.

All income is added together to produce **total income**.

Some items, such as loss relief, are deducted from total income to give **net income**.

Often a taxpayer will have no deductions from total income so here the terms total income and net income can be used interchangeably.

A personal allowance is then deducted from net income to give **taxable income**. This represents the amount of income they are allowed to earn tax free.

- Taxpayers are entitled to a personal allowance of £12,500.

- However, individuals with net income in excess of £100,000 will have their personal allowance reduced or removed completely.

Activity 1: Taxable income

An individual has the following gross income in 2020/21.

	£
Trading income	16,000
Property income	2,500

(handwritten margin note)
Trading income 16,000
Property income 2500
Total income 18500
Less PA (12500)
Taxable income. 6000

Required

His personal allowance is £12,500. His taxable income is:

£   6000.00 · *(handwritten)*

8.2 Income tax liability

Once we have taxable income, we can then tax the non-savings income. The rate of tax increases as the individual's taxable income increases:

Illustration 2: Calculation of tax liability

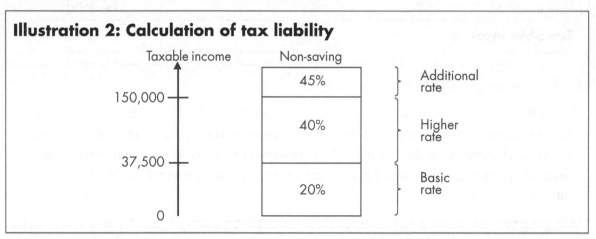

This gives us **tax liability** ie the total amount of tax that should be paid on our income.

Non-savings income is taxed in three bands:

1. Basic rate at 20% for income up to £37,500
2. Higher rate at 40% for income over £37,500 up to £150,000
3. Additional rate at 45% for income over £150,000

Illustration 3: Calculating tax liability

Zoë has taxable income (after the deduction of the personal allowance) of £40,000. This is all non-savings income.

Zoë's income tax liability for 2020/21 is calculated as follows:

Non-savings income	£
£37,500 × 20%	7,500
£2,500 × 40%	1,000
£40,000	
Tax liability	8,500

Illustration 4: Additional rate taxpayer

Clive has taxable income of £190,000 which is all non-savings income.

Clive's income tax liability for 2020/21 is calculated as follows:

Non-savings income	£
£37,500 × 20%	7,500
£112,500 × 40%	45,000
£40,000 × 45%	18,000
£190,000	
Tax liability	70,500

Activity 2: Calculation of income tax liability

Arthur has a salary of £17,000.

Required

Calculate the income tax liability for 2020/21.

Solution

	Non-savings income £
Employment income	17,000
Total income	17,000
Personal Allowance	(12,500)
Taxable income	4,500
NSI 4,500 × 20%	900
Tax liability	900

Assessment focus point

You will not be expected to produce a large income tax computation in your assessment. It is included here for background knowledge and will be useful when you come to study the chapter on Losses.

Chapter summary

- A business may be operated by a sole trader, partnership or company.
- Individuals trading as sole traders or in partnerships pay income tax, capital gains tax and NICs.
- Companies pay corporation tax.
- Companies and individuals must submit regular tax returns.
- It is important to be able to distinguish between tax evasion (illegal) and tax planning/avoidance (legal).
- When working in tax one should adhere to the AAT's five fundamental ethical principles of:
  - Confidentiality
  - Integrity
  - Objectivity
  - Professional behaviour
  - Professional competence and due care
- All of an individual's components of income for a tax year are added together to arrive at total income.
- Trading losses are deducted from total income to arrive at net income.
- A personal allowance is deducted from net income to arrive at taxable income.
- Taxable income is taxed at different rates, depending on which rate band it falls into.

Keywords

- **Confidentiality:** Respecting the confidentiality of client information, and keeping it confidential unless there is a legal or professional obligation to disclose it

- **Integrity:** Being straightforward and honest in all business relationships

- **Net income:** Total income minus, for example, trading losses

- **Objectivity:** Refusing to allow bias, conflicts of interest or undue influence to override professional judgements

- **Professional behaviour:** Compliance with relevant laws and regulations to avoid discrediting the profession

- **Professional competence and due care:** A professional accountant has an obligation to keep their knowledge and skills at a level that enables clients to receive a competent professional service, and to act diligently when providing those services

- **Tax avoidance:** Making use of loopholes in tax legislation in order to reduce tax liabilities. It is currently legal

- **Tax evasion:** To deliberately mislead the tax authorities in order to reduce a tax liability. Tax evasion is illegal

- **Tax planning:** Making use of tax planning opportunities to legally reduce a tax liability

- **Tax year:** The period for which personal tax computations are prepared which runs from 6th April to 5th April

- **Taxable income:** An individual's net income minus the personal allowance

- **Total income:** The total of an individual's components of income for a tax year, from all sources

Test your learning

1   You work in the tax department of a large company. You have prepared the tax return for the quarter, and submitted it to your Finance Director for her review. On reviewing your draft return, she has asked you to amend it to include some expenditure which was incurred shortly after the start of the next year in order reduce the profit for the year. She mentioned at the end of the conversation that your annual performance appraisal was due.

    Which fundamental principle(s) could be breached if you agreed to her request?

    Tick THREE boxes.

	✓
Integrity	✓
Objectivity	✓
Professional competence and due care	
Confidentiality	
Professional behaviour	✓

2   Tax avoidance is illegal and can lead to fines/imprisonment.

    Show whether this statement is true or false.

    Tick ONE box.

	✓
True	
False	✓

3   A company pays income tax on its total profits.

    Show whether this statement is true or false.

    Tick ONE box.

	✓
True	
False	✓

4   **Complete the following statement.**

Each tax year all of an individual's components of income are added together, then a personal allowance is deducted to arrive at:

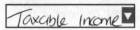 Taxable Income ▼

Picklist:

Net income
Taxable income
Total income

5   Arun (aged 35) has the following gross income in 2020/21:

Trading profits   £25,000
Property income   £12,000

Calculate Arun's income tax liability for 2020/21. Show your answer in whole pounds.

£   4900

37,000
(12500)
24,500   × 20%

4900

Computing trading income

2

Learning outcomes

1.1 and 2.1	**Analyse trading profits and losses for tax purposes for sole traders, partnerships and limited companies** • Apply rules relating to deductible and non-deductible expenditure • Classify expenditure as either revenue or capital expenditure • Adjust accounting profits and losses for tax purposes
1.6	**Complete the individual and partnership tax returns relevant to sole traders and partnerships** • Accurately complete self-employed tax returns • Accurately complete partnership tax returns
4.3	**Discuss the responsibilities relating to tax for the business and its agent** • What the badges of trade are and how they evolved

Assessment context

Adjustment of profits is highly examinable. In your assessment you could be required to show these adjustments on a self-employment tax return.

Qualification context

You will not see these areas again in your qualification.

Business context

Adjusting trading profit is one of the core tasks a tax adviser will have to perform for their client.

Chapter overview

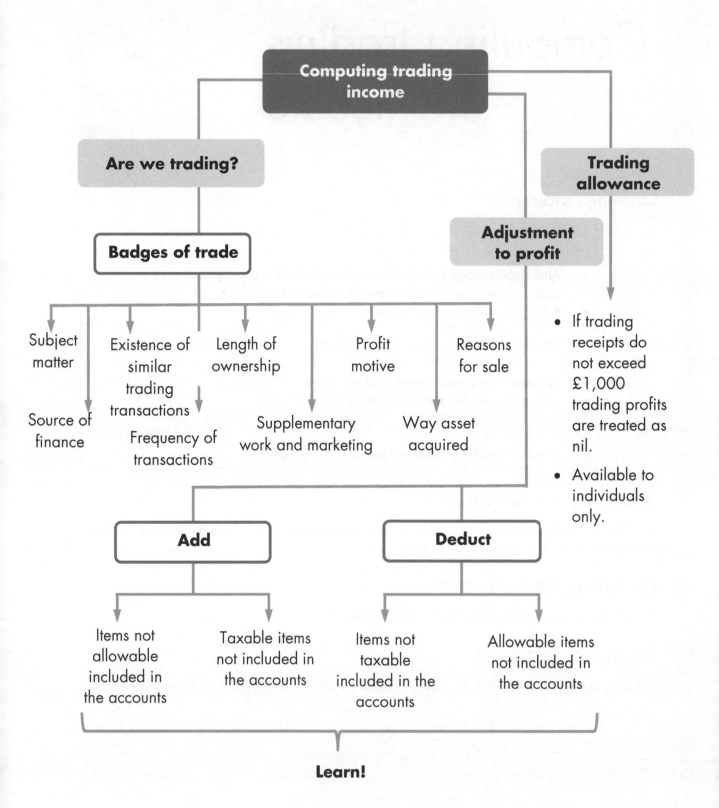

Computing trading income

Are we trading?

Trading allowance

Badges of trade

Adjustment to profit

Subject matter

Existence of similar trading transactions

Length of ownership

Profit motive

Reasons for sale

Source of finance

Frequency of transactions

Supplementary work and marketing

Way asset acquired

- If trading receipts do not exceed £1,000 trading profits are treated as nil.
- Available to individuals only.

Add

Deduct

Items not allowable included in the accounts

Taxable items not included in the accounts

Items not taxable included in the accounts

Allowable items not included in the accounts

Learn!

1 Introduction

In this chapter, we will look at the differences between earning a profit from trading and making a gain on an investment and how to treat them for tax purposes. We will also look at how to calculate a taxable trading profit figure for the tax return.

2 Is a trade being carried on?

It is important to know whether profits of an individual or company should be assessed as trading income.

For example, a person who buys and sells stamps may be trading as a stamp dealer. Alternatively, stamp collecting may be a hobby of that person. In this case, he is probably not trading.

If a trade is not being carried on, any profit arising from selling items could be exempt from tax or chargeable to capital gains tax.

2.1 Badges of trade

he badges
of trade

The following tests are used by the courts when distinguishing trading from investment or capital transactions and have evolved over the years as a result of the outcome of many court cases arguing trade versus investment:

2.1.1 Subject matter

Some items are commonly held as an **investment**, for example, works of art and antiques. A subsequent disposal may produce a gain of a capital nature rather than a trading profit. However, where the subject matter of a transaction is such that it would not normally be held as an investment (for example, 1,000,000 rolls of toilet paper), it is presumed that any profit on resale is a trading profit.

2.1.2 Ownership

Consider the length of ownership of the asset. The purchase of items followed by sale soon afterwards indicates trading. Conversely, if items are held for a long time before sale there is less likely to be a trade.

2.1.3 Frequency of transactions

A series of similar transactions indicates trading. Conversely, a single transaction is unlikely to be considered as a trade.

2.1.4 Improvement expenditure

If work is done to make an asset more marketable, or steps are taken to find purchasers, there is likely to be a trade. For example, when a group of accountants bought, blended and recasked a quantity of brandy, they were held to be taxable on a trading profit when the brandy was later sold. Advertisement of the goods for sale is also a factor which makes It more likely there is a trade.

2.1.5 Reason for sale

Where objective criteria clearly indicate that a trade is being carried on, the taxpayer's intentions are irrelevant. If, however, a transaction (objectively) has a dual purpose, you should consider the taxpayer's intentions. For example, the taxpayer could buy a property, restore it and sell it. You need to consider whether it was purchased purely for resale, which would indicate trade, or did the taxpayer buy it with the intention of making it their home and then changed their mind – not trade.

2.1.6 Motive for profit

If an item is bought with the intention of selling it at a profit, a trade is likely to exist.

2.1.7 Existence of similar trading transactions or interests

The existence of similar trading transactions or interests would suggest that a trade exist. If an accountant sold a car it would be unlikely to constitute a trade as there is no direct link between their existing interests and the sale. However, if a car mechanic sold a car there is a direct link between their existing trade and the sale. It would be likely that the sale of the car would be a trading transaction.

2.1.8 The source of finance

If an asset is acquired using short term finance, a trade is likely to exist. This is particularly the case where it will be necessary to dispose of the asset to repay the funds.

2.1.9 Method of acquisition

If goods are acquired unintentionally, for example, by gift or inheritance, their later sale is unlikely to constitute trading.

3 Adjustment of profits

Whether the business is unincorporated (sole trader or partnership) or incorporated (limited company) the tax computation will usually always start with the **adjustment of profits**. **This is a vital area for all business types**. Many of the rules are the same for unincorporated businesses and for companies, with some differences highlighted in this chapter.

The exception to using an adjustment to profit approach is if a sole trade business has trading receipts during a tax year of less than £1,000 when the **trading allowance** will be used. This is covered in more detail in Section 4 below.

3.1 Taxable trading profits

Taxable trading profits are not the same as accounting profits. The trader arrives at the profit for the year in the accounts by taking income and deducting various trading expenses. However, the trader is unlikely to follow tax rules in arriving at this profit as, for example, there are some costs for which tax legislation does not allow a tax deduction, even though the taxpayer quite legitimately deducts them for accounting purposes.

Profits before tax from the financial statements need adjusting in accordance with tax legislation as follows:

Adjustment of profits-le traders, artnerships and ompanies

	£
Net profit before tax per accounts	
Add back:	
(a) Items charged in the accounts but not deductible for trading profits purposes (eg depreciation)	
(b) Income taxable as trading profits which has not been included in the accounts (eg goods taken by owner for own use)	
Deduct:	
(a) Items included in the accounts but not taxable as trading profits (eg profit on disposal of fixed assets)	
(b) Expenditure which is deductible from trading profits but has not been charged in the accounts (eg capital allowances)	

Activity 1: Adjustment of profits (i)

Pratish trades as a car mechanic. His most recent accounts show a profit of £38,000. In arriving at this figure, he deducted entertaining expenses of £2,000 and depreciation of £4,000. These amounts are not allowable for tax purposes. Capital allowances of £3,500 are available for tax purposes.

Required

Using the proforma layout provided, calculate the taxable trading profit.

The starting figure has already been entered for you.

Solution

	£
Profit for the year in the accounts	38,000

3.2 General rule for disallowed expenditure

Expenditure incurred not **wholly and exclusively** for business purposes is disallowed.

3.3 Specific disallowed expenses:

3.3.1 Capital expenditure including depreciation

Capital expenditure is one-off expenditure leading to the creation or improvement of an asset (eg a piece of plant).

Revenue expenditure is regular ongoing expenditure required in the day to day running of the business (eg paying the gas bill).

Usually, revenue expenditure is allowable: it can be deducted from income before tax is calculated.

Capital expenditure is not allowable so must be added back if it has been charged in the statement of profit or loss. **Capital allowances** (see later) may sometimes be claimed on capital expenditure.

Repair expenditure can cause problems:

- Maintaining an asset (ie keeping it in its current condition) is allowable.

- Improving an asset is not allowable.

There are special rules where assets are repaired following acquisition:

- If the repairs are to make the asset usable, they are not allowable (eg repairs to an unseaworthy ship).

- If the repairs merely improve the appearance of an asset, they are allowable (eg refurbishing a cinema).

Activity 2: Capital versus revenue

Identify whether the following expenses are revenue or capital in nature by ticking the relevant box.

Solution

	Revenue ✓	Capital ✓
Paying employee wages		
Paying rent for premises		
Buying machinery		
Buying a van		
Building an extension to shop		
Paying for repairs to car		

3.3.2 Adjustments to general provisions/general allowances for doubtful debts

Only irrecoverable debts incurred wholly and exclusively for the purposes of the trade are deductible for taxation purposes. Thus loans to employees written off are not deductible unless the business is that of making loans, or it can be shown that the write-off was earnings paid out for the benefit of the trade.

Increases or decreases in a general provision are not allowable and an adjustment is needed.

Illustration 1: Irrecoverable debts account

The account below results in a credit to the statement of profit or loss of £124. What adjustment should be made to the profit for the year when calculating taxable trading profits?

2020	£	£	2020	£	£
			1 January		
			Provisions b/d		
			General	150	
			Specific	381	
					531
Provisions c/d					
General	207				
Specific	200				
		407			
Statement of profit or loss		124			
		531			531
			2021		
			1 January		
			Provisions b/d		407

The only adjustment you need to consider is the increase in general provision from £150 to £207. Thus £57 is added to the accounts profit to arrive at taxable profit.

3.3.3 Private expenditure of the owner

Unincorporated
businesses –
trading income

Strictly, expenditure incurred partly for private purposes and partly for business purposes has a dual purpose and is not deductible. However, HMRC sometimes allows taxpayers to apportion the expenditure between the part that is wholly for business purposes, and therefore deductible; and the part that is wholly for private purposes, and therefore not deductible.

Goods taken from stock by the proprietor of a business should be treated as if they had been sold for their market value. If correctly accounted for as drawings, this will require an adjustment for the profit, whereas if the cost is still reflected in cost of sales, the full selling price will need to be added back.

Illustration 2: Private use expenditure

A sole trader who runs his business from home incurs £500 on heating and lighting bills. 30% of these bills relate to the business use of his house. £500 has been deducted in arriving at the accounts profit. How much should be added back in the calculation of taxable trading profits?

The 30% relating to business use is allowable. Therefore, 70% × £500 = £350 must be added back to the accounts profit as disallowable expenditure.

Assessment focus point

In the CBT you may need to calculate adjusted profits for a sole trader/partnership (unincorporated business) or a company (incorporated business).

The calculation is basically the same; however, there are no private adjustments for a company.

Everybody who works for a company (including a director) is an employee, so any benefit they receive is taxed on them as part of their employment income (rules examinable in *Personal Tax*).

The cost is part of the company's cost of employing the workforce it needs to perform its trade, so the costs are allowable.

3.4 The treatment of various other items

Adjustment
of profits -
sole traders,
partnerships
and
companies

The table below details various types of allowable and **disallowable expenditure**, with mention of any differences between unincorporated businesses (sole traders and partnerships) and incorporated businesses (companies) where necessary.

Allowable expenditure	Disallowable expenditure	Comments
	Fines and penalties	HMRC usually allows parking fines incurred in parking an employee's car whilst on the employer's business. Fines relating to the owner of the business are, however, never allowed. Similarly, a company would not be able to deduct fines relating to directors
Costs of registering trademarks and patents		This is an exception to the rule of 'capital' related expenditure being disallowable
Incidental costs of obtaining loan finance		This deduction does not apply to companies because they get a deduction for the cost of borrowing in a different way. We look at this in Chapter 4 of this Course Book
	Depreciation or amortisation	In specific circumstances, a company can deduct these amounts, but this is outside the scope of this assessment
	Any salary or interest paid to a sole trader or partner	
	The private proportion of any expenses incurred by a sole trader or partner	The private proportion of a director's or employee's expenses is, however, deductible
Irrecoverable debts incurred in the course of a business. Specific provisions for irrecoverable debts	General provisions for irrecoverable debts (and other general provisions)	Loans to employees written off, despite being specific, are not allowable
Patent and copyright royalties		Patent and copyright royalties paid for trade purposes are deductible
Staff entertaining	Non-staff (eg customer) entertaining	

Allowable expenditure	Disallowable expenditure	Comments
Gifts for employees Gifts to customers as long as they: • Cost no more than £50 per donee per year • Carry a conspicuous advertisement for the business; and • Are not food, drink, tobacco or vouchers exchangeable for such goods Gifts to a small local charity if they benefit the trade	All other gifts including 'qualifying charitable donations'	'Qualifying charitable donations' are charitable gifts by companies on which tax relief is given. These are covered in Chapter 4 of this Course Book. The similar scheme relevant to individuals is not assessable in this *Business Tax* assessment
Subscriptions to a professional or trade association	Political donations	
Legal and professional charges relating directly to the trade	Legal and professional charges relating to capital or non-trading items	Deductible items include: • Charges incurred defending the taxpayer's title to non-current assets • Charges connected with an action for breach of contract
	Accountancy expenses relating to specialist consultancy work	Deductible items include: • Expenses for the renewal (not the original grant) of a lease for less than 50 years • Charges for trade debt collection • Normal charges for preparing accounts and assisting with the self-assessment of tax liabilities

Allowable expenditure	Disallowable expenditure	Comments
Interest on loans taken out for trade purposes	Interest on overdue tax	These rules are for unincorporated businesses. Companies have different rules for interest. We look at these in Chapter 4 of this Course Book
Costs of seconding employees to charities or educational establishments		
Expenditure incurred in the seven years prior to the commencement of a trade		Provided expenditure is of a type that would have been allowed had the trade started. Treat as an expense on the first day of trading
Removal expenses (to new business premises)		Only if not an expansionary move
Travelling expenses on the trader's business	Travel from home to the trader's place of business	
Redundancy payments		If the trade ceases, the limit on allowability is 3 × the statutory amount (in addition to the statutory amount)
	15% of leasing costs of car with CO_2 emissions in excess of 110g/km	

Activity 3: Calculation of add back

A sole trader charged the following expenses in computing his accounts profit:

	£
Fine for breach of Factories Act	1,000
Cost of specialist tax consultancy work	2,000
Redundancy payments	10,000
Salary for himself	15,000
Leasing cost of car (CO_2 emissions 150g/km)	3,000

The redundancy payments were made for trade purposes as a result of reorganisation of the business. The trade is continuing.

Required

Calculate how much must be added back in computing taxable trading profits.

Tick ONE box.

Solution

Amount to add back	✓
£17,450	
£16,000	
£18,450	
£11,450	

Activity 4: Entertainment and gifts

Decide whether each of the items in the entertainment account below should be added back in computing taxable trading profits.

Expenditure	£	Add back ✓
Staff tennis outing for 30 employees	1,800	
2,000 tee shirts with firm's logo given to race runners	4,500	
Advertising and sponsorship of an athletic event	2,000	
Entertaining customers	7,300	
Staff Christmas party (30 employees)	2,400	

Activity 5: Adjustment of profits (ii)

Hugo Drax, a sole trader, has the following statement of profit or loss for the year ended 31 December:

	£
Sales	100,000
Cost of sales	(50,000)
Gross profit	50,000
Add other income	
Bank interest	4,000
Less expenses	
Depreciation	(5,000)
Entertaining clients	(100)
Office costs	(2,000)
Staff wages and salaries	(15,000)
Hugo's personal council tax bill	(1,000)
Net profit	30,900

Salaries include £5,000 paid to Hugo and £10,000 paid to his wife. His wife's salary is reasonable in respect of the work she performs in the business.

Required

Complete the table below showing the calculation of adjusted trading profits before capital allowances. Complete the narrative by using the items in the picklist below the table.

Solution

Adjustment to profit	£	£
Net profit per the accounts		
Add back		
▼		
▼		
▼		
▼		
Total added back		
Deduct		
▼		
Adjusted profits before capital allowances		

Picklist:

Bank interest
Cost of sales
Council tax
Depreciation
Entertaining
Gross profit
Office costs
Sales
Staff wages

4 Trading allowance

From 2017/18, the trading allowance was introduced to simplify the calculation of trading profits for smaller sole traders.

Taxation
tables for
business tax
– 2020/21

If a sole trader has trading receipts (under the accruals basis) for a tax year which do not exceed the trading allowance of £1,000, the trading profits are treated as nil and there is no charge to income tax as a result of the trade. An election can be made for the trading allowance rules not to apply if, for example, the deduction of allowable costs would instead give rise to a trading loss.

If the sole trader has trading receipts exceeding the £1,000 trading allowance, then the usual adjustment to profits approach will be used to calculate trading profits as explained in Section 3 above. If the sole trader would prefer, perhaps if allowable costs were small, then an election can be made to deduct the £1,000 trading allowance from trading receipts in order to calculate the taxable trading profits instead of deducting allowable expenses.

5 Self-employment tax return pages

A sole trader needs to provide detailed information about the adjustment of profit in their tax return.

AAT have confirmed that the page shown below is the only page you should expect to see from the self-assessment tax return. You will notice that the boxes on the left side of the return show all a trader's expenses and the boxes on the right-hand side highlight which of those expenses are disallowable for tax purposes. For example, if a trader has a depreciation charge of £500, this will be shown in both box 29 and box 44.

You will be able to practise completing this form in the *Business Tax* Question Bank.

You may need to complete this page of the tax return as part of your CBE.

Illustration 3: Extract from self-employment tax return (using information from Activity 5)

Business expenses

Please read the 'Self-employment (full) notes' before filling in this section.

Total expenses	Disallowable expenses
If your annual turnover was below £85,000, you may just put your total expenses in box 31	Use this column if the figures in boxes 17 to 30 include disallowable amounts

17 Cost of goods bought for resale or goods used
£ 50 000 . 0 0

32 £ . 0 0

18 Construction industry – payments to subcontractors
£ . 0 0

33 £ . 0 0

19 Wages, salaries and other staff costs
£ 15 000 . 0 0

34 £ 5 000 . 0 0

20 Car, van and travel expenses
£ . 0 0

35 £ . . 0 0

21 Rent, rates, power and insurance costs
£ 1 000 . 0 0

36 £ 1 000 . 0 0

22 Repairs and maintenance of property and equipment
£ . 0 0

37 £ . 0 0

23 Phone, fax, stationery and other office costs
£ 2 000 . 0 0

38 £ . 0 0

24 Advertising and business entertainment costs
£ 1 0 0 . 0 0

39 £ 1 0 0 . 0 0

25 Interest on bank and other loans
£ . 0 0

40 £ . 0 0

26 Bank, credit card and other financial charges
£ . 0 0

41 £ . 0 0

27 Irrecoverable debts written off
£ . 0 0

42 £ . 0 0

28 Accountancy, legal and other professional fees
£ . 0 0

43 £ . 0 0

29 Depreciation and loss or profit on sale of assets
£ 5 000 . 0 0

44 £ 5 000 . 0 0

30 Other business expenses
£ . 0 0

45 £ . 0 0

31 Total expenses (total of boxes 17 to 30)
£ 73 100 . 0 0

46 Total disallowable expenses (total of boxes 32 to 45)
£ 11 100 . 0 0

SA103F 2021   Page SEF 2

(Adapted from HMRC, 2020(b))

29

Assessment focus point

Please refer to the reference material at the end of this Course Book to see which elements of this chapter will be available to you as a pop-up in the live assessment.

Chapter summary

- The badges of trade give guidance as to whether or not a trade is being carried on.

- Revenue expenses are generally allowable expenses for computing taxable trading profits but capital expenses are not (unless relieved through capital allowances – see later chapter).

- The main disallowable items that you must add back in computing taxable trading profits are:

  - Entertaining (other than staff entertaining)

  - Depreciation charges (deduct capital allowances instead)

  - Increase in general provisions

  - Fines

  - Legal fees relating to capital items

  - Wages or salary paid to a business owner

  - The private proportion of any expenses for a sole trader/partner (not applicable to a company)

- Deduct non-trading income/capital profits included in the accounts from the accounts profit to arrive at taxable trading profits.

- If a sole trader has trading receipts for the tax year not exceeding the trading allowance of £1,000, the trading profits are treated as nil.

Keywords

- **Adjustment of profits:** The adjustment of the accounting profits to comply with tax legislation

- **Badges of trade:** Indicate whether or not a trade is being carried on

- **Disallowable expenditure:** Expenditure that cannot be deducted in computing taxable trading profit

- **Expenditure wholly and exclusively for trade purposes:** Expenditure that is incidental to the trade and that does not have a dual purpose

- **Trading allowance:** An allowance of £1,000 which allows sole traders with trading receipts not exceeding the allowance to set their trade profits as nil and avoid the need for an adjustment to profit calculation.

Test your learning

1 **Which of the following expenses are allowable when computing taxable trading profits?**

	Allowable ✓
Legal fees incurred on the acquisition of a factory to be used for trade purposes	
Heating for factory	
Legal fees incurred on pursuing trade receivables	
Acquiring a machine to be used in the factory	

2 A sole trader incurs the following expenditure on entertaining and gifts.

	£
Staff entertaining	700
50 Christmas food hampers given to customers	240
Entertaining customers	900
	1,840

How much of the above expenditure is allowable for tax purposes?

£

3 **For each of the following expenses, show whether they are allowable or disallowable by ticking the relevant boxes.**

	Allowable ✓	Disallowable ✓
Parking fines incurred by the owner of the business		
Parking fines incurred by an employee while on the employer's business		
Parking fines incurred by the director of a company while on company business		
Legal costs incurred in relation to acquiring a 10-year lease of property for the first time		
Legal costs incurred in relation to the renewal of a lease for 20 years		

	Allowable ✓	Disallowable ✓
Gifts of calendars to customers, costing £4 each and displaying an advertisement for the company		
Gifts of bottles of whisky to customers, costing £12 each		

4   Herbert, a self-employed carpenter, makes various items of garden furniture for sale. He takes a bird table from stock and sets it up in his own garden. The cost of making the bird table amounts to £80, and Herbert would normally expect to achieve a mark-up of 20% on such goods.

Identify the adjustment Herbert needs to make to the accounts for tax purposes, assuming he has reflected in the accounts the deduction for the cost of making the table.

Tick ONE box.

	✓
£80 must be deducted from the accounts profit	
£80 must be added back to the accounts profit	
£96 must be deducted from the accounts profit	
£96 must be added back to the accounts profit	

5   Set out below is the irrecoverable debts account of Kingfisher, a sole trader:

Irrecoverable debts

	£	1.4.20	£
		Provisions b/d	
		General	2,500
		Specific (trade)	1,875
31.3.21			
Provisions c/d			
General	1,800		
Specific (trade)	4,059	Statement of profit or loss	1,484
	5,859		5,859

Insert the amount that needs adjusting and tick whether it should be added to, or deducted from, Kingfisher's accounts profit to arrive at taxable trading profits.

£ [ ]

Added back ✓	Deducted ✓

6   Trude works from home as a self-employed hairdresser. She incurs £450 on heating and lighting bills and this amount is deducted in her accounts. 20% of this expenditure relates to the business use of her home.

How much of the expenditure is disallowable for tax purposes?

£ [ ]

7   Calculate the taxable trading profits for the following sole traders, assuming they make any beneficial claim available to them. Their income and expenditure for 2020/21 is stated below:

	Zack	Mythili	Rohan	Arthur
Trading receipts	800	800	1,500	1,500
Allowable expenses	200	900	800	1,100

	Taxable trading profits
Zack	
Mythili	
Rohan	
Arthur	

Capital allowances

3

1.3	**Identify and calculate capital allowances for sole traders and partnerships**
	• Identify the types of capital allowances • Calculate capital allowances including adjustments for private use
2.2	**Identify and calculate capital allowances for limited companies**
	• Identify the types of capital allowances • Calculate capital allowances

Assessment context

All the rules in this chapter are highly examinable and could be examined in a variety of different combinations. Make sure you can deal with any scenario the assessment throws at you. Some students find the task on capital allowances quite challenging, so you must make sure you practise plenty of tasks to feel comfortable with applying your knowledge of this topic. In addition, you must ensure you know what information is available in your reference material.

Qualification context

You will not see these rules outside of this unit.

Business context

In practice, capital allowances are a significant form of tax relief for reducing a taxpayer's tax liability.

The government often uses capital allowances to encourage people to invest in new plant and machinery.

Chapter overview

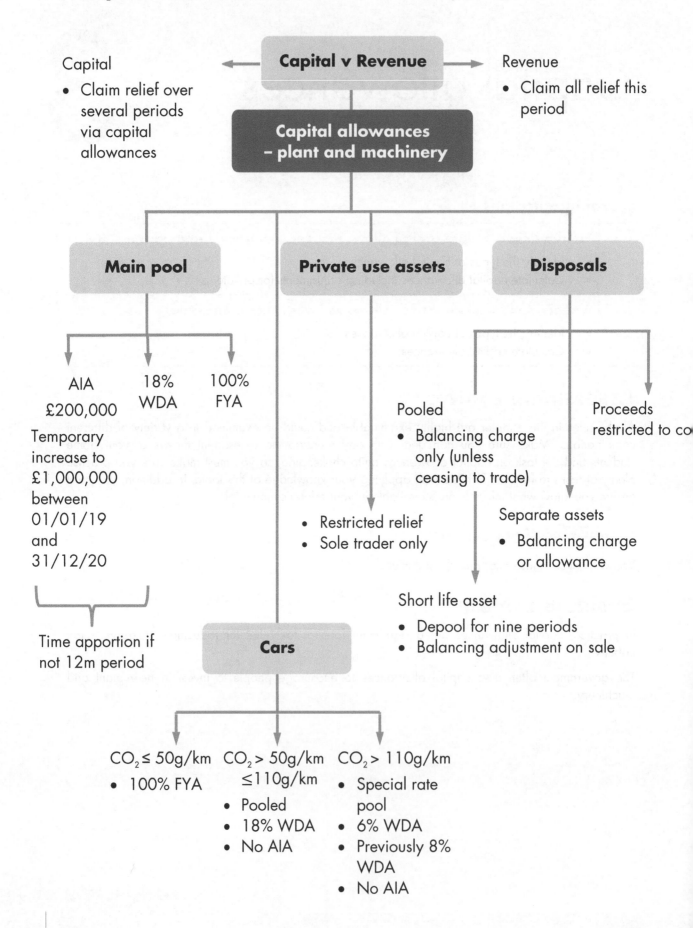

Capital v Revenue

Capital
- Claim relief over several periods via capital allowances

Revenue
- Claim all relief this period

Capital allowances – plant and machinery

Main pool

Private use assets

Disposals

AIA £200,000

Temporary increase to £1,000,000 between 01/01/19 and 31/12/20

18% WDA

100% FYA

Time apportion if not 12m period

- Restricted relief
- Sole trader only

Cars

Pooled
- Balancing charge only (unless ceasing to trade)

Separate assets
- Balancing charge or allowance

Short life asset
- Depool for nine periods
- Balancing adjustment on sale

Proceeds restricted to co

$CO_2 \le 50g/km$
- 100% FYA

$CO_2 > 50g/km$ $\le 110g/km$
- Pooled
- 18% WDA
- No AIA

$CO_2 > 110g/km$
- Special rate pool
- 6% WDA
- Previously 8% WDA
- No AIA

1 Introduction

This chapter looks at the difference between capital and revenue expenditure; and how to get tax relief for the different types of expenditure by either treating them as an expense, or **plant and machinery** for capital allowances.

2 Capital and revenue expenditure

Capital expenditure is one-off expenditure that will bring benefits to the business over a number of years (eg purchase of machinery).

Revenue expenditure is regular ongoing expenditure that only brings benefit in the period in which the expenditure is made (eg payment of electricity bill).

Revenue expenditure, generally, may be deducted against taxable profits before they are taxed (but we saw in the previous chapter that not all revenue expenditure is automatically allowable).

It may be possible to claim **capital allowances** on some capital expenditure. Capital allowances are just the tax version of accounts depreciation. They are calculated to replace the depreciation charged in the accounts.

Both individuals (sole traders and partners) and companies may claim capital allowances.

3 Expenditure qualifying for capital allowances

Plant and machinery is something which has a **function** within the trade as opposed to being part of the **setting** where the business takes place. Essentially, plant and machinery is any capital item used in the business other than buildings. For example, reference books could be plant and machinery.

Assessment focus point

There is much law determining what is allowable as plant and machinery and what is not. The AAT have confirmed that the very detailed rules on this do not form part of your syllabus but, for information, some examples include:

- Moveable office partitions are plant – but fixed partitions are not.
- Decorative items (eg paintings) in hotels are plant.

The more common items you will see in the assessment are:

- Cars, vans and lorries
- Furniture
- Computers

You may also be provided with a list of capital expenditure which includes costs incurred in altering premises. You are expected to understand that this forms part of the setting for the business and that therefore capital allowances will not be available.

4 Allowances on plant and machinery

4.1 When and how capital allowances are given

Allowances are computed by reference to the period for which accounts are drawn up.

They are deducted from the taxable profits of the period.

They include all additions and disposals occurring in the relevant accounting period. Expenditure must be of a capital nature.

4.2 Main pool for capital allowances

Most expenditure on plant and machinery is put into a 'pool' of assets known as the **main pool**. This includes expenditure on cars with CO_2 emissions of 110g/km or less.

Capital allowances on plant and machinery

Taxation tables for business tax – 2020/21

4.3 Annual investment allowance

A business can claim an **annual investment allowance (AIA)**, giving 100% tax relief on its expenditure on plant and machinery.

From 1 January 2021 a business can claim AIA on the first £200,000 of expenditure on plant and machinery in a 12-month **period of account**. Prior to 1 January 2021 the AIA had been temporarily increased to £1,000,000. The temporary, increased AIA was available from 1 January 2019 to 31 December 2020.

The AIA is not available for expenditure on cars.

The amount of the AIA is scaled up/down for long/short periods of account.

Note. Companies cannot have a corporation tax period that is longer than 12 months.

Activity 1: Annual investment allowance

Delson starts a business on 1 January 2021. In the nine-month period to 30 September 2021, he incurs the following expenditure:

		£
15 January 2021	Manufacturing equipment	50,000
16 January 2021	Computer equipment	60,000
7 May 2021	Office furniture	30,000
13 May 2021	Delivery vans	20,000
20 June 2021	Car	19,000

Required

Delson can claim an annual investment allowance of £ [   ] .

Workings (on-screen free text area provided in the CBT as part of larger question)

4.3.1 Periods of account which straddle the change in AIA

Capital allowances in plant and machinery

Taxation tables for business tax – 2020/21

Where a business has a period of account which straddles 1 January 2021, ie it starts before 1 January 2021 and ends after that date, the maximum AIA for that period of account is calculated by time apportioning the relevant AIA limits based on the number of months in the period of account which fall before 1 January 2021 and the number of months which fall after.

Where a business has a period of account which straddles 1 January 2019, ie it starts before 1 January 2019 and ends after that date, the same principle applies.

Assessment focus point

The rules for calculating the maximum AIA available for periods straddling 1 January 2021 and 1 January 2019 are slightly more complex than we have shown below. However, the AAT have advised us that the full complexity of this will not be needed and tasks in the Business Tax assessment will be designed to accommodate this.

Illustration 1

Matthew began trading on 1 April 2020 and prepared accounts for the year to 31 March 2021.

In the year ended 31 March 2021, Matthew buys equipment for his business at a cost of £600,000, all of which qualifies for the AIA. All expenditure was incurred prior to the 1 January 2021.

First we must calculate the maximum AIA that Matthew can claim. His period of account is 12 months long but nine of those months are before 1 January 2021 and three are after 1 January 2021. This means that the maximum AIA is as follows:

		£
1 April 2020 to 31 December 2020	9/12 × £1,000,000	750,000
1 January 2021 to 31 March 2021	3/12 × £200,000	50,000
Maximum AIA for the year ended 31 March 2021		800,000

So the maximum AIA for the year ended 31 March is £800,000, which will be sufficient to cover all of Matthew's £600,000 expenditure.

Illustration 2

Teddy began trading on 1 December 2018 and prepared accounts for the 16 months to 31 March 2020.

In the period ended 31 March 2020, Teddy buys equipment for his business at a cost of £850,000, all of which qualifies for the AIA.

First we must calculate the maximum AIA that Teddy can claim. His period of account is 16 months long but one of these months is before 1 January 2019 and 15 are after 1 January 2019. This means that the maximum AIA is as follows:

		£
1 December 2018 to 31 December 2018	1/12 × £200,000	16,667
1 January 2019 to 31 March 2020	15/12 × £1,000,000	1,250,000
Maximum AIA for the period ended 31 March 2020		1,266,667

So the maximum AIA for the period ended 31 March 2020 is £1,266,667, which will be sufficient to cover all of Teddy's £850,000 expenditure.

4.4 First year allowances (FYAs)

These are special allowances given in addition to the AIA.

First year allowances (FYAs) are available at 100% on expenditure incurred on:

- Low emission cars (ie cars with CO_2 emissions of 50g/km and below)
- Electrically propelled cars.

You must give FYAs at 100% to the assets that are eligible for them. Do not use the AIA against them.

FYAs are **never** time apportioned for short or long accounting periods.

The capital allowances on plant and machinery section of your reference data, which you can access in your assessment, reminds you of the assets on which the FYA is available and that it is never time apportioned. The CO_2 emissions for cars and their respective capital allowance treatment is also given in the taxation data section of your reference material.

Capital
llowances
plant and
machinery

Taxation
tables for
siness tax
2020/21

4.5 Writing-down allowances

A **writing-down allowance (WDA)** is given on the main pool at the rate of 18% per year (on a reducing balance basis). The WDA is calculated on the value of pooled plant, after adding current period additions and taking out current period disposals (as explained shortly).

The additions will include:

(a) Expenditure that qualifies for the AIA but is in excess of the maximum AIA available for the period.

(b) Cars with CO_2 emissions of between 51g/km and 110g/km. These are cars that do not qualify for 100% FYA and do not go into the special rate pool (see later). The emissions are stated clearly in the taxation tables for business tax – 2020/21 section of your reference material, which you can access in your assessment.

Illustration 3: Basic proforma for calculating WDAs

	Main pool £	Allowances £
TWDV b/f	X	
Additions (not eligible for AIA/FYA)	X	
Less disposals	(X)	
	X	
WDA @ 18%	(X)	X
TWDV c/f	X	

Note. TWDV = Tax Written-Down Value: this is the value of the pool of assets for tax purposes.

The total allowances for the accounting period can then be deducted in the adjustments to profit working.

WDAs are time apportioned for short/long accounting periods ($\frac{n}{12} \times 18\%$).

Note that the reference material provided in your assessment gives you a proforma capital allowance computation, together with lots of really useful facts, such as a reminder about time apportioning the allowances for the length of the accounting period. Make sure you can use your reference material effectively by practising tasks with it now.

Activity 2: Writing-down allowances in the main pool

Jamie draws up his accounts to 31 March. At 1 April 2020, he has a balance of £10,000 on his main pool.

In his period of account to 31 March 2021, he has the following transactions:

		£
13 June 2020	buys a car (CO$_2$ 105g/km)	18,000
31 August 2020	buys a van	9,000
30 October 2020	sells plant for	2,000
20 November 2020	buys manufacturing plant	850,000

Required

Jamie can claim an annual investment allowance of £ _____ .

Jamie can claim writing-down allowances of £ _____ .

Workings (on-screen free text area provided in the CBT as part of larger question)

4.6 WDA for small pools

If the balance on the main pool or special rate pool (before WDA) is less than the small pool limit at the end of the chargeable period, a WDA can be claimed up to the value of the small pool limit. This is known as a 'small pools allowance.'

This means that the pools may be written down to nil, rather than a small balance being carried forward.

The small pool limit is £1,000 for a 12-month period (pro rata for short and long chargeable periods). Note that this does not apply to any assets which are kept separate and not included in the pools.

5 Disposals

When an asset is sold in the year, we deduct the proceeds from the tax written down value of the pool brought forward. However, if an asset is sold for more than its original cost, we only deduct the original cost from the pool.

> **Illustration 4: Disposal proceeds**
>
> On 6 April 2020, a sole trader had a balance on his main pool of £47,000. Plant that had cost £7,000 was sold in the year for proceeds of:
>
> (a) £14,000
> (b) £4,000
>
> In (a) proceeds are more than original cost and so only £7,000 would be deducted from the main pool balance of £47,000.
>
> In (b) the actual proceeds are less than original cost and so the proceeds of £4,000 would be deducted from the main pool balance of £47,000.

6 Periods that are not 12 months long

The AIA limit and WDA are adjusted by the fraction: months/12.

The FYA is never adjusted.

A sole trader or partnership may have a period shorter or longer than 12 months. AIA and WDA can therefore be scaled up or down.

A company may have a corporation tax period shorter than 12 months but not longer than 12 months. AIA and WDA could therefore be scaled down but not up.

> **Assessment focus point**
>
> Note that the Chief Assessor has commented that short or long accounting periods are one of the scenarios which students find most challenging in this Task and so you must make sure you fully appreciate the consequences of the length of the accounting period on the calculation. Your reference material clearly reminds you to time apportion the AIA and the WDA but not the FYA for the length of the period, so make sure you use your reference material effectively and practise lots of tasks.

Activity 3: Short period of account

Edward Ltd has been in business a number of years, drawing up accounts to 31 March.

In 2020, Edward Ltd decided to change its year end to 31 December.

In the period ended 31 December 2020, Edward Ltd had the following additions:

		£
13 April	Car (CO$_2$ emissions 100g/km)	7,000
15 April	Plant	1,046,750

Edward Ltd sold a van for £2,000 on 7 July that had cost £3,000.

TWDV b/f at 1 April 2020 was £12,000.

Required

Edward Ltd can claim capital allowances of £ [   ].

Workings (on-screen free text area provided in the CBT as part of larger question)

7 Cessation of a business

When a business ceases to trade, no AIAs, FYAs or WDAs are given in the final period.

Additions in the final period are added to the pool in the normal way. Similarly, any disposal proceeds (limited to cost) of assets sold in the final period are deducted from the balance of qualifying expenditure. If assets are not sold, they are deemed to be disposed of on the final day of trading for their market value. For example, a sole trader may keep a car from the business that has just ceased trading and so must deduct the market value from the pool.

If, after the above adjustments, a positive balance of qualifying expenditure remains in the pool, then a **balancing allowance** equal to this amount is given. **The balancing allowance is deducted from taxable trading profits**. If, on the other hand, the balance on the pool has become negative, a **balancing charge** equal to the negative amount is given. **The balancing charge increases taxable trading profits.**

Balancing allowances on the main pool and the special rate pool (see below) can only arise on cessation of trade, whereas balancing charges on these pools, although most commonly happening on cessation, can arise whilst trade is still in progress.

Capital allowances on plant and machinery

Assessment focus point
This is another scenario which the Chief Assessor has said that students find challenging. The basic rules are available to you in your assessment.

Activity 4: Cessation of a business

Baxter normally has a June year end. On 1 July 2020, he has a TWDV in the pool of £12,000. He ceases to trade on 31 January 2021. His additions and disposals in his final period are as follows:

		£
5 September	Buys plant	2,000
12 October	Sells plant	See below

(a) Required

If Baxter sells his plant for £15,500 then he will have a

[▼] of £ [   ].

Picklist:

balancing allowance
balancing charge

Workings (on-screen free text area provided in the CBT as part of larger question)

(b) Required

If Baxter sells his plant for £11,500 then he will have a

[▼] of £ [   ].

Picklist:

balancing allowance
balancing charge

Workings (on-screen free text area provided in the CBT as part of larger question)

Notes.

1   A balancing allowance only arises in the main pool on the cessation of trade.

2   A balancing charge may arise on the main pool at any point in the business's life.

8 Assets that are not included in the main pool

We have seen above how to compute capital allowances on the main pool of plant and machinery. However, some special items are not put into the main pool. A separate record of allowances must be kept for these assets.

These assets are:

- Cars with CO_2 emissions greater than 110g/km

- Assets not wholly used for business purposes in **unincorporated businesses** (such as cars with private use by the proprietor)

- **Short life assets**

8.1 Cars with CO_2 emissions greater than 110g/km

Taxation tables for business tax – 2020/21

Cars with CO_2 emissions in excess of 110g/km are put in a pool known as the **special rate pool**. From 6 April 2019 (1 April 2019 for companies), the **WDA rate on the special rate pool is 6% for a 12-month period** calculated on the pool balance (after any additions and disposals) at the end of the chargeable period.

Activity 5: Special rate pool

Myles Ltd prepares accounts to 31 March each year and incurred the following transactions for the year ended 31 March 2021.

1.7.20   Bought car for £17,000, CO_2 emissions of 100g/km

1.10.20   Bought car for £8,000, CO_2 emissions of 160g/km

On 1 April 2020, the TWDV of plant and machinery were as follows:

	£
Main pool	25,000
Special rate pool	10,000

Required

Myles Ltd can claim capital allowances of £ [   ] .

Workings (on-screen free text area provided in the CBT as part of larger question)

Before 6 April 2019, the WDA rate on the special rate pool was 8%. For accounting periods straddling 6 April, a hybrid WDA is used for that period (rounded to 2 decimal places).

Illustration 5

Becky is preparing her tax-adjusted profits for the year ended 30 June 2019. After additions and disposals in the period the tax written down value of her special rate pool on 30 June 2019 is £75,000. What is the WDA that Becky can claim on her special rate pool in the year ended 30 June 2019?

The year ended 30 June 2019 has nine months which fall before 6 April 2019 and three which fall after 6 April 2019.

The hybrid WDA rate is used for that period. It is calculated as follows.

$(8\% \times 9/12) + (6\% \times 3/12) = 7.5\%$

The WDA is therefore $7.5\% \times £75,000 = £5,625$

Unincorporated businesses – trading income

8.2 Assets used partly for private purposes

If a proprietor of a sole trader business or a partner in a partnership uses a business asset for private purposes, the following treatment applies:

- The asset is put in a separate column.
- TWDV is reduced by **full amount** of AIA/FYA/WDA calculated as normal.
- A balancing allowance or charge will arise at the date of disposal.
- Only the business proportion of the allowance/charge is transferred into the allowances column.

We refer to these as **private-use assets**.

An asset with some private use by an employee (not the business owner) suffers no restriction. The employee may be taxed on the private use as a taxable benefit, so the business is entitled to full capital allowances on such assets. This means **there is never any private use restriction in a company's capital allowance computation**, whether the asset is used by an employee or a director.

The Unincorporated business – trading income section of the reference material you have access to in your assessment reminds you of the basics for private use adjustments.

Assessment focus point

The Chief Assessor has noted that making private use adjustments when they are not required is a common mistake, so please ensure you check who you are calculating capital allowances for.

- If it is a sole trader or partnership - make the adjustment **IF** it is the sole trader or partner who is using the asset privately.
- If it is a company – **do not** make the adjustment.

Activity 6: Private-use assets

At 1 January 2020, Sweeney has two cars used within his business: a car he uses himself with a TWDV b/f of £20,000 (20% private use, CO_2 emissions 180g/km); and a car used by his employee, Doris, with a TWDV b/f of £16,000 (35% private use, CO_2 emissions 100g/km). He draws up his accounts to 31 December 2020.

Sweeney has no other assets.

Required

(a) **Sweeney can claim capital allowances of** £ _____ .

Workings (on screen free text area provided in the CBT as part of larger question)

Required

(b) **What capital allowances would Sweeney claim if the business instead ceased in this period and both cars were sold for £15,000 each?**

_____ ▼ **of** £ _____ .

Picklist:

balancing allowance
balancing charge

Workings (on-screen free text area provided in the CBT as part of larger question)

8.3 Short life assets

Capital allowances on plant and machinery

A **short life asset** is an asset that a trader expects to dispose of within **eight years** of the end of the period of acquisition.

A trader can make a **depooling election** to keep such an asset in its own individual pool. **The advantage of this is that a balancing allowance can be given when the asset is disposed of**. Such an election would not be made if the asset is entitled to 100% FYA or AIA.

For an unincorporated business, the time limit for electing is the 31 January that is 22 months after the end of the tax year in which the period of account of the expenditure ends (for example, this would be 31 January 2023 for accounting periods ending in 2020/21). For a company, it is two years after the end of the accounting period of the expenditure.

If the asset is disposed of within eight years of the end of the period of account, or accounting period in which it was bought, a balancing charge or allowance is made on its disposal. However, if the asset is not disposed of within this period, the tax written-down value is transferred to the main pool at the end of that period. It would not be advisable to depool an asset that will be sold for more than its cost/tax written-down value as this would create a balancing charge. In this instance, the asset would just go into the main pool or special rate pool.

Short life asset treatment cannot be claimed for:

- Motor cars
- Plant used partly for private purposes

The AIA can be used against short life assets but it is more tax efficient to use it against expenditure that would fall into the main pool.

Activity 7: Short life asset election

Pyrocles buys an asset in his year ended 31 December 2020 and makes a depooling election for it. Its written down value at 1 January 2025 is £20,000.

Required

Explain the tax implications if the asset is sold on 1 December 2025 for either £5,000 or £50,000.

Workings (on-screen free text area provided in the CBT as part of larger question)

9 Differences between unincorporated and incorporated businesses

We have seen in this chapter that, broadly, the rules on capital allowances are the same for unincorporated businesses (sole traders and partnerships) and incorporated businesses (companies).

Two important differences in the calculation of capital allowances are as follows:

(a) There is never a **private use asset** column in a company's capital allowance computation.

- The director or employee may suffer a taxable benefit instead and so the company can deduct the allowance in full.

- If a sole trader or partner uses a business asset for private purposes, then we restrict the capital allowances claimed on this asset.

(b)   Long **period of account** (accounts that have been made up for more than 12 months).

- If a sole trader/partnership has a period shorter or longer than 12 months, we would scale down or scale up the calculation.

- If a company has a long period of account, we perform two capital allowances computations (see Chapter 4).

Assessment focus point

Both of these points are ones which the Chief Assessor has noted students find challenging in this task, so make sure you feel comfortable with these points.

Activity 8: Calculation of capital allowances

Oscar, a sole trader, makes up accounts for the 18 months to 30 June 2021. The brought forward value on his main pool on 1 January 2020 was £81,000. He bought and sold the following assets:

		£
10 July 2020	Plant	1,410,000
10 August 2020	Car for salesman (CO_2 emissions 49g/km)	11,000
12 September 2020	Plant	550,000
1 June 2021	Disposed of plant (cost £30,000)	32,000

Required

Calculate the capital allowances claim that Oscar can make for the period ended 30 June 2021.

Solution

Assessment focus point

In the live assessment, you will be provided with reference material that can be accessed through pop-up windows. The content of this reference material has been reproduced at the end of this Course Book.

Chapter summary

- Assets that perform a function in the trade are generally plant. Assets that are part of the setting are not plant.

- Most expenditure on plant and machinery goes into the main pool.

- An annual investment allowance (AIA) of £200,000 is available on expenditure other than on cars. The AIA was temporarily increased to £1 million between 1 January 2019 and 31 December 2020. The relevant limit is prorated for periods of more or less than 12 months.

- The AIA is time-apportioned on a monthly basis if the period of account straddles 1 January 2019 or 1 January 2021.

- FYAs at 100% are available on low emission cars and energy and water saving plant.

- There is a writing-down allowance (WDA) of 18% on the balance of the main pool in a 12-month period and 6% on the special rate pool.

- WDAs are time-apportioned in short or long periods.

- If an accounting period straddles 6 April 2019, a hybrid rate it used to calculate the WDA on the SR pool as WDA were given at 8% prior to this date.

- FYAs are never time-apportioned for short or long periods.

- If the WDV on the main or special rate pool is £1,000 or less then an election can be made to write off the pool balance, known as a 'small pools allowance'.

- Balancing allowances or balancing charges will be given when the trade ceases, and when an asset is disposed of, which is not included in the main pool or special rate pool.

- Private-use of assets by sole traders and partners restricts capital allowances.

- An election can be made to depool short life assets. If a depooled asset is not sold within eight years of the end of the period of acquisition, the value of the short life asset at the end of that period is transferred to the main pool.

- Cars are dealt with according to their CO_2 emissions:
    - Up to 50g/km – FYA at 100%
    - 51g/km to 110g/km – main pool with WDA of 18%
    - Above 110g/km – special rate pool with WDA 6%

Keywords

- **Annual investment allowance (AIA):** Available in a period in which expenditure is incurred on plant and machinery

- **Balancing allowance:** Given when a positive balance remains at cessation or disposal of certain assets

- **Balancing charge:** Given when a negative balance remains at cessation or disposal of certain assets

- **Capital expenditure** is one-off expenditure that will bring benefits to the business over a number of years (eg purchase of machinery).

- **Depooling election:** An election not to put an asset into the main pool of plant and machinery

- **First year allowance (FYA):** Available at 100% on low emission cars

- **Period of account:** The period for which a business prepares its accounts

- **Plant and machinery:** Apparatus that performs a function in the business. Apparatus that is merely part of the setting is not plant

- **Private-use asset:** Has restricted capital allowances but does not apply to companies

- **Revenue expenditure** is regular ongoing expenditure that only brings benefit in the period in which the expenditure is made (eg payment of electricity bill).

- **Short life asset:** An asset that a trader expects to dispose of within eight years of the end of the period of acquisition

- **Writing-down allowance (WDA):** A capital allowance of 18% per annum, given on the main pool of plant and machinery, or 6% per annum on the balance in the special rate pool

1 An item of plant is acquired for £2,000 and sold five years later for £3,200.

   The amount that will be deducted from the pool as proceeds when the disposal is made is:

   £ [   ]

2 Nitin, who prepares accounts to 30 September each year, had a balance on his main pool of £22,500 on 1 October 2020. In the year to 30 September 2021, he sold one asset and bought one asset as follows:

Addition (eligible for AIA) 1.12.20	£171,250
Disposal proceeds on sale on 1.8.21 (less than cost)	£7,800

   The amount of capital allowances available for the year ended 30 September 2021 is:

   £ [   ]

3 A company starts to trade on 1 July 2020, making up accounts to 31 December 2020 and buys a car with CO_2 emissions of 95g/km costing £18,000 on 15 July 2020. The company also buys a car with CO_2 emissions of 5g/km for £5,000 on 1 September 2020.

   The capital allowances available in the first period of account to 31 December 2020 are:

   £ [   ]

4 Abdul ceased trading on 31 December 2020, drawing up his final accounts for the year to 31 December 2020.

   The following facts are relevant:

Main pool balance at 1.1.20	£12,500
Addition – 31.5.20	£20,000
Disposal proceeds (in total – proceeds not exceeding cost on any item) – 31.12.20	£18,300

   Identify whether the following statement is true or false. Tick ONE box.

   There is a balancing charge of £14,200 arising for the year to 31 December 2020.

	✓
True	
False	

5   Raj, a sole trader who makes up accounts to 30 April each year, buys a Volvo estate car, with CO_2 emissions of 160g/km, for £30,000 on 31 March 2020. 60% of his usage of the car is for business purposes.

The capital allowance available to Raj in respect of the car for y/e 30 April 2020 is:

£ [   ]

6   Barry ceased trading on 31 December 2020, having been self-employed for many years. On 1 January 2020, the tax written down value of his plant and machinery main pool was £7,200. On 10 November 2020, Barry purchased a computer for £1,600. All of the items of plant and machinery were sold on 31 December 2020.

(a) Required

   If Barry sells all the plant and machinery for £10,000 then he will have a

   [▼] of £ [   ] .

   Picklist:

   balancing allowance
   balancing charge

   Workings (on-screen free text area provided in the CBT as part of larger question)

(b) Required

If Barry sells his plant for £6,000 then he will have a

[▼] **of** £ [   ].

Picklist:

balancing allowance
balancing charge

Workings (on-screen free text area provided in the CBT as part of larger question)

7   Peter is a sole trader and acquired a car for both business and private purposes on 1 July 2020. The car has CO_2 emissions of 160g/km and cost £19,000. The private mileage for the nine months ending 31 March 2021 represented 20% of his total mileage for that year.

Required

Peter can claim capital allowances for the period ending 31 March 2021

of £ [   ].

Workings (on-screen free text area provided in the CBT as part of larger question)

Computing corporation tax

4

Learning outcomes

2.2	Identify and calculate capital allowances
2.3	Calculate total taxable total profits and corporation tax payable
	• Calculate the taxable total profits from trading income, property income, investment income and chargeable gains
	• Calculate the total profits and corporation tax payable for accounting periods longer than, shorter than or equal to 12 months

Assessment context

In the assessment, you may be required you to calculate taxable total profits (TTP) and then go on to calculate corporation tax.

Qualification context

You will not see this topic outside of this assessment.

Business context

Companies need to know how much corporation tax they need to pay.

Chapter overview

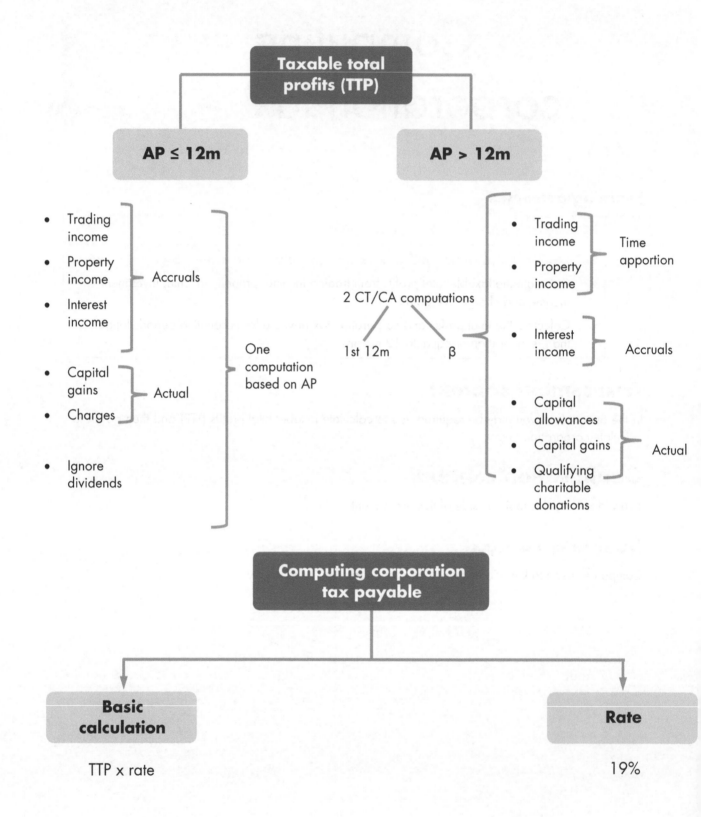

1 Introduction

In this chapter, we will look at the different types of income earned by a company, how this income is included on the tax return and how to calculate corporation tax.

2 Taxable total profits (TTP)

Key term

Corporation tax is a tax payable by companies.

Taxable total profits (TTP) are the profits on which a company must pay corporation tax.

Period of account is the period for which the company prepares its accounts.

ulation of rofits and ration tax payable

Set out below is an example of a proforma corporation tax computation. A proforma computation is also provided in the calculation of total profits and corporation tax payable section of the reference material which you can access during your assessment.

Illustration 1: Corporation tax computation for the X months to <date>

	£
Trading income	X
Interest income (NTL-R)	X
Property income	X
Chargeable gains	X
Less qualifying charitable donations	(X)
Taxable total profits	X

Much of the information covered below is shown in the calculation of total profits and corporation tax payable section of your reference material. Ensure you take a look to see what information you are given as you work this material.

2.1 Trading income

Trading income for a company is, broadly, computed in the same way that trading income for a sole trader is computed.

As a reminder, there are two important differences:

(a) There is never any private use adjustments for a company when either adjusting the accounting profit or calculating capital allowances.

(b)   Companies deal with a long period of account (accounts that have been made up for more than 12 months) in a different way to individuals or partnerships.

Note. Bad debts may be referred to as impairment losses in the financial statements of a company.

2.2 Interest

The calculation of total profits and corporation tax payable

In a corporation tax computation, interest income and expense is often referred to as a loan relationship. The taxation treatment of the interest income/expense will depend on whether the loan relationship exists for trade/non-trade reasons.

Virtually all interest received by companies will be a non-trading loan relationship (NTL-R). It is taxed as interest income/NTL-R income on the accruals basis. You may also see the income being referred to as a NTL-R credit.

Interest payable is deductible:

*   If the loan is for a **trading purpose** (eg to buy plant and machinery for use in the company's trade), **the interest is deductible when computing the company's trading income.** This means that if it is showing as an expense in the statement of profit or loss, **no** adjustment is needed.

*   If the loan is for a **non-trading purpose** (eg to buy investments such as shares or properties to rent out), the interest is **deductible from interest received** (eg from a bank or building society) **to give a net 'interest' figure to be used in computing taxable total profits**. The non-trading interest expense may be referred to as a NTL-R debit and it is the NTL-R credits and debits which are pooled to give the net 'interest' figure in TTP. In some cases, there may be a net deficit of non-trading interest paid over non-trading interest received, but the treatment of such a deficit is not in your syllabus.

2.3 Property income

A company with property business income must **pool the rents and expenses on all its properties, to give a single profit or loss**. Property business income is taxed on an **accruals basis** for companies.

Assessment focus point

You will not be expected to calculate property business income in your *Business Tax* assessment. However, you may be given a profit figure and be required to include it within the corporation tax computation, as appropriate.

2.4 Chargeable gains

Companies do not pay capital gains tax. Instead, their **net chargeable gains** (current period gains less current period and brought forward capital losses) **are brought into the computation of taxable total profits**.

We will look at gains in more detail later.

2.5 Qualifying charitable donations

Qualifying charitable donations are charitable gifts on which tax relief is given; however, they cannot be deducted as a trading expense. If a qualifying charitable donation has been deducted in computing the accounts profit, the amount deducted must be added back in computing taxable **trading** profits (adjustment of profits), but can then be deducted when computing taxable total profits.

2.6 Dividend income

Companies are not taxed on dividends they receive from other companies.

2.7 Dividends paid

Companies may not deduct dividends paid from their taxable total profits.

2.8 Income received/paid net of tax

Companies receive patent royalties from individuals net of 20% income tax. This means that the individual withholds 20% tax and pays it over to HM Revenue & Customs (HMRC) on the company's behalf.

Income received net of tax is included within the corporation tax computation at its gross equivalent. For example, £8,000 of patent royalties received net of tax would need to be grossed up by multiplying by 100/80 to include £10,000 within either trading profits or other income.

Patent royalties and interest, paid by a company to individuals, are paid net of 20% income tax which the company pays over to HMRC. It is the gross amount that is deducted in the corporation tax computation, either from trading profits or from interest or other income, as described above.

Payments of royalties and interest by a company to a company are made gross and so there are no income tax implications.

Illustration 2: Adjustment of profits and calculation of TTP

ST Ltd draws up accounts for the year ended 31 March 2021 which show the following results:

	£	£
Gross profit on trading		180,000
Dividends received from other companies		7,900
Bank interest received		222
Profit on sale of investments		20,000
Less: Trade expenses (all allowable)	83,400	
Bank interest payable (overdraft)	200	
Debenture interest payable (gross)	3,200	
Qualifying charitable donation	100	
Depreciation charge	9,022	(95,922)
Profit before taxation		112,200

Notes.

1   The capital allowances for the accounting period total £5,500.

2   The debentures were issued on 1 August 2020 to raise working capital. The £3,200 charged in the accounts represents six months' interest (£2,400) paid and two months accrued.

3   The profit on the sale of investments resulted in a chargeable gain of £13,867.

The calculation of the company's taxable total profits is as follows:

	£	£
Profit for the year per accounts		112,200
Less: Dividends received	7,900	
Profit on investments	20,000	
Interest received	222	
		(28,122)
		84,078
Add: Qualifying charitable donation	100	
Depreciation charge	9,022	
		9,122
		93,200
Less Capital allowances		(5,500)
Trading profits		87,700
Interest received (NTL-R income)		222
Chargeable gain		13,867
		101,789
Less Qualifying charitable donation		(100)
Taxable total profits		101,689

Note. The dividends received from other companies are not included within taxable total profits. Interest is deductible on the accruals basis.

Activity 1: Calculating taxable total profits

Abel Ltd, a UK trading company with no associated companies, produced the following results for the year ended 31 December 2020.

Income	£
Adjusted trading profits	2,440,000
Rental income	150,000
Bank deposit interest accrued	40,000
Chargeable gains: 25 September 2020	350,000
28 December 2020	70,000
(There were capital losses of £80,000 brought forward at 1 January 2020)	
Loan interest paid (loan was used to buy investments)	10,000
Qualifying charitable payment	70,000
Dividends received	135,000

Required

Complete the following table calculating taxable total profits for the year ended 31 December 2020.

Solution

Corporation tax computation y/e 31 December 2020

	£
Trading profits	
Rental income	
NTL-R income (Interest income)	
Chargeable gains	
Less qualifying charitable payments	
Taxable total profits	

3 Long periods of account

3.1 Accounting periods exceeding 12 months

A **period of account** is the period for which a company prepares its accounts.

An **accounting period** is the period for which corporation tax is charged.

A company's accounting period is usually the same as its period of account. However, **an accounting period cannot be longer than 12 months**. This means that **if a period of account exceeds 12 months, it must be divided into two accounting periods of**:

- The first 12 months
- The remaining balance of months

It is necessary to prepare separate computations of taxable total profits for each accounting period.

Splitting income and expenditure

Income and expenditure is split between the two computations using the following rules:

- Trading income (before deducting capital allowances) is apportioned on a time basis.

- Capital allowances and balancing charges are calculated separately for each accounting period. The annual investment allowance (AIA) and write-down allowances (WDAs) will need to be apportioned for the short period.

- Property income is time apportioned.

- Interest income (NTL-R income) is apportioned on an accruals basis.

- Qualifying charitable donations are allocated to the accounting period in which they are paid.

- Chargeable gains by reference to the date the asset is sold.

Assessment focus point

Dealing with long periods of account for corporation tax has been identified as a weak area in this task by the Chief Assessor. Make sure you know that the rules explaining how to split the long set of accounts into two accounting periods and how to split the profits between the two are clearly given in the calculation of total profits and corporation tax payable section of your reference material. The practice of applying these rules to tasks is also essential for you to be successful.

Activity 2: Calculating taxable total profits – long period of account

B plc prepared accounts for a 16-month period to 31 December 2020. The results for the period include the following:

	£
Adjusted trading profit before capital allowances	3,600,000
Bank interest receivable (accrued evenly over the period)	32,000
Chargeable gain (sale of asset on 13.10.20)	40,000
Qualifying charitable donation paid (annually on 31.7)	20,000

The tax written-down value of plant and machinery qualifying for capital allowances at 1 September 2019 was £37,500. The only capital transaction during the 16-month period was the purchase of a new van for £6,875 on 15 November 2020.

Required

Complete the following table, calculating taxable total profit for the two accounting periods that comprise the long period of account.

Solution

	months to £	months to £
Adjusted trading profits		
Less capital allowances		
Trading profits		
NTL-R income (Interest income)		
Chargeable gain		
Less qualifying charitable payment		
TTP		

4 Computing the corporation tax liability

Taxation
tables for
ness tax –
2020/21

Corporation tax rates are fixed for financial years. A **financial year** runs from 1 April to the following 31 March and is identified by the calendar year in which it begins.

For example, the year ended 31 March 2021 is the Financial Year 2020 (FY2020) as it begins on 1 April 2020. This should not be confused with a tax year for an individual, which runs from 6 April to the following 5 April.

The rate of corporation tax which applies from FY17 to FY20 is 19%.

Activity 3: Corporation tax payable

B plc has the following results for the year ended 31 March 2021:

	£
Trading profits	1,500,000
Chargeable gain	50,000
Qualifying charitable donations	30,000

Required

How much corporation tax is payable by B plc?

£ [   ]

Assessment focus point

In the live assessment you will be provided with reference material that can be accessed through pop-up windows. The content of this reference material has been reproduced at the back of this Course Book. Make sure you familiarise yourself with the content and practise referring to it as you work through this Course Book.

Chapter summary

- Adjustment of profit for companies is similar to that for individuals but there is no private use adjustment.

- To compute taxable total profits, aggregate all sources of income and chargeable gains. Deduct qualifying charitable donations.

- Patent royalties and interest are received/paid to individuals net of 20% tax. Include the gross amounts in the computation of taxable total profits.

- An accounting period cannot exceed 12 months in length.

- A long period of account must be split into two accounting periods: a period of 12 months and then a period covering the balance of the period of account.

- The taxable total profits will be charged to corporation tax at 19%

Keywords

- **Accounting period:** The period for which corporation tax is charged
- **Financial year:** Runs from 1 April to the following 31 March and is identified by the calendar year in which it begins
- **Period of account:** The period for which a company prepares its accounts
- **Qualifying charitable donations:** Charitable gifts on which tax relief is given
- **Taxable total profits:** The profits on which a company must pay corporation tax

Test your learning

1 **Indicate whether the following statements are true or false.**

	True ✓	False ✓
A company with a nine-month period of account will calculate capital allowances for nine months and deduct them from adjusted trading profits.		
A company with an 18-month period of account will calculate capital allowances for 18 months and deduct them from adjusted trading profits, and then prorate the answer between the appropriate accounting periods.		
A company with an 18-month period of account will calculate capital allowances for the first 12 months, then capital allowances for the remaining 6 months, and deduct them from the relevant prorated trading profits allocated to each accounting period.		
Dividends are not included in the taxable total profits. They are taxed separately.		

2 A company has accrued interest payable of £4,000 (gross) for the year ended 31 March 2021.

The interest payable was paid on a loan taken out to buy some machinery for use in the company's trade.

Identify how this will be treated in the corporation tax computation. Tick ONE box.

	✓
Added to trading income	
Added to net non-trading interest ie a NTL-R credit	
Deducted from trading income	
Deducted from net non-trading interest ie a NTLR debit	

3 On 30 June 2020, Edelweiss Ltd makes a donation to Help the Aged of £385. The donation is a qualifying charitable donation.

The amount of deduction available in respect of the charitable donation when calculating taxable total profits is:

£ [   ]

4   X Ltd had been making up accounts to 31 May for several years. Early in 2020, the directors decided to make accounts to 31 August 2020 (instead of 31 May 2020) and annually thereafter to 31 August.

Tick the box which correctly shows the two chargeable accounting periods for CT purposes for X Ltd.

	✓
1 June 2019 – 31 March 2020 and 1 April 2020 – 31 August 2020	
1 June 2019 – 31 May 2020 and 1 June 2020 – 31 August 2020	
1 June 2019 – 31 December 2019 and 1 January 2020 – 31 August 2020	
1 June 2019 – 31 August 2019 and 1 September 2019– 31 August 2020	

5   C Ltd prepares accounts for the 16 months to 30 April 2021. The results are as follows:

	£
Trading profits	320,000
Bank interest received (accrued evenly over period)	1,600
Chargeable gain (made 1 January 2021)	20,000
Qualifying charitable donation (paid 31 December 2020)	15,000

Using the proforma layout provided, calculate the taxable total profits for the accounting periods based on the above results. Input 0 if your answer is zero.

	[ ] ended [ ] £	[ ] ended [ ] £
Trading profits		
NTL-R income (Interest)		
Chargeable gain		
Qualifying charitable donation		
Taxable total profits		

6   P Ltd had taxable total profits of £255,000 for its six month accounting period to
    31 March 2021.

    Its corporation tax liability for the period will be:

    £

7   J Ltd had taxable total profits of £490,000 in the year ended 31 December 2020.

    The corporation tax liability for the year is:

    £

8   **Decide whether the following statement is true or false.**

    Financial Year 2020 (FY20) begins on 1 April 2020 and ends on 31 March 2021.

    Tick ONE box.

	✓
True	
False	

Taxing unincorporated businesses

5

Learning outcomes

1.2	Identify the correct basis period for each tax year
	• Identify the basis periods using opening year and closing year rules
	• Determine overlap periods and overlap profits
	• Explain the effect on the basis period of a change in accounting date

Assessment context

Basis period rules are highly examinable and need a lot of practice to ensure you are familiar with the different rules that apply in each circumstance.

Qualification context

You will not see these areas again in your studies.

Business context

Taxpayers need to know which fiscal year their profits fall into so they can determine when their tax is due. These rules will often influence when a taxpayer chooses to have his accounting period end.

Chapter overview

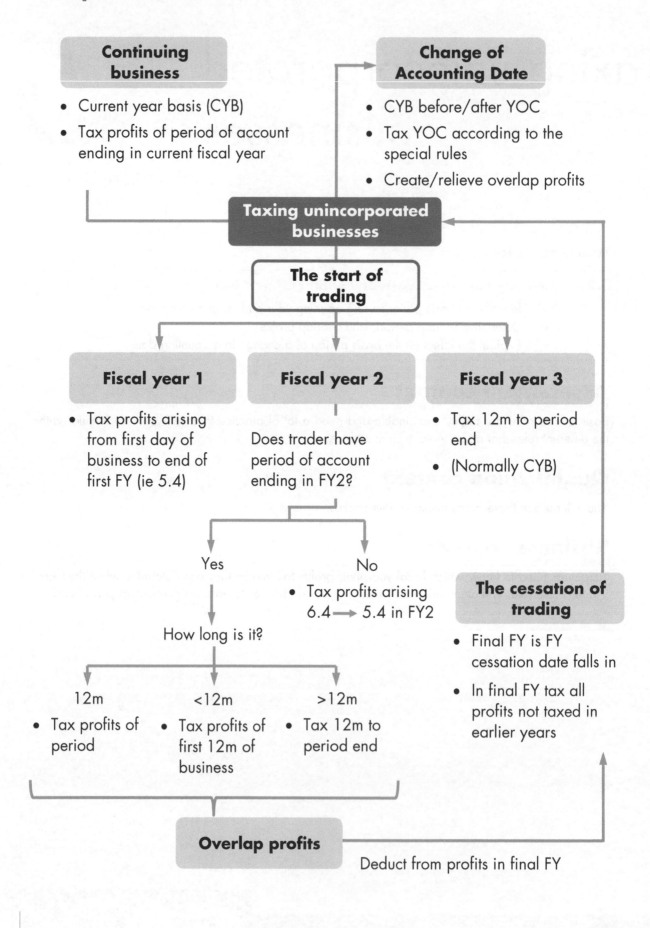

Continuing business
- Current year basis (CYB)
- Tax profits of period of account ending in current fiscal year

Change of Accounting Date
- CYB before/after YOC
- Tax YOC according to the special rules
- Create/relieve overlap profits

Taxing unincorporated businesses

The start of trading

Fiscal year 1
- Tax profits arising from first day of business to end of first FY (ie 5.4)

Fiscal year 2

Does trader have period of account ending in FY2?

Fiscal year 3
- Tax 12m to period end
- (Normally CYB)

Yes

No
- Tax profits arising 6.4 ⟶ 5.4 in FY2

How long is it?

The cessation of trading
- Final FY is FY cessation date falls in
- In final FY tax all profits not taxed in earlier years

12m
- Tax profits of period

<12m
- Tax profits of first 12m of business

>12m
- Tax 12m to period end

Overlap profits

Deduct from profits in final FY

1 Introduction

This chapter will concentrate on computing the figure to insert as **trading profit** in the income tax computation. These rules apply to unincorporated businesses only (ie individuals in business – sole traders and partners, **not** companies).

A sole trader/partnership may make up their accounts for any period they choose. As we have seen in earlier chapters, we use their accounting period as the basis for our adjustment of profit and capital allowances calculations.

However, income tax is calculated with reference to the **fiscal year** (also referred to as the **tax year** or **year of assessment**). The 2020/21 fiscal year runs 6 April 2020 to 5 April 2021.

1.1 Basis periods

A mechanism is needed to link the **taxable trading profits** (as adjusted for tax purposes and after the deduction of capital allowances) to a tax year. This mechanism is known as the **basis of assessment**, and the period whose profits are assessed in a tax year is called the **basis period**.

1.2 Current year basis

le traders
– basis
periods

The basis of assessment for a **continuing business** is the **12-month period** of account **ending** in a tax year. The profits resulting from those accounts are taxed in that tax year. This is known as the **current year basis of assessment**. This rule is stated in the sole traders – basis periods section of the reference material that you have access to within your assessment.

A sole trader who has been in business for several years and has prepared accounts for the year to 31 May each year will include **all** of the profits in the year ended 31 May 2019 in the tax return for 2019/20 because that is the tax year that the period of account ends in. Likewise all of the profits from the year ended 31 May 2020 will be included in the tax return for 2020/21.

Activity 1: Current year basis (i)

A trader prepares accounts to 31 December each year.

Required

Which year's profits will be assessed in 2020/21?

[_____ ▼]

Picklist:

Period 6 April 2020 – 5 April 2021
Year ended 31 December 2019
Year ended 31 December 2020
Year ended 31 December 2021

Activity 2: Current year basis (ii)

Required

(a) **Which fiscal year would the profits of year ended 30 June 2020 be taxed in?**

Picklist:

2019/20
2020/21

(b) **Which fiscal year would the profits of year ended 31 January 2020 be taxed in?**

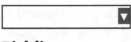

Picklist:

2019/20
2020/21

Sole traders
– basis
periods

2 The start of trading

On commencement of trade, the trader might not make up his first set of accounts for a 12-month period, therefore **special rules are needed to find the basis period in the first three tax years of a new business**. These rules always apply, even if the first set of accounts is for a 12-month period. Note that all these rules are summarised in the sole traders – basis periods section of the reference material that you have access to within your assessment.

2.1 The first fiscal year

The fiscal year in which an unincorporated business starts is the first fiscal year in which the profits will be taxed.

The profits are taxed on an actual basis in the first year, ie the profits accruing from the start date until the next 5 April. So if a trader starts to trade on 1 December 2020 and draws up accounts to 30 June 2021 making adjusted profits of £7,000, the first fiscal year is 2020/21 because that is the tax year they start their trade. In 2020/21, the basis period will be the date of commencement to the following 5 April, ie 1 December 2020 to 5 April 2021. Working to the nearest month, the profits made in that basis period is £7,000 × $\frac{4}{7}$ = £4,000.

BPP
LEARNING MEDIA

Activity 3: The first fiscal year

Christian starts trading on 1 January 2019. In the y/e 31 December 2020 he makes profits of £24,000.

Required

What is the first fiscal year of the trade? (XXXX/XX format)

What profits will be assessed in the first fiscal year?

£	

2.2 The second fiscal year

Finding the basis period for the second tax year may take more time, because there are four possibilities:

(a) If the period of account that ends in the second tax year is 12 months, tax the whole 12 months.

(b) If there is a period of account that ends in the second tax year, but it is less than 12 months, the basis period that must be used is the first 12 months of trading (ie increase the period to 12 months).

(c) If there is a period of account that ends in the second tax year, but it is longer than 12 months, the basis period that must be used is the 12 months leading up to the end of that period of account (ie reduce the period to 12 months).

(d) If there is no period of account that ends in the second tax year, because the first period of account is a very long one that does not end until a date in the third tax year, the basis period that must be used for the second tax year is the tax year itself (from 6 April to 5 April).

Illustration 1: Opening year rules – second fiscal year

Length of accounting period ending in second tax year	Taxed in second tax year
• 12 months	CYB (ie 12m period ending in fiscal year)
• <12 months	First 12 months of profits
• >12 months	12m to normal accounting year end
• No accounting period	**Actual basis** (ie 6.4 – 5.4)

The following flowchart may help you.

Illustration 2: Opening years – second fiscal year flowchart summary

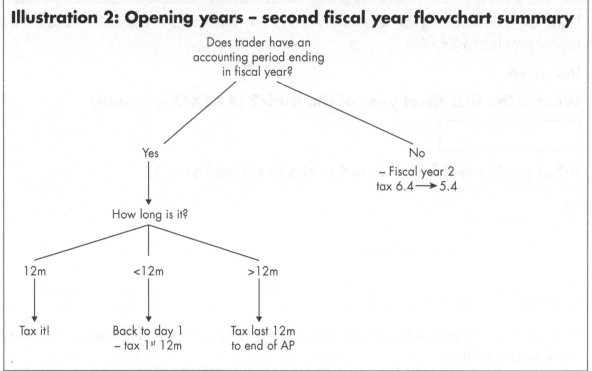

Activity 4: The second fiscal year (trader has 12-month accounting period)

Christian starts trading on 1 January 2019. In the y/e 31 December 2019 he makes profits of £24,000.

Required

What is the second fiscal year of the trade? (XXXX/XX format)

What profits will be assessed in the second fiscal year?

£

2.3 Overlap profits

You may have noticed in the previous example that some profits were taxed twice. This is a side effect of the opening year rules.

These profits are called **overlap profits**.

We will see shortly that overlap profits are deducted from profits in the trader's final fiscal year ensuring that, over the life of the business, all profits are only taxed once.

Overlap profits arise because HM Revenue & Customs (HMRC) would like all traders to have a 5 April year end.

If 5 April is selected as the year end, then no overlap profits can arise. This is a clear incentive for taxpayers to follow HMRC's wishes!

Assessment focus point

The calculation of overlap profits is an area which the Chief Assessor has identified as being a more challenging area for students in this task, so make sure you practise applying these rules to scenarios.

Activity 5: Overlap profits

Christian starts trading on 1 January 2019. In the y/e 31 December 2019 he makes profits of £24,000.

In his first fiscal year 2018/19, he is taxed on profits from 1 January 2019 to 5 April 2019 ie £6,000.

In his second fiscal year 2019/20, he is taxed on profits from 1 January 2019 to 31 December 2019 ie £24,000.

Required

His overlap period is (XX/XX/XX) ⬚⬚⬚ **to** ⬚⬚⬚.

His overlap profits are £ ⬚⬚⬚.

2.4 The third fiscal year

For the third fiscal year the basis period is the 12 months ending on the accounting date in the third fiscal year.

Further overlap profits may arise.

Activity 6: Opening year rules (short first period)

Linda starts trading on 1 January 2019. She decides on a 30 June year end and her results are:

	£
6m to 30/06/19	18,000
Y/e 30/06/20	48,000

Required

Complete the following table showing the results for the first three fiscal years of the business.

Solution

	Profits taxed			
	Fiscal year (XXXX/XX)	From (XX/XX/XX)	To (XX/XX/XX)	Amount taxed £
First fiscal year				
Second fiscal year				
Third fiscal year				
Overlap periods and profits				
First overlap period				
Second overlap period				
Total overlap				

Activity 7: Opening year rules (long first period ending in second fiscal year)

Peter begins trading on 1 July 2018. He decides on a December year end but draws up his first accounts to 31 December 2019.

He made £18,000 profits in the 18 months to 31 December 2019 and £30,000 in the 12 months to 31 December 2020.

Required

Complete the following table showing the results for the first three fiscal years of the business.

Solution

	Profits taxed			
	Fiscal year (XXXX/XX)	From (XX/XX/XX)	To (XX/XX/XX)	Amount taxed £
First fiscal year				
Second fiscal year				
Third fiscal year				
Overlap period and profits				

Activity 8: Opening year rules (long first period ending in third fiscal year)

Agnetha begins trading on 1 December 2018 and draws up her first accounts to 31 May 2020, her chosen year end. She makes £36,000 of profit in this period.

Required

Complete the following table showing the results for the first three fiscal years of the business.

Solution

	Profits taxed			
	Fiscal year (XXXX/XX)	From (XX/XX/XX)	To (XX/XX/XX)	Amount taxed £
First fiscal year				
Second fiscal year				
Third fiscal year				
Overlap period and profits				

3 The cessation of trading

Sole traders – basis periods

The final year of assessment is the tax year that the date of cessation falls into. **The basis period for this final tax year normally runs from the end of the basis period for the previous tax year to the date of cessation.**

The previous (penultimate) year is a normal year, so we apply current year basis.

In the final year, we tax all the profits arising since those taxed in the penultimate year.

We are allowed to deduct overlap profits from the profits taxed in the final fiscal year. This ensures all profits are only taxed once over the life of the business.

These rules are covered within the sole trader – basis periods section of the reference material that you have access to within your assessment.

Exceptionally, if a trade starts and ceases in the same tax year, the basis period for that year is the whole lifespan of the trade. If the final year is the second year, the basis period runs from 6 April at the start of the second year to the date of cessation.

Activity 9: Closing year rules (one period ending in final fiscal year)

Albert, who has been trading for some years making up his accounts to 31 December, ceases to trade on 30 April 2020 with profits as follows:

	Adjusted profits after capital allowances £
Year to 31/12/19	22,000
Four months to 30/04/20	12,000

Overlap profits at the start of the business were £4,000.

Required

Complete the following table showing the results for the final two fiscal years of the business.

Solution

	Profits taxed			
	Fiscal year (XXXX/XX)	**From (XX/XX/XX)**	**To (XX/XX/XX)**	**Amount taxed £**
Penultimate fiscal year				
Final fiscal year				

Activity 10: Closing year rules (two periods ending in final fiscal year)

Royce ceases trading on 31 March 2021. His recent results have been as follows:

	£
Y/e 31 December 2019	30,000
Y/e 31 December 2020	25,000
P/e 31 March 2021	4,000

Overlap profits on commencement were £12,000.

Required

Complete the following table showing the results for the final two fiscal years of the business.

Solution

	Profits taxed			
	Fiscal year (XXXX/XX)	**From (XX/XX/XX)**	**To (XX/XX/XX)**	**Amount taxed £**
Penultimate fiscal year				
Final fiscal year				

4 Change of accounting date

4.1 Introduction

A trader may change the date to which they prepare their annual accounts for a variety of reasons. For example, they may wish to move to a calendar year end or to fit in with seasonal variations of their trade. Special rules normally apply for taxing basis periods when a trader changes their accounting date.

On a change of accounting date, there may be:

- One set of accounts covering a period of less than 12 months
- One set of accounts covering a period of more than 12 months
- No accounts
- Two sets of accounts

ending in a tax year. In each case, the basis period for the year relates to the new accounting date.

The **steps** for dealing with a change of accounting date are:

1   Establish year of change (YOC) (ie. first year where CYB is not possible)

2   All years before YOC

     Basis period = 12 months to old year end

3   All years after YOC

     Basis period = 12 months to new year end

4   Year of change

     Basis period = period missed (gap) between (2) and (3) with the following adjustments:

     - If 'gap' > 12m, tax the profits of the 'gap' but bring down to 12m by relieving overlap profits from commencement

     - If 'gap' < 12m, create overlap by taxing 12m period to the end of the gap

5   Conditions

     First accounts to new date must be ≤ 18 months long and HMRC must be notified by 31 January following year of change

     Not permitted if previous change of accounting date in last five years (unless genuine commercial reasons)

 Assessment focus point

Note. that the sole traders – change of accounting date section of your reference material provided in the assessment does provide help on some of this data. However, this is remains a topic identified as weak by the Chief Assessor. Make sure you practice as many questions on this topic as you can.

4.2 Short accounting period

When a change of accounting date results in one short period of account ending in a tax year, the basis period for that year is always the 12 months to the new accounting date.

Illustration 3: Short accounting period

Sue prepares accounts to 31 December each year until she changes her accounting date to 30 June by preparing accounts for the six months to 30 June 2020.

There is one short period of account ending during 2020/21. This means the basis period for 2020/21 is the 12 months to 30 June 2020.

Sue's basis period for 2019/20 was the 12 months to 31 December 2019. This means the profits of the six months to 31 December 2019 are overlap profits that have been taxed twice. These overlap profits must be added to any overlap profits that arose when the business began. The total is either relieved when the business ceases or it is relieved on a subsequent change of accounting date.

Activity 11: Short accounting period

Harry makes up accounts to 31 August until changing to 31 May. His results are as follows:

	£
Y/e 31.8.19	20,000
9 months to 31.5.20	15,000
Y/e 31.5.21	30,000

Required

What are Harry's assessments for 2019/20, 2020/21, and 2021/22?

Solution

	£

4.3 One long period of account

When a change of accounting date results in one long period of account ending in a tax year, the basis period for that year ends on the new accounting date. It begins immediately after the basis period for the previous year ends. This means the basis period will exceed 12 months.

No overlap profits arise in this situation. However, more than 12 months' worth of profits are taxed in one income tax year and to compensate for this, relief is available for brought forward overlap profits. The overlap relief must reduce the number of months' worth of profits taxed in the year to no more than 12. So, if you have a 14 month basis period, you can give relief for up to two months' worth of overlap profits.

Illustration 4: Long period of account

Zoe started trading on 1 October 2017 and prepared accounts to 30 September until she changed her accounting date by preparing accounts for the 15 months to 31 December 2020. Her results were as follows.

Year to 30 September 2018	£24,000
Year to 30 September 2019	£48,000
Fifteen months to 31 December 2020	£75,000

Profits for the first three tax years of the business are:

2017/18 (1.10.17 – 5.4.18)	
6/12 × £24,000	£12,000
2018/19 (1.10.17 – 30.9.18)	£24,000
2019/20 (1.10.18 – 30.9.19)	£48,000

Overlap profits are £12,000. These arose in the six months to 5.4.18.

The change in accounting date results in one long period of account ending during 2020/21 which means the basis period for 2020/21 is the 15 months to 31 December 2020. Three months' worth of the brought forward overlap profits can be relieved.

2020/21 (1.10.19 – 31.12.20)	75,000
Less overlap profits 3/6 × £12,000	(6,000)
	69,000

The unrelieved overlap profits of £6,000 (£12,000 – £6,000) are carried forward for relief, either when the business ceases or on a further change of accounting date.

4.4 No accounting date ending in the year

If a change of accounting date results in there being no period of account ending in a tax year, there is a potential problem because basis periods usually end on an accounting date. To get round this problem, you must manufacture a basis period by taking the new accounting date and deducting one year. The basis period is then the 12 months to this date.

Illustration 5: No accounting date ending in the year

Anne had always prepared accounts to 31 March. She then changed her accounting date by preparing accounts for the 13 months to 30 April 2020.

There is no period of account ending during 2019/20, so the basis period for this year is the manufactured basis period of the 12 months to 30 April 2019.

You've probably spotted that this produces an overlap with the previous basis period. The overlap period is the 11 months from 1 May 2018 to 31 March 2019. The overlap profits arising in this period are added to any other unrelieved overlap profits and are carried forward for future relief.

4.5 Two accounting dates ending in the year

When two periods of account end in a tax year, the basis period for the year ends on the new accounting date. It begins immediately following the previous basis period. This means that the basis period will exceed 12 months and overlap relief can be allowed to ensure that only 12 months' worth of profits are assessed in the tax year.

Illustration 6: Two accounting dates ending in the year

Elizabeth prepared accounts to 30 September until 30 September 2020 when she changed her accounting date by preparing accounts for the six months to 31 March 2021.

The new accounting date is 31 March 2021. This is the end of the basis period for 2020/21. The basis period for 2019/20 ended on 30 September 2019. The 2020/21 basis period is therefore the 18 month period from 1 October 2019 to 31 March 2021. Six months' worth of overlap profits can be relieved in this year.

Activity 12: Two accounting periods ending in the year

Zoe makes up accounts to 30 June until changing to 31 December. Her results are as follows:

	£
Y/e 30.6.19	25,000
Y/e 30.6.20	30,000
6 months to 31.12.20	15,000
Y/e 31.12.21	35,000

Zoe has nine months of overlap profits totalling £21,000.

Required

What are Zoe's assessments for 2019/20, 2020/21 and 2021/22?

Solution

	£

 Assessment focus point

Please refer to the reference material at the end of this Course Book to see which elements of this chapter will be available to you as a pop-up window in the live assessment.

Chapter summary

- The profits of a 12-month period of account ending in a tax year are normally taxed in that tax year.
- In the first tax year, the basis period runs from the date the business starts to the following 5 April.
- There are three possibilities in the second tax year:
  - If a period of account of 12 months or more ends in the second tax year, the basis period for the second tax year is the 12 months to the end of that period of account.
  - If a period of account of less than 12 months ends in the second tax year, the basis period for the second tax year is the first 12 months from the start of trading.
  - If no period of account ends in the second tax year, the basis period for that year is 6 April to 5 April in the year.
- The basis period for the third tax year is the 12 months to the end of the period of account ending in that year.
- The basis period in the final tax year of a business runs from the end of the previous basis period to the date that the trade stops.
- When trade ceases, overlap profits are deducted from the final tax year's taxable profits.
- When a trader changes their accounting date it may result in:
  - One set of accounts covering a period of less than 12 months
  - One set of accounts covering a period of more than 12 months
  - No accounts
  - Two sets of accounts, ending in the year of change
- In each case, the basis period for the year relates to the new accounting date.

BPP
LEARNING MEDIA

Keywords

- **Basis period:** The period whose profits are taxed in a tax year
- **Current year basis of assessment:** Taxes the 12-month period of account ending in that tax year
- **Overlap profits:** The profits that are taxed more than once when a business starts
- **Tax year**, **fiscal year** or **year of assessment:** The year from 6 April in one year to 5 April in the next year

Test your learning

1 Oliver starts to trade on 1 May 2019. He makes his first set of accounts up to 31 December 2019 and annually thereafter.

Fill in the following table setting out the basis periods for the first three tax years and the overlap period of profits.

Tax year	Basis period
Overlap profits	

2 **Identify whether the following statement is true or false.**

When the trade ceases, overlap profits are deducted from the final tax year's taxable profits.

	✓
True	
False	

3 Barlow stops trading on 31 December 2020, having been in business since January 2013. Previously he has always made accounts up to 31 May. Overlap profits on commencement were £10,000.

Results for the last few years (as adjusted for tax) are:

Period	Profits £
Period to 31.12.20	15,000
Year ended 31.5.20	25,000
Year ended 31.5.19	32,000
Year ended 31.5.18	18,000

Using the proforma layout provided, compute the taxable profits for the final three tax years of trading.

Tax year	Basis period	Taxable profits £

4   Amarjat started trading on 1 February 2020. He prepared his first accounts to 30 June 2021. Taxable profits for this 17 month period were £34,000.

Show the taxable profits for 2019/20, 2020/21 and 2021/22.

Tax year	Basis period	Taxable profits £

His overlap profits are:

£	

5   Susi started to trade on 1 December 2019. Her first accounts were prepared to 30 June 2020. Taxable profits for the first two periods of account were:

Period to 30 June 2020: £70,000

Year to 30 June 2021: £60,000

(a) Her taxable profits for 2019/20 are:

£	

(b) Her taxable profits for 2020/21 are:

£	

(c) Her taxable profits for 2021/22 are:

£	

(d) Her overlap profits are:

£	

6   Barbara has been trading for many years with an accounting date of 31 October. She has no overlap from commencement of trade. She recently decided to change her year end to 30 April and made her accounts to 30 April 2020. Her taxable profits were as follows:

Year to 31 October 2019 £80,000

Period ended 30 April 2020 £50,000

Year to 30 April 2021 £120,000

(a) Her taxable profits for 2019/20 are:

£	

(b) Her taxable profits for 2020/21 are:

£ [   ]

(c) Her taxable profits for 2021/22 are:

£ [   ]

(d) Her overlap profits are:

£ [   ]

7 Stewart has always made accounts up to 31 July but in 2020 he decided to change his accounting date to 31 October and made up a 15 month set of accounts to 31 October 2020.

Results for the last few years (as adjusted for tax) are:

Period	Profits £
Year ended 31.7.19	15,000
Period to 31.10.20	25,000
Year ended 31.10.21	32,000

Overlap profits on commencement were £8,000 for eight months.

(a) Using the proforma layout provided, compute the taxable profits for the three tax years from 2019/20 to 2021/22.

Tax year	Basis period	Taxable profits £

(b) Overlap to carry forward:

£ [   ]

Partnerships

6

Learning outcomes

1.4	Analyse taxable profits and losses of a partnership between the partners
	• Apportion profits between a maximum of four partners • Determine the basis periods for continuing, new or departing partners • Allocate profits between the partners
1.6	Complete the individual and partnership tax returns relevant to sole traders and partnerships
	• Accurately complete partnership tax returns

Assessment context

In the assessment, you may be required to compute the split of partnership profits for new, continuing and leaving partners as well as the basis periods for the individual partners. The task involving analysing profits between partners is usually the best performing task within the asessement, so you must be able to demonstrate this skill.

You may also be required to complete extracts from the partnership tax return.

Qualification context

You will have seen partnerships in your accounting studies, so the basic treatment will not be a surprise to you. The tax treatment of partnerships is unique to this unit.

Business context

Partners need to know how much tax they owe to the Government.

Chapter overview

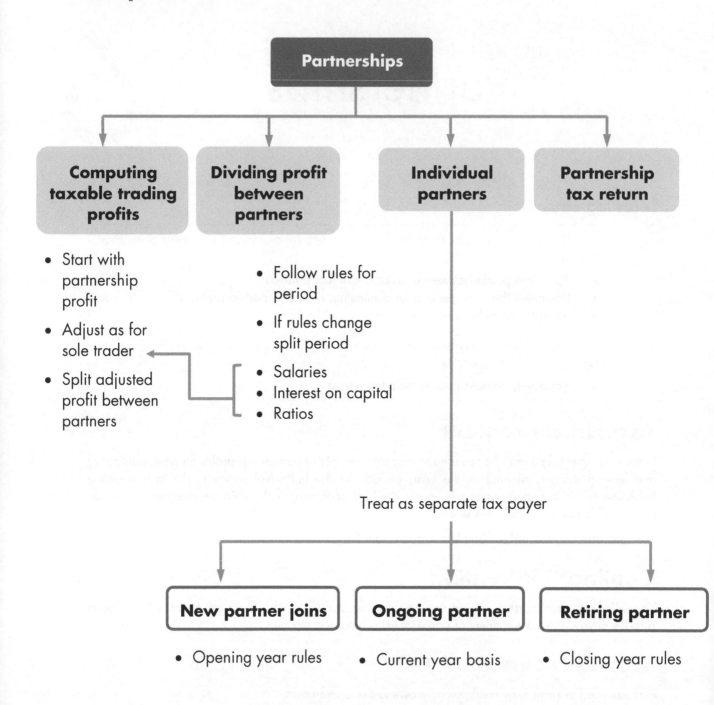

Partnerships

Computing taxable trading profits

- Start with partnership profit
- Adjust as for sole trader
- Split adjusted profit between partners

Dividing profit between partners

- Follow rules for period
- If rules change split period
- Salaries
- Interest on capital
- Ratios

Individual partners

Treat as separate tax payer

Partnership tax return

New partner joins

- Opening year rules

Ongoing partner

- Current year basis

Retiring partner

- Closing year rules

1 Introduction

In this chapter we look at the profits of a partnership, how these profits are shown on the tax return and how these profits are split between the individual partners. We then go on to look at how the individual partners are taxed on their share of the profits.

2 Computing taxable trading profits of partnerships

artnerships

A **partnership** is a group of self-employed people working together.

The partnership produces a statement of profit or loss for the whole business. Profits will be adjusted for tax purposes, and capital allowances will be calculated in exactly the same way as for a self-employed sole trader. This means that you must add back disallowable items. You must deduct specifically deductible items that have not been deducted in the accounts (for example, capital allowances) and also any income in the accounts that is not part of the taxable trading profit. Finally, add any amounts taxable as trading profits that have not been included in the accounts; for example, the market value of any goods taken for own use.

A particular point worth noting is that any partners' salaries or interest on capital deducted in the accounts must be added back when computing taxable trading profits of the partnership. These items are disallowable expenses because they are a form of drawings. They will be part of each partner's taxable trading profit as described below.

There is an additional stage here, though. The adjusted profits must be split between the partners.

Once profit has been split, each partner is treated as a sole trader and taxed separately.

3 Dividing taxable trading profits between partners

artnerships

Once you have computed a partnership's taxable trading profit for a period of account, you must divide it between the partners concerned.

The partners may agree to share profits in any way they wish. The agreed division of profits will be set out in the partnership agreement and will always be stated for you in assessment tasks. The partnerships section of your reference data provided in the assessment will give you some helpful reminders about partnerships – make sure you are aware of what information you are given.

Method:

- First, allocate any salaries and interest on capital to the partners.
- Second, share the residue of profits between the partners in the agreed ratio.

Illustration 1: Dividing profit between the partners

Pearl and Ruby are in partnership. The partnership's taxable trading profits (as adjusted for tax purposes) for the year ended 31 March 2021 were £110,000. The partnership agreement provides for Pearl to be paid a salary of £20,000 per annum and for Ruby to be paid a salary of £30,000 per annum. Any remaining profits are divided between Pearl and Ruby in the ratio 2:1.

First allocate the partners' salaries and then divide the balance of the profit in accordance with the profit-sharing ratio:

	Total £	Pearl £	Ruby £
Salary	50,000	20,000	30,000
Profit (£110,000 – £30,000 – £20,000) 2:1	60,000	40,000	20,000
	110,000	60,000	50,000

Pearl has taxable profits of £60,000 and Ruby has taxable profits of £50,000 for the year ended 31 March 2021. These profits will be taxable in 2020/21.

Activity 1: Partnership profit allocation

Ron and Steve have been in partnership as farmers since 1 July 1999 sharing profits and losses as follows.

	Ron	Steve
Salary	5,000	Nil
Balance – profit-share ratio	3	2

During y/e 30 June 2020 the partnership made a trading profit of £60,000.

Required

Complete the table showing how the profits are allocated between the partners.

Solution

	Ron £	Steve £
Profit share		

Workings (not provided in the CBT)

	Ron £	Steve £	Total £

4 Change in profit-sharing agreement

Sometimes the profit-sharing agreement may change during a period of account.

Here we apportion the profit before and after the change. We then split the profits before the change using the old rules, and the profits after the change using the new rules.

Do not forget interest and salaries are annual figures, so will need to be time apportioned.

Illustration 2: Change in partnership agreement

Jenny and Chris are in partnership. Taxable trading profits of the partnership for the year ended 31 March 2021 are £60,000. Until 30 September 2020 profits are shared equally. From 1 October 2020 Jenny and Chris agree that the profits should be shared in the ratio 2:1.

Show how the taxable trading profits of the year to 31 March 2021 are divided between Jenny and Chris.

Your first step should be to apportion the profits to the periods before and after the change in the profit-sharing ratio:

1.4.20 – 30.9.20   6/12 × £60,000 = £30,000

1.10.20 – 31.3.21   6/12 × £60,000 = £30,000

Next, divide these profits between the partners:

	Total £	Jenny £	Chris £
1.4.20 – 30.9.20 (1:1)	30,000	15,000	15,000
1.10.20 – 31.3.21 (2:1)	30,000	20,000	10,000
	60,000	35,000	25,000

For the year to 31 March 2021, Jenny's taxable trading profits are £35,000 and Chris's taxable trading profits are £25,000.

Activity 2: Change in profit-sharing arrangements

During the next year, ended 30 June, the Ron and Steve partnership made profits of £90,000.

On 1 January the partners decided to change their profit-sharing arrangement.

The old arrangement had been:

	Ron	Steve
Salary	5,000	Nil
Balance – profit-share ratio	3	2

After the change both partners receive an equal share of all profits and no one receives a salary.

Required

Complete the table showing how the profits are allocated between the partners.

Solution

	Ron £	Steve £
Profit share		

Workings (not provided in the CBT)

5 The tax positions of individual partners

Once we have allocated profits between partners, we treat each partner as an individual sole trader.

We follow normal current year basis, ie we tax each partner's profits in the fiscal year in which their period ends.

Note. It is the actual accounting period end that is important when determining the fiscal year in which the profits are taxed. If we have split the period to allocate profit because of a change in profit-sharing arrangements, we usually ignore the date of the split when deciding the fiscal year in which the profits will be taxed.

6 Changes in partners

artnerships A partnership may continue but individual partners may choose to leave while new partners may join.

If partners have joined or left the partnership, they will have their own periods with different starting or finishing dates to ongoing partners.

It is important to identify the periods of each partner. We then apply the relevant tax rules:

- A new partner will be taxed using the opening year rules.
- An ongoing partner will be taxed using the current year basis.
- A retiring partner will be taxed using the closing year rules.

Illustration 3: Partner joining partnership

Francis and Caroline have been in partnership for many years, making up accounts to 31 December each year. Profits were shared equally until 1 June 2018, when Charles joined the partnership. From 1 June 2018 profits were shared in the ratio 2:2:1.

Profits adjusted for tax purposes are as follows.

Period	Taxable profit £
1.1.18 – 31.12.18	48,000
1.1.19 – 31.12.19	18,000
1.1.20 – 31.12.20	24,000

We need to calculate the taxable profits for each partner for 2018/19 to 2020/21.

We must first share the profits between the partners.

	Total £	Francis £	Caroline £	Charles £
Year ended 31.12.18				
1.1.18 – 31.5.18 (5/12)				
Profits 50:50	20,000	10,000	10,000	
1.6.18 – 31.12.18 (7/12)				
Profits 2:2:1	28,000	11,200	11,200	5,600
Total	48,000	21,200	21,200	5,600
Year ended 31.12.19				
Profits 2:2:1	18,000	7,200	7,200	3,600
Total for y/e 31.12.19	18,000	7,200	7,200	3,600
Year ended 31.12.20				
Profits 2:2:1	24,000	9,600	9,600	4,800
Total for y/e 31.12.20	24,000	9,600	9,600	4,800

The next stage is to work out the basis periods and hence, the taxable profits for the partners in each tax year. The most important thing to remember at this stage is to **deal with each of the partners separately**.

Francis and Caroline are taxed on the current year basis of assessment throughout.

Year	Basis period	Francis £	Caroline £
2018/19	1.1.18 – 31.12.18	21,200	21,200
2019/20	1.1.19 – 31.12.19	7,200	7,200
2020/21	1.1.20 – 31.12.20	9,600	9,600

Charles joins the partnership on 1 June 2018, which falls in tax year 2018/19, so the opening year rules apply to him from 2018/19.

Year	Basis period	Working	Taxable profits £
2018/19	1.6.18 – 5.4.19	£5,600 + 3/12 × £3,600	6,500
2019/20	1.1.19 – 31.12.19		3,600
2020/21	1.1.20 – 31.12.20		4,800

Charles has overlap profits of £900 (£3,600 × 3/12) to carry forward and relieve in the tax year in which he leaves the partnership.

Illustration 4: Partner leaving a partnership

Dominic, Sebastian and India have traded in partnership, sharing profits equally for many years. On 1 May 2020 India left the partnership. Profits continue to be shared equally. Accounts have always been prepared to 30 September and recent results have been:

	Profit £
Y/e 30.9.18	36,000
Y/e 30.9.19	81,000
Y/e 30.9.20	60,000

Each of the partners had overlap profits of £10,000 on commencement of the business. We are asked to calculate the taxable trading profits of each partner for 2018/19 to 2020/21.

Firstly, allocate the profits of each period of account to the partners.

	Total £	Dominic £	Sebastian £	India £
Y/e 30.9.18	36,000	12,000	12,000	12,000
Y/e 30.9.19	81,000	27,000	27,000	27,000
Y/e 30.9.20				
1.10.19 – 30.4.20 (7/12)	35,000	11,667	11,667	11,666
1.5.20 – 30.9.20 (5/12)	25,000	12,500	12,500	–
	60,000	24,167	24,167	11,666

Dominic and Sebastian are taxed on the current year basis of assessment throughout:

	Dominic £	Sebastian £
2018/19 (y/e 30.9.18)	12,000	12,000
2019/20 (y/e 30.9.19)	27,000	27,000
2020/21 (y/e 30.9.20)	24,167	24,167

India is treated as ceasing to trade in 2020/21.

	£
2018/19 (y/e 30.9.18)	12,000
2019/20 (y/e 30.9.19)	27,000
2020/21 (p/e 30.4.20 less overlap profits)	
(£11,666 – £10,000)	1,666

Activity 3: Change in partnership personnel

M and G began a partnership on 1 June 2007, sharing profits and losses equally. On 1 December 2018, G retired and B joined them, the new arrangement being 2:1. Results have been as follows:

	£
Y/e 31.5.18	33,000
Y/e 31.5.19	51,000
Y/e 31.5.20	72,000

G's overlap profits were £5,000.

Required

Complete the following table showing the assessments on the partners for the tax years 2018/19 to 2020/21. If a partner has no taxable profit, show '0'. Identify B's overlap.

Solution

	M £	G £	B £
2018/19			
2019/20			
2020/21			
Overlap			

7 Partnership tax return

Familiarise yourself with the tax return; you may need to complete it in the CBT.

The following includes Ron's data from Activity 1: Partnership profit allocation

Partnership Statement (short) for the year ended 5 April 2021

Please read these instructions before completing the Statement

Use these pages to allocate partnership income if the only income for the relevant return period was trading and professional income or untaxed interest and alternative finance receipts from UK banks and building societies. Otherwise you must download the 'Partnership Statement (Full)' pages to record details of the allocation of all the partnership income. Go to www.gov.uk/taxreturnforms

Step 1   Fill in boxes 1 to 29 and boxes A and B as appropriate. Get the figures you need from the relevant boxes in the Partnership Tax Return. Complete a separate Statement for each accounting period covered by this Partnership Tax Return and for each trade or profession carried on by the partnership.

Step 2   Then allocate the amounts in boxes 11 to 29 attributable to each partner using the allocation columns on this page and page 7, read the Partnership Tax Return Guide, go to www.gov.uk/taxreturnforms
If the partnership has more than 3 partners, please photocopy page 7.

Step 3   Each partner will need a copy of their allocation of income to fill in their personal tax return.

PARTNERSHIP INFORMATION

If the partnership business includes a trade or profession, enter here the accounting period for which appropriate items in this statement are returned.

Start	**1**	01/05/19
End	**2**	30/06/20
Nature of trade	**3**	Farming

Individual partner details

6 Name of partner   Ron

Address

Postcode

MIXED PARTNERSHIPS

Tick here if this Statement is drawn up using Corporation Tax rules   **4**

Tick here if this Statement is drawn up using tax rules for non-residents   **5**

Date appointed as a partner
(if during 2019-20 or 2020-21) Partner's Unique Taxpayer Reference (UTR)

7   /   /   **8**

Date ceased to be a partner
(if during 2019-20 or 2020-21) Partner's National Insurance number

9   /   /   **10**

Partnership's profits, losses, income and tax credits

Tick this box if the items entered in the box had foreign tax taken off

Partner's share of profits, losses, income and tax credits

Copy figures in boxes 11 to 29 to boxes in the individual's Partnership (short) pages as shown below

- for an accounting period ended in 2020/21 ▼

from box 3.83	Profit from a trade or profession **A**	**11** £ 60,000	Profit **11** £ 38,000	Copy this figure to box 8
from box 3.82	Adjustment on change of basis	**11A** £	**11A** £	Copy this figure to box 10
from box 3.84	Loss from a trade or profession **B**	**12** £	Loss **12** £	Copy this figure to box 8
from box 3.94	Disguised remuneration	**12A**	**12A**	Copy to box 15

- for the period 6 April 2020 to 5 April 2021*

from box 7.9A	Income from untaxed UK savings	**13** £	**13** £	Copy this figure to box 28
from box 3.97	CIS deductions made by contractors on account of tax	**24** £	**24** £	Copy this figure to box 30
from box 3.98	Other tax taken off trading income	**24A** £	**24A** £	Copy this figure to box 31
from box 3.117	Partnership charges	**29** £	**29** £	Copy this figure to box 4, 'Other tax reliefs' section on page Ai 2 in your personal tax return

* If you're a 'CT Partnership' see the Partnership Tax Return Guide

SA800 2021   PARTNERSHIP TAX RETURN: PAGE 6

(Adapted from HMRC, 2020(c))

Assessment focus point

Please refer to the reference material at the end of this Course Book to see which elements of this chapter will be available to you as a pop-up in the live assessment.

Chapter summary

- A partnership is a group of self-employed individuals trading together.
- Calculate tax-adjusted profits for a partnership in the same way as you would calculate the tax-adjusted profits of a sole trader.
- Divide the tax-adjusted profits of a period of account between the partners in accordance with their profit-sharing arrangements during the period of account.
- If profit-sharing arrangements change during a period of account, time apportion profits to the periods before and after the change before allocating them to partners.
- Once you have found a partner's profit for a period of account you can consider which tax year that profit is taxed in. A continuing partner in a continuing business is taxed using the current year basis of assessment.
- The opening year rules apply to a partner joining the partnership. The closing year rules apply to a partner leaving the partnership.

Keywords

- **Partnership:** A group of self-employed individuals trading together

Test your learning

1 **The adjusted profit of a partnership is divided between the partners in accordance with the profit-sharing agreement in existence during what period?**

Tick ONE box.

	✓
The calendar year	
The tax year	
The period of account concerned	
The period agreed by the partners	

2 Dave and Joe are in partnership together and make a profit of £18,000 for the year to 31 December 2020. Up to 30 September 2020 they share profits and losses equally but thereafter, they share 3:2.

Dave's taxable profits for 2020/21 are:

£ [ ]

and Joe's taxable profits for 2020/21 are:

£ [ ]

3 Holly and Jasmine are in partnership sharing profits equally after paying a salary of £5,000 to Holly and a salary of £80,000 to Jasmine. Taxable profits for the year to 31 March 2021 were £200,000.

Using the proforma layout provided, show the taxable profits of each of the partners for the year.

	Total £	Holly £	Jasmine £
Salary			
Division of profits			

4 Barry and Steve have been in partnership for many years. Profits are shared three-quarters to Barry and one-quarter to Steve. For the year ended 31 March 2020, the partnership made a profit of £60,000 and for the year ended 31 March 2021, the profit was £80,000.

The profit taxable on Steve for 2020/21 is:

Tick ONE box.

	✓
£60,000	
£15,000	
£45,000	
£20,000	

5   Abdul and Ghita have been in partnership for many years. On 1 September 2020, Sase joins the partnership and profits are shared between the partners in the ratio 2:2:1 with Sase receiving the smallest profit share. For the year to 31 August 2021, the partnership makes a profit of £120,000.

The profits assessable on Sase in 2020/21 are:

£ _____

The profits assessable on Sase in 2021/22 are:

£ _____

The overlap profits arising for Sase are:

£ _____

6   William, Ann and John have been in partnership for many years, sharing profits equally. Accounts have always been prepared to 31 October each year. All partners had overlap profits of £5,000 on commencement. On 31 December 2020, William left the partnership. Profits continued to be shared equally. Recent results were:

	£
Y/e 31 October 2019	21,000
Y/e 31 October 2020	33,000
Y/e 31 October 2021	36,000

(a) **Using the proforma layout provided, show how the profits of each period will be divided between the partners.**

	Total £	William £	Ann £	John £
Y/e 31.10.19				
Y/e 31.10.20				
Y/e 31.10.21				

(b) **Using the proforma layout provided, show the taxable profits for each partner for 2019/20 to 2021/22.**

	William £	Ann £	John £

National insurance

7

Learning outcomes

1.5	**Calculate the NI contributions payable by self-employed taxpayers**
	• Determine who is liable to pay NI contributions
	• Calculate NI contributions

Assessment context

National insurance calculations are simple and straightforward and should earn you easy marks in the assessment. The task covering National Insurance calculations has been identified by the Chief Assessor as the best performing task in the assessment overall, so it is vital you can prepare these calculations.

Qualification context

You will not see these rules in detail outside of this unit.

Business context

These taxes are a significant extra cost for self-employed people.

Chapter overview

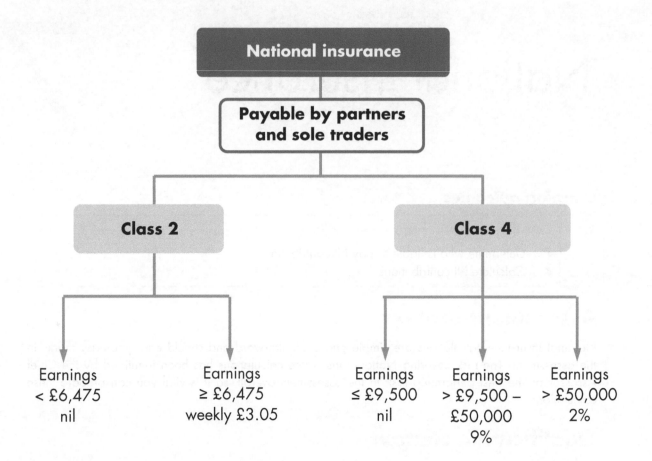

1 Introduction

Paying National Insurance Contributions (NICs) builds up an individual's entitlement to certain state benefits, such as pensions.

In the *Business Tax* assessment, you will only need to be aware of the NICs payable by the self-employed.

2 NICs payable by the self-employed

Self-employed people (ie partners and sole traders) must pay two types of NIC:

- **Class 2 contributions**
- **Class 4 contributions**

The information needed in order to calculate NIC is clearly stated in the taxation data and the national insurance contribution sections of the reference material you have access to in the assessment.

Taxation tables for ness tax – 2020/21

National insurance ntributions

2.1 Class 2 contributions

This is payable at a flat rate of £3.05 per week.

The amount of Class 2 contributions due are determined at the end of each tax year and are based on the number of weeks of self-employment in that year. This will then be collected through the self-assessment system, along with income tax and Class 4 contributions.

No contributions are due if trading profits for the year are less than the Small Profits Threshold of £6,475.

Taxation tables for ness tax – 2020/21

National insurance tributions

2.2 Class 4 contributions

This is payable in addition to Class 2.

Class 4 contributions are based on the level of the individual's trading profits after loss relief for a fiscal year.

They are calculated as:

- 9% of 'profits' between the lower earnings limit (LEL) of £9,500 and the upper earnings limit (UEL) of £50,000

- 2% of 'profits' above the UEL of £50,000

Activity 1: National insurance contributions

Note. You should calculate the following to pounds and pence.

(a)   Mr Bull, a trader, has trading income of £14,000 for 2020/21.

Required

His Class 2 NI contributions for the year are:

£

His Class 4 NI contributions at 9% are:

£

(b)   Mr Seye, a trader, has trading income of £78,000 in 2020/21.

Required

His Class 4 NI contributions at 9% are:

£

His Class 4 NI contributions at 2% are:

£

Assessment focus point

Please refer to the reference material at the end of this Course Book to see which elements of this chapter will be available to you as a pop-up window in the live assessment.

BPP
LEARNING MEDIA

Chapter summary

- Self-employed traders pay:
  - Class 2 contributions at a flat rate per week of £3.05 (in 2020/21), and
  - Class 4 contributions based on the level of their profits.
- Main rate Class 4 NICs are 9% of profits between the UEL and LEL.
- Additional Class 4 NICs are 2% of profits above the UEL.

Keywords

- **Class 2 contributions:** Flat rate contributions payable by the self-employed
- **Class 4 contributions:** Profit-related contributions payable by the self-employed

Test your learning

Compute the following total sole traders' liabilities to NICs for 2020/21.

Note. You should calculate the following to pounds and pence.

1 **Acker**

   Taxable trading profits   £5,050

£		.	

2 **Bailey**

   Taxable trading profits   £60,000

£		.	

3 **Cartwright**

   Taxable trading profits   £10,850

£		.	

Losses

8

Learning outcomes

4.1	**Appraise the effective use of trading losses**
	• Assess and calculate available loss relief
	• Advise on the best use of a trading loss for sole traders, partnerships and limited companies

Assessment context

Questions could focus on the rules for sole traders, partners or limited companies, so ensure you read the question carefully as the rules for companies are different to the rules for sole traders and partners.

Qualification context

You will not see these rules outside of this unit.

Business context

Using loss relief to generate a tax repayment is often a lifeline for struggling businesses.

Chapter overview

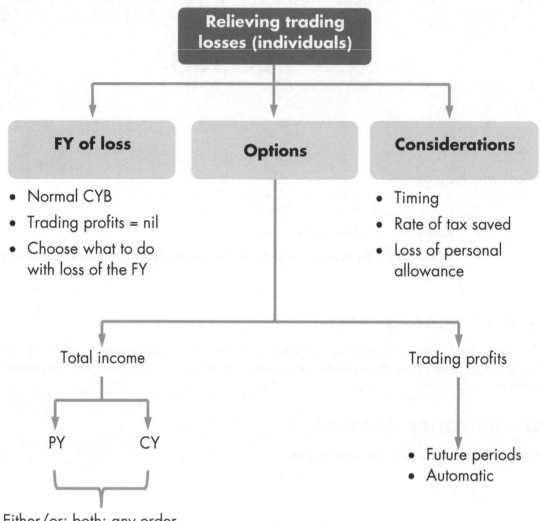

Relieving trading losses (individuals)

FY of loss

- Normal CYB
- Trading profits = nil
- Choose what to do with loss of the FY

Options

Total income

PY   CY

- Either/or; both; any order
- Optional
- May lose personal allowances

Trading profits

- Future periods
- Automatic

Considerations

- Timing
- Rate of tax saved
- Loss of personal allowance

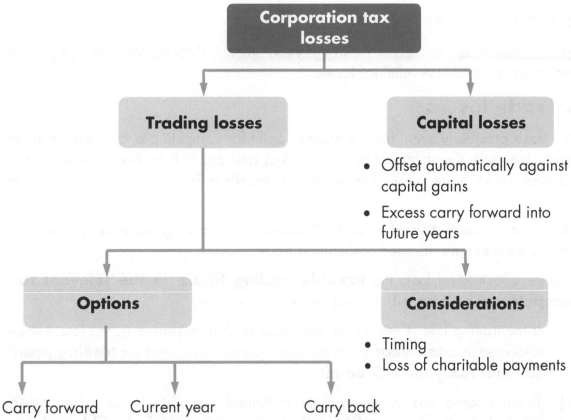

Carry forward

- Trade losses incurred post 1 April 2017 are carried forward and can be offset against total profits of a later accounting period if a claim is made

Current year

- Offset against profits before qualifying charitable donations
- Optional
- All or nothing

Carry back

- Offset against profits before qualifying charitable donations
- Optional
- All or nothing
- Must do CY first
- Previous 12 months

1 Introduction

Not all businesses make profits every year. In this chapter, we will see how a business can obtain tax relief for losses.

2 Trade losses

We have previously seen that the starting point for computing a business's trading results is to take the statement of profit or loss and adjust it for tax purposes. If this adjusted figure is negative, then there is a **trading loss**, rather than a taxable profit.

Note that the deduction of capital allowances can actually increase an adjusted loss, or even turn an adjusted profit into a trading loss.

If there is a trading loss, the **taxable trading figure in the relevant tax computation will be nil**; it is not the negative amount.

(a) If the trading loss is that of an individual (including partners), the loss will be allocated to a **tax year** using the basis period rules, and the **trading profit for that tax year will be nil**.

(b) If the trading loss is incurred by a limited company in an **accounting period**, the **trading profit for that accounting period will be nil**.

Note. Losses in a partnership are allocated to the partners in the same way as profits. Each partner will then decide on the best method of relief for their share of the loss.

Illustration 1: How it works

If a trader makes a loss of £5,000 in the year to 31 December 2020, the **2020/21** taxable profits based on that period will be **£nil**.

There will be a trading loss in **2020/21** of £5,000 which can be relieved by using it to reduce the taxpayer's other income.

The taxpayer has a choice as to how this loss is relieved, as follows:

- Carry forward of losses against future trading income
- Losses set against income in the tax year of the loss (current year CY)
- Losses set against income of the previous tax year (prior year PY)
- Losses set against capital gains

---

3 Trading loss relief options for individuals

Trading losses for sole traders and partners

3.1 Losses set against profits of the same trade

If no claim is made against total income (see below) or some of the loss is left after such a claim, then the balance must be relieved against profits of the same trade.

The loss is relieved against the first available future profits of the same trade.

Set-off is automatic and compulsory.

Any unrelieved loss may be carried forward indefinitely.

3.2 Losses set against total income

The loss is available for set-off against total income of:

- The fiscal year in which the loss-making accounting period ends (**year of the loss**); and/or

- The fiscal year immediately preceding the year of the loss.

A taxpayer does not have to deduct a loss under either method if he does not wish to do so. If he does wish to make either of these deductions, he would need to make a claim to do so.

If a claim is made, the maximum possible loss must be set off in that year (ie personal allowances cannot be saved). The taxpayer can choose which year to use the loss first eg current year and then preceding year or vice versa. Any loss left must be carried forward for use against first available profits of the same trade.

Claims to carry the loss forward must be made by 31 January, 22 months following the end of the tax year of the loss.

Illustration 2: Inclusion in the income tax computation	
	Non-savings £
Trading income	X
Relief against profits of the same trade	(X)
	X
Savings income	X
Rental income	X
Total income	X
Relief against total income	(X)
Net income	X
Personal Allowance	(X)
Taxable income	X

Illustration 3: Loss relief

Ahmed, a sole trader, has the following taxable trading profits/(loss):

	£
Year to 30 September 2019 (and so taxed in 2019/20)	10,000
Year to 30 September 2020 (loss, trading profits = nil in 2020/21)	(49,000)
Year to 30 September 2021 (and so taxed in 2021/22)	20,000

His only other income is rental income of £15,000 a year.

The loss of £49,000 is a loss of **2020/21** and could be deducted from:

- **Total income of £25,000** (trading income of £10,000 + rental income of £15,000) in 2019/20

- **Total income** (rental income) of £15,000 in **2020/21**

If both of these claims are made, the loss remaining unrelieved of £9,000 is automatically deducted from the **taxable trading profits** of £20,000 arising in **2021/22**.

Claiming to relieve the loss against total income of the current year and the prior year is optional. If he chooses not to make a claim to deduct the loss from total income, the loss is carried forward to deduct from taxable trading profits in future years.

The disadvantage of deducting a loss from total income in the year of the loss and/or in the preceding year is that **personal allowances may be wasted**. You will recall that every individual has a personal allowance that he can set against his net income. Income of up to the personal allowance is effectively tax-free income, so there is no benefit once the net income is reduced to an amount lower than the personal allowance.

Activity 1: Income tax trading loss options

Edward runs a gift card shop and his recent actual and budgeted trading results are as follows.

Year ended	£
31.12.18	5,000
31.12.19	(8,000)
31.12.20	20,000

He also receives £12,000 rental income per annum.

Required

Show if the following statements are true or false by ticking the correct box for each.

Solution

	True ✓	False ✓
Edward may offset the loss against total income in 2018/19 and then in 2017/18.		
Edward may offset the loss against total income in 2020/21.		
Edward may offset the loss against trading income only in 2018/19.		
Edward may offset the loss against the rental income in 2019/20.		

Activity 2: Utilisation of income tax losses

Pike commenced trading on 1 October 2002, making up his accounts to 30 September 2003 and annually thereafter. His recent actual and budgeted results are as follows:

Year ended	£
30.9.17	2,000
30.9.18	(15,000)
30.9.19	8,000
30.9.20	4,000

He has received rental income as follows:

	£
2017/18	400
2018/19	1,000
2019/20	1,000
2020/21	1,000

(a) Required

Complete the following table showing Pike's total income for 2017/18 to 2020/21 assuming maximum and earliest claims against total income are made. Enter '0' in cells as appropriate.

Solution

	2017/18 £	2018/19 £	2019/20 £	2020/21 £
Trading income				
Loss carried forward				
Property income				
Total Income				
CY loss relief				
PY loss relief				
Net income				

(b) Required

Show if the following statement is true or false by ticking the correct box.

Solution

	True ✓	False ✓
Pike has used his loss in the most tax-efficient way possible		

3.3 Relief against capital gains tax

If an individual has used **trading losses** in a tax year (current or prior year) to take their net income down to nil, they can then choose to make a further claim to use remaining losses against their capital gains for that year.

The claim is all or nothing so, if possible, the taxpayer must reduce the capital gains to nil.

The claim is deducted before the annual exempt amount (the capital gains tax equivalent of personal allowance), so this may be wasted if the claim is made.

BPP LEARNING MEDIA

An illustration is shown here for completeness but you should revisit this section after you have studied capital gains tax. Please note also that while the loss claims against total income are given in your reference material, it does not give you the information regarding the trade loss being used against capital gains.

Illustration 4: Loss relief against capital gains

Guy has the following results for 2020/21:

	2020/21 £
Trading loss	27,000
Total income	19,500
Capital gains less current year capital losses	14,000
Annual exempt amount	12,300

The loss would be relieved against income and gains as follows:

Income tax computation 2020/21	£
Total income	19,500
Less current year loss relief	(19,500)
Net income	0
Personal allowance (wasted)	0

Capital gains tax computation 2020/21	£
Current year gains less current year losses	14,000
Less relief for trading loss (27,000 – 19,500)	(7,500)
Chargeable gain	6,500
Annual exempt amount (partly wasted)	(6,500)
Taxable gain	0

4 Corporation tax losses

Corporation tax – trade losses

As we mentioned above, if the trading loss is incurred by a limited company in an **accounting period**, the trading profit for that accounting period will be nil.

You need to be aware of the following three methods by which a company may obtain relief for its trading losses:

- Carry forward
- Set off against current profits (optional)
- Carry back against earlier profits (optional)

You will also need to be aware of the impact that losses can have on qualifying charitable donations. This is included within the examples and tasks below.

We will look at each of the three methods of obtaining loss relief. These are similar to the rules for individuals but there are some significant differences.

4.1 Carry forward losses

4.1.1 Carry forward of trading losses incurred from 1 April 2017

Trading losses incurred from 1 April 2017 are carried forward in a flexible manner. Unused trading losses are carried forward and a claim can be made to offset some or all of the loss against total profits of future accounting periods. There is no requirement to allocate the loss against the first available profits and the claim specifies the amount of loss to be offset.

Trade losses incurred prior to 1 April 2017 are not examinable.

Assessment focus point

The AAT have confirmed that they will not examine a situation where a company claims to partially offset a loss.

Illustration 5: Carry forward loss relief

P Ltd has the following results for the three years to 31 March 2021:

	Year ended 31 March		
	2019 £	2020 £	2021 £
Trading profit/(loss)	(8,000)	3,000	6,000
NTL-R income	0	4,000	2,000

Carry forward loss relief would be relieved as follows, assuming that the company wants to use the carried forward losses as soon as possible and a claim is made:

	Year ended 31 March		
	2019 £	2020 £	2021 £
Trading profit	0	3,000	6,000
NTL-R income	–	4,000	2,000
Total profits	0	7,000	8,000
Less carry forward loss relief	–	(7,000)	(1,000)
Taxable total profits	0	0	7,000

BPP
LEARNING MEDIA

Activity 3: Carry forward loss relief

Strontium Ltd has the following actual and budgeted results for the three years to 31 March 2021.

	Year ended 31 March		
	2019 £	2020 £	2021 £
Trading profit/(loss)	(20,000)	5,000	6,000
Property income	–	2,000	2,000

Required

Assuming Strontium Ltd carries the loss forward and claims to utilise as much loss as possible, the loss carried forward at 31 March 2021 is:

£

4.2 Relief against total profits

4.2.1 Current year loss relief

Carrying the loss forward has a cash flow disadvantage for the company due to it only reducing future tax bills. The company may therefore prefer to consider using the loss to make a current year loss claim.

The trade loss may be relieved against total profits (including gains) before qualifying charitable donations in the period in which the loss arose.

The loss relief claim is 'all or nothing', so any qualifying charitable donations that become unrelieved are lost.

4.2.2 Carry back loss relief

Trading losses can be carried back against total profits (including gains) before qualifying charitable donations of the preceding 12 months.

The carry back claim may only be made **after** a current year claim (note that this is different to the rules for individuals).

This claim is also 'all or nothing' and any qualifying charitable donations which become unrelieved are lost.

Any loss remaining unrelieved after current period and **carry back loss relief** claims **must be carried forward** and offset according to the rules as to whether the trade loss was incurred before or after 1 April 2017, as explained above.

A company is permitted to carry back the loss for 12 months. If the loss is carried back to an accounting period that partly falls outside the permitted carry back period, then the total income before qualifying charitable donations of this period must be time apportioned to determine how much of the profits may be relieved.

Activity 4: Current year and carry back relief

Kay Ltd has the following actual and budgeted results.

| | Year ended 31 March | | |
	2019 £	2020 £	2021 £
Trading income	20,000	10,000	(100,000)
Capital gains	50,000	50,000	50,000

Required

Show if the following statements are true or false by ticking the correct box for each.

Solution

	True ✓	False ✓
Kay Ltd may claim to offset £60,000 of the loss against total profits in y/e 31.3.20.		
If Kay Ltd makes the maximum permissible claims, it will have £90,000 loss to carry forward at 31.3.21.		
Kay Ltd may claim to offset the loss against total profits in y/e 31.3.20 and then against total profits in y/e 31.3.21.		
Kay Ltd may claim to offset the loss against total profits in y/e 31.3.21 and carry the remaining loss forward to the y/e 31.3.22.		

Activity 5: Comprehensive example

Janet plc has the following actual and budgeted results.

	Y/e 30.9.18 £	P/e 31.3.19 £	Y/e 31.3.20 £	Y/e 31.3.21 £
Trading income	20,000	30,000	(155,000)	15,000
NTL-R income	10,000	10,000	10,000	10,000
Qualifying charitable payments	(5,000)	(5,000)	(5,000)	(5,000)

Required

Complete the following table, assuming the company will make the maximum permissible claims. Use the picklist for narrative entries. Insert '0' as appropriate.

Show all qualifying charitable donations, even if the company does not actually claim relief for them.

Solution

	Y/e 30.9.18 £	P/e 31.3.19 £	Y/e 31.3.20 £	Y/e 31.3.21 £
Trading profits	20,000	30,000	0	15,000
NTL-R income	10,000	10,000	10,000	10,000
Total profits				
▼				
▼				
▼				
▼				
Taxable total profits				

Picklist:

Current year relief
Losses carried forward
Prior year relief
Qualifying charitable donations

5 Individuals and companies – relieving non-trading losses

5.1 Capital losses

These can only be set against capital gains. The order of relief here is:

1   First, against current period/fiscal year gains

2   Second, any surplus losses are relieved against gains in future accounting periods/fiscal years

Note. Capital losses cannot be carried back to preceding years.

5.1.1 Companies

We have seen that capital gains form part of a company's taxable total profits (TTP) chargeable to corporation tax.

Any capital losses would be offset automatically against gains before considering how to allocate the trading loss.

5.1.2 Individuals

Capital gains are charged to capital gains tax and income is charged to income tax.

The rules concerning capital losses are therefore independent of the trading loss rules we have just looked at.

We will revisit the rules on capital losses for individuals in a later chapter.

6 Choosing loss relief

6.1 Individuals

As we have seen above, several alternative loss reliefs may be available for an individual, including:

- Carrying forward of losses
- Losses set against income in the tax year of the loss
- Losses set against income of the previous tax year
- Losses set against capital gains

In making a choice, consider:

(a)   **The rate at which relief will be obtained.**

We saw in Chapter 1 that individuals can pay income tax at the starting rate, the basic rate, the higher rate and the additional rate.

The most beneficial method is to try to offset losses against any income being taxed at the highest rate.

(b) **How quickly relief will be obtained.** It is quicker, and therefore could be more beneficial, to obtain loss relief against income of the previous year and current year rather than wait to carry forward loss relief.

(c) **The extent to which personal allowances and the (capital gains tax) annual exempt amount might be lost.**

6.2 Companies

We have also seen that there are several alternative loss reliefs available for a company, including:

- Carrying forward of losses
- Losses set against current profits
- Losses set against profits from earlier years

In making a choice consider:

(a) **How quickly relief will be obtained**: loss relief against total profits using a current year and carry back claim is quicker than carry forward loss relief.

(b) **The extent to which relief for qualifying charitable donations might be lost**.

Assessment focus point

Candidates often struggle with loss relief questions, so make sure you go over this chapter several times before attempting further questions to ensure you are well prepared for the assessment. It is not enough just to read the questions and answers - you need to prepare the computations yourself to fully understand them.

Chapter summary

- For an individual, a trading loss can be:
  - Carried forward to be deducted from the first available profits of the same trade
  - Deducted from total income in the tax year of the loss and/or in the preceding tax year
  - Deducted from net gains in the year of the claim against total income
- For a company, a trading loss can be:
  - Carried forward and set against future total profits if the loss was incurred post 1 April 2017 (offset if claim made)
  - Deducted from total profits in the accounting period of the loss
  - Deducted from total profits in the 12 months preceding the period of the loss
- Current year and carry back relief for a company is given against total profits before deducting qualifying charitable donations.
- An individual can choose the order in which to claim for current year loss relief and prior year loss relief.
- For a company, a claim for current year loss relief must be made before a loss is carried back.
- Capital losses can be set against current year gains or carried forward to gains in the future.
- When selecting a loss relief, consider the rate at which relief is obtained and the timing of relief.

Keywords

- **Carry back loss relief:** Allows a company to set a trading loss against total profits (before deducting qualifying charitable donations) in the 12 months preceding the period of the loss (after it has made a claim against current year total profits first); or an individual to set a trading loss against total income in the tax year prior to the tax year of the loss (no need to make a current year claim first)

- **Carry forward loss relief:** Allows an individual to set a trading loss against the first available profits from the same trade in the future. For a company, the trade loss is carried forward and can be offset with a claim against future period's total profits

- **Current year loss relief:** Allows a company to set a trading loss against total profits before deducting qualifying charitable donations in the loss-making accounting period; and an individual to set a trading loss against total income in the tax year of the loss

- **Trading losses:** These arise when the accounting profit is adjusted for tax purposes, and this adjusted figure is negative

1   Harold (a sole trader), who has been in business for many years, makes a trading loss of £20,000 in the year ended 31 January 2021.

In which year(s) may the loss be relieved against total income, assuming relief is claimed as soon as possible? Tick ONE box.

	✓
2020/21 only	
2021/22 and/or 2020/21	
2019/20 only	
2020/21 and/or 2019/20	

2   **Identify whether the following statement is true or false.**

For an individual, trading losses can only be carried forward for deduction in the six succeeding tax years.

	✓
True	
False	

3   **Where trade losses are carried forward by an individual, against what sort of income may they be relieved? Tick ONE box.**

	✓
Against non-savings income	
Against total income	
Against trading income arising in the same trade	
Against trading income arising in all trades carried on by the taxpayer	

4   Mallory (a sole trader), who has traded for many years, has the following recent tax-adjusted results:

Year ended 30 April 2019	Profit	£10,000
Year ended 30 April 2020	Loss	£(40,000)
Year ended 30 April 2021	Profit	£25,000

Mallory has other income of £9,000 each year.

Explain how the loss in the year to 30 April 2020 can be relieved.

5 **(a)** CR Ltd has the following results for the two years to 31 March 2021:

| | Year ended 31 March | |
	2020 £	2021 £
Trading profit (loss)	170,000	(320,000)
Interest	5,000	60,000
Chargeable gain (loss)	(20,000)	12,000
Qualifying charitable donation	5,000	5,000

Calculate the amount of trading loss remaining to be carried forward at 1 April 2021 assuming that all possible earlier loss relief claims against total profits are made.

£ [   ]

(b) Calculate the amount of capital loss remaining to be carried forward at 1 April 2021.

£ [   ]

6 JB Ltd had the following results in the three accounting periods to 31 March 2021:

	Year ended 30 September 2019 £	Six months to 31 March 2020 £	Year ended 31 March 2021 £
Trading profit/(loss)	4,000	6,000	(10,000)
Qualifying charitable donation	1,000	3,000	1,500

Identify the amount, if any, of the trading loss incurred in the year ended 31 March 2021 that may be relieved against total profits in the year ended 30 September 2019. Tick ONE box.

	✓
£Nil	
£2,000	
£4,000	
£3,000	

7 **State whether the following statements are true or false. Tick true or false for EACH row.**

	True	False
A sole trader's trade loss will be carried forward to offset against the first available trade profits of the same trade		
A company's trade loss incurred post 1 April 2017 will be carried forward to offset against the first available trade profits of the same trade		
A company's trade loss incurred post 1 April 2017 is carried forward and can be offset against total profits of future accounting periods		
A sole trader's trade loss must be offset against current year's total income before being offset against the total income of the prior year.		

Self-assessment for individuals

Learning outcomes

3.1	**Demonstrate an understanding of the tax return filing requirements and tax payments due**
	• Tax return filing deadlines
	• Payment rules for sole traders and partnerships: amounts and dates
3.2	**Demonstrate an understanding of the penalties and finance costs for non-compliance**
	• Penalties for late filing of tax returns and failing to notify chargeability
	• Late payment interest and surcharges
	• The enquiry window and penalties for incorrect returns
4.3	**Discuss the responsibilities relating to tax for the business and its agent**
	• What records need to be maintained by a business, for how long and the penalties for not keeping these records

Assessment context

There are a lot of very specific rules, dates and percentages in this chapter that could be tested in the assessment. Make sure you learn the detail.

Qualification context

You will not see the information in this chapter outside of this unit unless you are also studying *Personal Tax*.

Business context

It is vital for a tax adviser to ensure that their client's tax affairs are dealt with in a timely fashion and all information is properly submitted to HMRC. Serious financial penalties will arise if these deadlines are missed.

Chapter overview

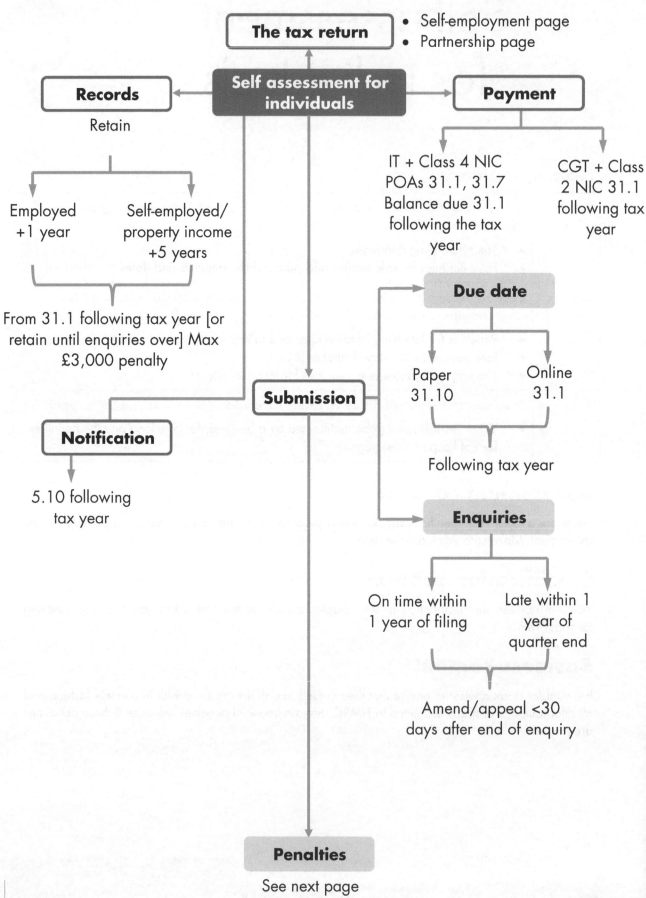

The tax return
- Self-employment page
- Partnership page

Self assessment for individuals

Records

Retain

Employed +1 year

Self-employed/ property income +5 years

From 31.1 following tax year [or retain until enquiries over] Max £3,000 penalty

Notification

5.10 following tax year

Submission

Payment

IT + Class 4 NIC POAs 31.1, 31.7 Balance due 31.1 following the tax year

CGT + Class 2 NIC 31.1 following tax year

Due date

Paper 31.10

Online 31.1

Following tax year

Enquiries

On time within 1 year of filing

Late within 1 year of quarter end

Amend/appeal <30 days after end of enquiry

Penalties

See next page

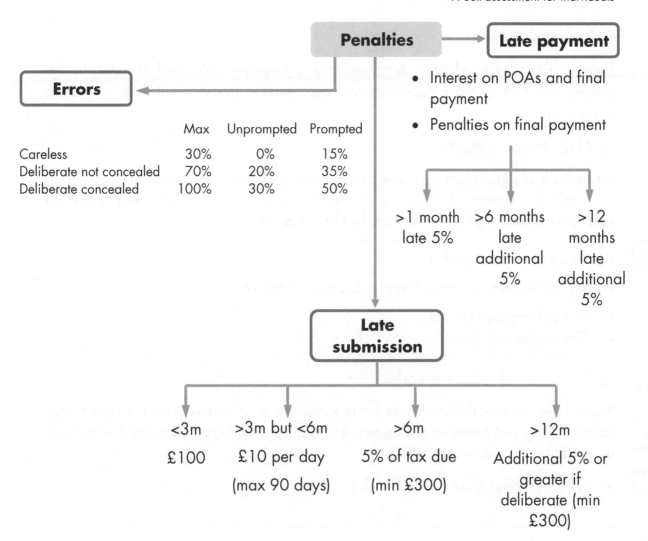

	Max	Unprompted	Prompted
Careless	30%	0%	15%
Deliberate not concealed	70%	20%	35%
Deliberate concealed	100%	30%	50%

Penalties

Late payment

- Interest on POAs and final payment
- Penalties on final payment

>1 month late 5%

>6 months late additional 5%

>12 months late additional 5%

Errors

Late submission

<3m
£100

>3m but <6m
£10 per day
(max 90 days)

>6m
5% of tax due
(min £300)

>12m
Additional 5% or greater if deliberate (min £300)

1 Introduction

There are a number of strict deadlines that a taxpayer will need to meet. In this chapter, we look at those deadlines and the penalties that occur if those deadlines are not met.

2 The tax return

An individual's tax return comprises a tax form, together with supplementary pages for particular sources of income and capital gains if required. **We will look at self-assessment of income tax in this chapter**.

> **Assessment focus point**
>
> In your assessment, you may have to complete either of:
> - The self-employment page
> - The partnership page

Payment and administration – sole traders and partners

3 Notice of chargeability

If you have income that needs to be reported on a self-assessment tax return, you have to notify HM Revenue & Customs (HMRC) by 5 October following the tax year in which the income was received.

Payment and administration – sole traders and partners

4 Timetable for 2020/21

31/10/2021	31/1/2022
Filing due date for paper returns	**Filing due date** for online returns
HMRC will calculate tax	Automatic electronic calculation of tax

Where a notice to make a return is issued after 31 July following the tax year, a period of three months is allowed for the filing of a paper return.

Where a notice to make a return is issued after 31 October following the tax year, a period of three months is allowed for the online filing of that return.

An individual may ask HMRC to make the tax computation if a paper return is filed. Where an online return is filed, the tax computation is made automatically.

Assessment focus point

In your assessment, take care if a task asks you to identify a date. The Chief Assessor has noted that some students are not careful enough in their application of the rules set out in the reference data. In addition, the Chief Assessor also notes that frequent errors are made when students calculate the period (in whole months) between two dates, meaning that the answer given is then wrong. On average, students finish this assessment with around eight minutes to spare – make sure you slow down to correctly calculate the length of time between two dates to help you apply your rules for penalties.

Illustration 1: Filing income tax returns

Advise the following clients of the latest filing date for their personal tax return for 2020/21 if notice to file the return is received on the following dates, and the return is:

(a) Paper
(b) Online

Notice to file tax return issued by HMRC:

Norma   on 6 April 2021
Melanie   on 10 August 2021
Olga   on 12 December 2021

The latest filing dates are:

	Paper	Online
Norma	31 October 2021	31 January 2022
Melanie	9 November 2021	31 January 2022
Olga	11 March 2022	11 March 2022

5 Retention of records

Enquiries and other penalties

All records must be retained until the later of:

- One year following 31 January after the end of the tax year (eg 31 January 2023 for tax year 2020/21)

- Five years following 31 January after the end of the tax year (eg 31 January 2027 for tax year 2020/21) for taxpayers who are self-employed or have property income. **Note.** All records must be retained for this time, not just property and self-employment records.

- Time at which enquiries can no longer be opened

- Time at which enquiries are concluded

The maximum penalty for failure to keep records is £3,000.

6 Penalties for errors

Payment and
administration
– sole traders
and partners

If a taxpayer makes an error in their tax return, they can amend it within 12 months of the filing date. They can also make a claim for overpayment relief within four years of the end of the tax year.

A penalty may be imposed where a taxpayer makes an inaccurate return if he has:

(a) **Been careless** because he has not taken reasonable care in making the return or discovers the error later but does not take reasonable steps to inform HMRC

(b) **Made a deliberate error** but does not make arrangements to conceal it

(c) **Made a deliberate error and has attempted to conceal it**, eg by submitting false evidence in support of an inaccurate figure

If there is more than one error, HMRC may charge more than one penalty.

Penalties may be reduced if the errors are brought to HMRC's attention by the taxpayer.

This could be **unprompted**, where the taxpayer admits the error before HMRC has any knowledge of irregularity, or **prompted**, when the taxpayer suspects the error has been, or is about to be, discovered.

Key term

Potential lost revenue (PLR) is the tax that would have been lost if the error had gone undetected.

Enquiries
and other
penalties

Penalties, which are given in the enquiries and other penalties section of the reference data provided in your assessment, are as follows:

Type of error	Maximum penalty	Minimum penalty with prompted disclosure	Minimum penalty with unprompted disclosure
Genuine mistake	No penalty	No penalty	No penalty
Careless	30%	15%	0%
Deliberate but not concealed	70%	35%	20%
Deliberate and concealed	100%	50%	30%

The scale of the reduction will vary depending upon the help the taxpayer has given HMRC in respect of:

- Advising about the error, making full disclosure and explaining how it was made
- Assisting HMRC to enable it to quantify the error
- Allowing access to records

A penalty for a careless error may be suspended by HMRC to allow the taxpayer to take action to ensure that the error does not occur again (eg where the error has arisen from failure to keep proper records).

HMRC will impose conditions which the taxpayer has to satisfy, eg establishing proper record-keeping systems.

The penalty will be cancelled if the conditions imposed by HMRC are complied with by the taxpayer within a period of up to two years.

A taxpayer may appeal against:

- The penalty being charged
- The amount of the penalty
- A decision by HMRC not to suspend a penalty
- Conditions set by HMRC in relation to the suspension of a penalty

Activity 1: Penalties

Kelly deliberately omitted an invoice from her trading income in her 2019/20 tax return, but did not destroy the evidence. She later disclosed this error, before she had reason to believe HMRC might investigate the matter.

Required

Complete the following sentence:

Kelly's penalty can be reduced from [   ] % of the potential lost

revenue (for a deliberate, but not concealed error) to [   ] %, with the unprompted disclosure of her error.

7 Penalties for late filing

The **filling due date** for a tax return is 31 October or 31 January in the following tax year, depending on whether paper or online returns are made. The penalties for filing a late tax return are:

Return outstanding	Penalty
⟶ 3 months	£100
3 ⟶ 6 months	Daily penalty of £10 per day (max 90 days)
6 ⟶ 12 months*	5% of the tax due (min £300)
12 months* ⟶	(a) 100% of the tax due where withholding of information is deliberate and concealed (b) 70% of the tax due where withholding of information is deliberate but not concealed (c) 5% of the tax due in other cases (eg careless)

*These tax-based penalties are subject to a minimum of £300

Penalties may be reduced for prompted and unprompted disclosures and cooperation with investigation.

These penalties are given in the payment and administration – sole traders and partners section of the reference material you will have access to in your assessment.

8 Due dates for 2020/21 self-assessed tax

8.1 Income tax

A taxpayer must usually make **three payments of tax**:

Date	Payment
31 January in the tax year	First payment on account
31 July after the tax year	Second payment on account
31 January after the tax year	Final payment to settle any remaining liability

Each **payment on account** (POA) is equal to 50% of the tax payable under self-assessment (ie not deducted at source) for the previous year.

If HMRC is late in requesting a tax return, then the final payment date is extended to three months following the 'notice to deliver' date (provided the taxpayer has notified chargeability on time).

POAs may be reduced if the taxpayer expects this year's liability to be lower than last year's. Interest will be charged if POAs are reduced and the final tax is greater than expected.

POAs are not required if the income tax payable for the previous year is less than £1,000 or if more than 80% of last year's liability was deducted at source.

This data is provided to you in your assessment in the payment and administration – sole traders and partners section of your reference material.

Illustration 2: Payments on account

Jeremy's tax liability for 2019/20 totalled £12,000. None of the tax was deducted at source.

Each payment on account for 2020/21 would therefore be £6,000 (50% × £12,000)

8.2 Capital gains tax

Capital gains tax is due on 31 January following the tax year. Capital gains tax is never paid by instalments (payments on account).

8.3 National insurance

Class 4 National Insurance contributions (NICs) are paid along with the income tax due. Instalments and balancing payments are calculated in the same way.

Class 2 NICs are paid on 31 January following the tax year.

Activity 2: Payments on account and balancing payments

Vorus's tax for 2019/20 was as follows:

	£
Income tax liability	7,000
PAYE (tax deducted at source from employment income)	4,000
Capital gains tax	5,000

His tax for 2020/21 is as follows:

	£
Income tax liability	8,000
PAYE (tax deducted at source from employment income)	2,500
Capital gains tax	1,000

Required

How is his tax liability for 2020/21 settled?

Solution

	£

Payment and administration – sole traders and partners

9 Penalties for late payment

Penalties for late payment of tax will be imposed in respect of balancing payments of income tax.

A penalty is chargeable where tax is paid after the penalty date. **The penalty date is 30 days after the due date for tax.** Therefore, no penalty arises if the tax is paid within 30 days of the due date.

Paid	Penalty
⟶ 30 days	0%
30 days – 6 months	5% of unpaid tax
6 months – 12 months	Further 5% of unpaid tax (10%)
12 months ⟶	Further 5% of unpaid tax (15%)

Penalties for late payment of tax **apply to balancing payments** of income tax only. They **do not apply to late payments on account**. The late payment penalties are set out for you in the payment and administration – sole traders and partners section of your reference data provided in your assessment.

10 Interest

Interest is chargeable on **late payment of payments on account and of balancing payments**. In both cases, interest runs from the **due date until the day before the actual date of payment**.

- POAs:
  - From 31 January during fiscal year
  - From 31 July following end of fiscal year
- Final payment:
  - From 31 January following end of fiscal year

If a taxpayer claims to reduce his payments on account and there is still a final payment to be made, interest is normally charged on the payments on account as if each of those payments had been the lower of:

(a) The reduced amount, plus 50% of the final income tax payable

(b) The amount which would have been payable had no claim for reduction been made

11 Repayment of tax and repayment interest

Overpaid tax is repaid unless a greater payment of tax is due in the following 30 days, in which case it is set off against that payment.

Repayment Interest is paid on overpayments of:

- Payments on account
- Final payments of tax
- Penalties

Interest runs from the later of the due date and the actual date of payment until the day before repayment is made.

12 Agent vs Principal

Where a taxpayer uses an agent, such as an accountant or tax adviser, to complete the tax return, it is the taxpayer's responsibility to ensure that the information disclosed in that return is correct. The taxpayer is referred to as the 'principal'.

The agent responsible for preparing the tax return must ensure confidentiality at all times. Only in limited circumstances may the agent disclose client information to third parties without the client's permission, for example if money laundering is suspected.

13 Compliance checks and enquiries

Usually, under self-assessment, HMRC will accept taxpayers' figures.

However, HMRC has the power to conduct a compliance check.

Some returns are selected for a compliance check at random, others for a particular reason – for example, if HMRC believes that there has been an underpayment of tax due to the taxpayer's failure to comply with tax legislation.

There are two types of compliance check:

- Pre-return check using information powers
- Enquiries into submitted returns

Examples of when a pre-return check may be carried out in practice include:

- To assist with clearances or ruling requests

- Where a previous check has identified poor record keeping

- To check that computer systems will produce the information needed to support a return

- To find out about planning or avoidance schemes

- Where fraud is suspected

HMRC must give notice of intention to conduct an enquiry not later than:

- 12 months after filing (if not late); or
- 12 months after quarter end in which return delivered

(Quarters are 31 January, 30 April, 31 July and 31 October if submitted late.)

HMRC has only one opportunity to open a formal enquiry and a tax return cannot be subject to a formal enquiry more than once.

In the course of the enquiries, the taxpayer may be required to produce documents, accounts or other information. There is a penalty of £300 for failing to produce these documents, with an additional £60 penalty charged each day the failure continues. The taxpayer can appeal to the Tax Tribunal against this.

HMRC must issue a closure notice when the enquiries are complete, state the conclusions and amend the self-assessment accordingly. If the taxpayer is not satisfied with the amendment, he may, within 30 days, appeal to the Tax Tribunal.

If the enquiry is complex or where there is avoidance or a large amount of tax at risk, then HMRC may issue a partial closure notice. This is issued ahead of a final closure notice and allows the tax payer certainty on discrete matters without having to wait for the full enquiry to be resolved.

The basic information about enquiries is covered in the enquiries and other penalties section of the taxation reference material you will be provided with in the assessment.

Assessment focus point

Please refer to the reference material at the end of this Course Book to see which elements of this chapter will be available to you as a pop-up window in the live assessment.

- Taxpayers must notify HMRC by 5 October following the end of the tax year if a tax return is needed.

- A tax return must be filed by 31 January following a tax year, provided it is filed online. Paper returns must be filed by 31 October following the tax year.

- Taxpayers must keep records until the later of:

  (a) One year after 31 January following the tax year

  (b) Five years after 31 January following the tax year if in business or with property income

- A taxpayer can amend a tax return within 12 months of filing date or make a claim for overpayment relief within 4 years of the end of the tax year.

- A penalty may be imposed if the taxpayer makes an error in his tax return based on the potential lost revenue as a result of the error.

- A fixed penalty of £100 applies if a return is filed late; followed by a potential daily penalty of £10 if the return is filed between three and six months late.

- A tax-geared penalty will also apply if a return is filed more than 6 months late, with a further penalty if this is over 12 months late.

- Payments on account of income tax are required on 31 January in the tax year and on 31 July following the tax year.

- Balancing payments of income tax are due on 31 January following the tax year.

- Late payment penalties apply to balancing payments of income tax. They do not apply to late payments on account.

- Interest is chargeable on late payment of both payments on account and balancing payments.

- HMRC can enquire into a return, usually within one year of receipt of the return. There is a penalty of £300 for failing to produce documents requested in an enquiry which increases by £60 per day that the failure continues.

- An accountant or tax adviser may act as the 'agent' for a client by preparing their tax return, but it remains the responsibility of the client, 'principal', to ensure the accuracy of the information submitted.

Keywords

- **Filing due date:** The date by which a return must be filed
- **Interest:** Charged on late payments on account and on late balancing payments
- **Payment on account:** An amount paid on account of income tax
- **Repayment interest:** Payable by HMRC on overpaid payments on account, balancing payments and penalties

1 **The due filing date for an income tax return for 2020/21, assuming the taxpayer will submit the return online, is (insert date as XX/XX/XX):**

2 **Select the correct answers to the four questions from the four picklists provided.**

   The 2020/21 payments on account will be calculated as

   of the income tax payable for

   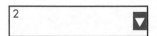

   and will be due on

   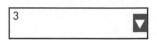

   and

   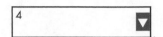

Picklist 1:	Picklist 2:	Picklist 3:	Picklist 4:
25%	2018/19	31 January 2020	31 July 2021
50%	2019/20	1 January 2021	31 December 2021
100%	2020/21	31 January 2021	31 January 2022

3 A notice requiring a tax return for 2020/21 is issued in April 2021 and the return is filed online in May 2022. All income tax was paid in May 2022. No payments on account were due.

   Explain what charges will be made on the taxpayer.

4 Susie filed her 2019/20 tax return online on 28 January 2021.

   By what date must HMRC give notice that it is going to enquire into the return?

   Tick ONE box.

	✓
31 January 2022	
31 March 2022	
6 April 2022	
28 January 2022	

5   Jamie paid income tax of £12,000 for 2019/20. In 2020/21, his tax payable was
    £16,000.

    Jamie's 2020/21 payments on account will each be

    £ [   ]

    and will be due on (insert date as XX/XX/XX)

    [   ]

    and

    [   ]

    Jamie's balancing payment will be

    £ [   ]

    and will be due on (insert date as XX/XX/XX)

    [   ].

6   Tim should have made two payments on account of his 2020/21 income tax
    payable of £5,000 each. He actually made both of these payments on
    31 August 2021.

    State the amount of any penalties for late payment.

    £ [   ]

7   **(a) By what date must a taxpayer generally submit a tax return for
         2020/21 if it is filed as a paper return?**

	✓
30 September 2021	
31 October 2021	
31 December 2021	
31 January 2022	

    (b) On which dates are payment on accounts due for 2020/21?

	✓
31 January 2022 and 31 July 2022	
31 January 2021 and 31 July 2021	
31 October 2021 and 31 January 2022	
31 July 2021 and 31 January 2022	

8   Lola accidentally fails to include an invoice of £17,000 on her 2020/21 tax return. She pays basic rate tax at 20%, and has not yet disclosed this error.

Identify the maximum penalty that could be imposed on her. Tick ONE box.

	✓
£5,100	
£3,400	
£1,020	
£2,380	

Self-assessment for companies

10

Learning outcomes

3.1	**Demonstrate an understanding of the tax return filing requirements and tax payments due**
	• Tax return filing deadlines
	• Payment rules for limited companies: amounts and dates
3.2	**Demonstrate an understanding of the penalties and finance costs for non-compliance**
	• Penalties for late filing of tax returns and failing to notify chargeability
	• Late payment interest and surcharges
	• The enquiry window and penalties for incorrect returns
4.2	**Demonstrate an understanding of the current tax reliefs and other tax issues**
	• Current tax reliefs available to businesses
	• Current tax issues and their implications for businesses

Assessment context

The assessment may require you to explain various aspects of the taxation rules, specifically including payments, penalties, filing dates and payment dates.

You may have to explain the effect of IR35 and the reliefs obtained for research and development expenditure.

Qualification context

You will not see these rules outside of this unit.

Business context

Serious financial consequences will arise if a company pays tax late or fails to file a tax return on time.

Chapter overview

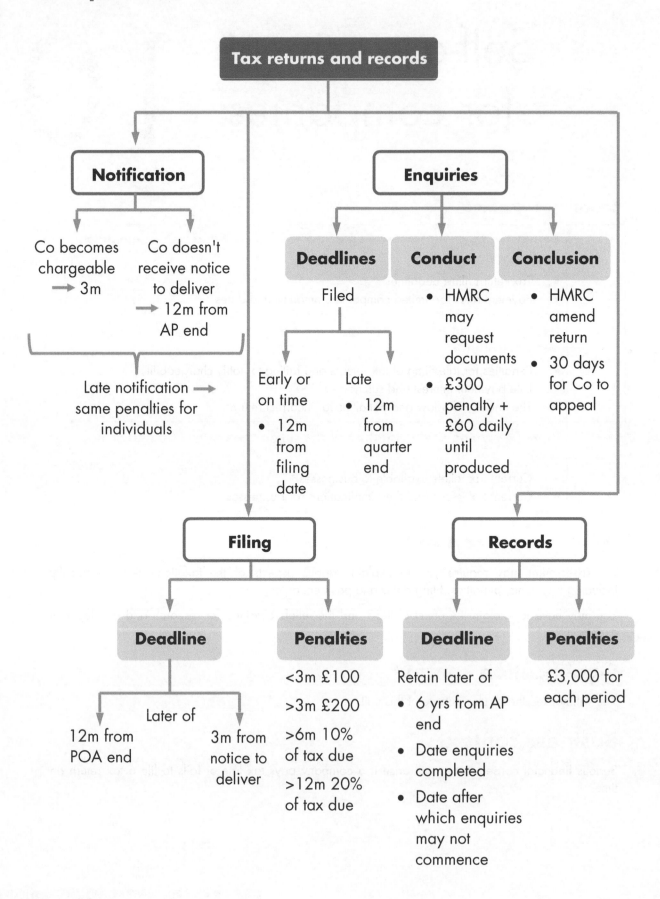

BPP
LEARNING MEDIA

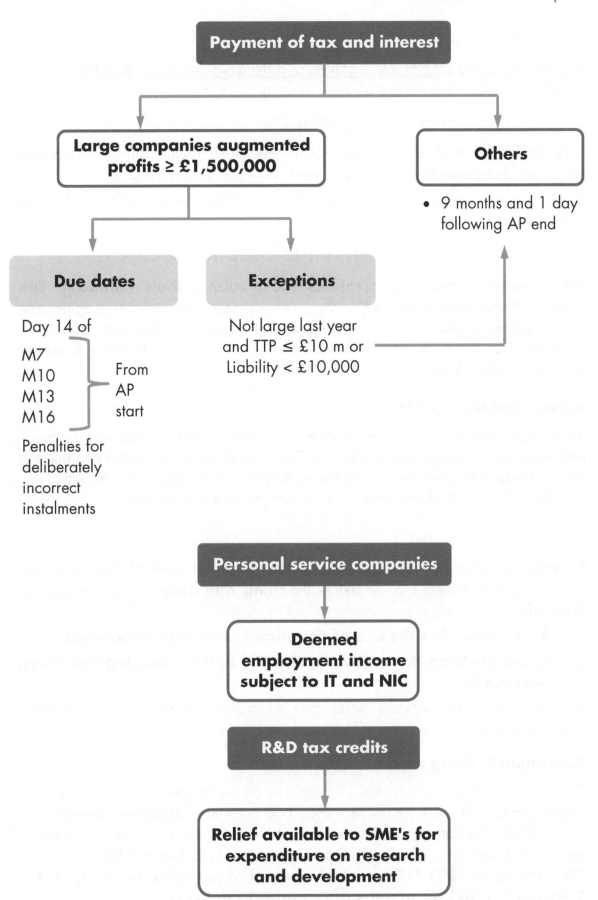

Payment of tax and interest

Large companies augmented profits ≥ £1,500,000

Others

- 9 months and 1 day following AP end

Due dates

Day 14 of

M7
M10
M13
M16

From AP start

Penalties for deliberately incorrect instalments

Exceptions

Not large last year and TTP ≤ £10 m or Liability < £10,000

Personal service companies

Deemed employment income subject to IT and NIC

R&D tax credits

Relief available to SME's for expenditure on research and development

1 Introduction

We saw in the last chapter the deadlines and penalties that apply to individuals. In this chapter, we look at those that apply to companies.

2 Notification of chargeability

A company must notify HM Revenue & Customs (HMRC) when it first comes within the scope of corporation tax. This will usually be when it starts trading.

The notice must be made within three months of the date when it first became chargeable.

3 Company tax returns and keeping records

All companies and organisations must submit their Company Tax Return (Form CT600) online, except in exceptional circumstances. Additionally, tax computations and (with very few exceptions) the accounts that form part of the Company Tax Return must be submitted in 'Inline eXtensible Business Reporting Language' (iXBRL) format.

Assessment focus point

If your assessment asks for a specific date to be determined from a calendar, you must remember that precision is essential. The Chief Assessor has noted that students do not always take sufficient care in this style of task. In addition, take care in identifying the length of time between two dates to identify a penalty due.

3.1 Filing date

Corporation tax – payment and administration

Complete accounts, computations and a tax return for each of the company's accounting periods is due on or before the **filing due date**. This is normally the **later of**:

(a) **12 months after the end of the period of account concerned**

(b) **3 months from the date on which the notice requiring the return was made**

An obligation to file a return arises only when the company receives a notice requiring a return.

Illustration 1: Filing date

Size Ltd prepares accounts for the 12 months to 30 September 2020. A notice requiring a CT600 return for the year ended 30 September 2020 was issued on 1 June 2021. The date by which Size Ltd must file its Company Tax Return for the year to 30 September 2020 is **30 September 2021, being the later of: 30 September 2021 (12 months from end of period of account) and 1 September 2021 (3 months after notice to deliver)**.

If a **period of account** is more than 12 months long, there will be **two accounting periods** based on the period of account. The first accounting period is 12 months long; the second is for the remainder of the period of account (PA).

A tax return must be filed for each accounting period. The tax returns for both accounting periods must be filed within 12 months of the end of the **period of account**.

> **Illustration 2: Long period of account**
>
> Octo Ltd prepares accounts for the 18 months to 30 June 2020.
>
> The two accounting periods relating to this period of account are **year ended 31 December 2019 and six months to 30 June 2020**.
>
> The date by which Octo Ltd must file its Company Tax Returns based on this period of account, assuming a notice requiring the returns was issued shortly after the end of the period of account, is **30 June 2021**.

3.2 Penalties

poration
payment
and
istration

Companies are subject to the following late filing penalties:

Return outstanding	Penalty
<3 months late	£100
>3 months late	£200
>6 months late	10% of tax due per return
>12 months late	20% of tax due per return

3.3 Record keeping

poration
payment
and
istration

Companies must keep records until the latest of:

(a) **Six years from the end of the accounting period**
(b) The date any enquiries (compliance checks) are completed
(c) The date after which enquiries may not be commenced

All business records and accounts, including contracts and receipts, must be kept.

Failure to keep records can lead to a penalty of up to £3,000 for each accounting period affected.

3.4 Penalties for errors

poration
payment
and
istration

The rules that apply to individuals also apply to companies.

3.5 Compliance checks and enquiries

As with an individual, HMRC may conduct a compliance check into a company's tax return.

An enquiry is a compliance check into a return that has already been filed.

HMRC must give written notice of an enquiry within:

- 12 months of actual filing date (if not late); or
- If the return is filed after the due filing date the date becomes 12 months from quarter-end that the return was filed in (31 January, 30 April, 31 July, 31 October).

Only one enquiry may be made in respect of any one return.

HMRC may request documents.

- There is a £300 penalty if the company does not provide them.
- HMRC may then charge £60 a day until these are produced.

An enquiry ends when HMRC gives notice that it has been completed.

- HMRC will amend the return.
- The company may appeal the amendments to the Tax Tribunal within 30 days.

In the same way that we saw for individuals, HMRC can issue a partial closure notice over certain matters where the enquiry is complex.

Illustration 3: Enquiries

Green Ltd prepares accounts for the 12 months to 30 April 2020. The Company Tax Return for the year was filed on 31 March 2021.

The date by which HMRC may commence an enquiry into the return based on these accounts is:

31 March 2022 (12 months from the actual filing date).

4 Payment of tax and interest

All tax must be paid electronically.

4.1 Non-large companies

Corporation tax is due for payment nine months and one day after the end of the accounting period for a company with augmented profits (taxable total profits plus dividends) **of less than £1,500,000** for a 12-month accounting period, where there are no related 51%-group companies.

If a company owns more than 50% of another company, then the £1,500,000 limit is divided by the number of related 51%-group companies; eg if Co A owns 100% of both Co B and Co C, the £1,500,000 limit is divided by 3.

Illustration 4: Corporation tax due date

K Ltd makes up accounts to 31 March 2021. Its profits do not exceed £1,500,000 and it has no dividend income. The corporation tax for the year to 31 March 2021 is £30,000.

The corporation tax is due on 1 January 2022.

4.2 Large companies

Large companies, which have augmented profits of £1,500,000 or above (adjusted by the length of the period and the number of 51%-related group companies), are required to pay their estimated tax liability in four quarterly instalments, due:

- 6 months and 14 days after the start of the accounting period (CAP)
- 9 months and 14 days after the start of the CAP
- 14 days after the end of the CAP
- 3 months and 14 days after the end of the CAP

Assessment focus point

You will not be expected to deal with periods other than 12-month periods in your assessment.

You will not be expected to deal with **very large companies** with annual augmented profits over £20 million.

Illustration 5: Payment in instalments

A company which draws up accounts to 31 December 2020 will pay instalments as follows:

Instalment	Due date
1	14 July 2020
2	14 October 2020
3	14 January 2021
4	14 April 2021

Activity 1: Payment of corporation tax

A plc has taxable total profits (TTP) of £2.1m in the year to 31 March 2021. It has no related-51% group companies.

Required

Show how the corporation tax in respect of the year to 31 March 2021 will be paid.

Solution

	£

You will note that tax must be paid before the end of the accounting period on profits that have not yet been earned.

(a) At each quarter end, the directors will have to estimate how much the total tax bill will be for the year.

(b) They then calculate the proportion of this tax due to date (eg by the time of the second instalment ²⁄₄, ie ½ of the tax is due).

(c) They will then pay over the difference compared to what they have paid to date.

Corporation tax – payment and administration

4.3 Interest to HMRC

Interest arises on late-paid instalments (from the due date to the actual payment date).

4.4 Interest from HMRC

Interest on overpaid instalments will run from the date that the tax was originally paid to the repayment date (note that interest on overpaid tax cannot run any earlier than from the due date of the first instalment).

Interest on tax paid late is a deductible expense and interest on overpaid tax is taxable. This will be added to, or subtracted from, interest income.

poration
payment
and
nistration

4.5 Exceptions

If a 'small' company is treated as large as a result of the related 51%-group companies rule, it will not have to pay corporation tax by instalments if its own liability is less than £10,000.

If a company is a large company for an accounting period, it will not have to pay corporation tax by instalments for that period if:

(a) **Its augmented profits do not exceed £10 million** (reduced to reflect any related 51%-group companies at the end of the previous period); and

(b) **It was not a large company in the previous year**.

4.6 Incorrect instalments

Penalties will be applied if the company deliberately underpays its instalments.

HMRC may require the company to justify why it paid the instalments it did. HMRC may request working papers. A fixed penalty, followed by a daily penalty, may be imposed until the information is supplied.

4.7 Long period of account

A long period of account gives rise to two accounting periods. Each accounting period will have its own due date(s).

Illustration 6: Long period of account

Z Ltd, which is not a large company, has a 15-month period to 30 September 2020.

Z Ltd will have two chargeable accounting periods:

- 12 months to 30 June 2020
- 3 months to 30 September 2020

Z Ltd will therefore have two payment dates:

- 1 April 2021
- 1 July 2021

---

5 Current tax reliefs available to businesses

Assessment focus point

In your assessment, one of your tasks will relate to you applying relevant knowledge when presenting professional advice. The topics covered below could be topics that you are expected to explain to a client and you should take careful note of the information provided to you in the reference material available to you in your assessment.

The Chief Assessor has noted that while students perform reasonably well in this task, there is a clear separation between the strongest and weakest performances. In order to meet the requirements, you need to apply the facts from the reference material to the scenario in your task; but to exceed the pass requirements, you must apply the facts from the reference material, use suitable communication skills and add relevant advice for the task scenario.

The Assessor also noted that students should familiarise themselves with the content and the layout of the reference material available to them in their assessment in order to reduce time taken gathering information for this task.

Current tax reliefs and other tax issues

5.1 Research and development

Tax reliefs are available to small and medium enterprises (SME) which incur expenditure on research and development (R&D).

An SME is a company with less than 500 employees and either:

- An annual turnover under €100 million; or
- A balance sheet total under €86 million.

5.1.1 Qualifying R&D

To qualify as R&D, any activity must contribute directly to seeking an advance in science or technology or must be a qualifying indirect activity. The costs must relate to the company's trade – either an existing one, or one that they intend to start up based on the results of the R&D.

Examples of qualifying R&D expenditure include revenue expenditure on:

- Staff directly or indirectly engaged in R&D
- Consumables or transformable material
- Computer software
- Power, water and fuel

5.1.2 The relief

An SME is allowed to deduct 230% of its research and development expenditure from its taxable profits, giving it lower profits and therefore a lower corporation tax liability.

If the deduction of this amount turns the profit into a loss, or if the company is already loss making, the company can choose not to carry forward the loss to offset against future trade profit but to surrender this loss for an R&D tax credit.

This tax credit is 14.5% of the surrenderable loss figure.

6 Current tax issues

6.1 Employment vs self-employment

Current tax reliefs and other tax issues

It is important to distinguish between employment and self-employment for tax purposes. Self-employment usually results in a lower tax burden than employment and as such, some individuals claim self-employment when they actually meet the criteria of employee. This is an issue which is often challenged by HMRC.

An employed person usually has a contract **of** service, whereas a self-employed person will have a contract **for** services.

Factors to consider when deciding if an individual is employed rather than self-employed are such things as:

- Provision of own equipment – you are usually provided with equipment if you are an employee

- Sick and holiday pay – you are not entitled to this if you are self-employed

- Financial risk – as an employee, you have little financial risk as you will receive your salary, regardless of how well the company is performing

- Control – as an employee, you will have little control over how/when and what work you do

- Exclusivity – as an employee, you usually only work for one employer

6.2 Tax differences

As an employee, there is Income Tax on salary, bonus and benefits plus NIC on salary and bonus. As a sole trader, there is also Income Tax but NIC is at a lower rate. As the owner of a company, an individual can extract cash via dividends, on which there is Income Tax (at a lower rate than salary/profits) but no NIC.

6.3 Personal service companies (PSC) (IR35)

This anti-avoidance legislation was developed in order to stop individuals selling their services to clients through an intermediary (a company). IR35 applies if an individual would be an employee of the client if the intermediary was not there. For example, I set myself up as the 100% shareholder of a company and my company sends me to work for my old employer doing the same job. Instead of receiving a salary, I take dividends from my company and consequently, end up paying less tax. My company would be referred to as a **personal service company** if this legislation were to apply.

6.4 Consequences of IR35

If IR35 applies then the individual is taxed on deemed employment income. This is the amount received from the client, less any allowable employment expenses such as business travel costs. This amount is then subject to Income Tax and NIC.

> **Assessment focus point**
>
> Much of this information is included in the reference material which is available to you as a pop up window in the live assessment.

Chapter summary

- A company must usually file its CT600 online return within 12 months of the end of the period of account concerned.

- Fixed penalties arise if the return is up to six months late. If the return is over six months late, there may be a tax-geared penalty.

- Companies must normally keep records until six years after the end of the accounting period concerned.

- HMRC can enquire into a return. Notice of an enquiry must usually be given within 12 months of the actual filing date.

- Large companies must pay their CT liability in four instalments, starting in the seventh month of the accounting period. The final instalment is due in the fourth month following the end of the accounting period.

- Other companies must pay their corporation tax liability nine months and one day after the end of an accounting period.

- An SME can deduct 230% of its R&D expenditure from its trading profits.

- If the company is loss making, it can claim an R&D tax credit instead of the expense deduction.

- Employment – a contract of service vs self-employment – a contract for service.

- Personal service company (PSC) IR35 anti-avoidance legislation is applied if the relationship between the worker and the client would be considered employment if the existence of the PSC was ignored.

- If IR35 applies – the worker is taxed on deemed employment income.

Keywords

- **Filing due date:** The date by which a tax return must be filed
- **Large companies:** Companies with augmented profits that exceed £1,500,000 for a 12-month accounting period, where there are no related 51%-group companies
- **Personal service company:** An intermediary set up to disguise permanent employment

Test your learning

1 A company has been preparing accounts to 30 June for many years. It submitted its CT600 return for the year to 30 June 2019 on 1 June 2020.

By what date must HMRC give notice that it is going to commence an enquiry into the return?

[   ]

2 A company filed its CT600 return for the year to 31 December 2019 on 28 February 2021.

What is the maximum penalty in respect of the late filing of the return for the year to 31 December 2019?

£ [   ]

3 Girton Ltd has no related 51% group companies.

When will the first payment of corporation tax be due on its taxable profits of £150,000 arising in the year ended 31 December 2020?

	✓
14 July 2020	
1 October 2021	
31 December 2021	
1 January 2022	

4 Eaton Ltd has taxable total profits of £2,400,000 for both its year ended 31 December 2018 and its year ended 31 December 2020.

The final payment of the corporation tax liability for the year ended 31 December 2020 will be due on:

	✓
14 July 2020	
14 April 2021	
1 October 2021	
31 December 2021	

5 M Ltd, a large company, has an estimated corporation tax liability of £240,000 in respect of its accounting year to 31 March 2021.

What will be the amount of each of the company's quarterly instalments?

£ [   ]

6   S Ltd, an SME, spends £125,000 on qualifying R&D in the year ended
    31 March 2021.

    **How much would be deductible from profits in respect of this
    expenditure?**

£	

7   Gavin works for Gavin Ltd. 90% of Gavin Ltd's income comes from one client who
    Gavin works for 3 days a week, on their premises, using a laptop provided by the
    client and for a fixed daily fee.

    Identify whether the following statement is true or false.

    Gavin Ltd is a Personal Service Company.

	✓
True	
False	

Chargeable gains – the basics

11

Learning outcomes

5.1	Calculate the capital gains tax payable by self-employed taxpayers
	• Apply the rules relating to chargeable persons, disposals and assets • Calculate chargeable gains and allowable losses • Apply current reliefs and allowances • Apply the capital gains tax rates
5.2	Calculate chargeable gains and allowable losses for limited companies
	• Apply the rules relating to disposal and assets • Calculate the computation of chargeable gains and allowable losses • Apply current reliefs and allowances

Assessment context

The assessment will test the basics of capital gains tax as well as other matters such as exemptions, losses and tax payable, all of which are covered in this chapter.

Qualification context

You will not see the information in this chapter outside of this unit unless you are also studying *Personal Tax*.

Business context

People and companies sell assets for a variety of reasons. It is important to realise when a charge to tax arises and when capital gains tax needs to be paid if a taxpayer is to avoid paying interest and penalties.

Chapter overview

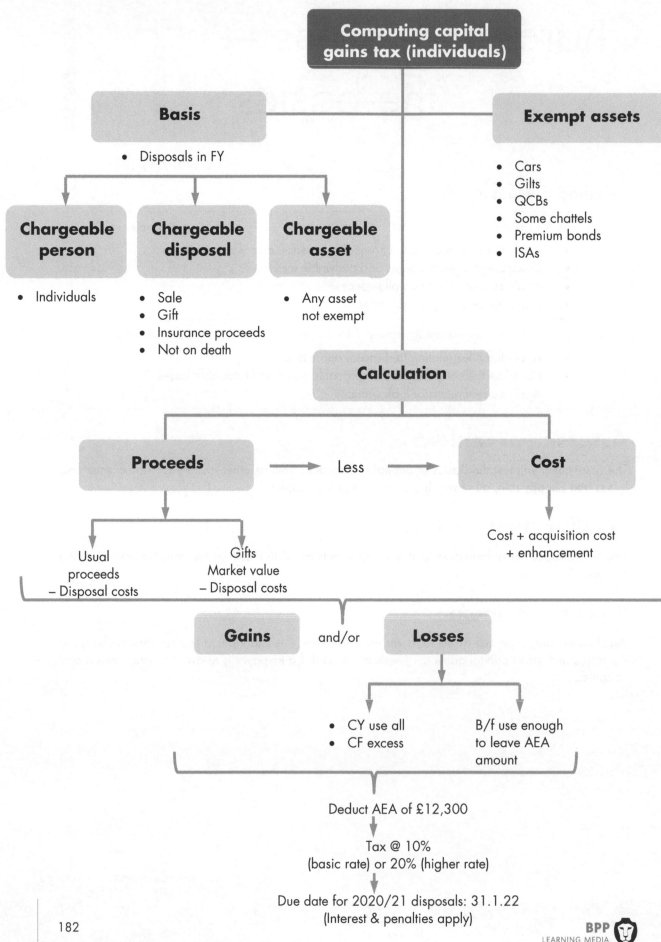

Computing capital gains tax (individuals)

Basis

- Disposals in FY

Chargeable person

- Individuals

Chargeable disposal

- Sale
- Gift
- Insurance proceeds
- Not on death

Chargeable asset

- Any asset not exempt

Exempt assets

- Cars
- Gilts
- QCBs
- Some chattels
- Premium bonds
- ISAs

Calculation

Proceeds → Less → **Cost**

Usual proceeds – Disposal costs

Gifts Market value – Disposal costs

Cost + acquisition cost + enhancement

Gains and/or **Losses**

- CY use all
- CF excess

B/f use enough to leave AEA amount

Deduct AEA of £12,300

Tax @ 10% (basic rate) or 20% (higher rate)

Due date for 2020/21 disposals: 31.1.22 (Interest & penalties apply)

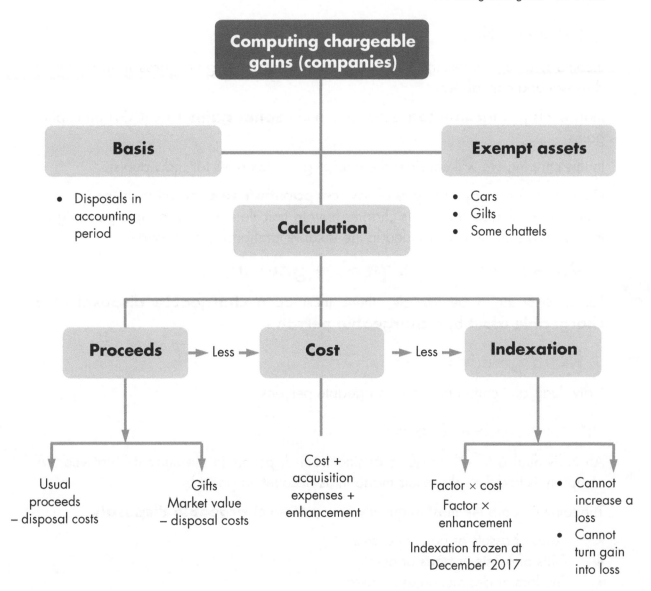

1 Introduction

Income is a regular receipt that is expected to recur. A gain arises from a one-off disposal of a capital item.

Individuals pay **income tax** on income and **capital gains tax** (CGT) on capital gains.

In this chapter, we will consider the capital gains tax rules for individuals.

Companies only pay one type of tax, **corporation tax**, on all their income and gains. We will also see in this chapter how to calculate the chargeable gains figure that we have previously included in the taxable total profits calculation.

2 When does a chargeable gain arise?

Introduction to chargeable gains

For a disposal to be taxable, there must be a **chargeable disposal** of a **chargeable asset** by a **chargeable person**.

2.1 Chargeable person

Individuals and companies are chargeable persons.

2.2 Chargeable disposal

An individual is taxed on gains arising from disposals in the current fiscal year. A company is taxed on disposals made in its accounting period.

The following are the most frequently encountered **chargeable disposals**:

- Sales of assets or parts of assets
- Gifts of assets or parts of assets
- The loss or destruction of an asset

A chargeable disposal occurs on the date of the contract (where there is one, whether written or oral), or the date of a conditional contract becoming unconditional.

Exempt Disposals include:

- Transfers on death
- Gifts to charities

On death, the heirs inherit assets as if they bought them at death for their then market values. There is no capital gain or allowable loss on death.

2.3 Chargeable assets

All assets are chargeable unless they are classified as exempt. The following are exempt:

- Motor vehicles suitable for private use
- UK government stocks (gilt-edged securities) (individuals only)
- Qualifying corporate bonds (individuals only)

- Wasting chattels (greyhounds, racehorses) eg greyhounds, racehorses (see later)
- Premium bonds (individuals only)
- Investments held in an ISA (individuals only)

Remember that sales of assets as part of the trade of a business (ie sales of inventory) give rise to trading profits and not chargeable gains.

Assessment focus point

Make sure you identify an exempt asset, state that it is exempt and do not tax it.

3 Calculation of chargeable gains and allowable losses for individuals

Illustration 1: Basic capital gains computation

Disposal consideration (or market value)	X
Less incidental costs of disposal	(X)
Net proceeds	X
Less allowable cost (including acquisition cost)	(X)
Less enhancement expenditure	(X)
Capital gain/(capital loss)	X/(X)

We now look at each of the items in the above proforma in turn.

3.1 Disposal consideration

Usually, this is proceeds received. Note though, that a disposal is deemed to take place at market value (MV) when the disposal is:

- A gift
- A sale at undervalue (for example, a sale to a friend for less than MV)
- Made for a consideration that cannot be valued
- Made to a connected person (see later)

3.2 Costs

The following costs are deducted in the above proforma:

(a) **Incidental costs of disposal**

These are the costs of selling an asset. They may include advertising costs, estate agents' fees, legal costs and valuation fees. These costs should be deducted separately from any other allowable costs.

(b) **Allowable costs**

These include:

(i) The original purchase price of the asset
(ii) Costs incurred in purchasing the asset (estate agents' fees, legal fees, etc)

(c) **Enhancement expenditure**

Enhancement expenditure is capital expenditure which enhances the value of the asset and is reflected in the state or nature of the asset at the time of disposal.

Illustration 2: Calculation of capital gain

Jack bought a holiday cottage for £25,000. He paid legal costs of £600 on the purchase.

Jack spent £8,000 building an extension to the cottage.

Jack sold the cottage for £60,000. He paid estate agents' fees of £1,200 and legal costs of £750.

Jack's gain on sale is:

£	24,450

	£
Disposal consideration	60,000
Less: incidental costs of disposal (1,200 + 750)	(1,950)
Net proceeds	58,050
Less: allowable costs (25,000 + 600)	(25,600)
Less: enhancement expenditure	(8,000)
Chargeable gain	24,450

Activity 1: Capital gain calculation (Individuals)

Mr Dunstable bought an asset for £15,000 in February 1986. He incurred legal fees of £500. He sold the asset for £38,500 incurring expenses of £1,500. While he owned the asset, he improved it at a cost of £3,000.

Required

Complete the table showing Mr Dunstable's gain.

Solution

	£
Proceeds	
Less selling expenses	
Net proceeds	
Less cost	
Less legal fees on purchase	
Less enhancement	
Capital gain	

4 Computing taxable gains in a tax year

Introduction
to
chargeable
gains

An individual pays capital gains tax on any **taxable gains** arising in a **tax year** (6 April to 5 April).

All the chargeable gains made in the tax year are added together, and any capital losses made in the same tax year are deducted to give net gains (or losses) for the year. Trading losses that can be offset against gains (which we saw in Chapter 8) are deducted next, and then the annual exempt amount is deducted. Finally, any unrelieved capital losses brought forward from previous years is deducted to arrive at taxable gains, on which CGT will be applied.

Year-end computation

	£
Current gains	X
Current losses (all)	(X)
Net gains	X
Annual exempt amount	(12,300)
	X
Losses b/fwd from earlier years	(X)
Taxable gains	X

Note. Unused annual exempt amounts cannot be carried forward.

Introduction to
chargeable gains

4.1 Annual exempt amount

Key term

> **Annual exempt amount (AEA)/annual exemption** is the amount of gain
> that will be tax free. For 2020/21, this is £12,300.

This may also be referred to as an **annual exemption** in your assessment. It is
deducted from net gains in the tax year after any current year capital losses but
before any brought forward losses. This means that for 2020/21, the first £12,300
of chargeable gains are tax free for an individual.

Introduction to
chargeable gains

4.2 Losses

If losses have been made in the current year, they must be offset against the gains of
that year, even if this means that some or all of the annual exempt amount is
wasted.

If the losses in a year are greater than the gains, then the excess losses are carried
forward. When a capital loss is carried forward, it is set against gains **after** the
annual exempt amount. This means the taxpayer does not lose the benefit of the
annual exempt amount. Any further loss remaining is carried forward.

> **Illustration 3: Capital losses**
>
> (a) Tim has chargeable gains in 2020/21 of £25,000 and allowable losses of
>   £16,000. As the losses are current year losses, they must be fully relieved
>   against the gains to produce net gains of £9,000, despite the fact that net gains
>   are below the annual exempt amount.
>
> | | £ |
> | --- | --- |
> | Chargeable gains in tax year | 25,000 |
> | Less losses in tax year | (16,000) |
> | Net chargeable gains | 9,000 |
> | Less annual exempt amount | (12,300) |
> | Taxable gain | 0 |
>
> (b) Hattie has gains of £22,200 in 2020/21 and allowable losses brought
>   forward of £16,000. Hattie offsets the annual exempt amount to leave £9,900
>   of gains to be covered by her brought forward capital losses.
>
> | | £ |
> | --- | --- |
> | Net chargeable gains | 22,200 |
> | Less annual exempt amount | (12,300) |
> | Less losses brought forward | (9,900) |
> | Taxable gain | 0 |
>
> The remaining £6,100 (16,000 – 9,900) of losses are carried forward to
> 2021/22.

Activity 2: Current year losses

In 2020/21, Ted makes gains of £45,000 and £10,000. He also makes a loss of £48,000. Ted has no losses to bring forward from earlier years.

Required

Ted's net capital gain for 2020/21 before the annual exempt amount is:

£ [   ]

Ted has a loss to carry forward of £ [   ].

Workings (not provided in the CBT)

	£

Activity 3: Prior year losses

Tara disposes of a property in 2020/21 for proceeds of £27,000. Her total allowable costs of the property are £13,000. She makes no other disposals in the tax year. Tara has losses brought forward from the previous year of £10,000.

Required

Tara's net capital gain for 2020/21 before the deduction of losses is:

£ [   ]

Tara has a loss to carry forward of £ [   ].

Workings (not provided in the CBT)

	£

Taxation tables for business tax – 2020/21

5 Computing capital gains tax payable

An individual's taxable gains are chargeable to CGT at the rate of 10% or 20% depending on the individual's taxable income in the fiscal year.

If the individual is a basic rate taxpayer, then CGT is payable at 10% on an amount of taxable gains up to the amount of the taxpayer's **unused** basic rate band; and at 20% on the excess.

If the individual is a higher or additional rate taxpayer, then CGT is payable at 20% on all their taxable gains. Note that the basic rate band covers taxable income and gains up to £37,500 (in 2020/21).

Illustration 4: Calculating capital gains tax

(a) In 2020/21, Sally has taxable income (ie the amount after the deduction of the personal allowance) of £10,000 and taxable gains (ie after the deduction of the annual exempt amount) of £20,000.

Sally's CGT liability is:

£20,000 × 10%   £2,000
The taxable income uses £10,000 of the basic rate band, leaving £27,500 of the basic rate band unused, therefore all of the taxable gain is taxed at 10%.

(b) In 2020/21 Hector has taxable income of £60,000 (ie he is a higher rate taxpayer), and made taxable gains of £10,000.

Hector's CGT liability is:

£10,000 × 20%   £2,000
All of Hector's basic rate band has been taken up by the taxable income, therefore the taxable gain is taxed at 20%.

(c) Isabel has taxable income of £30,000 in 2020/21 as well as taxable gains of £25,000.

Isabel has (£37,500 – £30,000) = £7,500 of her basic rate band unused. Isabel's CGT liability is:

	£
7,500 × 10%	750
£17,500 × 20%	3,500
£25,000	4,250

Activity 4: Computing capital gains tax payable

Mr Dunstable had a chargeable gain of £18,800 in 2020/21 and taxable income of £34,000.

Required

What is Mr Dunstable's capital gains tax payable?

£ [   ].

Workings (not provided in the CBT)

	£

6 Self-assessment for capital gains tax

CGT is payable on 31 January following the end of the tax year.

There are no payments on account.

An individual taxpayer who makes chargeable gains in a tax year is usually required to file details of the gains in a tax return. In many cases, the taxpayer will be filing a tax return for income tax purposes and will include the capital gains supplementary pages. If, however, the taxpayer only has chargeable gains to report, **he must notify his chargeability to HMRC by 5 October following the end of the tax year**.

The consequences of late notification, late filing, late payment of CGT and errors are the same as for income tax, so penalties and interest may be charged where applicable. Repayment interest may be paid on overpayments of CGT.

Calculation of gains and losses for companies

7 Computing chargeable gains and allowable losses for companies

The calculation of a chargeable gain or allowable loss for a company is very similar to the calculations we have already seen for individuals, with just a few significant differences:

- Companies claim an allowance for inflation called 'indexation'.

- Companies do not get an annual exempt amount.

- Loss relief is more straightforward. Current year gains and losses net off against each other. We then deduct capital losses brought forward.

Calculation of gains and losses for companies

7.1 Calculation of chargeable gains for companies

Basic capital gains computation

	£
Disposal consideration (or market value)	X
Less incidental costs of disposal	(X)
Net proceeds	X
Less allowable costs (including acquisition costs)	(X)
Less enhancement expenditure	(X)
Unindexed gain	X
Less indexation on cost	(X)
Less indexation on enhancement expenditure	(X)
Indexed gain	X

7.2 Indexation allowance

Indexation allowance (IA) is given as a deduction to remove the effects of inflation from a gain.

It is calculated with reference to the movement of the retail price index (RPI) over the period of ownership. However, it was frozen in December 2017 and so indexation can only ever be given for ownership up to December 2017.

The allowance is applied to the cost.

If the asset has subsequently been enhanced, IA must be applied separately to the enhancement as there will be different levels of inflation on the differing time periods.

You will be given the IA factor to use in your assessment.

Illustration 5: Indexation allowance

K Ltd bought an asset on 19 August 2000 for £10,000. Enhancement expenditure of £1,000 was incurred on 12 June 2007. The asset was sold for £41,500 on 20 February 2021. The disposal costs were £1,500.

Calculate the chargeable gain arising on the sale of the asset. Indexation factors: August 2000 to December 2017 = 0.631; June 2007 to December 2017 = 0.342.

	£
Disposal consideration	41,500
Less incidental costs of disposal	(1,500)
Net proceeds	40,000
Less purchase price	(10,000)
Less enhancement expenditure	(1,000)
	29,000
Less indexation on purchase price	
£10,000 × 0.631	(6,310)
Less indexation on enhancement expenditure	
£1,000 × 0.342	(342)
Chargeable gain	22,348

Activity 5: Capital gain calculation (companies)

Dunstable Ltd

	£
Asset purchased February 1986	15,000
Legal fees on purchase	500
Sale July 2020	58,500
Selling expenses July 2020	1,500
Enhancement expenditure October 1995	3,000
IA February 1986 – December 2017	1.879
IA October 1995 – December 2017	0.856

Required

Complete the table showing Dunstable Ltd's gain.

Solution

	£
Proceeds	
Less selling expenses	
Net proceeds	
Less cost	
Less legal fees on purchase	
Less enhancement	
Unindexed gain	
Less indexation on cost	
Less indexation on enhancement expenditure	
Capital gain	

The indexation allowance cannot create or increase an allowable loss. If there is a gain before the indexation allowance, the allowance can reduce that gain to zero, but no further. If there is a loss before the indexation allowance, there is no indexation allowance.

Activity 6: Indexation

JEK Ltd bought an asset for £50,000. Indexation is 0.761.

Required

What is the capital gain/(loss) if it was sold for:

(a) **£20,000?**   £ _____

(b) **£70,000?**   £ _____

(c) **£150,000?**   £ _____

Workings (not provided in the CBT)

Assessment focus point

In the live assessment you will be provided with reference material that can be accessed through pop-up windows. The content of this reference material has been reproduced at the back of this Course Book.

Chapter summary

- A chargeable gain arises when there is a chargeable disposal of a chargeable asset by a chargeable person.

- Enhancement expenditure can be deducted in computing a chargeable gain if it is reflected in the state and nature of the asset at the time of disposal.

- Chargeable gains are computed for individuals and companies in a similar way but for companies, there is an indexation allowance.

- Taxable gains for an individual are net chargeable gains for a tax year (ie minus allowable losses of the current tax year, the annual exempt amount and any unrelieved capital losses brought forward).

- The annual exempt amount is deducted before losses brought forward by an individual.

- The rates of CGT are 10% and 20%, but the lower rate of 10% only applies if, and to the extent that, the individual has any unused basic rate band.

- CGT is payable by 31 January following the end of the tax year.

- CGT is self-assessed and has the same rules about notification of chargeability, penalties and interest as income tax.

- The indexation allowance gives relief for the inflation element of a gain for a company. It was frozen in December 2017.

Keywords

- **Annual exempt amount (AEA):** The amount of gains an individual can make before they have to pay CGT (£12,300 for 2020/21)

- **Chargeable disposal:** A sale or gift of an asset

- **Chargeable asset:** Any asset that is not an exempt asset

- **Chargeable person:** An individual or company

- **Exempt disposal:** A disposal on which no chargeable gain or allowable loss arises

- **Enhancement expenditure:** Capital expenditure that enhances the value of the asset and is reflected in the state or nature of the asset at the time of disposal

- **Taxable gains:** The chargeable gains of an individual for a tax year, after deducting allowable losses of the same tax year, the annual exempt amount and any unrelieved capital losses brought forward.

1   **Tick to show if the following disposals would be chargeable or exempt for CGT.**

	Chargeable ✓	Exempt ✓
A gift of an antique necklace		
The sale of a building		

2   Yvette buys an investment property for £325,000. She sells the property on 12 December 2020 for £560,000.

   Her chargeable gain on sale is:

   £ [   ]

3   Philip has chargeable gains of £171,000 and allowable losses of £5,300 in 2020/21. Losses brought forward at 6 April 2020 were £10,000.

   The amount liable to CGT in 2020/21 is:

   £ [   ]

   The losses carried forward are:

   £ [   ]

4   Martha is a higher rate taxpayer who made chargeable gains (before the annual exempt amount) of £24,200 in October 2020.

   Martha's CGT liability for 2020/21 is:

   £ [   ]

5   **The payment date for capital gains tax on 2020/21 disposals is (insert date as XX/XX/XX):**

   [   ]

6   **Fill in the blanks with words of explanation.**

   Indexation allowance runs from the date [   ] **to** [   ].

7   J plc bought a plot of land in July 2006 for £80,000. It spent £10,000 on drainage in April 2009, and sold the land for £200,000 in August 2020. The indexation factor from July 2006 to December 2017 is 0.401 and from April 2009 to December 2017 it is 0.315.

Using the proforma layout provided, compute the gain on sale.

	£
Proceeds of sale	
Less cost	
Less enhancement expenditure	
Less indexation allowance on cost	
Less indexation allowance on enhancement	
Chargeable gain	

Further aspects of chargeable gains

12

Learning outcomes

5.1	Calculate the capital gains tax payable by self-employed taxpayers
	• Apply the rules relating to chargeable persons, disposals and assets
	• Calculate chargeable gain and allowable losses
	• Apply the rules relating to the disposal of chattels and wasting assets
	• Apply current reliefs and allowances

Assessment context

There are lots of rules regarding different assets so be sure you watch out for them in the assessment. It is crucial that you also notice if you are calculating a gain for an individual or a company as the tax treatment is different.

Qualification context

You will not see the information in this chapter outside of this unit unless you are also studying *Personal Tax*.

Business context

There are a number of very specific rules that apply in particular circumstances. It is vital to spot when these apply and use them correctly to ensure a business pays the right amount of tax on time and avoids penalties.

Chapter overview

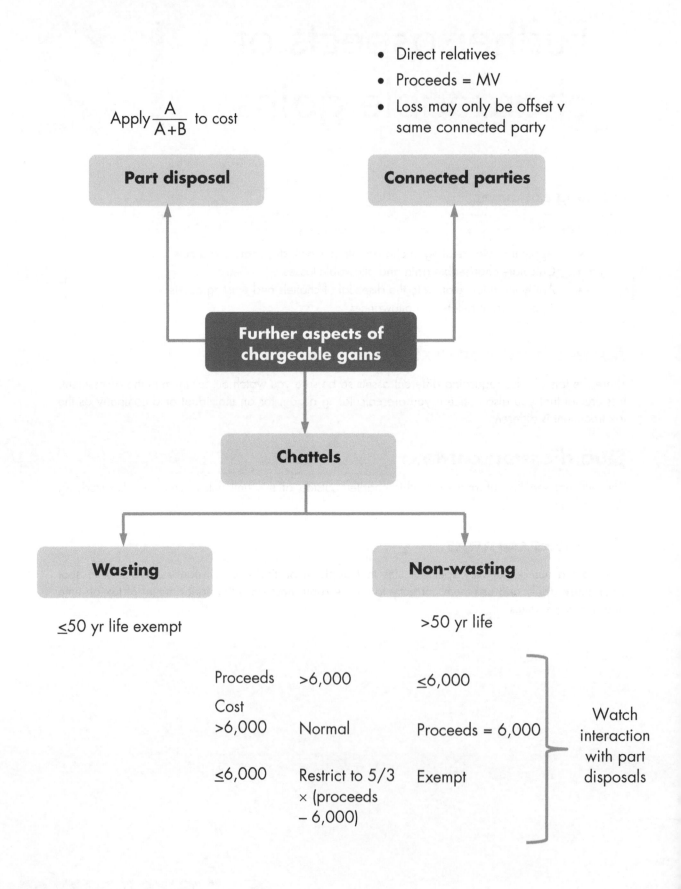

Apply $\dfrac{A}{A+B}$ to cost

Part disposal

- Direct relatives
- Proceeds = MV
- Loss may only be offset v same connected party

Connected parties

Further aspects of chargeable gains

Chattels

Wasting

≤50 yr life exempt

Non-wasting

>50 yr life

Proceeds	>6,000	≤6,000
Cost >6,000	Normal	Proceeds = 6,000
≤6,000	Restrict to 5/3 × (proceeds − 6,000)	Exempt

Watch interaction with part disposals

1 Introduction

This chapter looks in more detail at specific aspects of capital gains.

We will consider how to deal with part disposals of assets, and the calculation for disposals of a particular type of asset – a chattel.

There are special capital gains rules applying to disposals to certain individuals such as a spouse and other family members, so we will consider how these calculations are different.

2 Part disposals and chattels for individuals

2.1 Part disposals

A **part disposal** occurs when only part, rather than the whole, of an asset is disposed of. For instance, one-third of a piece of land may be sold. In this case, we need to be able to compute the chargeable gain or allowable loss arising on the part of the asset disposed of.

The problem is that although we know what the disposal proceeds are for the part of the asset disposed of, we do not usually know what proportion of the 'cost' of the whole asset relates to that part. The solution to this is to **use the following fraction to determine the cost of the part disposed of**.

The fraction is:

ulation of gains and losses for individuals

$$\frac{A}{A+B} = \frac{\text{Value of the part disposed of}}{\text{Value of the part disposed of} + \text{Market value of the remainder}}$$

A is the 'gross' proceeds (or market value) before deducting incidental costs of disposal.

B is the market value of the part of the asset that was not sold.

Assessment focus point

The formula for a part disposal is given to you in the calculation of gains and losses for individuals section of your reference material which you have access to in your assessment. These calculations are identified by the Chief Assessor as a common weakness, so make sure you practise applying these rules.

Part disposal calculation

	£
Gross proceeds	X
Less selling costs	(X)
	X
Less:	
Original cost of the whole asset $\times \dfrac{A}{A+B}$	(C)
Gain	X

Illustration 1: Part disposal

Mr Jones bought four acres of land for £270,000. He sold one acre of the land at auction for £200,000, before auction expenses of 15%. The market value of the three remaining acres is £460,000.

The cost of the land being sold is:

$$\frac{200,000}{200,000+460,000} \times £270,000 = £81,818$$

	£
Disposal proceeds	200,000
Less incidental costs of sale (15% × £200,000)	(30,000)
Net proceeds	170,000
Less cost (see above)	(81,818)
Chargeable gain	88,182

Activity 1: Part disposal

Tom bought ten acres of land for £20,000.

He sold three acres of land for £10,000, incurring disposal costs of £950, when the remaining seven acres were worth £36,000.

Required

The gain on the disposal of the land is £ ⬚ .

The cost of the remaining land carried forward is £ ⬚ .

Workings (not provided in the CBT)

	£

*tion of
*ns and
*ses for
*viduals

2.2 Chattels

Key term

Chattels are tangible moveable properties.

Wasting chattel is a chattel with an estimated remaining useful life of 50 years or less, eg a racehorse or greyhound.

Wasting chattels are exempt from capital gains tax (CGT) so there are no chargeable gains and no allowable losses.

Non-wasting chattels are chargeable to CGT in the normal way, subject to the following exceptions/restrictions:

Cost	Proceeds		
≤ 6,000	≤ 6,000	Wholly exempt	No need to calculate any gain.
≤ 6,000	> 6,000	Any gain restricted to max of: $\frac{5}{3}$ (Gross proceeds – £6,000)	Calculate gain, compare to the maximum, take the lower figure.
>6,000	≤ 6,000	Gross proceeds deemed to be £6,000	Do normal calculation but always use £6,000 as proceeds figure.
>6,000	>6,000	Wholly Taxable	Calculate a gain using the normal rules

Assessment focus point

Note that these rules are identified by the Chief Assessor as being where students give a weak performance in their assessment. You should note that the rules are clearly given in the calculation of gains and losses for individuals section of the reference material which you have access to in your assessment and you need to ensure you have plenty of practice in applying these rules to scenarios.

Illustration 2: Proceeds > £6,000 cost < £6,000

John purchased a painting for £3,000. On 1 January 2021, he sold the painting at auction.

If the gross sale proceeds are £4,000, the gain on sale will be exempt.

If the gross sale proceeds are £8,000 with costs of sale of 10%, the gain arising on the disposal of the painting will be calculated as follows:

	£
Gross proceeds	8,000
Less incidental costs of sale (10% × £8,000)	(800)
Net proceeds	7,200
Less cost	(3,000)
Chargeable gain	4,200
Gain cannot exceed $\frac{5}{3}$ × £(8,000 – 6,000) Therefore chargeable gain is £3,333.	£3,333

Illustration 3: Proceeds < £6,000 cost > £6,000

Magee purchased an antique desk for £8,000. She sold the desk in an auction for £4,750 net of auctioneer's fees of 5% in November 2019.

Magee obviously has a loss and therefore the allowable loss is calculated on deemed proceeds of £6,000. The costs of disposal can be deducted from the deemed proceeds of £6,000.

	£
Deemed disposal proceeds	6,000
Less incidental costs of disposal (£4,750 × 5/95)	(250)
	5,750
Less cost	(8,000)
Allowable loss	(2,250)

Activity 2: Chattels

(a) Orlando Gibbons purchased a rare manuscript for £500. He sold it several years later for £9,000, before deducting the auctioneer's commission of £1,000.

(b) Antique bought for £7,000 and sold two years later for £3,000.

Required

(a) **The chargeable gain on the disposal is** £ [   ] .

(b) **The loss on the disposal is** £ [   ] .

3 Further rules for individuals

3.1 Transfers to connected persons

ulation of gains and losses for dividuals

If a disposal by an individual is made to a connected person, **the disposal is deemed to take place at the market value (MV) of the asset**.

If an **allowable loss arises** on the disposal, it can **only be set against gains** arising in the same or future tax years from disposals **to the same connected person**, and the loss can only be set off if he or she is still connected with the person making the loss.

For this purpose, an individual is connected with:

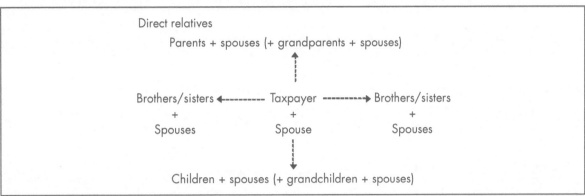

3.2 Transfers between spouses/civil partners

Spouses/civil partners are taxed as two separate people. Each individual has a separate annual exempt amount each year, and allowable losses of one individual cannot be set against gains of the other.

Disposals between spouses/civil partners do not give rise to chargeable gains or allowable losses. The disposal is said to be on a **'no gain/no loss'** basis. The acquiring spouse/civil partner takes the base cost of the disposing spouse/civil partner.

Activity 3: Transfers between spouses/civil partners

William sold an asset to his wife Kate in May 2020 for £32,000 when its market value was £45,000. William acquired the asset for £14,000 in June 2005.

Calculate the chargeable gain on this transfer. Tick ONE box.

Solution

	✓
Nil	
£18,000	
£31,000	
£13,000	

Assessment focus point

Please refer to the reference material at the end of this Course Book to see which elements of this chapter will be available to you as a pop-up window in the live assessment.

Chapter summary

- On the part disposal of an asset, the formula A/(A + B) must be applied to work out the cost attributable to the part disposed of.

- Wasting chattels are exempt assets (eg racehorses and greyhounds).

- If a non-wasting chattel is sold for gross proceeds of £6,000 or less, any gain arising is exempt.

- If gross proceeds exceed £6,000 on the sale of a non-wasting chattel, but the cost is less than £6,000, any gain arising on the disposal of the asset is limited to $\frac{5}{3}$ × (Gross proceeds – £6,000).

- If the gross proceeds are less than £6,000 on the sale of a non-wasting chattel, any loss otherwise arising is restricted by deeming the gross proceeds to be £6,000.

- A disposal to a connected person takes place at market value.

- For individuals, connected people are, broadly, brothers, sisters, lineal ancestors and descendants and their spouses/civil partners, plus similar relations of a spouse/civil partner.

- Losses on disposals to connected people can only be set against gains on disposals to the same connected person.

- Disposals between spouses/civil partners take place on a no gain/no loss basis.

Keywords

- **Chattel:** Tangible moveable property
- **Part disposal:** When part of an asset, rather than a whole asset, is disposed of
- **Wasting chattel:** A chattel with an estimated remaining useful life of 50 years or less

Test your learning

1 **Tick to show the correct answer.**

Richard sells four acres of land (out of a plot of ten acres) for £38,000 in July 2020. Costs of disposal amount to £3,000. The ten-acre plot cost £41,500. The market value of the six acres remaining is £48,000.

The chargeable gain/allowable loss arising is:

	✓
£16,663	
£17,500	
£19,663	
£18,337	

2 Mustafa bought a non-wasting chattel for £3,500.

The gain arising if he sells it for:

(a) **£5,800 after deducting selling expenses of £180 is:**

£ [   ]

(b) **£8,200 after deducting selling expenses of £220 is:**

£ [   ]

3 Simon bought a racehorse for £4,500. He sold the racehorse for £9,000 in December 2020.

The gain arising is:

£ [   ]

4 Santa bought a painting for £7,000. He sold the painting in June 2020 for £5,000.

The loss arising is (both minus signs and brackets can be used to indicate negative numbers):

£ [   ]

5   X Ltd bought four acres of land for £50,000 in December 2010. In February 2021, it sold one acre of the land for £80,000. At the time of the sale, the value of the three remaining acres was £120,000. The indexation factor between December 2010 and December 2017 is 0.218.

(a)   The cost of the part of the land sold is:

£ [ ]

(b)   The chargeable gain arising on the disposal is:

£ [ ]

6   M plc purchased a non-wasting chattel for £3,500 in August 2013. In October 2020, it sold the chattel at auction for £8,000. The indexation factor between August 2013 and December 2017 is 0.108.

The gain arising is:

£ [ ]

7   S Ltd bought a non-wasting chattel for £8,700 in October 2009. It sold the chattel for £4,300 in May 2020. The indexation factor between October 2009 and December 2017 is 0.288.

Calculate the allowable loss on sale. Tick ONE box.

	✓
£(6,906)	
£(4,400)	
£(2,700)	
£(5,206)	

8   **Decide whether the following statement is true or false.**

A loss arising on a disposal to a connected person can be set against any gains arising in the same tax year or in subsequent tax years.

	✓
True	
False	

9 **Decide whether the following statement is true or false.**

No gain or loss arises on a disposal to a spouse/civil partner.

	✓
True	
False	

10 **Complete the table by ticking the appropriate box for each scenario.**

	Actual proceeds used ✓	Deemed proceeds (market value) used ✓	No gain or loss basis ✓
Paul sells an asset to his civil partner Joe for £3,600			
Grandmother gives an asset to her grandchild worth £1,000			
Sarah knowingly sells an asset worth £20,000 to her best friend Cathy for just £12,000			

Share disposals 13

Learning outcomes

5.1	Calculate the capital gains tax payable by self-employed taxpayers
	• Apply the rules relating to the disposal of shares
5.2	Calculate chargeable gains and allowable losses for limited companies
	• Apply the rules relating to the disposal of shares

Assessment context

This task is likely to be assessed by free data entry of all workings and will be human marked.

Qualification context

Share disposals by individuals also feature in *Personal Tax*. You will not see these rules anywhere else in your qualification.

Business context

A tax practitioner needs to be able to calculate capital gains tax payable on the disposal of shares for their clients.

Chapter overview

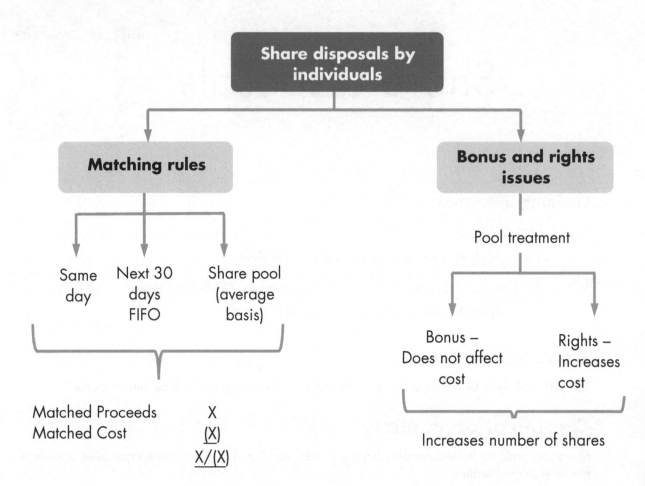

Share disposals by individuals

Matching rules

- Same day
- Next 30 days FIFO
- Share pool (average basis)

Matched Proceeds   X
Matched Cost   (X)
                 X/(X)

Bonus and rights issues

Pool treatment

- Bonus – Does not affect cost
- Rights – Increases cost

Increases number of shares

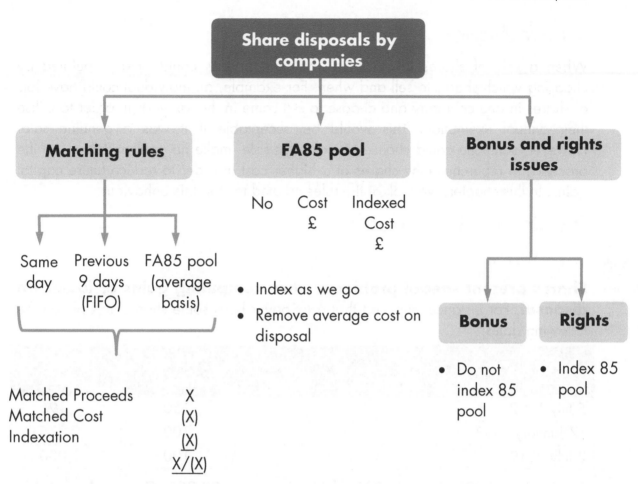

1 Introduction

When a sale of shares takes place, the gain or loss could be manipulated by choosing which shares to sell and when. For example, an individual could have lots of shares in one company and choose to sell some in the tax year in order to utilise their annual exemption. This would be acceptable if it was a genuine sale. However, someone could choose to make this sale, make no gain and then use the proceeds to repurchase the shares at a higher cost in order to reduce future capital gains. In this chapter, we look at the rules created to stop this behaviour.

2 Rules for individuals

2.1 Matching rules for individuals

Shares and
securities –
disposals by
individuals

Shares present special problems when computing gains or losses on disposal. For instance, suppose that a taxpayer buys some shares in X plc on the following dates:

	No of shares	Cost £
5 July 1992	150	195
17 January 1997	100	375
2 July 2019	100	1,000

On 15 June 2020, he sells 220 of his shares for £3,300. **To work out his chargeable gain, we need to be able to identify which shares** out of his three holdings **were actually sold**. Since one share is identical to any other, it is not possible to work this out by reference to factual evidence.

As a result, it has been necessary to devise 'matching rules'. These allow us to identify, on a disposal, which shares have been sold and so **work out what the allowable cost** (and therefore the gain) **on disposal should be**. These matching rules are considered in detail below.

Assessment focus point

It is very important that you understand the matching rules. These rules are very regularly assessed and if you do not understand them, you will not be able to get any of this part of a task right. The Chief Assessor has noted that this is usually where student performance is weakest in this task, so make sure you practise plenty of tasks.

Matching rules

Shares sold should be matched with purchases in the following order:

1   Acquisitions on the same day as disposal

2   Acquisitions within the following 30 days, on a first in, first out (FIFO) basis

3   Shares from the share pool. The share pool includes all other shares not acquired on the dates above, and is explained below.

Illustration 1: Matching rules

Noah acquired shares in Ark Ltd as follows.

2 August 2012	10,000 shares
25 April 2014	10,000 shares
17 June 2020	1,000 shares
19 June 2020	2,000 shares

Noah sold 15,000 shares on 17 June 2020.

Which shares is he selling for capital gains tax purposes?

Noah will match his disposal of 15,000 shares on 17 June 2020 as follows:

1   1,000 shares bought on 17 June 2020 (same day)
2   2,000 shares bought on 19 June 2020 (next 30 days, FIFO basis)
3   12,000 shares from the 20,000 shares in the share pool

Basic computation

	£	£
For each batch of matched shares:		
Proportion of proceeds	X	
Less cost (if from share pool W1)	(X)	
		X

(W1) Share pool

	No of shares	Cost £
Shares bought/sold	X	X

2.2 Share pool

ares and
curities –
posals by
dividuals

The share pool includes shares acquired up to the day before the disposal on which we are calculating the gain or loss. It grows when an acquisition is made and shrinks when a disposal is made.

2.2.1 The calculation of the share pool value

To compute the value of the share pool, set up two columns of figures:

(a)   The number of shares
(b)   The cost of the shares

Each time shares are acquired, both the number and the cost of the acquired shares are added to those already in the pool.

When there is a disposal from the pool, both the number of shares being disposed of, and a cost relating to those shares, are deducted from the pool. The cost of the disposal is calculated as a proportion of total cost in the pool, based on the number of shares being sold.

Illustration 2: The share pool

Jackie bought 10,000 shares in X plc for £6,000 in August 1996 and another 10,000 shares for £9,000 in December 2008.

She sold 12,000 shares for £24,000 in August 2020.

The gain is:

	£
Proceeds of sale	24,000
Less allowable cost (W1)	(9,000)
Chargeable gain	15,000

(W1) The share pool is:

	No of shares	Cost £
August 1996 acquisition	10,000	6,000
December 2008 acquisition	10,000	9,000
	20,000	15,000
August 2020 disposal (£15,000 × $\frac{12,000}{20,000}$ = £9,000)	(12,000)	(9,000)
c/f	8,000	6,000

Activity 1: Matching rules for individuals

Mr L made the following purchases of ordinary shares in H plc:

Date	Number	Cost
15.5.02	2,200	8,800
1.5.20	400	3,000
17.5.20	500	4,500

On 1.5.20, Mr L sold 1,600 shares for £14,000.

Required

What is the chargeable gain or allowable loss on the disposal of these shares? Clearly show the balance of shares to be carried forward.

Solution

	£	£

Activity 2: Share pool for individuals

Mr Lambert purchased the following holdings in Grande plc:

Date	Number	Cost £
January 1985	3,000	5,000
February 1987	1,000	4,000

In May 2020, he sold 2,000 shares for £14,000.

Required

What is the chargeable gain or allowable loss on the disposal of these shares? Clearly show the balance of shares to be carried forward.

Solution

	£	£

BPP
LEARNING MEDIA

ares and
curities –
posals by
dividuals

2.3 Bonus and rights issues for individuals

2.3.1 Bonus issues

Bonus issues are free shares given to existing shareholders in proportion to their existing shareholding. For example, a shareholder may own 2,000 shares. The company makes a 1 share for every 2 shares held bonus issue (called a 1 for 2 bonus issue). The shareholder will then have an extra 1,000 shares, giving him 3,000 shares overall.

Bonus shares are treated as being acquired at the date of the original acquisition of the underlying shares giving rise to the bonus issue.

Since bonus shares are issued at no cost, there is **no need to adjust the original cost**.

2.3.2 Rights issues

In a **rights issue**, a **shareholder is offered the right to buy additional shares by the company in proportion to the shares already held**.

The difference between a bonus issue and a rights issue is that, in a rights issue, the new shares are paid for. This results in an **adjustment to the original cost**.

For matching purposes, bonus and rights shares are treated as if they were acquired on the same day as the shareholder's original holdings.

Illustration 3: Bonus and rights issues

Jonah acquired 20,000 shares for £34,200 in T plc in April 2005. There was a 1 for 2 bonus issue in May 2010 and a 1 for 5 rights issue in August 2015 at £1.20 per share.

Jonah sold 30,000 shares for £45,000 in December 2020.

The gain on sale is:

	£
Proceeds of sale	45,000
Less allowable cost (W1)	(34,500)
Chargeable gain	10,500

(W1) The share pool is constructed as follows:

	No of shares	Cost £
April 2005 acquisition	20,000	34,200
May 2010 bonus 1 for 2 ($\frac{1}{2}$ × 20,000 = 10,000)	10,000	–
	30,000	34,200
August 2015 rights 1 for 5 @ £1.20 ($\frac{1}{5}$ × 30,000 = 6,000 shares × £1.20 = £7,200)	6,000	7,200
	36,000	41,400
December 2020 disposal (£41,400 × $\frac{30,000}{36,000}$ = £34,500)	(30,000)	(34,500)
c/f	6,000	6,900

Activity 3: Bonus and rights issues for individuals

Richard had the following transactions in S plc.

1.10.95	Bought 10,000 shares for £15,000
11.9.99	Bought 2,000 shares for £5,000
1.2.00	Took up rights issue 1 for 2 at £2.75 per share
5.9.05	2 for 1 bonus issue
14.10.20	Sold 15,000 shares for £15,000

Required

Calculate the gain or loss made on these shares. All workings must be shown in your calculations.

Solution

	£	£

	£	£

3 Rules for companies

3.1 Matching rules for companies

There are different matching rules for companies.

Matching rules for companies

Shares sold should be matched with purchases in the following order:

1   Acquisitions on the same day
2   Acquisitions in the previous nine days – FIFO basis
3   Shares from the FA 1985 pool

There is no indexation allowance on shares acquired in the previous nine days, even if the acquisition is in the previous month to the disposal.

Assessment focus point

Application of the matching rules for companies is the area the Chief Assessor has noted as being where student performance is weakest. Make sure you know that the shares and securities – disposal by companies section of your reference material, available in the assessment, covers most of the rules you need to apply and ensure you practise plenty of tasks on this topic.

Illustration 4: The application of the matching rules for companies

Z Ltd acquired the following shares in L plc:

9 November 2007   10,000 shares

15 December 2009   20,000 shares

11 July 2020   5,000 shares

15 July 2020   5,000 shares

Z Ltd disposed of 20,000 of the shares on 15 July 2020.

We match the 20,000 shares sold to acquisitions as follows.

(a)   Acquisition on same day: 5,000 shares acquired 15 July 2020.

(b)   Acquisitions in previous 9 days: 5,000 shares acquired 11 July 2020.

(c)   FA 1985 share pool: 10,000 shares out of 30,000 shares in FA 1985 share pool (9 November 2007 and 15 December 2009).

A disposal computation is produced for each matching rule.

3.2 The FA 1985 pool

Shares and securities – disposals by companies

The FA 1985 pool comprises the following shares:

Shares acquired by that company on or after 1 April 1985.

We must keep track of:

(a)   The number of shares
(b)   The cost of the shares ignoring indexation
(c)   The indexed cost of the shares

Basic computation

	£	£
For each batch of matched shares:		
Proportion of proceeds	X	
Less cost (if from share pool W1)	(X)	
		X

(W1) Share pool

Contains 3 columns

	No of shares	Cost £	Indexed cost £
Shares bought/sold	X	X	X

You must reflect each **operative event** in the FA 1985 pool. An operative event is a disposal/acquisition of shares that decrease/increase the amount of expenditure within the FA 1985 pool. However, prior to reflecting an operative event within the FA 1985 share pool, a further indexation allowance (sometimes described as an indexed rise) must be computed up to the date of the operative event you are looking at. You must look at each operative event in chronological order.

As explained in Chapter 11, the indexation allowance was frozen in December 2017. Therefore, for any share acquisitions after this date, add in the number of shares and cost, but do not add in any indexed rise.

Illustration 5: FA85 pool (from 1 April 1985)

J Ltd has a share pool at 1 April 1985 containing 20,000 shares with a cost of £15,000 and an indexed cost of £16,329. Now assume that J Ltd acquired 4,000 more shares on 1 January 1990 at a cost of £6,000.

Show the value of the FA 1985 pool on 1 January 1990 following the acquisition. The indexation factor April 1985 – January 1990 = 0.261.

	No of shares	Cost £	Indexed cost £
1 April 1985	20,000	15,000	16,329
Index to January 1990			
0.261 × £16,329			4,262
			20,591
January 1990 acquisition	4,000	6,000	6,000
	24,000	21,000	26,591

If there are several operative events, the procedure described must be performed several times over. In the case of a disposal, following the calculation of the indexed rise, the cost and the indexed cost attributable to the shares disposed of are deducted from the cost and the indexed cost columns within the FA 1985 pool. This is computed on a pro-rata basis if only part of the holding is being sold.

Illustration 6: FA85 pool – a disposal from the pool

Following on from the above example, suppose that J Ltd now disposes of 12,000 shares on 9 January 2021 for £26,000.

Show the value of the FA 1985 pool on 10 January 2021 following the disposal. Compute the gain on the disposal. The indexation factor for the period of January 1990 – December 2017 = 1.327.

(W1)

	No of shares	Cost £	Indexed cost £
Value at January 1990	24,000	21,000	26,591
Indexed rise to December 2017			
(1.327 × £26,591)			35,286
	24,000	21,000	61,877
Disposal			
(cost or indexed cost × $^{12,000}/_{24,000}$)	(12,000)	(10,500)	(30,939)
Pool c/f	12,000	10,500	30,938

The gain on the disposal is calculated as follows:

	£
Sale proceeds	26,000
Less cost (W1)	(10,500)
	15,500
Less indexation (£30,939 – £10,500)	(20,439)
Gain	Nil

Note that the indexation for the shares sold is the difference between the indexed cost and the cost, and that the indexation cannot create or increase a loss.

Activity 4: Matching rules for companies

ABC Ltd bought 1,000 shares in XYZ Ltd for £2,750 in August 1996 and another 1,000 for £3,250 in December 1998. On 4 July 2020, it bought 500 shares for £2,511 and on 10 July 2020, it bought 1,000 shares for £4,822.

ABC Ltd sold 2,500 shares on 10 July 2020 for £12,500.

Indexed rises: August 1996 to December 1998   =   0.008

December 1998 to December 2017   =   0.692

Required

Compute the gain on the disposal of these shares. Clearly show the balance to be carried forward.

Solution

		£	£

		£	£

3.3 Bonus and rights issues for companies

Indexation is not required when bonus shares are received, as there is no additional cost.

Indexation will be required if there is a rights issue, as the shares are acquired at a cost. The FA 1985 pool will need to be indexed to the date of the rights issue as this is classed as an 'operative event'.

Activity 5: Bonus and rights issues for companies

Wotan Ltd sold 800 shares in Krimpton Ltd on 5 September 2020 for £10,000. The holding had been built up as follows:

- 500 acquired for £1,000 on 1 May 1985
- 1 for 2 rights issue for £5 per share on 5 August 1987
- 1 for 1 bonus issue on 15 September 1989
- 1 for 3 rights issue for £6 per share on 10 March 2019

Indexation factors are as follows:

May 1985 → August 1987	0.072
August 1987 → September 1989	0.142
September 1989 → December 2017	1.385
August 1987 → December 2017	1.724

Required

Calculate the chargeable gain in September 2020.

Solution

		£	£

Assessment focus point

Please refer to the reference material at the end of this Course Book to see which elements of this chapter will be available to you as a pop-up window in the live assessment.

- The matching rules for individuals are:

    – Same-day acquisitions
    – Next 30 days' acquisitions, on a FIFO basis
    – Shares in the share pool

- The share pool runs up to the day before disposal.

- Bonus issue and rights issue shares are acquired in proportion to the shareholder's existing holding.

- The difference between a bonus and a rights issue is that in a rights issue, shares are paid for.

- The matching rules for companies are:

    – Same-day acquisitions
    – Previous 9 days' acquisitions on a FIFO basis
    – Shares in the FA 1985 share pool

- In the FA 1985 share pool, we must keep track of the number of shares, the cost of the shares and the indexed cost.

- Operative events increase or decrease the amount of expenditure within the FA 1985 pool.

- For a company, a rights issue is treated as an operative event, whereas a bonus issue is not.

Keywords

- **Bonus shares:** Shares that are issued free to shareholders, based on original holdings

- **Operative events:** Disposals/acquisitions of shares that decrease/increase the amount of expenditure within the FA 1985 pool

- **Rights issues:** Similar to bonus issues except that in a rights issue, shares must be paid for

1   Tasha bought 10,000 shares in V plc in August 1994 for £5,000 and a further 10,000 shares for £16,000 in April 2009. She sold 15,000 shares for £30,000 in November 2020.

Tick to show what her chargeable gain is.

	✓
£15,750	
£11,500	
£17,000	
£14,250	

2   **Tick to show whether the following statement is true or false.**

In both a bonus issue and a rights issue, there is an adjustment to the original cost of the shares.

	✓
True	
False	

3   Marcus bought 2,000 shares in X plc in May 2003 for £12,000. There was a 1 for 2 rights issue at £7.50 per share in December 2004. Marcus sold 2,500 shares for £20,000 in March 2021.

His chargeable gain is:

£ [   ]

4   Mildred bought 6,000 shares in George plc in June 2011 for £15,000. There was a 1 for 3 bonus issue in August 2012. Mildred sold 8,000 shares for £22,000 in December 2020.

Her chargeable gain is:

£ [   ]

5   **What are the share matching rules for disposals by companies?**

6   Q Ltd bought 10,000 shares in R plc in May 2003 at a cost of £90,000. There was a 1 for 4 rights issue in June 2009 at the cost of £12 per share and Q Ltd took up all of its rights entitlement.

Q Ltd sold 10,000 shares in R plc for £150,000 in January 2021.

The indexed rise between May 2003 and June 2009 is 0.176; and between June 2009 and December 2017, is 0.303.

(a) Using the proforma layout provided, show the share pool.

		No of shares	Cost £	Indexed cost £

(b) Using the proforma layout provided, compute the gain on sale.

	£

Reliefs for chargeable gains 14

Learning outcomes

4.2	**Demonstrate an understanding of current tax reliefs and other tax issues**
	• Current tax reliefs available to businesses
5.1	**Calculate capital gains tax payable by self-employed taxpayers**
	• Calculate chargeable gains and allowable losses • Apply current reliefs and allowances • Apply the capital gains tax rates
5.2	**Calculate chargeable gains and allowable losses for limited companies**
	• Calculate the computation of chargeable gains and allowable losses • Apply current reliefs and allowances

Assessment context

In the assessment you could be tested on capital gains tax exemptions, losses, reliefs and tax payable.

Qualification context

You will not see these rules outside of this unit.

Business context

Nobody likes to pay tax! These reliefs are extremely useful in the real world to postpone, reduce or eliminate a tax liability.

Chapter overview

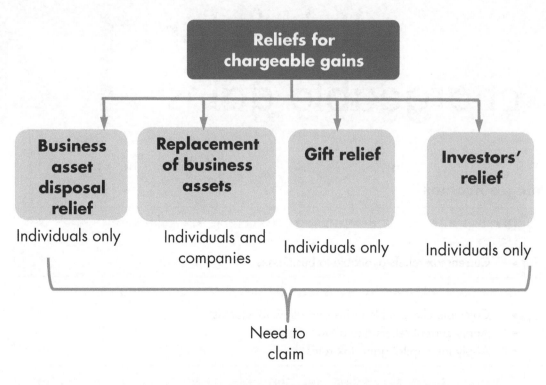

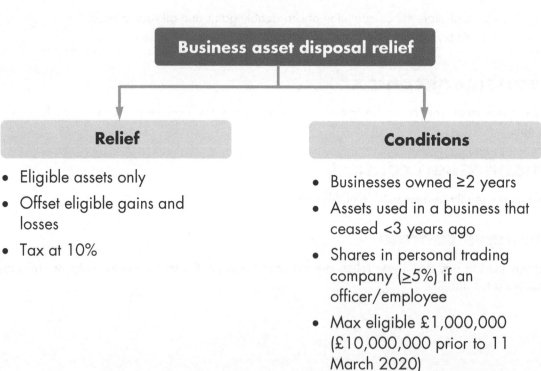

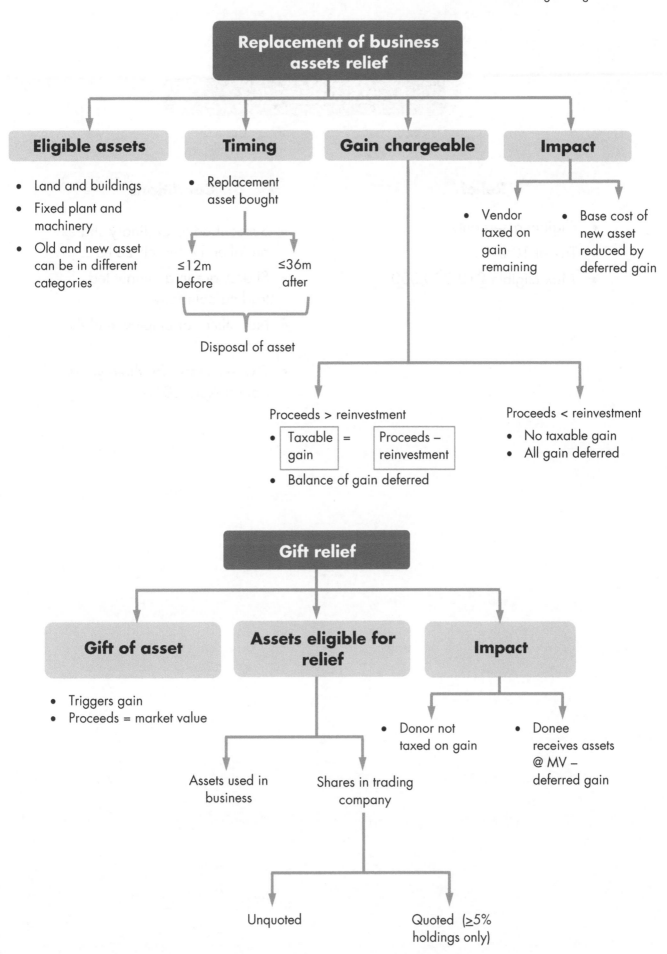

Investors' relief

Relief

- Eligible assets only
- Tax at 10%
- Max eligible £10,000,000

Conditions

- Subscribed to Ordinary shares on/after 17 March 2016
- Shares are in an unquoted trading company
- Not officer or employee of the company
- Owned shares for three years from 6 April 2016

1 Introduction

This chapter looks at the reliefs available to individuals and companies to reduce their capital gains liabilities. Business asset disposal relief and gift relief are available to individuals only. Replacement of business assets relief is available to both individuals and companies.

Assessment focus point

Note that most of the rules are available to you in your assessment and so it is vital that you practise using the reference material as you attempt tasks on these topics.

2 Business asset disposal relief

Chargeable
ains – reliefs
available to
individuals

2.1 The relief

Individuals can claim business asset disposal relief to reduce the rate of capital gains tax (CGT) on a material disposal of business assets.

Gains on assets qualifying for **business asset disposal relief (BADR)** are **taxed at 10%** regardless of the level of a person's taxable income.

This relief was previously called entrepreneurs relief but was renamed in FA20.

If a taxpayer has both gains that are eligible for business asset disposal relief and gains that are ineligible, they should offset the annual exempt amount, and any ineligible losses against the ineligible gains first.

Although gains eligible for the relief are taxed at 10%, they are deemed to be taxed before ineligible gains when deciding whether any of the basic rate band remains available.

Illustration 1: Losses, annual exempt amount and basic rate band

Steve makes gains eligible for business asset disposal relief (BADR) of £15,000, and gains not eligible for business asset disposal relief of £40,000. He has taxable income of £25,000 and capital losses brought forward of £3,700.

The CGT payable is:

Equity	£	£
Gains eligible for BADR	15,000	
Gains not eligible for BADR		40,000
Annual exemption		(12,300)
Capital losses brought forward		(3,700)
Taxable gains	15,000	24,000
Tax:		
£15,000 × 10% (gains eligible for BADR)		1,500
£24,000 × 20%		4,800
CGT due:		6,300

Note. There is no basic rate band remaining after taxing income and the gain eligible for business asset disposal relief (£25,000 + £15,000)

Activity 1: Business asset disposal relief – calculation of capital gains tax

Poins disposes of his business on 21 August 2020, realising a gain of £10,000 which qualifies for business asset disposal relief. He has other gains in the year of £50,300 which do not qualify for business asset disposal relief.

Poins has taxable income of £22,370.

Required

Capital gains tax payable at 10% due to BADR is £ _____.

Capital gains tax payable at 10% to utilise the remaining basic rate band is £ _____.

Capital gains tax payable at 20% is £ _____.

Workings (not provided in the CBT)

	Eligible gains £	Other gains £

2.2 Conditions

Business asset disposal relief applies when there has been a material disposal of business assets, such as a:

- disposal of the whole/ part of an unincorporated business
- disposal of assets used in an unincorporated business that has ceased trading; or
- disposal of certain shares/ securities.

These are explained in further detail below.

2.2.1 Disposal of an unincorporated business

The disposal of the whole or part of a business (as a going concern) which has been owned by the individual throughout the period of two years ending with the date of the disposal.

A business includes one carried on as a partnership of which the individual is a partner.

The business must be a trade, profession or vocation conducted on a commercial basis with a view to the realisation of profits.

Relief is only available on relevant business assets. These are assets used for the purposes of the business and cannot include shares and securities or assets held by the business as investments. Gains and losses on relevant business assets are netted off.

2.2.2 Disposal of assets used in an unincorporated business that has ceased trading

The disposal of assets used in the business prior to the cessation of the business, provided that:

- The business was owned for two years prior to the cessation
- The assets were sold within three years of the cessation

2.2.3 Disposal of shares

The disposal of shares or securities will qualify for business asset disposal relief where:

- The company is the individual's personal company (ie owns at least 5% of the shares and can exercise 5% of the votes);
- The company is a trading company; and
- The individual is an officer or employee of the company.

For business asset disposal relief to be available the conditions above must have been met:

- For two years before the date of disposal; or
- For two years up to the date at which the company ceases to trade. The shares must then be sold within three years of this date.

Activity 2: Disposals eligible for business asset disposal relief

The following assets are disposed of in 2020/21 by various individuals.

Identify which, if any, are qualifying disposals for business asset disposal relief. Tick the relevant box.

Solution

	✓
Part of a business in which the individual has been a partner since August 2014	
A freehold factory which the individual uses in his business and has owned for ten years	
Unquoted shares (≥5%) held by the individual in a personal trading company in which he is employed and which he has owned for the previous three years.	
Quoted shares (≥5%) held by the individual in a personal trading company in which he is employed and which he has owned for the previous three years.	

2.3 Lifetime limit

There is a lifetime limit of £1 million of gains on which business asset disposal relief can be claimed. Prior to the 11 March 2020 this was £10,000,000

Illustration 2: Lifetime limit

Carrie has made several disposals qualifying for business asset disposal relief (BADR). The gains on these disposals are as follows:

1 May 2017   £5,750,000
1 June 2017   £2,300,000
1 February 2021   £2,200,000

Business asset disposal relief will be given on the following amounts:

Disposal	Gain qualifying for BADR	Gain not qualifying for BADR	Notes
1 May 2017	£5,750,000	£0	Less than the lifetime limit of £10,000,000
1 June 2017	£2,300,000	£0	Cumulative total is still less than the lifetime limit of £10,000,000
1 February 2021	£0	£2,200,000	Lifetime limit of £1,000,000 applies which has been used up by earlier qualifying disposals.

Activity 3: Business asset disposal relief – calculating gains eligible for relief

Hal has run his business for many years. In January 2021, he sells it, realising the following gains and (losses).

Equity	£
Goodwill	500,000
Factory	300,000
Office block	(100,000)
Shares	80,000

All the assets were used in his business except the shares.

He has never previously claimed business asset disposal relief.

Required

(a) **The total net taxable gain eligible for business asset disposal relief is**

£ _____ .

The total net taxable gain not eligible for business asset disposal relief is

£ _____ .

Workings (not provided in the CBT)

	£	£

(b) **If the gain on the factory was £9,800,000, then the total net taxable gain eligible for business asset disposal relief is**

£ [   ] .

The total net taxable gain not eligible for business asset disposal relief is

£ [   ] .

Workings (not provided in the CBT)

	£	£

	£	£

2.4 Claim

The relief must be claimed within one year following the 31 January after the tax year of disposal. Relief for 2020/21 must, therefore, be claimed by 31 January 2023.

Chargeable gains – reliefs available to individuals

3 Replacement of business assets (rollover) relief

3.1 The relief

Rollover relief is available to **both individuals and companies**.

A gain may be 'rolled over' where it arises **on the disposal of a business asset** (the 'old' asset) **if another business asset** (the 'new' asset) **is acquired**.

The following conditions must be met:

(a) The old asset and the new asset must **both be used in a trade**.
(b) The old asset and the new asset must **both be qualifying assets**.

The 'new' asset can be one asset or more than one asset and the new asset can be for use in a different trade from the old asset.

Deferral is usually obtained by deducting the gain on the old asset from the cost of the new asset.

3.2 Qualifying assets

Both the old and new assets must fall into one of the following categories:

- Land and buildings used for the purpose of the trade
- Fixed plant and machinery
- Goodwill (for individuals only)

3.3 Timing

Reinvestment of the proceeds of the old asset must take place in a period beginning **one year before**; and ending **three years after**, the date of the disposal.

Illustration 3: Rollover relief – all proceeds reinvested

A freehold factory was purchased by a sole trader on 13 May 2002 for £60,000 and sold for £90,000 on 18 September 2020. A replacement factory was purchased on 6 December 2020 for £100,000. Rollover relief was claimed on the sale of the first factory.

(a)   Gain on sale September 2020

	£
Disposal proceeds	90,000
Less cost	(60,000)
Gain (all proceeds reinvested therefore defer full gain)	30,000

(b)   Revised base cost of asset purchased in December 2020

	£
Original cost	100,000
Less rolled over gain	(30,000)
Revised base cost (this will be used to calculate gain on subsequent sale of new asset)	70,000

3.4 Taxed now

For all the gain to be deferred, all the proceeds of the old asset must be reinvested in the new asset. Any proceeds not reinvested in a qualifying asset are deducted from the gain to be rolled over.

If the amount of proceeds not reinvested exceeds the gain, no amount of the gain can therefore be rolled over. This is the same as saying the amount chargeable is the lower of the gain and the amount not reinvested.

Illustration 4: Rollover relief – not all proceeds reinvested

Susannah realised a gain of £300,000 on the disposal of an office block used in her business. The office block was sold for £700,000. A new office block was bought for £600,000 in the following month.

The proceeds not reinvested are £100,000 so this amount of the gain is immediately chargeable. The remaining gain of £200,000 can be rolled over and set against the base cost of the new office block. This means the base cost of the new office block is £(600,000 – 200,000) = £400,000.

Calculation of gains and losses for companies

3.5 Rollover relief for companies

Rollover relief is the only relief available to companies. It is calculated in the same way as we have seen for individuals, with the following key differences:

- Indexation is given on the disposal of the original asset.
- Goodwill is not a qualifying asset for companies.
- The gain deferred is the indexed gain.
- On disposal of the replacement asset, indexation is calculated on the base cost, not the actual cost.

Activity 4: Rollover relief

Henry Ltd sells fixed plant for £200,000. It cost £150,000, indexation allowance is 10%. Six months later, Henry Ltd buys a building for £190,000.

Both assets are used in the trade.

Required

The gain taxed on Henry Ltd now is

£ _____ .

The base cost of the building is

£ _____ .

Workings (not provided in the CBT)

4 Gift relief

4.1 The relief

Individuals can claim **gift relief** to defer a gain arising **on the gift of a business asset**.

The gift is deemed to be made at market value (MV).

The transferee is deemed to acquire the asset for its market value, less the deferred gain.

> **Illustration 5: Gift relief**
>
> John bought a business asset in 2010 for £20,000. On 1 May 2020, John gave the asset to Marie-Louise. The market value of the asset on the date of the gift was £90,000.
>
> John is deemed to dispose of the asset for its market value of £90,000, so the gain arising on the gift is:
>
> | | £ |
> | --- | --- |
> | Deemed disposal proceeds | 90,000 |
> | Less cost | (20,000) |
> | Gain | 70,000 |
>
> The gain of £70,000 is deferred by setting it against the value of £90,000, at which Marie-Louise is deemed to acquire the gift. Therefore, Marie-Louise is deemed to acquire the gift for £20,000 (£90,000 – £70,000) and this will be used as the base cost for future disposals.

4.2 Conditions

The disposal must be made to a UK individual.

Qualifying assets for gift relief purposes include:

(a) Assets used in a trade carried on:

  (i) By the donor; or
  (ii) By the donor's personal company

(b) Shares in:

  (i) An unquoted trading company; or
  (ii) The donor's personal trading company

A 'personal company' is one in which not less than 5% of the voting rights are controlled by the donor.

4.3 Impact of claim

The donor's gain in relation to the gifted asset is reduced to nil.

The gain is rolled over into (deducted from) the base cost of the asset now owned by the recipient.

The gift relief claim to defer the gain must be made jointly by the donor and the recipient.

Activity 5: Gift relief

Bill gave a workshop used in his trade to his son, Ludovic. Its market value was £25,000.

Bill had purchased the workshop for £7,000.

A valid gift relief claim is made.

Required

The gift relief claim must be signed by [▼].

Picklist:

Bill and Ludovic
Bill only
Ludovic only

Bill's chargeable gain on disposal is

£ [   ].

Ludovic's base cost is

£ [   ].

Workings (not provided in the CBT)

Activity 6: With and without gift relief

Julie bought 10,000 shares in an unquoted trading company for £50,000 in July 2008. Julie gave her shares to Jack in May 2020, when they were worth £85,000. Jack sold the shares for £95,000 in December 2020.

Required

(a) **If gift relief is not claimed, Julie's chargeable gain is**

£ [   ]

and Jack's chargeable gain is

£ [   ] .

(b) **If gift relief is claimed, Julie's chargeable gain is**

£ [   ]

and Jack's chargeable gain is

£ [   ] .

Workings (not provided in the CBT)

Chargeable gains – reliefs available to individuals

5 Investors' relief

5.1 The relief

Individuals can claim investors' relief to reduce the rate of capital gains tax (CGT) on certain qualifying share disposals.

Gains on assets qualifying for **investors' relief** are **taxed at 10%** regardless of the level of a person's taxable income.

As we saw for business asset disposal relief, if a taxpayer has both gains that are eligible for investors' relief, and gains that are ineligible, they should offset the annual exempt amount, and any ineligible losses against the ineligible gains first.

Although gains eligible for the relief are taxed at 10%, they are deemed to be taxed before ineligible gains when deciding whether any of the basic rate band remains available.

5.2 Conditions

Investors' relief applies when there has been a disposal of shares which meet the following conditions:

- the individual **subscribes** for shares which are issued **on or after 17 March 2016**

- the shares are **ordinary** shares
- the issuing company is a **trading** company or holding company of a trading group
- the shares are **not listed** on a recognised stock exchange
- the individual has **not been an officer or employee** of the issuing company at any point during the ownership period; and
- the shares are held **continuously for three years** from the date of issue or from 6 April 2016 where the shares are issued between 17 March and 5 April 2016.

Unlike disposal of business asset relief, there is no minimum shareholding required, and the relief allows non-employee shareholders in unquoted trading companies to get the preferential 10% tax rate for shares they have subscribed for and held for more than three years.

Activity 7: Disposals eligible for investors' relief

The following assets are disposed of on 30 June 2020 by various individuals.

Identify which, if any, are qualifying disposals for investors' relief or business asset disposal relief. Tick or cross the relevant boxes.

Solution

	Investors' relief ✓	Business asset disposal relief ✓
4% holding in A Ltd, an unquoted trading company in which the individual is not employed. The shares were subscribed for on 30 April 2016.		
20% holding in B Ltd, an unquoted trading company in which the individual is employed. The shares were subscribed for on 30 April 2016.		
1% holding in C Ltd, a quoted trading company in which the individual is not employed. The shares were subscribed for on 30 June 2016.		
15% holding in D Ltd, an unquoted trading company in which the individual is not employed. The shares were subscribed for on 30 June 2018.		
10% holding in E Ltd, an unquoted trading company in which the individual is not employed. The shares were bought on 30 April 2016.		

5.3 Lifetime limit

There is a lifetime limit of £10 million of gains on which investors' relief can be claimed.

5.4 Claim

The relief must be claimed within one year following the 31 January after the tax year of disposal. Relief for 2020/21 must, therefore, be claimed by 31 January 2023.

Assessment focus point

In the live assessment you will be provided with the reference material which has been reproduced at the end of this Course Book. Please review this material to see which elements of this chapter will be available to you as a pop-up window in the live assessment.

Chapter summary

- Business asset disposal relief reduces the rate of CGT on gains made by an individual, on certain business disposals, to 10%. This relief was previously called entrepreneur's relief.

- There is a lifetime limit of £1 million for business asset disposal relief since 11 March 2020.

- Business asset disposal relief applies to disposals of an unincorporated business (or part of a business), disposals of business assets on cessation, and shares in a trading company that is the individual's personal company and of which he is an officer or employee.

- Rollover relief can be used by individuals and companies to defer a gain when a qualifying business asset is replaced with another qualifying business asset.

- Qualifying business assets for rollover relief include land and buildings, fixed plant and machinery and, for individuals, goodwill. Both the old and the new assets must be used for the purposes of a trade.

- If sale proceeds are not fully reinvested, an amount of the gain equal to the proceeds not reinvested is immediately chargeable. The remainder of the gain may be rolled over.

- The rolled-over gain reduces the cost of the new asset.

- The new asset must be acquired in the period commencing one year before, and ending three years after, the disposal.

- Gift relief can be used by an individual to defer a gain on the gift of business assets.

- The recipient acquires the gift at its market value, less the amount of the deferred gain.

- Qualifying assets for gift relief include assets used in a trade by the donor or his personal company, unquoted shares in a trading company and shares in a personal trading company.

- Investors' relief reduces the rate of CGT on gains made by an individual, on disposals of certain shares, to 10%.

- Unlike for business asset disposal relief the investor must not be an officer/employee and there is no minimum percentage shareholding. The shares must be ordinary shares subscribed for in an unquoted trading company and held for a minimum period of three years.

- There is a separate lifetime limit of £10 million for investors' relief.

Keywords

- **Business asset disposal relief:** Reduces the effective rate of tax on the disposal of certain business assets from 20% (if they would be taxed at the higher rate) to 10%

- **Gift relief:** Can defer a gain on a gift of business assets by an individual

- **Rollover relief:** Can defer a gain when business assets are replaced

- **Investors' relief:** Reduces the effective rate of tax on the disposal of certain shares from 20% (if they would be taxed at the higher rate) to 10%

Test your learning

1   Ian sold his business as a going concern to John in May 2020. The gains on sale were £1,400,000. Ian had not previously made any claims for business asset disposal relief, and made no other disposals in 2020/21. Ian is a higher rate taxpayer.

Ian's CGT liability for 2020/21 is:

£ [   ]

2   Jemma sold her shareholding in J Ltd in January 2021. She had acquired the shares in August 2007 for £10,000. The proceeds of sale were £80,000. The disposal qualified for business asset disposal relief.

Jemma's CGT on the disposal, assuming she has already used the annual exempt amount for 2020/21, is:

£ [   ]

3   K Ltd sold a factory on 10 November 2020. It purchased the following assets:

Date of purchase	Asset
21 September 2019	Office block
15 February 2021	Freehold factory
4 June 2022	Fork lift truck
8 December 2023	Freehold warehouse

All of the above assets are used for the purpose of the trade of K Ltd.

Against which purchase may K Ltd claim rollover relief in respect of the gain arising on disposal of the factory?

	✓
Office block	
Freehold factory	
Fork lift truck	
Freehold warehouse	

4   Trevor bought land for £100,000 in March 2008. In March 2020, this land was sold for £400,000 and replacement land was bought for £380,000. The replacement land was sold in May 2021 for £500,000. Both pieces of land were used in Trevor's trade, which is still continuing.

What is the chargeable gain arising in May 2021? Assume all available reliefs were claimed.

	✓
£120,000	
£200,000	
£400,000	
£420,000	

5   **Decide whether the following statement is true or false.**

Provided both assets are used in Mr Astro's trade, a gain arising on the sale of freehold land and buildings can be rolled over against the cost of goodwill.

	✓
True	
False	

6   **Fill in the blank boxes.**

A company sells freehold land and buildings.

If relief for replacement of business assets is to be claimed, reinvestment of the proceeds must take place in a period beginning

[   ] **months before and ending**

[   ] **months after the date of disposal.**

7   H Ltd sells a warehouse for £400,000. The warehouse cost £220,000 and the indexation allowance available is £40,000. The company acquires another warehouse 10 months later for £375,000 and claims rollover relief.

The chargeable gain after rollover relief is:

£ [   ]

8 **Decide whether the following statement is true or false.**

If Sara gives some jewellery to her daughter Emily, gift relief can be claimed.

	✓
True	
False	

9 Tommy gave Sinbad a factory in June 2020 that had been used in his trade. The factory cost £50,000 in October 2007 and was worth £200,000 at the date of the gift. Sinbad sold the factory for £350,000 in May 2021. Ignore the annual exempt amount.

If gift relief is claimed, the gain on the gift by Tommy is:

£ [   ]

and the gain on the sale by Sinbad is:

£ [   ]

10 Sunil sold his shareholding in W Ltd in February 2021. He had subscribed for the shares in June 2016 for £20,000. The proceeds of sale were £50,000. W Ltd is an unquoted trading company of which Sunil is not an employee. Sunil also makes a gain of £30,000 on the sale of shares in X Ltd, an investment company during 2020/21. Sunil is a higher rate tax payer.

Sunil's CGT liability for 2020/21 is:

£ [   ]

Activity answers

CHAPTER 1 Tax framework

Activity 1: Taxable income

£	6,000

	Non-savings income £
Trading income	16,000
Property income	2,500
Dividends	
Net income	18,500
Less personal allowance	(12,500)
Taxable income	6,000

Activity 2: Calculation of income tax liability

	Non-savings income £
Employment income	17,000
Total income	17,000
PA	(12,500)
Taxable income	4,500
Non-savings income	
4,500 × 20%	900
Tax liability	**900**

Activity 1: Adjustment of profits (i)

	£
Profit for the year in accounts	38,000
Add **entertaining expenses**	2,000
Add **depreciation**	4,000
	44,000
Less **capital allowances**	(3,500)
Taxable trading profit	40,500

Activity 2: Capital versus revenue

	Revenue ✓	Capital ✓
Paying employee wages	✓	
Paying rent for premises	✓	
Buying machinery		✓
Buying a van		✓
Building an extension to shop		✓
Paying for repairs to car	✓	

Activity 3: Calculation of add back

Amount to add back	✓
£17,450	
£16,000	
£18,450	✓
£11,450	

The fine will not be deductible and will therefore need to be added back as will the cost of the specialist tax consultancy work. The redundancy payments are allowable because they were incurred wholly and exclusively for the purposes of the trade. The payment of a salary to the proprietor of a business is not deductible because it is just a method of extracting a profit from the business and that profit is taxable in the normal way as part of the taxable trading profits. 15% of leasing costs of car with CO_2 emissions exceeding 110g/km are disallowable. Add back 1,000 + 2000 + 15,000 + 15% x 3,000 = £18,450.

Activity 4: Entertainment and gifts

Expenditure	£	Add back ✓
Staff tennis outing for 30 employees	1,800	
2,000 tee shirts with firm's logo given to race runners	4,500	
Advertising and sponsorship of an athletic event	2,000	
Entertaining customers	7,300	✓
Staff Christmas party (30 employees)	2,400	

Activity 5: Adjustment of profits (ii)

Adjustment to profit	£	£
Net profit per the accounts		30,900
Add back		
Depreciation	5,000	
Entertaining	100	
Staff wages	5,000	
Council tax	1,000	
Total added back		11,100
Deduct		
Bank interest		(4,000)
Adjusted profits before capital allowances		38,000

Activity 1: Annual investment allowance

Delson can claim an annual investment allowance of | £ | 150,000 |.

Workings (on-screen free text area provided in the CBT as part of larger question)

Nine-month period.

Max entitlement is therefore $\frac{9}{12} \times £200,000 = £150,000$

Assets eligible are:

		£
15 January 2021	Manufacturing equipment	50,000
16 January 2021	Computer equipment	60,000
7 May 2021	Office furniture	30,000
13 May 2021	Delivery vans	20,000
		160,000

As the eligible assets are greater than the limit, Delson may only claim £150,000.

Note. The balance of expenditure will be eligible for other allowances.

Activity 2: Writing-down allowances in the main pool

Jamie can claim an annual investment allowance of | £ | 800,000 |.

Jamie can claim writing-down allowances of | £ | 15,300 |.

Workings (on-screen free text area provided in the CBT as part of larger question)

	AIA £	Main pool £	Total £
TWDV b/f		10,000	
Additions			
Car		18,000	
Van	9,000		
Manufacturing plant (Total = £850,000)	791,000	59,000	
AIA (see note)	(800,000)		800,000
Disposals		(2,000)	

	AIA £	Main pool £	Total £
		85,000	
WDA @ 18%		(15,300)	15,300
			815,300
TWDV c/f		69,700	

Note. The AIA limit is (£1,000,000 × 9/12) + (£200,000 × 3/12) = £800,000.

Activity 3: Short period of account

Edward Ltd can claim capital allowances of **£** | 792,356 | .

Workings (on-screen free text area provided in the CBT as part of larger question)

	AIA £	Main pool £	Allowances £
TWDV b/f		12,000	
P/e 31.12.20			
Disposal			
7.7 van		(2,000)	
AIA additions			
15.4 Plant (total £1,046,750)	750,000	296,750	
AIA 1,000,000 × $\frac{9}{12}$	(750,000)		750,000
Non-AIA addition			
13.4 car		7,000	
		313,750	
WDA @ 18% × $\frac{9}{12}$		(42,356)	42,356
TWDV c/f		271,394	
			792,356

Activity 4: Cessation of a business

(a) If Baxter sells his plant for £15,500 then he will have a ⌐balancing charge⌐

of ☐£☐ 1,500 ☐.

Workings (on-screen free text area provided in the CBT as part of larger question)

	Main pool £	Allowances £
TWDV b/f	12,000	
Additions	2,000	
Disposals	(15,500)	
	(1,500)	
Balancing charge	1,500	(1,500)
TWDV c/f	–	

(b) If Baxter sells his plant for £11,500 then he will have a ⌐balancing allowance⌐

of ☐£☐ 2,500 ☐.

Workings (on-screen free text area provided in the CBT as part of larger question)

	Main pool £	Allowances £
TWDV b/f	12,000	
Additions	2,000	
Disposals	(11,500)	
	2,500	
Balancing allowance	(2,500)	2,500
TWDV c/f	–	

Activity 5: Special rate pool

Myles Ltd can claim capital allowances of │ **£** │ 8,640 │.

Workings (on-screen free text area provided in the CBT as part of larger question)

	Main pool £	Special rate £	Allowances £
Y/e 31.3.21			
TWDV b/f	25,000	10,000	
Additions	17,000	8,000	
	42,000	18,000	
WDA 18%/6%	(7,560)	(1,080)	8,640
TWDV c/f	34,440	16,920	

Activity 6: Private-use assets

(a) Sweeney can claim capital allowances of │ **£** │ 3,840 │.

Workings (on-screen free text area provided in the CBT as part of larger question)

	Main pool £	Sweeney's car 80% business use £	Restriction £	Total £
TWDV b/f	16,000	20,000		
WDA @ 18%	(2,880)			2,880
WDA @ 6%		(1,200)	× 80%	960
				3,840
TWDV c/f	13,120	18,800		

Note. As there is no restriction for the private use of an employee, Doris's car would be in the main pool.

Sweeney's car has CO_2 emissions in excess of 110g/km so it is written down at the special rate rather than the main rate.

(b) What capital allowances would Sweeney claim if the business ceased in this period and both cars were sold for £15,000 each?

Sweeney would have a [balancing allowance] of [£ | 5,000] .

Workings (on-screen free text area provided in the CBT as part of larger question)

	£
Sweeney's car	
Balancing allowance (20,000 – 15,000) × 80% =	4,000
Main pool (Doris's car)	
Balancing allowance (16,000 – 15,000) =	1,000
	5,000

Note. There is no restriction for the private use of an employee.

Activity 7: Short life asset election

Workings (on-screen free text area provided in the CBT as part of larger question)

By making the election, the asset is depooled for eight years until 31 December 2028.
The asset has been sold before the election expires. It is therefore treated separately to the assets in the main pool, so a balancing allowance or charge will arise on disposal.
If the asset is sold for £5,000 there will be a balancing allowance of £20,000 – £5,000 = £15,000.
If the asset is sold for £50,000 there will be a balancing charge of £50,000 – £20,000 = £30,000.

Activity 8: Calculation of capital allowances

The capital allowances claim that Oscar can make for the period ended 30 June 2021 is calculated as follows:

	AIA/FYA £	Main pool £	Allowances £
18 m/e 30 June 2021			
B/f		81,000	
Disposal 1.6.21		(30,000)	
AIA acquisition			
10.7.20 Plant	1,410,000		
12.9.20 Plant	550,000		
AIA (see note)	(1,100,000)		1,100,000
	860,000		
Transfer balance to pool	(860,000)	860,000	
FYA acquisition			
10.8.20 Car	11,000		
FYA @ 100%	(11,000)		11,000
		911,000	
WDA @ 18% × 18/12		(245,970)	245,970
C/f		665,030	
Allowances			1,356,970

Notes.

1   The AIA limit and WDA are scaled up for the 18 month period, whereas the FYA is never scaled up or down. The limit is calculated by adding together the pro rated AIA for the part of the period prior to 1 January 2021 to the pro rated AIA to the part of the period starting on 1 January 2021. This is (£1,000,000 × 12/12) + (£200,000 × 6/12). The total AIA is therefore £1,100,000.

2   This working would not be the same had it related to a company, as the 18-month period would be split into two accounting periods (a 12-month period and a 6-month period). We look at accounting periods for companies later in the Course Book.

Activity 1: Calculating taxable total profits

Corporation tax computation y/e 31 December 2020

	£
Trading profits	2,440,000
Rental income	150,000
NTL-R income (Interest income) (40,000 - 10,000)	30,000
Chargeable gains (350,000 + 70,000 – 80,000)	340,000
Less qualifying charitable payment	(70,000)
Taxable total profits	2,890,000

Note. The dividends received are not taxable.

Activity 2: Calculating taxable total profits – long period of account

Long period of account

	12 months to 31.8.20 £	4 months to 31.12.20 £
Adjusted trading profits (12:4)	2,700,000	900,000
Less capital allowances (W1)	(6,750)	(8,720)
Trading profits	2,693,250	891,280
NTL-R income (Interest income) (12:4)	24,000	8,000
Chargeable gain	–	40,000
Less qualifying charitable payment	(20,000)	–
TTP	2,697,250	939,280

Workings (not provided in CBT)

	AIA £	Main pool £	Allowances £
1.9.19 to 31.8.20 (12m)			
TWDV @ 1.9.19		37,500	
WDA (18%)		(6,750)	6,750
		30,750	
1.9.20 to 31.12.20 (4m)			
Addition	6,875		
AIA*	(6,875)		6,875
WDA (18%) × $\frac{4}{12}$		(1,845)	1,845
		28,905	
			8,720

*AIA available = $1,000,000 \times \frac{4}{12} = \underline{333,333}$

Activity 3: Corporation tax payable

£	288,800

Workings (not provided in CBT)

	£
Trading profits	1,500,000
Chargeable gain	50,000
Qualifying charitable donations	(30,000)
Taxable total profits	1,520,000
Corporation tax due £1,520,000 × 19%	£288,800

Activity 1: Current year basis (i)

Correct option is year ended 31 December 2020.

Workings (not provided in the CBT)

Tax the profits arising in the accounting period ending in fiscal year 2020/21 ie the accounting period that ends between 6 April 2020 and 5 April 2021.

Activity 2: Current year basis (ii)

(a) Correct option is fiscal year 2020/21

Workings (not provided in the CBT)

Period ended 30 June 2020 ends between 6 April 2020 and 5 April 2021, ie fiscal year 2020/21.

(b) Correct option is fiscal year 2019/20

Workings (not provided in the CBT)

Period ended 31 January 2020 ends between 6 April 2019 and 5 April 2020, ie fiscal year 2019/20.

Activity 3: The first fiscal year

What is the first fiscal year of the trade? (XXXX/XX format) | 2018/19

What profits will be assessed in the first fiscal year?

£ | 6,000

Workings (not provided in the CBT)

2018/19
Actual basis 01/01/19 to 05/04/19
$\frac{3}{12} \times 24{,}000 = £6{,}000$

Activity 4: The second fiscal year (trader has 12 month accounting period)

What is the second fiscal year of the trade? (XXXX/XX format) | 2019/20

What profits will be assessed in the second fiscal year?

£ | 24,000

Workings (not provided in the CBT)

Trade begins in fiscal year 2018/19 so this is the first year.
The second year is therefore 2019/20
12m period ending in 2019/20 ⇒ basis period = 12 months to the end of AP
ie. y/e 31.12.19 = £24,000

Activity 5: Overlap profits

His overlap period is (XX/XX/XX) | 01/01/19 | to | 05/04/19

His overlap profits are | £ | 6,000

Activity 6: Opening year rules (short first period)

	Fiscal year (XXXX/XX)	Profits taxed From (XX/XX/XX)	To (XX/XX/XX)	Amount taxed £
First fiscal year	2018/19	01/01/19	05/04/19	9,000
Second fiscal year	2019/20	01/01/19	31/12/19	42,000
Third fiscal year	2020/21	01/07/19	30/06/20	48,000
Overlap periods and profits				
First overlap period		01/01/19	05/04/19	9,000
Second overlap period		01/07/19	31/12/19	24,000
Total overlap				33,000

Workings (not provided in the CBT)

	£
2018/19 **Actual** 01/01/19 to 05/04/19	
$\frac{3}{6}$ × 18,000 = £9,000	
2019/20	
6m period ending in 2019/20 $\Rightarrow$ tax first 12 months of profits	
6m to 30/06/19	18,000
6m to 31/12/19 ($\frac{6}{12}$ × 48,000)	24,000
	42,000
2020/21 – CYB 12m period ending 30/06/20	48,000
Overlap 01/01/19 to 05/04/19	
$\frac{3}{6}$ × 18,000	9,000
Plus 01/07/19 to 31/12/19	
$\frac{6}{12}$ × 48,000	24,000
Total	33,000

Activity 7: Opening year rules (long first period ending in second fiscal year)

	Profits taxed			
	Fiscal year (XXXX/XX)	From (XX/XX/XX)	To (XX/XX/XX)	Amount taxed £
First fiscal year	2018/19	01/07/18	05/04/19	9,000
Second fiscal year	2019/20	01/01/19	31/12/19	12,000
Third fiscal year	2020/21	01/01/20	31/12/20	30,000
Overlap period and profits		01/01/19	05/04/19	3,000

Workings (not provided in the CBT)

2018/19
Actual 01/07/18 to 05/04/19
$\frac{9}{18} \times 18,000 = £9,000$
2019/20
18m period ending in 2019/20 $\Rightarrow$ tax 12m to accounting year end $\Rightarrow$ 01/01/19 to 31/12/19
$\frac{12}{18} \times 18,000 = £12,000$
2020/21
Y/e 31/12/20   £30,000
Overlap 01/01/19 to 05/04/19
$\frac{3}{18} \times 18,000 = £3,000$

Activity 8: Opening year rules (long first period ending in third fiscal year)

		Profits taxed		
	Fiscal year (XXXX/XX)	From (XX/XX/XX)	To (XX/XX/XX)	Amount taxed £
First fiscal year	2018/19	01/12/18	05/04/19	8,000
Second fiscal year	2019/20	06/04/19	05/04/20	24,000
Third fiscal year	2020/21	01/06/19	31/05/20	24,000
Overlap period and profits		01/06/19	05/04/20	20,000

Workings (not provided in the CBT)

2018/19
Actual 01/12/18 to 05/04/19
$\frac{4}{18}$ × 36,000   = £8,000
2019/20
– no accounting period ending in 2019/20 ⇒ **Actual** 06/04/19 to 05/04/20
$\frac{12}{18}$ × 36,000   = £24,000
2020/21
12m to y/e ⇒ 12m to 31/05/20
$\frac{12}{18}$ × 36,000   = £24,000
Overlap 01/06/19 to 05/04/20
$\frac{10}{18}$ × 36,000   = £20,000

Activity 9: Closing year rules (one period ending in final fiscal year)

		Profits taxed		
	Fiscal year (XXXX/XX)	From (XX/XX/XX)	To (XX/XX/XX)	Amount taxed £
Penultimate fiscal year	2019/20	01/01/2019	31/12/2019	22,000
Final fiscal year	2020/21	01/01/2020	30/04/2020	8,000

Workings (not provided in the CBT)

Business finishes 30/04/20 so final year is 2020/21	
2019/20 CYB (y/e 31/12/19)	22,000
2020/21 4 months: 01/01/20 – 30/04/20	12,000
Less overlap profits	(4,000)
	8,000

Activity 10: Closing year rules (two periods ending in final fiscal year)

	Profits taxed			
	Fiscal year (XXXX/XX)	From (XX/XX/XX)	To (XX/XX/XX)	Amount taxed £
Penultimate fiscal year	2019/20	01/01/2019	31/12/2019	30,000
Final fiscal year	2020/21	01/01/2020	31/03/2021	17,000

Workings (not provided in the CBT)

Business finishes on 31 March 2021 ie in fiscal year 2020/21. This is his final year.

2019/20 y/e 31 December 2019	30,000
2020/21 y/e 31 December 2020	25,000
p/e 31 March 2021	4,000
	29,000
Less overlap profits	(12,000)
	17,000

Activity 11: Short accounting period

Year of change 2020/21

	£
2019/20 y/e 31 August 2018 (1.9.18 to 31.8.19)	20,000
2020/21 gap 9 months to 31 May 2020	
Tax 12 months to 31 May 2020 (1.6.19 to 31.5.20)	
$\frac{3}{12}$ × 20,000 + 15,000	20,000
2021/22 y/e 31.5.21	30,000

Creates overlap profits

1.6.19 – 31.8.19 ie 3/12 x 20,000 = £5,000

Activity 12: Two accounting periods ending in the year
Year of change 2020/21

	£
2019/20 y/e 30.6.19	25,000
2020/21 Gap 18 months to 31.12.20	45,000
Less $\frac{6}{9}$ × 21,000	(14,000)
	31,000
2021/22 y/e 31.12.21	35,000

CHAPTER 6 Partnerships

Activity 1: Partnership profit allocation

	Ron £	Steve £
Profit share	38,000	22,000

Workings (not provided in the CBT)

	Ron £	Steve £	Total £
Year ended 30 June			
Salary	5,000	–	5,000
Balance (3:2)	33,000	22,000	55,000 (bal)
Assessments	38,000	22,000	60,000

Activity 2: Change in profit-sharing arrangements

	Ron £	Steve £
Profit share	50,500	39,500

Workings (not provided in the CBT)

	Ron £	Steve £	Total £
Year ended 30 June			
1 July – 31 December			
Salary $^{6}/_{12} \times 5,000$	2,500		2,500
Balance (3:2)	25,500	17,000	42,500
$^{6}/_{12} \times 90,000$			45,000
1 January – 30 June			
$^{6}/_{12} \times 90,000$			
Split 1:1	22,500	22,500	45,000
	50,500	39,500	90,000

Activity 3: Change in partnership personnel

	M £	G £	B £
2018/19	16,500	24,250	5,667
2019/20	29,750	0	20,500
2020/21	48,000	0	24,000
Overlap			17,667

Workings (not provided in the CBT)

Sharing of profits

	Total £	M £	G £	B £
Y/e 31.5.18, ie £33,000				
(1:1)	33,000	16,500	16,500	–
Y/e 31.5.19, ie £51,000				
Up to 1.12.18 (1:1) 51,000 × $^6/_{12}$	25,500	12,750	12,750	–
From 1.12.18 (2:1 each) 51,000 × $^6/_{12}$	25,500	17,000		8,500
	51,000	29,750	12,750	8,500
Y/e 31.5.20, ie £72,000				
(2:1)	72,000	48,000		24,000

New partner (B): Trading profits

	£
Started trading 1.12.18	
6 months to 31.5.19	8,500
Year ended 31.5.20	24,000

New partner (B): Trading assessments

	£
2018/19 actual 1.12.18 – 5.4.19 8,500 × $^4/_6$	5,667
2019/20 (first 12 months), ie 1.12.18 – 30.11.19 8,500 + $^6/_{12}$ × 24,000	20,500
2020/21 (y/e 31.5.20)	24,000

New partner (B): Overlap

	£
1.12.18 – 5.4.19	5,667
1.6.19 – 30.11.19 ($^6/_{12}$ × 24,000)	12,000
	17,667

Retiring partner (G): Trading assessments

	£
Retires on 1.12.18, ie 2018/19	
2018/19 (y/e 31.5.18)	16,500
2018/19 (p/e 1.12.18)	12,750
Less overlap	(5,000)
Total 2018/19	24,250

Continuing partner (M): Trading assessments

	£
2018/19 (y/e 31.5.18)	£16,500
2019/20 (y/e 31.5.19)	£29,750
2020/21 (y/e 31.5.20)	£48,000

CHAPTER 7 National insurance

Activity 1: National insurance contributions

(a) Mr Bull

His Class 2 NI contributions for the year are:

£	158.60

His Class 4 NI contributions at 9% are:

£	405.00

Workings (not provided in the CBT)

Class 2	52 × £3.05	£158.60
Class 4	(£14,000 – £9,500) × 9%	£405.00

(b) Mr Seye

His Class 4 NI contributions at 9% are:

£	3,645.00

His Class 4 NI contributions at 2% are:

£	560.00

Workings (not provided in the CBT)

Class 4 at 9%	(£50,000 – £9,500) × 9%	£3,645.00
Class 4 at 2%	(£78,000 – £50,000) × 2%	£560.00

CHAPTER 8 Losses

Activity 1: Income tax trading loss options

Show if the following statements are true or false by ticking the correct box for each.

	True ✓	False ✓
Edward may offset the loss against total income in 2018/19 and then in 2017/18.		✓
Edward may offset the loss against total income in 2020/21.		✓
Edward may offset the loss against trading income only in 2018/19.		✓
Edward may offset the loss against the rental income in 2019/20.	✓	

Notes.

1   The loss has been made in fiscal year 2019/20. It can, therefore, be used in 2019/20 and/or 2018/19, so the first option is false.

2   If Edward lets the loss carry forward to 2020/21, then it offsets automatically against trading income only, so the second option is false.

3   If Edward chooses to carry the loss back to 2018/19, it will offset against total income, not just trading income, so the third option is false.

4   If Edward makes a claim for 2019/20, it will offset against his total income. The only income he has is rental income so the fourth option is true.

Activity 2: Utilisation of income tax losses

(a) Complete the following table showing Pike's total income for 2017/18 to 2020/21, assuming maximum and earliest claims against total income are made. Enter '0' in cells as appropriate.

	2017/18 £	2018/19 £	2019/20 £	2020/21 £
Trading income	2,000	0	8,000	4,000
Loss carried forward	0	0	(8,000)	(3,600)
	0	0	0	400
Property income	400	1,000	1,000	1,000
Total Income	2,400	1,000	1,000	1,400
CY loss relief	0	(1,000)	0	0
PY loss relief	(2,400)	0	0	0
Net income	0	0	1,000	1,400

Workings (not provided in the CBT)

	Trading loss
Loss made in 2018/19	15,000
Carry back against total income in 2017/18	(2,400)
Use against total income in current year 2018/19	(1,000)
Carry forward against trading income in year 2019/20	(8,000)
Carry forward against trading income in year 2020/21 (balancing figure)	(3,600)
	0

(b) Show if the following statement is true or false by ticking the correct box.

	True ✓	False ✓
Pike has used his loss in the most tax-efficient way possible		✓

Explanation

Pike's income is below the personal allowance in all years, so it is a waste to carry back the loss or use it in the year of the loss.

It is wasteful to use it in the future years as well but Pike has no control over this. The carry forward is automatic.

Note. The question told you to use the loss as soon as possible, so prior year relief should be claimed before current year.

Activity 3: Carry forward loss relief

The loss carried forward at 31 March 2021 is

£	5,000

Workings (not provided in the CBT)

	Year ended 31 March		
	2019 £	**2020** £	**2021** £
Trading profit	–	5,000	6,000
Property income	–	2,000	2,000
Total profits	–	7,000	8,000
Less trade loss carried forward		(7,000)	(8,000)
TTP	–	–	–

Loss memorandum			£
Y/e 31 March 2019			20,000
Loss relief y/e 31 March 2020			(7,000)
			13,000
Loss relief y/e 31 March 2021			(8,000)
c/f			5,000

Activity 4: Current year and carry back relief

	True ✓	False ✓
Kay Ltd may claim to offset £60,000 of the loss against total profits in y/e 31.3.20.		✓
If Kay Ltd makes the maximum permissible claims, it will have £90,000 loss to carry forward at 31.3.21.		✓
Kay Ltd may claim to offset the loss against total profits in y/e 31.3.20 and then against total profits in y/e 31.3.21.		✓
Kay Ltd may claim to offset the loss against total profits in y/e 31.3.21 and carry the remaining loss forward to the y/e 31.3.22.	✓	

Workings (not provided in CBT)

The loss arises in year ended 31 March 2021, so this is the current year.

We cannot carry back to the prior year of 31 March 2020 unless we have used the loss in y/e 31.3.21 first, so the first statement is false because only £50,000 of the loss would remain after a current year claim.

If the company makes the maximum permissible claims, it will offset in the current year of 31.3.21, then carry back to y/e 31.3.20, setting losses against total profits including gains (see below). It will have insufficient losses to reduce the y/e 31.3.20 income to nil so there will be no losses to carry forward. The second statement is, therefore, false.

If we wish to offset in y/e 31.3.20 and y/e 31.3.21, we must offset y/e 31.3.21 before y/e 31.3.20, so the third statement is false.

We can choose to offset the loss in y/e 31.3.21 only, so the fourth statement is true. Once we have offset in y/e 31.3.21, we could choose to make a further claim to offset in y/e 31.3.20 or to carry it forward into future accounting periods.

	Year ended 31 March		
	2019 £	2020 £	2021 £
Trading income	20,000	10,000	–
Capital gains	50,000	50,000	50,000
Total profits	70,000	60,000	50,000
Loss relief		(ii) (50,000)	(i) (50,000)
TTP	70,000	10,000	–

Workings (not provided in CBT)

Loss memorandum

	£
Y/e 31.3.21	100,000
Less relief y/e 31.3.21(optional claim)	(50,000)(i)
Less relief y/e 31.3.20 (additional optional claim after y/e 31.3.21 claim)	(50,000)(ii)
	Nil

Activity 5: Comprehensive example

	Y/e 30.9.18 £	P/e 31.3.19 £	Y/e 31.3.20 £	Y/e 31.3.21 £
Trading profits	20,000	30,000	0	15,000
NTL-R income	10,000	10,000	10,000	10,000
Total profits	30,000	40,000	10,000	25,000
Current year relief	0	0	(10,000)(i)	0
Prior year relief	(15,000)(iii)	(40,000)(ii)	0	0
Losses carried forward				(25,000)
	15,000	0	0	0
Qualifying charitable donations	(5,000)	(5,000)	(5,000)	(5,000)
Taxable total profits	10,000	0	0	0

Picklist:

Current year relief
Losses carried forward
Prior year relief
Qualifying charitable donations

Workings (not provided in CBT)

Loss memo £

Y/e 31.3.20		155,000
Current – y/e 31.3.20	(i)	(10,000)
Carry back – 6m P/E 31.3.19	(ii)	(40,000)
– Y/e 30.9.18 – max claim 6/12 × 30,000	(iii)	(15,000)
		90,000
C/fwd y/e 31.3.21	(iv)	(25,000)
C/fwd		65,000

Tutorial note. Full relief has been claimed in the y/e 31.3.21 because the question stated that maximum reliefs must be taken as early as possible. However, it would be possible in this scenario to restrict the relief in y/e 31.3.21 to £20,000 in keep the relief from the qualifying charitable donation and carry the remaining loss of £5,000 for offset in y/e 31.3.22.

CHAPTER 9 Self-assessment for individuals

Activity 1: Penalties

Kelly's penalty can be reduced from [70] % of the potential lost revenue (for a deliberate, but not concealed error) to [20] %, with the unprompted disclosure of her error.

Activity 2: Payments on account and balancing payments

	£
2019/20 income tax payable 7,000 − 4,000 =	3,000
The payments on account for 2020/21 are therefore:	
31.1.21 $\frac{1}{2}$ × 3,000	1,500
31.7.21 $\frac{1}{2}$ × 3,000	1,500
The final payment is therefore:	
Income tax liability	8,000
Less PAYE	(2,500)
Less payments on account (2 × 1,500)	(3,000)
	2,500
Capital gains tax liability	1,000
31.1.22 Final payment	3,500

CHAPTER 10 Self-assessment for companies

Activity 1: Payment of corporation tax

A plc has a 31 March year end and has TTP of £2.1m per year.

	£
Corporation tax due	
2,100,000 × 19%	399,000
Due by instalments on the 14th day of month 7, 10, 13 and 16, counting from the start of the period – ie 1 April 2020.	
14 October 2020	99,750
14 January 2021	99,750
14 April 2021	99,750
14 July 2021	99,750

CHAPTER 11 Chargeable gains – the basics

Activity 1: Capital gain calculation (individuals)

Complete the table showing Mr Dunstable's gain.

	£
Proceeds	38,500
Less selling expenses	(1,500)
Net proceeds	37,000
Less cost	(15,000)
Less legal fees on purchase	(500)
Less enhancement	(3,000)
Capital gain	18,500

Activity 2: Current year losses

Ted's net capital gain for 2020/21 before the annual exempt amount is:

£ | 7,000

Ted has a loss to carry forward of £ | nil

Workings (not provided in the CBT)

	£
Gains 45,000 + 10,000	55,000
Less loss	(48,000)
Net capital gains	7,000
Less annual exempt amount	(12,300)
Taxable gains	Nil
The balance of the annual exempt amount is wasted.	

Activity 3: Prior year losses

Tara's net capital gain for 2020/21 before the deduction of losses is:

£ | 1,700

Tara has a loss to carry forward of £ | 8,300 .

Workings (not provided in the CBT)

	£
Gain in 2020/21	14,000
Less annual exempt amount	(12,300)
Net gain before the deduction of losses	1,700
Less losses b/f	(1,700)
Taxable gains	Nil
Losses to c/f £(10,000 – 1,700)	8,300

Activity 4: Computing capital gains tax payable

What is Mr Dunstable's capital gains tax payable? £ | 950 |.

Workings (not provided in the CBT)

	£
Capital gain	18,800
Less annual exempt amount	(12,300)
Taxable gain	6,500
Basic rate band	37,500
Taxable income	(34,000)
Basic rate band remaining	3,500

	£
Capital gains tax payable	
3,500 × 10%	350
3,000 × 20%	600
6,500	950

Activity 5: Capital gain calculation (companies)

	£
Proceeds	58,500
Less selling expenses	(1,500)
Net proceeds	57,000
Less cost	(15,000)
Less legal fees on purchase	(500)
Less enhancement	(3,000)
Unindexed gain	38,500
Less indexation on cost ((15,000 + 500) × 1.879)	(29,125)
Less indexation on enhancement expenditure (3,000 × 0.856)	(2,568)
Capital gain	6,807

Activity 6: Indexation

JEK Ltd bought an asset for £50,000.

What is the capital gain/(loss) if it was sold for:

(a) £20,000?

£	(30,000)

(b) £70,000?

£	nil

(c) £150,000?

£	61,950

Workings (not provided in the CBT)

		£	£	£
Proceeds		20,000	70,000	150,000
Less cost		(50,000)	(50,000)	(50,000)
		(30,000)	20,000	100,000
IA (a) N/A		–		
(b) 50,000 × 0.761 = 38,050				
restrict to 20,000			(20,000)	
(c) 50,000 × 0.761				(38,050)
Indexed gain/(loss)		(30,000)	–	61,950

CHAPTER 12 Further aspects of chargeable gains

Activity 1: Part disposal

The gain on the disposal of the land is £ | 4,702 |.

The cost of the remaining land carried forward is £ | 15,652 |.

Workings (not provided in the CBT)

	£
Gross proceeds	10,000
Less disposal costs	(950)
Net proceeds	9,050
Cost $\dfrac{10}{10+36} \times 20,000$	(4,348)
	4,702
Cost of remaining land for future CGT calculations: = 20,000 – 4,348	15,652

Activity 2: Chattels

(a)   The chargeable gain on the disposal is £ | 5,000 |.

Workings (not provided in the CBT)

Non-wasting chattel: cost ≤ £6,000, proceeds > £6,000	£
Proceeds	9,000
Less commission	(1,000)
	8,000
Less cost	(500)
	7,500
$\frac{5}{3}$ (Gross proceeds – 6,000)	
= $\frac{5}{3}$ (9,000 – 6,000)	
= 5,000	
∴ take lower gain 5,000	5,000

(b) The loss on the disposal is | **£** | 1,000 | .

Workings (not provided in the CBT)

Non-wasting chattel: cost > £6,000, proceeds ≤ £6,000	£
Proceeds (deemed)	6,000
Less cost	(7,000)
Allowable loss	(1,000)

Activity 3: Transfers between spouses/civil partners

The chargeable gain on transfer is:

	✓
Nil	✓
£18,000	
£31,000	
£13,000	,

The transfer takes place at no gain/no loss and Kate assumes the base cost of £14,000 as her cost.

CHAPTER 13 Share disposals

Activity 1: Matching rules for individuals

	Shares
Same day	400
Next 30 days	500
Share pool	700 ß
Disposal	1,600

ß is a balancing figure

1   Match with same day

	£	£
Proceeds $\frac{400}{1,600} \times 14,000$	3,500	
Cost	(3,000)	
		500

2   Match with next 30 days

	£	£
Proceeds $\frac{500}{1,600} \times 14,000$	4,375	
Cost	(4,500)	
		(125)

3   Match with share pool

	£	£
Proceeds $\frac{700}{1,600} \times 14,000$	6,125	
Cost (W)	(2,800)	
		3,325
Net gain		£3,700

(W) Share pool

	Number	Cost
15.5.02	2,200	8,800
Disposal $\frac{700}{2,200} \times 8,800$	(700)	(2,800)
	1,500	£6,000

Activity 2: Share pool for individuals

Matching rules: The shares were all acquired prior to the date of disposal, so they are all in the share pool.

	£
Proceeds	14,000
Cost (W1)	(4,500)
Gain	9,500

Share pool (W1)

	Number	Cost £
January 1985		
Purchase	3,000	5,000
February 1987		
Purchase	1,000	4,000
	4,000	9,000
May 2020		
Disposal $2,000/_{4,000} \times 9,000$	(2,000)	(4,500)
	2,000	4,500

Activity 3: Bonus and rights issues for individuals

Matching rules: All bought prior to date of disposal so all from share pool.

Gain

	£
Proceeds	15,000
Less cost (W1)	(10,139)
Gain	4,861

(W1) Share pool

	Number	Cost £
1.10.95	10,000	15,000
11.9.99 acquisition	2,000	5,000
	12,000	20,000
1.2.00 1:2 rights @ £2.75	6,000	16,500
	18,000	36,500
5.9.05 2:1 bonus	36,000	–
	54,000	36,500
14.10.20 sale 15000/54000 × 36,500	(15,000)	(10,139)
	39,000	26,361

Activity 4: Matching rules for companies

	£
Match same day	1,000
Last 9 days	500
FA85 pool	1,000
	2,500

Same-day sale	£
Proceeds $\frac{1,000}{2,500} \times 12,500$	5,000
Cost	(4,822)
	178

Last 9 days	£
Proceeds $\frac{500}{2,500} \times 12,500$	2,500
Cost	(2,511)
	(11)

FA85 pool	Number	Cost £	Indexed cost £
Aug 1996	1,000	2,750	2,750
Index up to December 1998			
0.008 × 2,750 =			22
	1,000	2,750	2,772
Addition December 1998	1,000	3,250	3,250
	2,000	6,000	6,022
Index up to December 2017			
0.692 × 6,022 =			4,167
	2,000	6,000	10,189
Disposal 1,000/2,000 × 6,000 1,000/2,000 × 10,189	(1,000)	(3,000)	(5,095)
C/f	1,000	3,000	5,094

	£
Proceeds 1,000/2,500 × 12,500	5,000
Cost	(3,000)
Unindexed gain	2,000
IA (5,095 − 3,000)	(2,095)
Indexed gain	0

Total gains	£
Same day	178
Last 9 days	(11)
FA85 pool	0
	167

Activity 5: Bonus and rights issues for companies

Matching rules: The shares were all acquired prior to the date of disposal so they are all in the share pool.

Total gains	£
Proceeds	10,000
Less cost (W)	(2,100)
Less indexation (3,730 – 2,100)	(1,630)
Chargeable gain	6,270

1985 pool working	Number	Cost £	Indexed cost £
1.5.85	500	1,000	1,000
5.8.87 rights			
Index up to August 87			
1,000 × 0.072			72
	500	1,000	1,072
Rights 1:2 @ £5	250	1,250	1,250
	750	2,250	2,322
15.9.89 bonus	750	–	–
	1,500	2,250	2,322
5.9.19 disposal			
Index up to 17 December			
2,322 × 1.724			4,003
	1,500	2,250	6,325
10.3.2019 Rights issue 1:3 @ £6	500	3,000	3,000
	2,000	5,250	9,325
Disposal 800/2,000 × 5,250 800/2,000 × 9,325	(800)	(2,100)	(3,730)
	1,200	3,150	5,595

CHAPTER 14 Reliefs for chargeable gains

Activity 1: Business asset disposal relief – calculation of capital gains tax

Capital gains tax payable at 10% due to business asset disposal relief is

£ | 1,000 | .

Capital gains tax payable at 10% to utilise the remaining basic rate band is

£ | 513 | .

Capital gains tax on other gains payable at 20% is

£ | 6,574 | .

Workings (not provided in the CBT)

	Eligible gains £	Other gains £
Chargeable gains	10,000	50,300
Less annual exempt amount		(12,300)
	10,000	38,000
	£	
Basic rate band	37,500	
Taxable income	(22,370)	
Basic rate band remaining	15,130	
Eligible gains	£	
10,000 × 10%	1,000	
Other gains		
5,130 × 10% (15,130 – 10,000)	513	
32,870 × 20%	6,574	
38,000		
	8,087	

Activity 2: Disposals eligible for business asset disposal relief

Identify which, if any, are qualifying disposals for business asset disposal relief. Tick the relevant box.

	✓
Part of a business in which the individual has been a partner since August 2014	✓
A freehold factory which the individual uses in his business and has owned for ten years – this is not disposal of the whole/ part of a business (as a going concern)	
Unquoted shares held by the individual in a personal trading company in which he is employed and which he has owned for the previous three years	✓
Quoted shares held by the individual in a personal trading company in which he is employed and which he has owned for the previous three years	✓

Activity 3: Business asset disposal relief – calculating gains eligible for relief

(a) The total net taxable gain eligible for business asset disposal relief is

£ | 700,000 | .

The total net taxable gain not eligible for business asset disposal relief is

£ | 67,700 | .

Workings (not provided in the CBT)

	£
Eligible gains	
Goodwill	500,000
Factory	300,000
Office block	(100,000)
	700,000
Other gains	
Shares	80,000

	Eligible gains £	Other gains £
Chargeable gains	700,000	80,000
Less annual exempt amount		(12,300)
Taxable gains	700,000	67,700

(b) If the gain on the factory was £9,800,000 then the total net taxable gain eligible for business asset disposal relief is

£	1,000,000

.

The total net taxable gain not eligible for business asset disposal relief is

£	9,267,700

.

Workings (not provided in the CBT)

	£	£
Eligible gains		
Goodwill	500,000	
Factory	9,800,000	
Office block	(100,000)	
	10,200,000	
Less business asset disposal relief		
Max	(1,000,000)	
Gain not eligible		9,200,000
Shares		80,000
Other gains		9,280,000

	Eligible gains £	Other gains £
Chargeable gains	1,000,000	9,280,000
Less annual exempt amount		(12,300)
Taxable gains	1,000,000	9,267,700

Activity 4: Rollover relief

The gain taxed on Henry Ltd now is:

£ | 10,000 .

The base cost of the new building is:

£ | 165,000 .

Workings (not provided in the CBT)

	£
Disposal of fixed plant	
Proceeds	200,000
Less cost	(150,000)
IA 150,000 × 10%	(15,000)
Indexed gain	35,000
Rollover relief (balancing figure)	(25,000)
Proceeds not reinvested taxed now (200,000 – 190,000)	10,000
Base cost of building = £190,000 – £25,000	165,000

Activity 5: Gift relief

The gift relief claim must be signed by: | Bill and Ludovic | .

Bill's chargeable gain on disposal is | £ | Nil | .   Ludovic's base cost is | £ | 7,000 | .

Picklist:

Bill and Ludovic
Bill only
Ludovic only

Workings (not provided in the CBT)

	£
Proceeds (deemed)	25,000
Less cost	(7,000)
	18,000
Gain rolled over	(18,000)
Chargeable gain	Nil
Base cost for Ludovic:	
MV (deemed consideration)	25,000
Less gain held over	(18,000)
Adjusted base cost	7,000

Activity 6: With and without gift relief

(a) If gift relief is not claimed, Julie's chargeable gain is:

£ | 35,000

	£
Deemed sale proceeds (MV)	85,000
Less cost	(50,000)
Gain	35,000

and Jack's chargeable gain is:

£ | 10,000

	£
Proceeds	95,000
Less cost (MV)	(85,000)
Gain	10,000

(b) If gift relief is claimed, Julie's chargeable gain is:

£ | 0

	£
Deemed sale proceeds	85,000
Less cost	(50,000)
	35,000
Less gift relief	(35,000)
Gain	0

and Jack's chargeable gain is:

£ | 45,000

	£	£
Proceeds		95,000
Less cost	85,000	
Less gift relief	(35,000)	
		(50,000)
Gain		45,000

Activity 7: Disposals eligible for investors' relief

	IR ✓	BADR ✓
4% holding in A Ltd, an unquoted trading company in which the individual is not employed. The shares were subscribed for on 30 April 2016. This meets the conditions for investors' relief. However, note that business asset disposal relief (BADR) will not be available as the individual is not an employee.	✓	x
20% holding in B Ltd, an unquoted trading company in which the individual is employed. The shares were subscribed for on 30 April 2016. As the individual is employed, investors' relief will not be available. However, note that BADR will be available.	X	✓

	IR ✓	BADR ✓
1% holding in C Ltd, a quoted trading company in which the individual is not employed. The shares were subscribed for on 30 June 2016. As the shares are in a quoted company investor's relief will not be available. Note that BADR will also not be available due to the individual not having a 5% shareholding (and also not being an employee).	X	X
15% holding in D Ltd, an unquoted trading company in which the individual is not employed. The shares were subscribed for on 30 June 2018. As the shares have not been held for three years investors' relief will not be available. Note that BADR will also not be available as the individual is not an employee of the company.	X	X
10% holding in E Ltd, an unquoted trading company in which the individual is not employed. The shares were bought on 30 April 2016. As the shares were bought rather than subscribed for investors' relief will not be available. Note that BADR will also not be available as the individual is not an employee.	X	X

Test your learning: answers

CHAPTER 1   Tax framework

1

	✓
Integrity	✓
Objectivity	✓
Professional competence and due care	
Confidentiality	
Professional behaviour	✓

Integrity: It would not be honest to knowingly reduce profits by including expenditure that was not incurred in the year.

Objectivity: If you agreed to her request because of your job prospects, you are allowing bias to affect your judgement.

Professional behaviour: Submitting a tax return that does not follow tax law is illegal.

2

	✓
True	
False	✓

Tax evasion can lead to fines/imprisonment.

3

	✓
True	
False	✓

A company pays **corporation tax** on its total profits.

4   Each tax year all of an individual's components of income are added together, then a personal allowance is deducted to arrive at taxable income .

5

£	4,900

	Non-savings income £
Trading profits	25,000
Property income	12,000
Total income	37,000
Personal allowance	(12,500)
Taxable income	24,500

Tax	£
Non-savings income	
£24,500 × 20%	4,900
Tax liability	**4,900**

CHAPTER 2 Computing trading income

1

	Allowable ✓
Legal fees incurred on the acquisition of a factory to be used for trade purposes	
Heating for factory	✓
Legal fees incurred on pursuing trade receivables	✓
Acquiring a machine to be used in the factory	

Legal fees on the acquisition of factory are capital expenditure and so not allowable. Heating is a revenue expense and so allowable. Legal fees incurred on pursuing trade receivables are allowable as they relate to a revenue source. Acquiring a machine is a capital expense and so not allowable (although capital allowances will be available for this expenditure).

2

£	700

The cost of staff entertaining is allowable. Gifts of food to customers are never allowable. The entertaining of customers is never allowable.

3

	Allowable ✓	Disallowable ✓
Parking fines incurred by business owner		✓
Parking fines incurred by an employee while on the employer's business	✓	
Parking fines incurred by the director of a company while on company business		✓
Legal costs incurred in relation to acquiring a 10-year lease of property for the first time		✓
Legal costs incurred in relation to the renewal of a lease for 20 years	✓	
Gifts of calendars to customers, costing £4 each and displaying an advertisement for the company	✓	
Gifts of bottles of whisky to customers, costing £12 each		✓

4

	✓
£80 must be deducted from the accounts profit	
£80 must be added back to the accounts profit	
£96 must be deducted from the accounts profit	
£96 must be added back to the accounts profit	✓

The normal selling price of £80 + (20% × £80) = £96 must be added to the accounts profit.

5

£	700

Added back	Deducted
✓	✓
	✓

The movement on the general provision is disallowable (if an increase)/not taxable (if a decrease). This means that the decrease in the general provision of **£700** (£2,500 – £1,800) must be deducted from the accounts profit.

6

£	360

80% × £450 is disallowable for tax purposes.

7

	Taxable trading profits
Zack • As trading receipts do not exceed £1,000 the trading allowance means trade profits will be nil.	0
Mythili • As trading profits do not exceed £1,000 the trading allowance means trade profits will be nil. However, Mythili should elect for the trading allowance not to apply and instead deduct allowable costs, thus giving rise to a trading loss.	(100)
Rohan • As trading profits exceed £1,000 the normal adjustment to profits will apply, meaning Rohan will be taxed on £700 of trade profits. However, as the allowable expenses are less than £1,000, Rohan should elect to instead deduct the trading allowance, which will give lower trade profits of £500.	500
Arthur • As Arthur's trading receipts exceed £1,000 the normal adjustment to profits will apply, giving trading profits of £400. It would not be preferable to elect to deduct the trading allowance instead.	400

CHAPTER 3   Capital allowances

1

£	2,000

A maximum of the original cost is deducted from the pool.

2

£	173,896

Workings

Year ended 30 September 2021

	AIA £	Main pool £	Allowances £
B/f		22,500	
Addition qualifying for AIA			
Addition 1.12.20	171,250		
AIA (See Note)	(171,250)		171,250
Disposal 1.8.21			
Proceeds		(7,800)	
		14,700	
WDA @ 18%		(2,646)	2,646
C/f		12,054	
Allowances			173,896

Note. Maximum AIA = (3/12 x £1,000,000) + (9/12 x £200,000)= £400,000. This is sufficient to cover all of the expenditure on qualifying assets.

3

| £ | 6,620 |

6 months ended 31 December 2020

	FYA @ 100% £	Main pool £	Allowances £
Addition (no AIA)		18,000	
WDA @ 18% × $\frac{6}{12}$		(1,620)	1,620
		16,380	
Addition	5,000		
FYA @ 100%	(5,000)		5,000
C/f		16,380	
			6,620

Note. The AIA and WDAs are time apportioned in a short period. FYAs are not. AIAs and FYAs are not available on a car with CO_2 emissions of 95g/km.

4

	✓
True	
False	✓

There is no AIA or WDA in the final period so a **balancing allowance** arises as follows:

	£
B/f	12,500
Addition	20,000
Proceeds	(18,300)
	14,200
Balancing allowance	**(14,200)**

5

£	1,080

Year ended 30 April 2020

	Private use asset @ 60% £	Allowances £
Addition	30,000	
WDA @ 6%	(1,800) × 60%	**1,080**
C/f	28,200	

6 **(a) If Barry sells all the plant for £10,000 then he will have a**

balancing charge	of	£	1,200

Picklist:

balancing allowance
balancing charge

Workings (on-screen free text area provided in the CBT as part of larger question)

TWDV b/f		7,200
Addition		1,600
		8,800
Disposal		(10,000)
		(1,200)
Balancing charge		1,200

(b) **If Barry sells his plant for £6,000 then he will have a**

balancing allowance	**of**	**£**	2,800

Picklist:

balancing allowance
balancing charge

Workings (on-screen free text area provided in the CBT as part of larger question)

TWDV b/f		7,200
Addition		1,600
		8,800
Disposal		(6,000)
		2,800
Balancing allowance		(2,800)

7 **Peter can claim capital allowances for the period ending 31 March 2021 of**

£	684

Workings (on-screen free text area provided in the CBT as part of larger question)

Cars are not entitled to the AIA.	
The car will be treated as a special rate item and be entitled to 6% WDA.	
The WDA will be prorated by 9/12 as it is a 9-month accounting period.	
The WDA claimed will be restricted to 80% due to the private use.	
WDA = £19,000 × 6% × 9/12 × 80% =	£684

CHAPTER 4 Computing corporation tax

1

	True	False
A company with a nine-month period of account will calculate capital allowances for nine months and deduct them from adjusted trading profits.	✓	
A company with an 18-month period of account will calculate capital allowances for 18 months and deduct them from adjusted trading profits, and then prorate the answer between the appropriate accounting periods.		✓
A company with an 18-month period of account will calculate capital allowances for the first 12 months, then capital allowances for the remaining 6 months, and deduct them from the relevant prorated trading profits allocated to each accounting period.	✓	
Dividends are not included in the taxable total profits. They are taxed separately.		✓

Capital allowances are calculated separately for each accounting period and then deducted from the prorated adjusted profits.

Dividends are not taxable for the company (for the purpose of the *Business Tax* assessment).

2

	✓
Added to trading income	
Added to net non-trading interest ie a NTL-R credit	
Deducted from trading income	✓
Deducted from net non-trading interest ie a NTL-R debit	

The loan is for trading purposes and is interest **paid**, not received, so it is included as an expense.

3

£	385

Companies make donations gross, so the actual amount given to the charity is deducted from TTP.

4

	✓
1 June 2019 – 31 March 2020 and 1 April 2020 – 31 August 2020	
1 June 2019 – 31 May 2020 and 1 June 2020 – 31 August 2020	✓
1 June 2019 – 31 December 2019 and 1 January 2020 – 31 August 2020	
1 June 2019 – 31 August 2019 and 1 September 2019 – 31 August 2020	

The first accounting period is always 12 months in length in a long period of account.

5

	Year ended 31.12.20 £	4 months ended 30.4.21 £
Trading profits ($^{12}/_{16} : ^{4}/_{16}$)	240,000	80,000
NTL-R income (Interest) (accrued for each period)	1,200	400
Chargeable gain (allocate to period made)	0	20,000
Qualifying charitable donation (allocate to period paid)	(15,000)	0
Taxable total profits	226,200	100,400

6

£	48,450

£255,000 × 19% = **£48,450**

7

£	93,100

£490,000 × 19% = **£93,100**

8

	✓
True	✓
False	

Financial Year 2020 (FY20) begins on 1 April 2020 and ends on 31 March 2021.

CHAPTER 5   Taxing unincorporated businesses

1

Tax year	Basis period
2019/20	1 May 2019 – 5 April 2020
2020/21	Year ended 31 December 2020
2021/22	Year ended 31 December 2021
Overlap profits	1 January 2020 – 5 April 2020

2   When the trade ceases, overlap profits are deducted from the final tax year's taxable profits.

	✓
True	✓
False	

3

Tax year	Basis period	Taxable profits £
2018/19	1 June 2017 to 31 May 2018	18,000
2019/20	1 June 2018 to 31 May 2019	32,000
2020/21	1 June 2019 to 31 December 2020	30,000

In 2020/21, taxable profits are (£25,000 + £15,000 – £10,000) = £30,000

4

Tax year	Basis period	Taxable profits £
2019/20	1 February 2020 – 5 April 2020	34,000 × 2/17 = 4,000
2020/21	6 April 2020 – 5 April 2021	34,000 × 12/17 = 24,000
2021/22	12 months ended 30 June 2021	34,000 × 12/17 = 24,000

His overlap profits are:

£	18,000

(1 July 2020 to 5 April 2021)

9/17 × £34,000

5 (a)   Her taxable profits for 2019/20 are:

£ | 40,000

(1 December 2019 – 5 April 2020)   4/7 × £70,000

   (b)   Her taxable profits for 2020/21 are:

£ | 95,000

(1 December 2019– 30 November 2020) £70,000 + 5/12 × £60,000

   (c)   Her taxable profits for 2021/22 are:

£ | 60,000

(1 July 2020 to 30 June 2021)

   (d)   Her overlap profits are:

£ | 65,000

	£
1 December 2019 – 5 April 2020	40,000
1 July 2020 – 30 November 2020	25,000
	65,000

6 (a)   Her taxable profits for 2019/20 are:

£ | 80,000

(Current year basis 12 months to 31 October 2019)

   (b)   Her taxable profits for 2020/21 are:

£ | 90,000

(Short period therefore tax 12 months to new date, 30 April 2020: $\frac{6}{12}$ × £80,000 + 50,000)

   (c)   Her taxable profits for 2021/22 are:

£ | 120,000

(Current year basis 12 months to 30 April 2021)

   (d)   Her overlap profits are:

£ | 40,000

(1 May 2019 to 31 October 2019) $\frac{6}{12}$ × £80,000

7 (a)

Tax year	Basis period	Taxable profits £
2019/20	1/8/18 – 31/7/19	15,000
2020/21	1/8/19 – 31/10/20 (15 months less overlap)	22,000
2021/22	1/11/20 – 31/10/21	32,000

(b)

£	5,000

2020/21: 15 months to 31/10/20 £25,000 less £3,000 $\frac{3}{8}$ × £8,000

3 months overlap can be deducted from the profits for the 15 month period to leave a 12 month period taxable. The remainder of the overlap profit is carried forward (£8,000 – £3,000).

CHAPTER 6 Partnerships

1

	✓
The calendar year	
The tax year	
The period of account concerned	✓
The period agreed by the partners	

2 Dave's taxable profits for 2020/21 are:

£	9,450

and Joe's taxable profits for 2020/21 are:

£	8,550

Working

	Total £	Dave £	Joe £
1.1.20 – 30.9.20 (9/12) 1:1	13,500	6,750	6,750
1.10.20 – 31.12.20 (3/12) 3:2	4,500	2,700	1,800
	18,000	**9,450**	**8,550**

3

	Total £	Holly £	Jasmine £
Salary	85,000	5,000	80,000
Division of profits 1:1	115,000	57,500	57,500
	200,000	62,500	137,500

4

	✓
£60,000	
£15,000	
£45,000	
£20,000	✓

2020/21 (year ended 31 March 2021)

Taxable profits on Steve for 2020/21 are £20,000 ($\frac{1}{4}$ × £80,000).

5   The profits assessable on Sase in 2020/21 are:

£	14,000

The opening year rules apply to Sase.
(1 September 2020 – 5 April 2021) $\frac{7}{12}$ × £24,000

The profits assessable on Sase in 2021/22 are:

£	24,000

(Year ended 31 August 2021)

The overlap profits arising for Sase are:

£	14,000

(1/9/20 – 5/4/21)

Workings

Year ended 31 August 2021

	Total £	Abdul £	Ghita £	Sase £
Profits (2:2:1)	120,000	48,000	48,000	24,000

6 (a)

	Total £	William £	Ann £	John £
Y/e 31.10.19	21,000	7,000	7,000	7,000
Y/e 31.10.20	33,000	11,000	11,000	11,000
Y/e 31.10.21				
1.11.20 – 31.12.20 (2/12)	6,000	2,000	2,000	2,000
1.1.21 – 31.10.21 (10/12)	30,000	0	15,000	15,000
	36,000	2,000	17,000	17,000

(b)

	William £	Ann £	John £
2019/20 (y/e 31.10.19)	7,000	7,000	7,000
2020/21 (y/e 31.10.20)	8,000	11,000	11,000
2021/22 (y/e 31.10.21)	0	17,000	17,000

Ann and John will be taxed on the current year basis of assessment throughout. The cessation rules apply to William in 2020/21, the year he left the business:

1 November 2019 – 31 December 2020 (£11,000 + £2,000 – £5,000) = £8,000

CHAPTER 7 National insurance

1 Acker

£	0	.	00

No Class 2 NICs, as earnings below small earnings exemption of £6,475

No Class 4 NICs due, as profits below annual lower earnings limit of £9,500

2 Bailey

£	4,003	.	60

		£
Class 2 NICs	52 × £3.05	158.60
Class 4 NICs	(£50,000 – £9,500) × 9%	3,645.00
	(£60,000 – £50,000) × 2%	200.00
Total NICs		**4,003.60**

3 Cartwright

£	280	.	10

Class 2 NICs 52 × £3.05 = £158.60

Class 4 NICs (£10,850 – £9,500) × 9% = £121.50

Total NICs = **£280.10**

CHAPTER 8 Losses

1

	✓
2020/21 only	
2021/22 and/or 2020/21	
2019/20 only	
2020/21 and/or 2019/20	✓

The tax year of the loss is 2020/21. Claims against total income are for this year and/or 2019/20.

2

	✓
True	
False	✓

Trading losses can be carried forward indefinitely.

3

	✓
Against non-savings income	
Against total income	
Against trading income arising in the same trade	✓
Against trading income arising in all trades carried on by the taxpayer	

4 The loss is a loss of 2020/21.

It can be:

(a) Deducted from total income of £9,000 in 2020/21 and/or from total income of £19,000 in 2019/20; and/or

(b) Carried forward to be deducted from taxable trading profits of £25,000 in 2021/22 and then in later years.

5　(a)　The amount of trading loss remaining to be carried forward at 1 April 2021 (assuming that all possible earlier loss relief claims against total profits are made) is:

£ | (85,000)

(£320,000 – £60,000 – £175,000)

| | Year ended 31 March | |
	2020 £	2021 £
Trading profit	170,000	0
Interest	5,000	60,000
Capital gain £(12,000 – 20,000)	0	0
Total profits	175,000	60,000
Less: Current period loss relief	0	(60,000)
Carry back loss relief	(175,000)	0
Less Qualifying charitable donation	0	0
	0	0
Unrelieved qualifying charitable donations	5,000	5,000

(b)　The amount of capital loss remaining to be carried forward at 1 April 2021 is:

£ | (8,000)

(£20,000 – £12,000)

6

	✓
£Nil	
£2,000	✓
£4,000	
£3,000	

	Year ended 30.9.19 £	Six months 31.3.20 £	Year ended 31.3.21 £
Trading profit	4,000	6,000	0
Less: Current period loss relief	0	0	0
Carry back loss relief	(2,000)	(6,000)	0
Qualifying charitable donation	(1,000)	–	–
Taxable total profits	1,000	–	–

The maximum relief for year ended 30.9.19 is £4,000 × $\frac{6}{12}$.

7

	True	False
A sole trader's trade loss will be carried forward to offset against the first available trade profits of the same trade	✓	
A company's trade loss incurred post 1 April 2017 will be carried forward to offset against the first available trade profits of the same trade • The loss will be offset against future total profits as and when a claim is made.		✓
A company's trade loss incurred post 1 April 2017 is carried forward and can be offset against total profits of future accounting periods	✓	
A sole trader's trade loss must be offset against current year's total income before being offset against the total income of the prior year. • A sole trader can claim to offset the loss against total income of the prior year and/or the current year. This can be in any order. A company must make a claim to offset its trade loss against total profits of the current period before it can carry back the loss to the prior 12 months.		✓

CHAPTER 9   Self-assessment for individuals

1   The due filing date for an income tax return for 2020/21, assuming the taxpayer will submit the return online is:

31/01/22

2   The 2020/21 payments on account will be calculated as

¹   50%

of the income tax payable for

²   2019/20

and will be due on

³ 31 January 2021

and

⁴   31 July 2021

3   £100 penalty for failure to deliver return on time.

Possible £10 per day penalty from 1 May 2022 until date of filing.

5% penalty on tax paid late. Interest on tax paid late.

4

	✓
31 January 2022	
31 March 2022	
6 April 2022	
28 January 2022	✓

A year after the actual filing date, because Susie filed the return before the due filing date (31 January 2021).

5   Jamie's 2020/21 payments on account will each be

£	6,000

and will be due on

31/01/21

and

31/07/21

Jamie's balancing payment will be

£	4,000

and will be due on

31/01/22

.

6

£	0

No penalties for late payment are due on late payments on account.

7   (a)

	✓
30 September 2021	
31 October 2021	✓
31 December 2021	
31 January 2022	

Paper returns must usually be submitted by 31 October following the end of the tax year.

(b)

	✓
31 January 2022 and 31 July 2022	
31 January 2021 and 31 July 2021	✓
31 October 2021 and 31 January 2022	
31 July 2021 and 31 January 2022	

Payments on account are due on 31 January in the tax year and 31 July following the end of the tax year.

8

	✓
£5,100	
£3,400	
£1,020	✓
£2,380	

30% × PLR = **£1,020**

PLR = £17,000 × 20% = £3,400

CHAPTER 10   Self-assessment for companies

1

1 June 2021

(12 months after the actual filing date)

2

£	100

(The return is less than 3 months late)

3

	✓
14 July 2020	
1 October 2021	✓
31 December 2021	
1 January 2022	

Girton Ltd is not a large company, so all CT is due nine months and one day after the end of the accounting period.

4

	✓
14 July 2020	
14 April 2021	✓
1 October 2021	
31 December 2021	

Eaton Ltd is a large company and is required to pay corporation tax by instalments. The instalments are due in the seventh and tenth months of the accounting period and in the first and fourth months after the accounting period.

5

£	60,000

¼ × £240,000

6

£	287,500

230% of £125,000

7

	✓
True	✓
False	

The structure shows several indicators of an employment relationship.

CHAPTER 11 Chargeable gains – the basics

1

	Chargeable ✓	Exempt ✓
A gift of an antique necklace	✓	
The sale of a building	✓	

2   Her chargeable gain on sale is:

£ | 235,000

	£
Proceeds	560,000
Less cost	(325,000)
Chargeable gain	235,000

3   The amount liable to CGT in 2020/21 is:

£ | 143,400

The losses carried forward are:

£ | 0

	£
Gains	171,000
Less current year losses	(5,300)
	165,700
Less annual exempt amount	(12,300)
	153,400
Less losses b/f	(10,000)
Taxable gains	143,400

4   Martha's CGT liability for 2020/21 is:

£ | 2,380

	£
Chargeable gains	24,200
Less annual exempt amount	(12,300)
Taxable gains	11,900
CGT on £11,900 @ 20%	2,380

5   The payment date for capital gains tax for 2020/21 is:

31/01/22

6   Indexation allowance runs from the date | the expenditure was incurred | to

December 2017 .

7

	£
Proceeds of sale	200,000
Less cost	(80,000)
Less enhancement expenditure	(10,000)
	110,000
Less indexation allowance on cost £80,000 × 0.401	(32,080)
Less indexation allowance on enhancement £10,000 × 0.315	(3,150)
Chargeable gain	74,770

CHAPTER 12   Further aspects of chargeable gains

1   The chargeable gain/allowable loss arising is:

	✓
£16,663	✓
£17,500	
£19,663	
£18,337	

	£
Proceeds	38,000
Less costs of disposal	(3,000)
	35,000
Less £41,500 × $\dfrac{38,000}{38,000+48,000}$	(18,337)
Chargeable gain	16,663

2   The gain arising if he sells it for:

(a)   £5,800 after deducting selling expenses of £180 is:

£	Nil

There is no gain as the chattel is sold for gross proceeds of less than £6,000.

(b)   £8,200 after deducting selling expenses of £220 is:

£	4,033

	£
Gross proceeds	8,420
Less selling expenses	(220)
Net proceeds	8,200
Less cost	(3,500)
	4,700

Gain cannot exceed 5/3 (8,420 – 6,000) = £4,033

Therefore, gain is £4,033

3   The gain arising is:

£	Nil

A racehorse is an exempt asset as it is a wasting chattel, so no chargeable gain or allowable loss arises.

4   The loss arising is:

£	(1,000)

	£
Deemed proceeds	6,000
Less cost	(7,000)
Allowable loss	(1,000)

5

(a)   The cost of the part of the land sold is:

£	20,000

$$\frac{80,000}{80,000+120,000} \times £50,000 = \underline{\textbf{£20,000}}$$

(b)   The chargeable gain arising on the disposal is:

£	55,640

	£
Proceeds of sale	80,000
Less cost (W)	(20,000)
	60,000
Less indexation allowance £20,000 × 0.218	(4,360)
Chargeable gain	**55,640**

6   The gain arising is:

£	3,333

	£
Proceeds of sale	8,000
Less cost	(3,500)
	4,500
Less indexation allowance £3,500 × 0.108	(378)
Chargeable gain	4,122
Gain cannot exceed £(8,000 – 6,000) × $\frac{5}{3}$	**3,333**

7

	✓
£(6,906)	
£(4,400)	
£(2,700)	✓
£(5,206)	

	£
Deemed proceeds of sale	6,000
Less cost	(8,700)
Allowable loss	**(2,700)**

No indexation allowance is due as indexation cannot create or increase a loss.

8

	✓
True	
False	✓

A loss on a disposal to a connected person can be set only against gains arising on disposals to the same connected person.

9

	✓
True	✓
False	

10

	Actual proceeds used ✓	Deemed proceeds (market value) used ✓	No gain or loss basis ✓
Paul sells an asset to his civil partner Joe for £3,600			✓
Grandmother gives an asset to her grandchild worth £1,000		✓	
Sarah sells an asset worth £20,000 to her best friend Cathy for £12,000		✓	

CHAPTER 13 Share disposals

1   Her chargeable gain is:

	✓
£15,750	
£11,500	
£17,000	
£14,250	✓

Workings

	No of shares £	Cost £
August 1994 acquisition	10,000	5,000
April 2009 acquisition	10,000	16,000
	20,000	21,000
November 2020 disposal	(15,000)	(15,750)
(£21,000 × 15,000/20,000 = £15,750)		
c/f	5,000	5,250

		£
Proceeds of sale		30,000
Less allowable cost		(15,750)
Chargeable gain		**14,250**

2

	✓
True	
False	✓

In a rights issue, shares are paid for and this amount is added to the original cost. In a bonus issue, shares are not paid for and so there is no adjustment to the original cost.

3   His chargeable gain is:

£ | 3,750

	No of shares	Cost £
May 2003 acquisition	2,000	12,000
December 2004 1 for 2 rights issue @ £7.50	1,000	7,500
($\frac{1}{2}$ × 2,000 = 1,000 shares × £7.50 = £7,500)		
	3,000	19,500
March 2021 disposal	(2,500)	(16,250)
(£19,500 × $\frac{2,500}{3,000}$)		
c/f	500	3,250
		£
Proceeds of sale		20,000
Less allowable costs		(16,250)
Chargeable gain		**3,750**

4   Her chargeable gain is:

£ | 7,000

	No of shares	Cost £
June 2011 acquisition	6,000	15,000
August 2012 1 for 3 bonus issue		
($\frac{1}{3}$ × 6,000 = 2,000 shares)	2,000	nil
	8,000	15,000
December 2020 disposal (ie all the shares)	(8,000)	(15,000)
c/f	nil	nil
		£
Proceeds of sale		22,000
Less allowable costs		(15,000)
Chargeable gain		**7,000**

5 The matching rules for shares disposed of by a company are:

(a) Shares acquired on the same day
(b) Shares acquired in the previous nine days (FIFO)
(c) Shares from the FA 1985 pool

6 (a) **Share pool**

		No of shares	Cost £	Indexed cost £
5.03	Acquisition	10,000	90,000	90,000
6.09	Indexed rise			
	£90,000 × 0.176			15,840
	Rights 1:4 @ £12	2,500	30,000	30,000
		12,500	120,000	135,840
12.17	Indexed rise			
	£135,840 × 0.303			41,160
				177,000
	Disposal (× $\frac{10,000}{12,500}$)	(10,000)	(96,000)	(141,600)
		2,500	24,000	35,400

(b) **Gain on Sale**

	£
Proceeds	150,000
Less cost	(96,000)
	54,000
Less indexation allowance £(141,600 – 96,000)	(45,600)
Chargeable gain	8,400

CHAPTER 14 Reliefs for chargeable gains

1 Ian's CGT liability for 2020/21 is:

£ | 177,540

	£
Gains	1,400,000
Less annual exempt amount	(12,300)
Taxable gain	1,387,700
CGT:	
1,000,000 @ 10%	100,000
387,700 @ 20%	77,540
	177,540

2 Jemma's CGT on the disposal, assuming she has already used the annual exempt amount for 2020/21, is:

£ | 7,000

	£
Proceeds of sale	80,000
Less allowable cost	(10,000)
Taxable gain (no annual exempt amount available)	70,000
CGT @ 10%	**7,000**

3

	✓
Office block	
Freehold factory	✓
Fork lift truck	
Freehold warehouse	

The office block and the freehold warehouse were acquired outside the qualifying reinvestment period, commencing one year before and ending three years after, the disposal.

The fork lift truck is not fixed plant and machinery.

4

	✓
£120,000	
£200,000	
£400,000	✓
£420,000	

Land

	£
Sales proceeds	400,000
Less cost	(100,000)
Gain	300,000

£20,000 of the proceeds are not reinvested, so £20,000 of the gain remains chargeable; £280,000 is rolled over.

Replacement land

	£	£
Sale proceeds		500,000
Less cost	380,000	
Rolled-over gain	(280,000)	
Revised base cost		(100,000)
Chargeable gain		400,000

5

	✓
True	✓
False	

6 If relief for replacement of business assets is to be claimed, reinvestment of the proceeds must take place in a period beginning

| 12 | months before and ending

| 36 | months after the date of disposal.

7 The chargeable gain after rollover relief is:

£ | 25,000

The gain on the sale of first warehouse is:

	£
Proceeds	400,000
Less cost	(220,000)
	180,000
Less indexation allowance	(40,000)
	140,000
Less rollover relief (balancing figure)	(115,000)
Chargeable gain: amount not reinvested £(400,000 – 375,000)	**25,000**

8

	✓
True	
False	✓

Jewellery is not a qualifying asset for gift relief purposes. It is not used in Sara's trade.

9 If gift relief is claimed, the gain on the gift by Tommy is:

£ | 0

	£
Market value	200,000
Less cost	(50,000)
Gain	150,000
Less gift relief	(150,000)
Gain left in charge	**0**

and the gain on the sale by Sinbad is:

£ | 300,000

	£
Sale proceeds	350,000
Less cost (£200,000 – £150,000)	(50,000)
Gain	**300,000**

10 Sunil's CGT liability for 2020/21 is:

£	6,540

	Investors' relief gains £	Ineligible gains £
Chargeable gains (£50,000 – £20,000)	30,000	30,000
Less annual exempt amount		(12,300)
Taxable gains	30,000	17,700
CGT due:		
£30,000 × 10% (IR gains)		3,000
£17,700 × 20% (ineligible gains)		3,540
Total CGT		6,540

1 Taxation tables for business tax – 2020/21

1.1 Capital allowances

Annual investment allowance
 Prior to 1 January 2019 £200,000
 Between 1 January 2019 and 31 December 2020 £1,000,000
 From 1 January 2021 £200,000

Plant and machinery writing down allowance
 Assets other than motor cars 18%

Motor cars
 CO_2 emissions up to 50 g/km 100%
 CO_2 emissions between 51 and 110 g/km 18%
 CO_2 emissions over 110 g/km – Prior to 1 April 2019/6 April 2019 8%
 CO_2 emissions over 110 g/km – From 1 April 2019/6 April 2019 6%

1.2 Capital gains

Annual exempt amount £12,300

Basic rate 10%
Higher rate 20%
Business asset disposal relief rate 10%
Investors' relief rate 10%

Business asset disposal relief lifetime allowance £1,000,000
Investors' relief lifetime allowance £10,000,000

1.3 National Insurance rates

Class 2 contributions: £3.05 per week
Small profits threshold £6,475p.a.

Class 4 contributions:
Main rate 9%
Additional rate 2%
Lower profits limit £9,500
Upper profits limit £50,000

1.4 Trading allowance

This allowance is available to individuals only. £1,000

1.5 Corporation tax

Financial year	**2020**	**2019**
All profits and gains	19%	19%

2 Introduction to business tax

2.1 Administration

- Taxation administered by HM Revenue & Customs (HMRC).

- Rules covering tax are contained in statute (law) which is passed every year (*Finance Act*).

- Decisions reached by the courts interpreting the law are known as case law.

- HMRC also issue guidance – Extra Statutory Concessions and Statements of Practice.

2.2 Taxes

- Corporation Tax – paid by companies on both income and chargeable gains.

- Income Tax – paid by individuals on their income.

- Capital Gains Tax – paid by individuals on their capital gains.

2.3 Tax evasion, tax avoidance and tax planning

- Tax evasion: any action taken to evade tax by illegal means; this carries a risk of criminal prosecution. Examples of tax evasion include failing to declare income and claiming false expenses.

- Tax avoidance: bending the rules of the tax system to gain a tax advantage that Parliament never intended. It involves operating within the letter of the law but not the spirit of the law.

- Tax planning: use of legitimate means to minimise taxpayer's tax liability, for example by investing in a tax-free ISA (Individual Savings Account).

3 Adjustment of profits – sole traders, partnerships and companies

3.1 Pro forma for adjustment of profits

	£	£
Net profit as per accounts		X
Add: Expenses charged in the accounts that are not allowable as trading expenses	X̲	
		X̲
		X
Less: Income included in the accounts which is not assessable as trading income	X̲	
		(X)̲
Adjusted profit/(loss)		X̲

3.2 Disallowed expenses

- Expenses that fail the remoteness test so not "wholly and exclusively" for trading purposes.

- Fines on the business or fraud by directors/owners.

- Donations to charity are generally disallowed in calculating trading profits (however qualifying charitable donations are deductible in the corporation tax computation).

- Political donations are never allowable.

- Capital expenditure e.g. purchase of equipment included in profit and loss account.

- Depreciation. Capital allowances granted instead.

- Costs of bringing newly acquired second-hand assets to useable condition.

- Legal and professional expenses relating to capital items or breaking the law.

- Customer entertaining. Staff entertaining can be allowable.

- Customer gifts, unless gift incorporates business advertising, cost is less than £50 per annum per customer, and gift is not food, drink, tobacco or cash vouchers.

3.3 Non-assessable income

- Income taxed in any other way, e.g. interest or property income for individuals.

- Profits on sale of fixed assets.

4 Unincorporated businesses – trading income

4.1 Trading income calculated for each period of account:

	£
Adjusted accounting profit	X
Less: Capital allowances:	(X)
Less: Balancing allowances	(X)
Plus: Balancing charges	X
Trading income for the period of account	X

4.2 Expenses charged in the accounts which are not allowable as trading expenses

- See adjustment of profits – sole traders, partnerships and companies.

- Transactions with the owner of the business. For example:

    - Add back salary paid to owner. Salaries paid to family members do not need to be added back.

    - Private expenditure included in accounts.

    - Class 2 and Class 4 National Insurance contributions.

    - Goods taken for own use.

5 Sole traders – basis periods

Tax year – 2020/21 tax year runs from 6 April 2020 to 5 April 2021.

5.1 Basis period rules

- First year – runs from start date of trading to the next 5 April.
- Second year and third year.

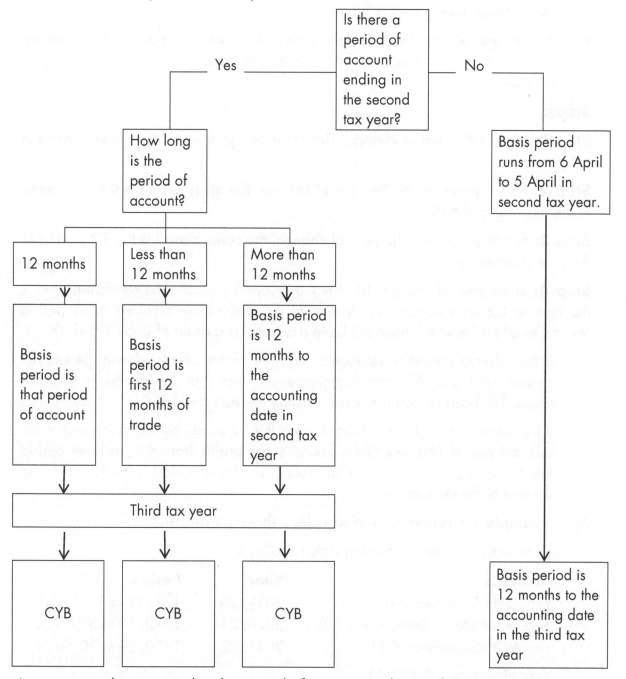

Later years – basis period is the period of account ending in the tax year = Current Year basis (CYB).

Final year – basis period is the period from the end of the basis period for the previous tax year to cessation date.

Overlap profits – opening year rules may lead to profits being taxed twice. Relief is given on cessation of the business.

6 Sole traders – change of accounting date

For an accounting date change to be recognised for tax purposes the following conditions must be satisfied:

- the first accounts ending on the new date must not exceed 18 months in length

- the sole trader or partnership must give notice of the change in the tax return by the filing date of the tax return

- the change will not be permitted if there has been a change of accounting date in the previous five years unless there are genuine commercial reasons for the change.

Steps:

Step 1: Identify the year of change. This is the first year when current year basis is not possible.

Step 2: For all years before the year of change, the basis period is the 12 months to the old year end date.

Step 3: For all years after the year of change, the basis period is the 12 months to the new year end date.

Step 4: In the year of change, identify the relevant period'. The relevant period is the time to the new accounting date from the end of the previous basis period (example: all profits which have not been assessed as a result of steps 2 and 3)

- If the relevant period > 12 months, tax the profits of the relevant period but deduct overlap profits from commencement such that 12 months in total are taxed. The basis period is the same as the relevant period.

- If the relevant period is < 12 months, tax the 12 month period to the end of the relevant period (this will mean taxing some profits from the previous period twice, creating additional overlap profits). The basis period is the 12 months to the end of the relevant period.

6.1 Example 1 – relevant period is less than 12 months

Jasmin changes her accounting date as follows:

Accounts	Year	Period
Year to 31 December 2019	2019/20	1/1/19 to 31/12/19
Nine months to 30 September 2020	2020/21	1/10/19 to 30/9/20
Year to 30 September 2021	2021/22	1/10/20 to 30/9/21

Year of change – 2020/21

Relevant period – nine months to 30 September 2020

Basis period for 20/21 – 12 months to 30 September 2020

6.2 Example 2 – relevant period is greater than 12 months

Vaughan changes his accounting date as follows:

Accounts	Year	Period
Year to 31 December 2019	2019/20	1/1/19 to 31/12/19
15 months to 31 March 2021	2020/21	1/1/20 to 31/3/21
Year to 31 March 2022	2021/22	1/4/21 to 31/3/22

Year of change – 2020/21

Relevant period – 15 months to 31 March 2021

Basis period for 20/21 – 15 months to 31 March 2021

7 Capital allowances on plant and machinery

7.1 Layout of capital allowances on plant and machinery computation

(see taxation tables for rates)

	First Year Allowance (FYA) £	Annual Investment Allowance (AIA) £	General pool £	Special rate pool £	Short Life Asset £	Total allowances £
WDV b/f			X	X	X	
Additions	X	X	X			
Disposals	—	—	(X)	—	(X)	
	X	X	X	X	X	
Balancing allowance/balancing charge (BA/BC)					X/(X)	X/(X)
					Nil	
AIA/FYA	(X)	(X)				X
Writing down allowance @ 18% pa			(X)			X
Writing down allowance @ X% pa	—	—	—	(X)		X
WDV c/f	Nil	Nil	X	X		—
Total allowances						X

- Plant – defined by 'function/setting' distinction and case law.

- AIA – 100% allowance for expenditure (other than cars) in 12-month period (pro rata). Expenditure in excess of AIA qualifies for writing down allowance (WDA). If the accounting period straddles 1 January 2019 or 1 January 2021, the AIA must be pro-rated.

- Full WDA for the period is given regardless of date of purchase of item. WDA is scaled for periods other than 12 months.

- The WDA % on the special rate pool is calculated as: ((8 × number of months before 1 April 2019) + (6 × number of months after 1 April 2019))/number of months in the chargeable period. This % should be rounded to two decimal places.

- FYA – 100% allowance given on purchase of low CO2 emission cars. FYA is not scaled for short accounting periods.

- If the written down value (WDV) on the general pool (= WDV b/f + additions-disposals) is £1,000 or less then an election can be made to write off the pool balance, known as a 'small pools allowance'.

- Short life assets (SLA) – de-pool asset if life expected to be less than 8 years. Not available for cars.

7.2 Unincorporated businesses – Private use assets

- Private use assets have separate column in Capital Allowance computation.

- Disallow private use % of WDA/AIA/FYA.

7.3 Capital allowances – business cessation

- In the cessation period of account, no WDA/AIA/FYA.

- Include additions and disposals as normal. Any asset taken over by owner, treat as a disposal at market value. Balancing adjustment made (balancing charge or balancing allowance).

8 Partnerships

- Each partner is taxed like a sole trader on their share of the partnership profits.

- First step is to share accounting profits between partners:

    - allocate the correct salaries and interest on capital for the period to each partner

    - divide the remaining profit for each set of accounts between the partners based upon the profit sharing arrangement

    - you may need to split the period if there is a change such as a partner joining or leaving.

- Opening year and cessation rules apply to partners individually when they join or leave the partnership.

- Allocate the profit for each partner to the correct tax year using usual basis period rules.

- Basis periods for continuing partners are unaffected by joiners or leavers.

- Each partner enters their share of profits for a tax year in the partnership pages of their own tax return.

9 Trading losses for sole traders and partners

9.1 Trading losses for sole traders and partners

- A loss is computed in the same way as a profit, making the same adjustments to the net profit as per the accounts and deducting capital allowances.

9.2 Set off of trading loss against total income

- Set off loss against total income of the preceding tax year and/or the tax year of loss, e.g. loss in 2020/21 set off against total income in 2019/20 and/or 2020/21.

- Cannot restrict loss to preserve use of personal allowance so personal allowance may be wasted.

- For 2020/21 loss claim needed by 31 January 2023.

9.3 Carry forward of trading losses

- If any loss remains unrelieved after current year and carry back claim has been made, or no such claims are made, then carry forward the loss against first available profits of the same trade.

9.4 Choice of loss relief – consider the following:

- utilise loss in the tax year in which income is taxed at a higher rate

- possible wastage of personal allowance

- review the projected future profits to ensure the loss can be utilised

- if cash flow is important, a loss carry back claim may result in a tax refund being paid to the business.

10 Payment and administration – sole traders and partners

10.1 The return must be filed by:

- 31 October following the end of the tax year if filing a paper return
- 31 January following the end of the tax year if filing online.

10.2 Penalties for late filing and payment

Late filing	Late payment	Penalty
Miss filing deadline		£100
	30 days late	5% of tax outstanding at that date
3 months late		Daily penalty £10 per day for up to 90 days (max £900)
6 months late		5% of tax due or £300, if greater
	6 months late	5% of tax outstanding at that date
12 months late		5% of tax due or £300, if greater
	12 months late	5% of tax outstanding at that date
12 months and information deliberately withheld		Based on behaviour: • deliberate and concealed withholding 100% of tax due, or • £300 if greater. • deliberate but not concealed 70% of tax due, or £300 if greater. Reductions apply for prompted and unprompted disclosures and for cooperation with investigation.

10.3 Disclosure and errors

- Taxpayer must notify HMRC by 5 October following end of the tax year if a tax return is needed.

- Taxpayer can amend a tax return within 12 months of filing date or make a claim for overpayment relief within four years of the end of the tax year.

10.4 Payments on account (POA)

- Due 31 January (in tax year) and 31 July (after tax year end). Each instalment is 50% of the previous year's tax and Class 4 National Insurance contribution (NIC) liability after taking into account any tax deducted at source.

- Balancing payment made 31 January after tax year end.

- No POA due if:
    - last year's tax and Class 4 NIC liability is less than £1,000 or
    - if greater than 80% of last year's liability was deducted at source.

- Can reduce this year's POA if this year's liability expected to be less than last year's. Penalties and interest will be charged if a deliberate incorrect claim is made.

- Capital gains tax (CGT) liability and Class 2 National Insurance is paid 31 January following the tax year end. No POA needed for CGT and Class 2 National Insurance.

10.5 Interest on tax paid late/overpaid tax

- Interest charged daily on late payment.

11 Enquiries and other penalties

- HMRC must notify individual of enquiry within 12 months of submission of return.

- Basis of enquiry – random or HMRC believe income/expenses misstated.

- Penalty for failure to produce enquiry documents = £300 + £60 per day.

- Penalty for failure to keep proper records is up to £3,000. Records must be kept for five years after the filing date for the relevant tax year.

- Penalties for incorrect returns are detailed in the table below:

Type of behaviour	Maximum	Unprompted (minimum)	Prompted (minimum)
Genuine mistake: despite taking reasonable care	0%	0%	0%
Careless error and inaccuracy are due to failure to take reasonable care	30%	0%	15%
Deliberate error but not concealed	70%	20%	35%
Deliberate error and concealed	100%	30%	50%

12 National Insurance contributions

- Self-employed individuals pay Class 2 and Class 4 contributions.

- Class 4 contributions are at 9% on profits between the lower and upper limits, then 2% on profits above the upper limit.

- Percentages and limits are provided in the Taxation Tables.

13 An outline of corporation tax

- Companies pay corporation tax on their profits for each accounting period.

- There is one rate of corporation tax set each financial year.

- Profits = Income + Gains – Qualifying charitable donations

- Accounting periods are usually 12 months long but can be shorter.

- If a company's accounts are longer than 12 months, the first 12 months will be one accounting period and the remainder a second accounting period.

- All UK property income is pooled as a single source of income and taxed on an accruals basis.

- Borrowing or lending money by a company is a loan relationship.

- Trading loan relationships are part of trading income.

- Non-trading loan relationships (NTL-R) are pooled to give NTL-R credits or deficits.

- Donations to charities are qualifying charitable donations.

- Company A is a related 51% group company of company B if:

    - A is a 51% subsidiary of B, or
    - B is a 51% subsidiary of A, or
    - A and B are both 51% subsidiaries of the same company.

'A' is a 51% subsidiary of 'B' if more than 50% of its ordinary share capital is beneficially owned (directly or indirectly) by 'B'.

14 The calculation of total profits and corporation tax payable

ABC Ltd

Corporation tax computation for the year/period ended DD/MM/20XX

	£
Trading income – accruals basis	X
Interest income (NTL-R) – accrual basis	X
Property income – accruals basis	X
Chargeable gains	X
	X
Less Qualifying charitable donations	(X)
Total taxable profits	X
Corporation tax payable – Total taxable profits × Corporation tax rate	X

14.1 Key points

- Trading income is adjusted from net profit per company accounts less capital allowances.
- Companies receive interest gross.
- Virtually all interest receivable is taxed as interest income (NTL-R).
- Dividends payable by a company are not an allowable expense.
- UK dividends receivable by a company are not taxable.
- Net-off current year capital losses against current year capital gains. If there is a net capital loss carry it forward.
- See taxation tables for corporation tax rates.

14.2 Long periods of account

- Will consist of two accounting periods = first 12 months and remainder of period.
- Split profits as follows:
- Adjusted trading profit – time apportion.
- Capital allowances – separate computations for each accounting period.
- Interest income (NTL-R) and property income – accruals basis.
- Chargeable gains – according to date of disposal.
- Qualifying charitable donations– according to date paid.

15 Corporation tax – trade losses

- Can elect to set trading losses against current accounting period 'total profits'. Qualifying charitable donations will remain unrelieved.

- If the above election is made, can also carry back trading loss to set against 'total profits' within the previous 12 months.

- Losses not relieved in the current accounting period or previous 12 months are carried forward and an election can be made to set against total profits in future periods.

- If there is a choice of loss relief, firstly consider when the loss was incurred, the rate of loss relief and then the timing of relief.

- Set out the use of the losses in a loss memorandum.

16 Corporation tax – payment and administration

16.1 Payment dates

- Small companies (annual profits less than £1.5 million): nine months + 1 day after end of the accounting period (AP).

- Large companies (annual profits greater than £1.5 million) must estimate year's tax liability and pay 25% of the year's liability:
    - six months and 14 days after start of AP
    - nine months and 14 days after start of AP
    - 14 days after end of AP
    - three months and 14 days after end of AP.

- Estimate must be revised for each quarter. Penalties may be charged if company deliberately fails to pay sufficient instalments.

- No instalments due for first year company is large unless profits are greater than £10 million.

- 51% group companies share the annual profit limit of £1.5 million equally.

16.2 Interest on late payments

- Interest charged daily on late payment. Overpayment of tax receives interest from HMRC. Interest is taxable/tax allowable as interest income.

16.3 Filing the return

- Filed on the later of 12 months after end of AP or three months after the notice to deliver a tax return has been issued.

- Late filing penalties are: less than three months late: £100; greater than three months late: £200; greater than six months late: 10% of tax due per return; greater than 12 months late: 20% of tax due per return.

- Company must notify HMRC it is within scope of corporation tax within 3 months of starting to trade.

- Company can amend return within 12 months of the filing date.

16.4 Enquiries and other penalties

- HMRC must notify company of enquiry within 12 months of submission of return.

- Basis of enquiry – random or HMRC believe income/expenses misstated.

- Penalty for failure to produce enquiry documents: £300 + £60 per day.

- Penalty for failure to keep proper records is up to £3,000. Records must be retained for six years after the end of the relevant accounting period.

- Penalties for incorrect returns are the same as for sole traders and partners – see sole traders and partners link.

17 Current tax reliefs and other tax issues

17.1 Research and development (R&D) tax credits for small and medium sized companies

A small or medium sized enterprise (SME) is a company with less than 500 employees with either:

- an annual turnover under €100 million, or
- a balance sheet under €86 million.

17.2 The SME tax relief scheme

The tax relief on allowable R&D costs is 230%.

17.3 R&D tax credits

If a company makes a loss, it can choose to receive R&D tax credits instead of carrying forward a loss.

17.4 Costs that qualify for R&D tax relief

To qualify as R&D, any activity must contribute directly to seeking an advance in science or technology or must be a qualifying indirect activity. The costs must relate to the company's trade – either an existing one, or one that they intend to start up based on the results of the R&D.

17.5 Intermediaries (IR35) legislation

IR35 legislation prevents personal service companies ("PSC") being used to disguise permanent employment.

The rules apply where the relationship between the worker and the client, would be considered to be an employment relationship if the existence of the PSC was ignored.

If the rules apply, a **deemed employment income tax charge** is charged on the PSC.

The **deemed employment income tax charge** is calculated based upon the actual payments made to the PSC by the client.

18 Introduction to capital/chargeable gains

- Individual pays Capital Gains Tax (CGT) on net chargeable gains in a tax year.

- For companies, chargeable gains are included as income in calculating total profits.

- Individuals receive an annual exempt amount from CGT – for 2020/21 this is £12,300.

- Gains/losses arise when a chargeable person makes a chargeable disposal of a chargeable asset.

- Chargeable person – individual or company.

- Chargeable disposal – sale, gift or loss/destruction of the whole or part of an asset. Exempt disposals – on death and gifts to approved charities.

- Chargeable asset – all assets unless exempt. Exempt assets include motor cars and some chattels.

18.1 Calculation of capital gains tax

Net chargeable gains – total gains in the tax year after netting off any current year or brought forward losses and the annual exempt amount.

18.2 Annual exempt amount (AEA)

- For individuals only.

- AEA cannot be carried forward or carried back.

- Current year losses must be netted off against current year gains before AEA. This means AEA can be wasted.

- Brought forward capital losses are set off against current year gains after AEA so AEA is not wasted.

19 Calculation of gains and losses for individuals

19.1 Pro forma computation

	£	£
Consideration received		X
Less Incidental costs of sale		(X)
Net sale proceeds		NSP
Less Allowable expenditure		
– Acquisition cost	X	
– Incidental costs of acquisition	X	
– Enhancement expenditure	X	
		(Cost)
Gain/(Loss)		X/(X)

- Consideration received is usually sales proceeds, but market value will be used instead of actual consideration where the transaction is a gift or between connected persons.

- An individual is connected with their spouse, relatives (and their spouses) and spouse's relatives (and their spouses). Relative means brother, sister, lineal ancestor or lineal descendent.

- Husband and wife/civil partner transfers – nil gain nil loss.

Part disposals – the cost allocated to the disposal = Cost × (A/(A + B))

A = consideration received on part disposal

B = market value of the remainder of the asset

Chattels – tangible moveable object.

Two types:

- Wasting – expected life of 50 years or less (e.g. racehorse or boat). CGT exempt.

- Non-wasting – expected life greater than 50 years (e.g. antiques or jewellery).

19.2 CGT, £6,000 rule

Sell \ Buy	£6,000 or less	More than £6,000
Less than £6,000	Exempt	Allowable loss but proceeds are deemed = £6,000
More than £6,000	Normal calculation of the gain, then compare with 5/3 (gross proceeds – £6,000) – Take the lower gain	Chargeable in full

20 Shares and securities – disposals by individuals

20.1 CGT on shares and securities

Disposal of shares and securities are subject to CGT except for listed government securities (gilt-edged securities or 'gilts'), qualifying corporate bonds (e.g. company loan notes/debentures) and shares held in an Individual Savings Account (ISA).

20.2 The identification rules

Used to determine which shares have been sold and so what acquisition cost can be deducted from the sale proceeds (e.g. match the disposal and acquisition).

Disposals are matched:

- firstly, with acquisitions on the same day as the day of disposal

- secondly, with acquisitions made in the 30 days following the date of disposal (FIFO basis)

- thirdly, with shares from the share pool.

20.3 The Share Pool

- The share pool contains all shares acquired prior to the disposal date.

- Each acquisition is not kept separately, but is 'pooled' together with other acquisitions and a running total kept of the number of shares and the cost of those shares.

- When a disposal from the pool is made, the appropriate number of shares are taken from the pool along with the average cost of those shares.

- The gain on disposal is then calculated.

20.4 Bonus issues and rights issues

- Bonus issue – no adjustment to cost needed.
- Rights issue – adjustment to cost needed.

21 Chargeable gains – reliefs available to individuals

Replacement of business assets (Rollover) relief – when a qualifying business asset is sold at a gain, taxpayer can defer gain by reinvesting proceeds in a qualifying replacement asset.

- Deferred gain is deducted from the cost of the replacement asset so gain crystallises when the replacement asset is sold.

- Qualifying assets (original and replacement) – must be used in a trade by the vendor and be land and buildings, fixed plant and machinery or goodwill.

- Qualifying time period – replacement asset must be purchased between 1 year before and 3 years after the sale of the original asset.

- Partial reinvestment – only some of the sales proceeds reinvested then the gain taxable is the lower of the full gain and the proceeds not reinvested.

Gift relief (holdover relief) – donee takes over asset at donor's base cost i.e. the gain is given away along with the asset.

- Qualifying assets – trade assets of donor or shares in any unquoted trading company or personal trading company (donor owns at least 5% of company).

Business asset disposal relief – gain taxable at 10% capital gains tax rate.

- The £1 million limit is a lifetime limit which is reduced each time a claim for the relief is made.

- For 2020/21 a claim must be made by 31 January 2023.

- Qualifying business disposals (assets must be owned for at least 24 months prior to sale).

    - The whole or part of a business carried on by the individual (alone or in partnership).

    - Assets of the individual's or partnership's trading business that has now ceased.

    - Shares in the individual's 'personal trading company' where they have at least 5% of shares, voting rights, entitlement to distributable profits and entitlement to net assets. Individual must have owned the shares and been an employee of the company for 24 months prior to sale.

Investors relief – gain taxable at 10% capital gains tax rate

- The £10 million limit is a lifetime limit which is reduced each time a claim for the relief is made.
- For 2020/21 a claim must be made by 31 January 2023:
  - the individual subscribes for shares which are issued on or after 17 March 2016
  - the shares are ordinary shares
  - the issuing company is a trading company or holding company of a trading group
  - the shares are not listed on a recognised stock exchange
  - the individual has not been an officer or employee of the issuing company at any point during the ownership period
  - the shares are held continuously for three years.

22 Calculation of gains and losses for companies

22.1 Pro forma computation

	£	£
Consideration received		X
Less Incidental costs of sale		(X)
Net sale proceeds		NSP
Less Allowable expenditure		
Acquisition cost + incidental costs of acquisition	X	
Indexation allowance [indexation factor × expenditure]	X	
Enhancement expenditure	X	
Indexation allowance	X	
		(Cost)
Chargeable gain		Gain

- Companies are entitled to an indexation allowance, based on the changes in the retail price index (RPI) from the date when expenditure was incurred to the date of disposal (or deemed disposal).

- Indexation allowance is frozen at 31 December 2017.

- Disposals taking place from 1 January 2018 will use the RPI at 31 December 2017 for indexation allowance purposes.

- Indexation allowance is not available where there is an unindexed loss; nor can it turn an unindexed gain into an indexed loss.

- Note that companies do not get an annual exempt amount.

- Losses relieved in order – current year first followed by losses brought forward.

22.2 Only relief available to companies is rollover relief:

- Rollover relief is a deferral relief – see Chargeable gains – reliefs available to individuals for main rollover relief rules.

- Key differences applying for companies:

    - indexation is given on disposal of the original asset.

    - goodwill is not a qualifying asset for companies.

    - gain deferred is the indexed gain.

    - on disposal of the replacement asset, indexation is calculated on the 'base cost' not actual cost.

23 Shares and securities – disposals by companies

The identification rules – a disposal of shares is matched:

- firstly, with same-day transactions

- secondly, with transactions in the previous nine days (FIFO). No indexation allowance is available.

- thirdly, with shares from the 1985 pool (shares bought from 1 April 1982 onwards).

1985 pool – pro forma working	No.	Cost	Indexed cost
		£	£
Purchase	X	X	X
Index to next operative event			X
			X
Operative event (purchase)	X	X	X
	X	X	X
Index to next operative event			X
			X
Operative event (sale)	(X)	(X)	(X) A
Pool carried forward	X	X	X

Operative event = purchase, sale, rights issue. Bonus issue is not an operative event.

Computation

	£
Proceeds	X
Less indexed cost (A from pool)	(X)
Indexed gain	X

24 The badges of trade

- Profit seeking motive
- Number of transactions
- Nature of asset
- Existence of similar trading transactions or interests
- Changes to the asset
- The way the sale was carried out
- The source of finance
- Interval of time between purchase and sale
- Method of acquisition

25 Duties and responsibilities of a tax advisor

- Maintain client confidentiality at all times.

- AAT members must adopt an ethical approach and maintain an objective outlook.

- Give timely and constructive advice to clients.

- Honest and professional conduct with HMRC.

- A tax advisor is liable to a penalty if they assist in making an incorrect return.

These Reference Materials have been produced by the AAT

Bibliography

AAT (2017) AAT Code of Professional Ethics. [Online.] Available from: https://www.aat.org.uk/prod/s3fs-public/assets/AAT-Code-Professional-Ethics.pdf [Accessed 4 July 2018].

Contains public sector information licensed under the Open Government Licence v3.0. www.nationalarchives.gov.uk/doc/open-government-licence/version/3/.

HMRC (2018(a)) *Tackling tax evasion and avoidance.* [Online.] Available from: https://assets.publishing.service.gov.uk/government/uploads/system/uploads/atta chment_data/file/413931/Tax_evasion_FINAL__with_covers_and_right_sig_.pdf [accessed 4 July 2018].

HMRC (2020(b)) *Self-employment (full).* [Online.] Available from: https://assets.publishing.service.gov.uk/government/uploads/system/uploads/atta chment_data/file/874594/sa103f_English_Form.pdf [Accessed 15 May 2020)

HMRC (2020(c)) Partnership tax return. [Online] Available from: https://assets.publishing.service.gov.uk/government/uploads/system/uploads/atta chment_data/file/879470/sa800man_English_Form.pdf [Accessed 15 May 2020].

Index

A

Accountancy expenses, 24
Accounting period, 169
Accounting period, 71, 75
Additional rate, 8
Adjustment of profits, 18, 32
Agent vs Principal, 157
Agent, 157
Amortisation, 23
**Annual exempt amount (AEA)/annual
exemption, 188**, 192, 197
Annual investment allowance (AIA), 40, 59
Appeal, 153
Assets used partly for private purposes, 52
Augmented profits, 170

B

Badges of trade, 17, 32
Balancing allowance, 48, 59
Balancing charge, 48, 59
Basic rate band, 190
Basic rate, 8
Basis period, 81, 96
Bonus issues, 223, 231
Bonus shares, 235
Business asset disposal relief (BADR), 245,
258

C

Capital allowances, 20, 39
Capital expenditure, 20, 39, 59
Capital gains tax (CGT), 184, 190
Capital losses, 140
Careless, 152
Carry back loss relief, 143
Carry forward loss relief, 143
Case law, 5
Cessation, 48, 88
Change of accounting date, 90
Chargeable asset, 184, 197
Chargeable disposal, 184, 197
Chargeable gains, 67
Chargeable person, 184, 197
Chattels, 205, 210
Choosing loss relief, 140
Class 2 contributions, 121, 124
Class 2 NICs, 155

Class 4 contributions, 121, 124, 155
Closure notice, 158
Companies, 4, 170
Company tax returns, 168
Compliance checks, 158, 170
Connected persons, 207
Corporation tax, 65, 184
Costs of registering trademarks and patents,
23
Costs
    disposal, 185
    original purchase price, 186
Current tax reliefs, 173
Current year basis of assessment, 81, 96,
107
Current year loss relief, 137, 143

D

Date, 168
Deliberate error, 152
Deliberate, 152
Depooling election, 54, 59
Depreciation, 23
Disallowable expenditure, 32
Disallowed expenditure, 20
Discovered, 152
Disposals, 46
Dividend income, 67
Dividends paid, 67

E

Employment vs self-employment, 174
Enhancement expenditure, 186, 197
Enquiries, 158, 170
Entertaining, 23
Entrepreneurs' relief, 262
Errors, 169
Ethics, 5
Exempt disposal, 197
Expenditure wholly and exclusively for trade
    purposes, 32

F

FA 1985 pool, 226
Filing due date
    companies, 168, 177

Filing due date, 161
Filling due date, 154
Finance Act, 5
Financial year, 73, 75
Fines, 23
First year allowance (FYAs) , 43, 59
Fiscal year, 81, 96
Fundamental principles, 5

G

General provisions, 21
Gift relief, 255, 263
Gifts, 24
Goods taken from stock, 22

H

Higher rate, 8
HMRC (FY), 5

I

Incidental costs of disposal, 185
Incidental costs of obtaining loan finance, 23
Income tax liability, 8
Income tax, 7, 184
Incorporated businesses, 4
Indexation, 192, 228
Inline eXtensible Business Reporting Language'
    (iXBRL), 168
Interest on late paid tax, 157, 172
Interest on over paid tax, 157
Interest, 25, 66, 161
IR35, 175
Irrecoverable debts, 23

K

Keeping records, 168

L

Large companies, 171, 177
Late filing, 154
Leasing costs of car, 25
Legal and professional charges, 24
Lifetime limit, 247, 258
Loan relationship, 66
Long period of account, 66, 71, 169, 173
Losses, 188, 192
Low emission cars, 43
Lower earnings limit (LEL), 121

M

Main pool, 40
Matching rules, 218, 225

N

National Insurance Contributions (NICs), 121
Net income, 7, 12
No gain/no loss disposal, 208
Non-trading loan relationship (NTL-R), 66
Notice of chargeability, 150
Notice to make a return, 150
Notification of chargeability, 168

O

Opening year rules, 82, 107
Operative event, 227, 231, 235
Overlap profits, 84, 88, 90, 96

P

Part disposal, 203, 210
Partial closure notice, 158, 170
Partnership tax return, 111
Partnership, 4, 103, 113, 114
Payment of capital gains tax, 192
Payment of corporation tax, 170
Payment of income tax, 154
Payment on account, 154, 161
Penalties for error, 152
Penalties for failure to keep records, 169
Penalties, 23, 152, 156, 169
Period of account, 40, 56, 59, **65**, 71,
    75, 169
Personal allowance, 7
Personal service companies, 175
Personal service company, 177
Plant, 59
Political donations, 24
Potential lost revenue (PLR), **152**
Principal, 157
Private expenditure, 22
Private use adjustments, 65
Private use asset, 53, 55, 59
Professional behaviour, 6, 12
Professional competence, 5, 12
Profit-sharing agreement, 105
Prompted, 152
Property business income, 66

Q

Qualifying assets, 252
Qualifying charitable donations, 67, 75

R

Redundancy payments, 25
Repair expenditure, 20
Repayment interest, 161
Research and development, 174
Retail price index (RPI), 193
Retention of records, 151
Revenue expenditure, 20, 39, 59
Rights issues, 223, 231, 235
Rollover relief, 252, 260
Royalties, 23, 67

S

Share pool, 219
Short life asset, 54, 59
Small Profits Threshold, 121
Sole traders, 4
Special rate pool, 50
Spouses/civil partners, 208
Statue law, 5
Statutory Instruments, 5
Subscriptions, 24

T

Tax avoidance, 6, 12
Tax evasion, 6

Tax liability, 8
Tax planning, 6, 12
Tax return, 28
Tax Written-Down Value, 44
Tax year, 12, 81, 96, 187
Taxable gain, 187, 197
Taxable income, 7, 12, 190
Taxable total profits (TTP), **65**, 75
The tax return, 150
Total income, 7, 12
Trading losses, 130, 143
    companies, 135
    individuals, 130
Trading profits
    companies, 65

U

Unincorporated businesses, 4
Unprompted, 152
Upper earnings limit (UEL), 121

W

Wasting chattel, **205**, 210
Wholly and exclusively, 20
Writing down allowance (WDA), 43, 59

Y

Year of assessment, 96
Year of change (YOC), 90

REVIEW FORM

How have you used this Course Book?
(Tick one box only)

☐ Self study

☐ On a course_____

☐ Other _____

Why did you decide to purchase this Course Book? *(Tick one box only)*

☐ Have used BPP materials in the past

☐ Recommendation by friend/colleague

☐ Recommendation by a college lecturer

☐ Saw advertising

☐ Other _____

During the past six months do you recall seeing/receiving either of the following?
(Tick as many boxes as are relevant)

☐ Our advertisement in Accounting Technician

☐ Our Publishing Catalogue

Which (if any) aspects of our advertising do you think are useful?
(Tick as many boxes as are relevant)

☐ Prices and publication dates of new editions

☐ Information on Course Book content

☐ Details of our free online offering

☐ None of the above

Your ratings, comments and suggestions would be appreciated on the following areas of this Course Book.

	Very useful	Useful	Not useful
Chapter overviews	☐	☐	☐
Introductory section	☐	☐	☐
Quality of explanations	☐	☐	☐
Illustrations	☐	☐	☐
Chapter activities	☐	☐	☐
Test your learning	☐	☐	☐
Keywords	☐	☐	☐

	Excellent	Good	Adequate	Poor
Overall opinion of this Course Book	☐	☐	☐	☐

Do you intend to continue using BPP Products?   ☐ Yes ☐ No

The BPP author of this edition can be emailed at: learningmedia@bpp.com

REVIEW FORM (continued)

TELL US WHAT YOU THINK

Please note any further comments and suggestions/errors below